W9-BWV-956

Praise for *The Equity Trader Course*

"There is always more to learn about equity trading—I learned this again by reading this wonderfully insightful book."

—Dr. Stefan Jentzsch, Member of the Board
of Managing Directors, Dresdner Bank AG

"*The Equity Trader Course* captures what we do every day in the market. It offers a clear, concise, and compelling assessment of the equity trading environment. As we say, 'Take it to where it trades!!'"

—Andrew M. Brooks, Vice President,
Head of Equity Trading, T. Rowe Price Group

"Global equity markets and the operations of the equity traders are rapidly changing. This book is on the forefront of that change. I strongly recommend it as one of the best guides available through the intricate environment that we face today."

—Kurt Viermetz, Chairman of the Supervisory Board,
Hypo Real Estate Holding AG, and Chairman
of the Supervisory Board, Deutsche Börse AG

"Without trading, investing is an academic exercise. This book and its computer simulation bridge the gap and should be required reading for traders, old and new, and anyone who wants to understand why America's equity markets are the richest and deepest in the world. Part primer and part advanced discussion of modern trading techniques and technology, this book should be in every trading room. Authors Schwartz, Francioni, and Weber—along with a slew of important contributors—have created a definitive course on equity trading. Ignore this book at your investing peril!"

—Theodore R. Aronson, CFA,
Aronson+Johnson+Ortiz, and former Chair
of the Board of Governors, CFA Institute

"Back in the early days of Island, we all read Bob Schwartz's articles on Limit Order Trading. Now, with *The Equity Trader Course*, tomorrow's traders can benefit from this comprehensive overview of stock trading."

—Matt Andresen, President,
Citadel Execution Services,
and former CEO, Island ECN

"Smart investing is one thing, and efficient trading quite another. But effectively targeted material on the intricacies of trading is scarce. I recommend this book as one that impressively fills a critical need."

—Raymond J. Bär, Chairman of the Board of
Directors, Julius Bär Holding AG

"Many seek to understand the mysteries of stock trading—this book represents a unique opportunity to gain deep insights into a cornerstone of the American economy: stocks and the market."

—John C. Giesea, President and CEO,
Security Traders Association

The Equity Trader Course

Founded in 1807, John Wiley & Sons is the oldest independent publishing company in the United States. With offices in North America, Europe, Australia and Asia, Wiley is globally committed to developing and marketing print and electronic products and services for our customers' professional and personal knowledge and understanding.

The Wiley Trading series features books by traders who have survived the market's ever changing temperament and have prospered—some by reinventing systems, others by getting back to basics. Whether a novice trader, professional or somewhere in-between, these books will provide the advice and strategies needed to prosper today and well into the future.

For a list of available titles, please visit our Web site at www.WileyFinance.com.

The Equity Trader Course

ROBERT A. SCHWARTZ
RETO FRANCIONI
BRUCE W. WEBER

WILEY

John Wiley & Sons, Inc.

Published by John Wiley & Sons, Inc., Hoboken, New Jersey.
Published simultaneously in Canada.

For general information on our other products and services or for technical support, please contact our Customer Care Department within the United States at (800) 762-2974, outside the United States at (317) 572-3993 or fax (317) 572-4002.

Wiley also publishes its books in a variety of electronic formats. Some content that appears in print may not be available in electronic books. For more information about Wiley products, visit our web site at www.wiley.com.

Library of Congress Cataloging-in-Publication Data:

Schwartz, Robert A. (Robert Alan), 1937–
   The equity trader course / by Robert A. Schwartz, Reto Francioni, Bruce W. Weber.
      p.   cm.—(Wiley trading series)
   Includes bibliographical references and index.
   ISBN-13: 978-0-471-74155-8 (cloth/cd-rom)
   ISBN-10: 0-471-74155-8 (cloth/cd-rom)
   1. Stocks.   I. Francioni, Reto.   II. Weber, Bruce W., 1961–   III. Title.
IV. Series.
HG4661.S344 2006
332.63'22—dc22

                                                                    2005034340

Printed in the United States of America.

10   9   8   7   6   5   4   3   2   1

To our wives, Jody, Karin, and Teri.
We thank them for their patience,
and for the support and resistance levels
that they have provided.

Contents

Foreword

It is a great time to be a trader. But to thrive today, you need to know more than ever before.

Readers interested in trading have a wonderful opportunity to make money, due principally to the confluence of several well-intentioned federal initiatives that have tilted the markets ever so slightly in favor of traders and against investors. Wayne Wagner of Plexus Group,[1] who does a credible job measuring transaction costs, indicates that more than $40 billion a year moves from investors to traders as a result of the structural issues with the market. That's your opportunity.

First, as this book explains, the rules of the traditional exchanges and the newer electronic communications networks, called ECNs in the slang of the Street, force investors to display their trading intentions for the specialists and dealers to see. Economists say that investors are forced to give the market a valuable option when they reveal their trading intentions in displaying a limit order. Today, you have the same visibility as the pros concerning what is available to buy and to sell.

Second, in 1997, new Federal regulations forced the dealers to allow the public to interact directly with what had been dealer-only trading opportunities. Traders have the privilege of trading with the investors' orders. The wholesale/retail distinction is gone. You now have the same access to the merchandise as the pros.

Finally, more recently, additional federal legislation in 2001 reduced the cost of stepping ahead of an investor's order to only a penny a share, an economically insignificant amount. This means that when you identify an imbalance in the supply and the demand of buyers and sellers, you can, for very little money, step to the head of the line and trade ahead of slower parties. You face the same economics as the pros. This book is all about how you can win a piece of that $40 billion-plus that Mr. Wagner identifies.

---

[1]On January 3, 2006, Plexus Group was acquired by Investment Technology Group, Inc., with whom Wayne Wagner is now a consultant.

In this book you will learn the distinct differences between investing and trading. Investors put money at risk because they have a view about the value of a particular company. They have confidence in the company's management team and its ability to wring profits from a business in a dynamic, competitive industry. Investors care about the supply of and demand for a company's goods and services.

Traders are different. Traders can trade profitably without much, if any knowledge of the company or its business. I am taking an extreme position here to make this point (some traders are experts in the details of the company's business). Traders put money at risk because they have a view of the short-term movement of the stock's price. Traders are interested in the supply and demand of buyers and sellers in the company's stock. That is very different from being interested in the supply and demand of the company's goods and services.

You will also learn here how to take advantage of asymmetries in the rules of the markets that today favor traders over investors. You will learn that the game underlying the market is a problem called "the Prisoners' Dilemma." It is all about the risks inherent in trusting other parties when you show your hand, revealing valuable information that cannot be recalled and which has consequences.

You will learn that the rules of the market are counterintuitive: The person who goes first is penalized and the person who waits is rewarded. Going first, you get exactly the price you stated on your order, even if the person who goes last would have been willing to pay more or receive less. This is the arcane world of what is called *price improvement*, which is Orwellian doublespeak at its best.

You will learn that the person who provides liquidity by leaving a limit order in the market can be hurt by the market's rules. The person who hangs back and only takes liquidity by hitting exposed orders benefits, despite that fact that if everyone hangs back all the time there is no liquidity. In other words, you will learn that the markets reward just the opposite of what they should reward. You will see how in certain situations you will want to wait for the other fellow to reveal his intentions, while in others you will need to show your hand first. But you will also find out that limit orders can be used to capture profits from high intraday volatility, and that intraday volatility must in fact be accentuated for a limit order book market to be viable.

You will learn that large institutions are the main victims of the tilt in the market's rules. You will see them trying to hide their presence in the market by entering ever smaller orders and leaving their orders exposed for ever shorter periods. In today's markets, stealth is the name of the game.

I spend my days and nights working hard at Pipeline to rebalance the structure of the market to neutral, where neither the investor nor the trader is advantaged, where everyone receives exactly the same information at exactly the same time. But we are not there yet. In the meantime, if trading interests you, you should trade now while the rules are on your side.

Alfred R. Berkeley III
CEO, Pipeline Trading Systems LLC

Preface

Would you like to know more about how to drive down your trading costs and effectively exploit intraday trading opportunities? This book has one overriding purpose: to help you do so and thereby enhance your trading performance by delivering highly readable, key information about the dynamics of equity trading. You may be one of a spectrum of individuals who are serious participants in, or observers of, the markets. We have in mind people at trading desks, hedge funds, day traders, market professionals, and technicians; retail investors who in increasing numbers are entering and executing their orders electronically; and anyone else who is curious about how the equity market operates.

If you fit into one of these categories, you might realize that pricing inefficiencies exist, but do you know why and how? Research into market structure issues over the past years has provided tremendous insights into these matters but, for the most part, the material has not been conveyed in an easily accessible, practical manner. Our objective is to close the gap between research insights and practical application.

For a simple and crucially important reason, this book could have been titled *Investing for the Next 30 Minutes*. Each purchase or sale of stock is made within a brief trading interval (perhaps a day, or 30 minutes, or less), during which time, because of trading costs, blockages, and other frictions, share prices may be highly volatile. The accentuated intraday volatility makes it possible for a nimble trader to be on the profitable side of these price swings, and perhaps turn a position into a realized profit within a day, 30 minutes, or less.

But far more is involved. A trader who buys at the wrong moment pays more, and one who sells at the wrong moment receives less because of bad market timing and poor order handling. Consequently, the return that you might realize over a far more extended holding period (perhaps a month, a year, or more) depends critically on precisely when and how, in a very brief interval, your position was first established and then, in another brief interval, unwound. This is in sharp contrast with a frictionless, perfectly liquid market where there would be no trading as we know it—only a costless push of a magic button that would continuously maintain your optimal portfolio weights.

The frictionless, perfectly liquid market is far from reality. In the real world, poor trading can seriously undermine the profitability of good investment decisions. Consequently, short-run trading decisions are critically important, along with the longer-run investment decisions that they are implementing. As memories of the broad bull markets of the mid-1980s and the late 1990s fade and expectations for returns are lowered, trading decisions and costs have an increasingly important impact on investor profits. In the real world, trading stands on its own as an important operation, and as one that is distinct from investing.

Markets and trading operations in the United States and Europe are changing rapidly. Each passing year brings new technology, market structures, and regulations. New operating procedures, trading tools, and analytics keep emerging. The major stock exchanges evolve, new firms enter the playing field, and some old ones disappear. This is exciting and demanding, all at the same time, and it certainly challenges anyone writing a book in this field. We assure you that the basic, driving economic forces will remain, and that the energy spent to understand them will deliver you an asset that will not deteriorate. But, with the passage of time, some of our institutional description will start to look out of date. To clarify the context within which this book was written, the writing was completed by the end of October 2005.

Many of the important points presented in the text will be illustrated with the use of a computer-based simulation model, TraderEx, which is packaged with the book. TraderEx is introduced in Chapter 1. TraderEx has been a foundation of our MBA and executive teaching on trading and market structure, and we think you will benefit from the chance to make your own hands-on trading decisions and see the results live on your computer screen. We clarify certain ideas by presenting TraderEx screen shots and charts based on the simulation. We employ terms defined in the context of the simulation and suggest computer exercises that use TraderEx. Run the simulations to see the ideas discussed come to life.

GUEST CONTRIBUTORS

A number of industry leaders have contributed special pieces for the chapters of this book. Each piece brings valuable reflections and further perspective to various institutional arrangements, activities, and issues that we discuss. We are deeply grateful to these contributors:

Alfred R. Berkeley III, CEO, Pipeline Trading Systems LLC

Paul L. Davis, retired Managing Director, TIAA-CREF Investment Management LLC

Robert Greifeld, President and CEO, NASDAQ Stock Market, Inc.

Frank M. Hatheway, Chief Economist, NASDAQ Stock Market, Inc.

Richard D. Holowczak, Director, Wasserman Trading Floor, Subotnick Center, Zicklin School of Business, Baruch College, City University of New York

Marcus Hooper, Global Electronic Trading Solutions, Bear Stearns International Limited

Peter Jenkins, Senior Vice President, New York Stock Exchange

Michael S. Pagano, Associate Professor of Finance, Villanova University

John H. Porter, Managing Director, Barclays Capital

Gerald Putnam, Chairman and CEO, Archipelago Exchange

Martin Reck, Managing Director, Deutsche Börse AG

Rainer Riess, Managing Director, Deutsche Börse AG

Frank L. Romanelli, Vice President, SWX Swiss Exchange

James Ross, CEO, MatchPoint Trading, Inc.

Uwe Schweickert, Deutsche Börse AG

David Segel, Founder & CEO, the Mako Group

Melissa Spurlock, Senior Consultant, ITG, Inc., former Vice President, Plexus Group

John A. Thain, CEO, New York Stock Exchange

Jean-François Théodore, Chairman and CEO, Euronext NV

Wayne H. Wagner, Consultant, ITG, Inc., Former Chairman, Plexus Group

René Weber, Senior Vice President, Bank Vontobel AG

Claudio Werder, Senior Vice President, Bank Vontobel AG

OVERVIEW OF THE BOOK

The book is structured as follows. Chapter 1 establishes some of the basic features of equity trading and motives for trading, knowledge of which you, as a successful trader, must have. Concurrently, the chapter discusses simulated trading as a learning tool and tells you how to use TraderEx, the simulation software that comes with this book. You will see that a simulated trading environment offers an excellent way to (1) assess your aptitude for trading in different market structures, and (2) improve the speed and accuracy with which you are able to exploit profit opportunities in a fast-moving market. Chapter 1 also tells you how to get TraderEx started; describes alternative plays of the game that are available; and shows you how to enter your orders, interpret screen information, and assess your performance.

Chapter 2 deals with liquidity, the dimension of portfolio analysis that typically receives far less attention in finance courses and elsewhere than it deserves (the other two dimensions are risk and return). Smart trading is all about coping effectively with trading costs that characterize illiquid markets. This chapter explains what is involved. In so doing, we (1) show why liquidity is difficult to define and not easy to measure; (2) establish the relationship between liquidity, trading costs, and intraday price changes; and (3) better enable you to understand why trading is a competitive, zero-sum game that you will want to win. We also present the generic market structures within which liquidity is produced.

The two basic, generic order types that traders use are limit orders (which establish prices) and market orders (which execute at the prices set by the limit orders). In Chapter 3, we turn to the use of limit orders and market orders. Our context, for the most part, is the electronic limit order platforms that form the basic trading systems offered by most equity markets around the world. Accordingly, the fundamental knowledge that you must have as an equity trader is how and when to submit limit orders, and when alternatively to submit market orders. Equivalently, you must know when to pay the bid-ask spread as a cost of immediacy, and when to trade patiently and earn the spread as a liquidity provider. You must also understand when and how to break a large order into smaller pieces to be entered over a succession of trades.

The market structure discussed in Chapter 3 is a continuous trading environment (a trade can be made at any moment that a buy and a sell order meet or cross in price). In Chapter 4, we contrast order entry and trade execution in the continuous trading regime with its alternative, a periodic call auction that batches multiple orders together for simultaneous execution, at a single price, at a predetermined point in time. The call auction alternative is now offered by every major market center around the world. You should understand the call auction's advantages and disadvantages when establishing and unwinding your positions. You should know when to go to the continuous market and when to send your orders to the call when both alternatives are available to you.

Chapter 5 is about the nuts and bolts of intermediary operations. It provides an overview of the New York Stock Exchange (NYSE) and NASDAQ marketplaces, as well as the newer alternative trading systems (ATSs) and electronic communications networks (ECNs). It explains market maker operations, the services they provide, their revenue sources, and their costs. Key aspects of market maker operations are set forth with reference to the TraderEx simulation model. The chapter also discusses special order handling by intermediaries that might help you reduce your trading costs.

In Chapter 6, we turn to two procedures that are widely used by traders: technical analysis and algorithmic trading. Both have been extensively written about and discussed, but we approach them differently. Rather than explaining how to develop and implement technical trading rules and algorithms, we establish the economic logic that underlies their value to you as a trader. Our discussion is linked to price discovery and quantity discovery, two economic functions of a marketplace that are of overriding importance.

The book's final chapter is about performance measurement. Market participants (and you, when using the TraderEx software) need to know how well they are doing as traders. This chapter addresses the complexities involved in performance measurement, and considers alternative performance benchmarks. It then expands the discussion to include transaction cost analysis, risk management, and best execution obligations. We conclude by emphasizing the importance of market structure, and by suggesting that market centers share a best execution responsibility.

PRIOR PUBLICATION

This book builds on a foundation established by Robert A. Schwartz and Reto Francioni in their prior book, *Equity Markets in Action: The Fundamentals of Liquidity, Market Structure, and Trading* (New York: John Wiley and Sons, Inc., 2004). The current, practice-oriented book is distinguished not only in contents but also in form from its predecessor. In *The Equity Trader Course*, we focus primarily on delivering information that a trader will want to know to drive costs down when entering his or her orders, while the prior text is more broadly focused on the role of exchanges, market structure, clearance and settlement, public policy, and regulatory issues. Nevertheless, there is overlap between the two books, and some repetition is inevitable. But much new material has been added, old material reworked, and the TraderEx simulation, which was presented as the final chapter in *Equity Markets in Action*, has been expanded in scope and moved up to become Chapter 1. The simulation now includes order-driven trading, quote-driven trading, and call auction trading, and is integrated into the chapters that follow. Additionally, there are new ideas, examples, and illustrations, along with the contributed pieces.

ACKNOWLEDGMENTS

A number of people have contributed substantially to the production of this book. In particular, we thank Antoinette Colaninno and Nelly Baccaro for their assistance in gathering and assembling information, and helping to keep us organized. Bill Abrams (Schwartz's and Weber's partner in TraderEx LLC) has, as always, given invaluable advice and assistance. Special thanks are also due to Al Berkeley who, along with having written the Foreword for this book and a contributed piece for Chapter 4, has given us very helpful feedback on earlier drafts of the manuscript. We further thank Paul Davis, Frank Romanelli, and Wayne Wagner for their helpful comments on earlier drafts of these chapters. Some of the material in the book is based on recent research undertaken with co-authors to whom we are most grateful: Archishman Chakraborty, Puneet Handa, Mike Pagano, Jacob Paroush, Asani Sarkar, Ashish Tiwari, Avner Wolf, and Bob Wood. We also thank Oliver Rockwell who programmed the TraderEx software, and Bernard Donefer, who developed a Users Guide to TraderEx that has been adapted for use in Chapter 1. Leigh Woods produced the graphs and figures, and we are grateful. Shahzad Hashmi and Aniket Deshpande provided very useful research assistance, for which we are most appreciative. As always, we are deeply grateful to our editor, Pamela Van Giessen, for having given us excellent advice, direction, and encouragement to complete this manuscript on a timely basis; and to Jennifer McDonald at Wiley, who has helped us throughout the publication process.

Robert A. Schwartz
Reto Francioni
Bruce W. Weber

New York, New York
Zurich, Switzerland
London, England
October 2005

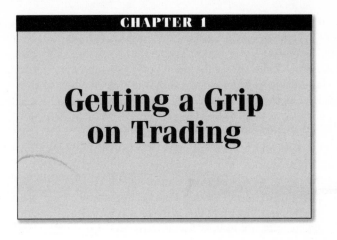

CHAPTER 1

Getting a Grip on Trading

Trading is not investing. Trading is all about converting an investment decision (either yours or your portfolio manager's) into a desired portfolio position. You will want to do this at the least possible cost and in the most timely fashion. Trading is also about finding pricing discrepancies in the market, jumping on them, and realizing a profit. This book deals with these actions.

You might be a novice at all of this. If so, we will lead you carefully through the terms, thoughts, and analytic tools that you will need as you approach a marketplace with your orders. You might be an experienced trader or portfolio manager who understands intuitively much of what we deal with in this book. For you, our goal is to make your knowledge explicit so that you can have greater confidence in your good instincts and decision making, and more successfully avoid some of the pitfalls that all traders inevitably fall into from time to time. You might also use this book as an effective tool to train your new recruits and to sharpen further the skills of your more advanced traders.

A deeper, more structured understanding of the myriad forces that impact on and permeate the markets requires organized discussion, illustration, and experience that does not result in your losing money. The illustration and trading experience should be simplified, precise, and focused. To this end, a trading simulation can help. We introduce a computer simulation in this chapter that will enable you to experience tangibly the dynamics of a marketplace. Just as chess software can help a chess novice or an experienced player prepare for a tournament, the simulation will accelerate your gaining proficiency as an equity trader.

We make numerous references to the simulation throughout the rest of the book and suggest exercises that use it at the end of several of the chapters. Our simulation, called TraderEx, is on the CD that is packaged with this book.[1] TraderEx will enable you to gain hands-on trading experience from multiple perspectives, including that of a day trader, an institutional trader working a large order for a fund manager, a market maker intermediary, or a proprietary trader who wishes to end the day with a zero (typically called *flat*) position. TraderEx offers an excellent way to assess your aptitude for trading and to improve the speed and accuracy with which you handle your orders in a fast-moving market.

Trading is very different from investing. Investing calls for research, analysis, and reasoned judgment. This all takes time, for you and for others as well. A portfolio manager at a large mutual or pension fund may spend days, weeks, or longer formulating an investment decision. In a 2001 Schwartz and Steil survey of chief investment officers and head equity traders at 72 major asset management firms, only 9 percent of the respondents said that their buy orders are regularly generated by a decision process lasting under one hour, and 77 percent said that this is "never" or "infrequently" the case. At the other end of the spectrum, 48 percent said that the decision process "regularly" or "very frequently" takes between a week and a month, and 38 percent said it "regularly" or "very frequently" takes over a month. The responses are summarized in Exhibit 1.1.[2]

But once a decision is made and has been passed on to the trading desk, time acquires a different meaning. The clock suddenly accelerates. Prices in the marketplace can move with startling velocity in brief intervals of time. As they do, trading opportunities may pop up and quickly vanish. Your own order handling can cause a price to move away from you. Poor order placement and imperfect order timing can be very costly. Consequently, a hefty portion of the gains that an asset manager might otherwise have realized from a good investment decision can be nullified by a poor trading decision.

EXHIBIT 1.1   Time Typically Taken by Professional Fund Managers to Make a Buy or Sell Decision

	5	4	3	2	1	Mean
Less than one hour	3.1%	6.2%	13.8%	46.1%	30.8%	2.05
One hour to one day	7.7	9.2	41.6	24.6	17.0	2.66
One day to one week	10.7	32.3	27.7	20.0	9.2	3.15
One week to one month	7.5	40.9	21.2	18.2	12.1	3.14
Over one month	15.2	22.7	19.7	24.2	18.2	2.92

Scale: 5 ("very frequently," or 75-100 percent of the time) to 1 ("never")

In *Blink*, a fascinating book about how we can think quickly and intuitively without literally figuring out our answers, Malcolm Gladwell analyzes decision making from a perspective that is germane for a trader.[3] Perhaps you are at the trading desk of a mutual fund, a hedge fund, or a pension fund. You are an active, short-term trader, and you have orders to work. You see the numbers flicker on your screen. You follow the market as it becomes fast-moving and then, sensing the situation, you act. Without having the luxury of time to figure it all out, you buy the shares, you sell the shares, or you hold back.

When you act, you may take liquidity or supply it. Traders who are successful often choose to wait and then become active. They will not alter their approach when losses arise, and they remain steady on the plow. Decisions must be made effectively under a spectrum of conditions, including when the market is under stress, such as when stabilizing orders are cancelled and a rush of one-sided orders arrives, or at a daily opening or closing when volume is high, volatility accentuated, and the clock is ticking.

Some people are better suited to trading than others. Regardless, it takes training to gain the experience needed to think and act instinctively. Professional traders are good only after lengthy training. Think of the basketball player who, having spent hundreds of hours shooting baskets for practice, makes a clutch shot on instinct just before the buzzer at the end of a championship game. So, too, with the equity trader. Only after many months of training will the good trader trade well on instinct. In his contributed piece for this chapter, David Segel explains the characteristics that his firm, Mako Global, looks for in a trader, and the learning stages that comprise Mako's very carefully structured training program.

ORDER ARRIVAL

Good traders have a good feel for the order flow. They keep their fingers on the pulse of trading. What is the color of the market at the current time? Are buy orders dominating the sells? How sharply might the buy-sell imbalance push prices up? Are the sell orders rolling in and banging against the buys? How sharply might the sell-buy imbalance push prices down?

To get a sense of the economics that can underlie these forces, let's look at a simple model in which orders to buy and to sell have arrival rates that vary with current market prices and with a fundamental, *equilibrium* value of the security (described more fully later in this chapter). We call this equilibrium value "P*." In Exhibit 1.2, buy orders are generated at the

EXHIBIT 1.2 Buy and Sell Order Arrival Rates for Institutional Sized Orders
At higher prices, the arrival rate for sell orders increases, while it decreases for buy orders.

average rates indicated by the downward-sloping buy curve in place at a given time—let's call it t. Sell orders are generated at the rates given by the upward-sloping sell curve.

For this particular setting, with the market bid and ask quotes centered on P* equaling $48, the buy and sell orders are both expected to arrive at the rate of seven orders per hour. If the quotes were centered on a price above $48, the arrival of sell orders would, on expectation, exceed the arrival of buy orders. Or, if the quotes were centered on a price below $48, the arrival of buy orders would, on expectation, exceed the arrival of sell orders. Absent changes in P*, the market quotes will tend to self-correct and remain centered on P*. That is, at higher quotes, selling pressure will move the market back down toward $48, and at lower quotes, buying pressure will move the market back up to $48. But if P* were to shift up from $48 to, say, $48.50, the graph would then center on $48.50. If the quotes did not move up with P*, buy order arrivals would (on expectation) be greater than sell order arrivals, and the buying pressure would push the quotes up until they centered on the new value of P*. The opposite would occur if P* were to shift down from $48 to, say, $47.50.

What lies behind the order arrival rates? To dig into this, we identify three types of traders: information traders, liquidity traders, and technical traders. The information traders and liquidity traders respond to external events—the former to the advent of new information, and the latter to whatever drives their own individual desires to trade. The technical traders respond to the price and quote behavior that they observe in the marketplace. Before we consider each of these three types in greater detail, let's focus on how *arrival rates* for orders and events can be understood as a statistical process.

Poisson Arrival Rates

The arrival of information-driven and liquidity-driven orders can be described with the use of a stochastic statistical model known as the *Poisson Arrival Process*. The Poisson process has some useful properties and it plays a central role in our simulation model. The arrival of new information (news) occurs randomly over time. In the TraderEx simulation, the random arrival of news events conforms to the Poisson process. So, too, does the arrival of liquidity-motivated orders. Let's take a closer look at this statistical process.

The Poisson process has the interesting property of being *memoryless*, meaning that no matter how much time has passed since the last information event, the probability that news will cause P* to jump again in the next segment of time (e.g., minute) remains constant. Consequently, it is not possible to predict when new information change will occur based on the amount of time that has passed since P*-changing news last arrived.

To illustrate, imagine that you are waiting to catch a number 3 city transit bus. While the timetable says that a number 3 bus should arrive every 20 minutes, you do not believe bus timetables and have observed that, in fact, buses arrive, on expectation, every 20 minutes according to a Poisson process. When you get to the bus stop, what is your expected wait time for the number 3? It is 20 minutes. After waiting five minutes, what then is your expected wait time? Again, it is 20 minutes.

Think about this while you are waiting. Knowing that, when on schedule, a number 3 bus arrives every 20 minutes, you figure that the probability that one will arrive in the next minute should increase with each passing minute. But what if you are not sure that you are standing at the correct stop for the number 3? In this case, as the minutes go by, the probability of a number 3 appearing could start to fall off. Now, if in some cases the probability of the next event occurring increases with the passage of time, and if in other cases the probability falls, you might conceive of a third case, a neutral one, one where the probability of a new arrival neither increases nor decreases with the passage of time. This is the Poisson.

The Poisson has some nice properties. First, it has the frictionless,

efficient markets property that it is not possible to predict when information change will next occur (or, for that matter, if the news will be good or
bad). Second, the Poisson is simple. The order arrival rate, signified by the
Greek letter lambda (λ), is its one and only parameter. This parameter describes both the mean and the variance of the distribution. An active stock
will have a high λ value; an inactive stock will have a low λ value. By
changing λ, we can change the rate at which orders arrive and information
events occur in a TraderEx simulation run.

The Impact of Information Change

The magnitude of information change, when it occurs, is reflected by the
size of the jump in P*. For TraderEx, this too is determined by a random
draw. Each change in P* is a return. If P* jumps up (a positive return) it
means that the stock has become more valued, while P* jumping down
(a negative return) means bad news. If you are a stat type, you might
like to know that, in our TraderEx simulation, the P* returns are lognormally distributed with a mean of zero. Each new value of P* is obtained
by multiplying its previous value by one plus the return given by the
draw from a lognormal distribution. Further details on the measurement of returns, and return means, variances, and correlations, are
given in the Appendix, "Prices and Returns," at the end of the book.

Over any simulation run, P* may drift up or it may drift down but,
with a mean return of zero, there is no built-in tendency for it to move in
one direction or the other over any simulation run. We can change the
magnitude of the information events, and thus the underlying level of market volatility, by changing the variance parameter of the (lognormal) returns distribution. One last point: Because the P* returns are obtained by
random draw, successive changes in P* are not serially correlated. P*
moves randomly through time.

Informed Traders

It is useful to categorize the participants in a marketplace as fitting into
one of three groups: informed (fundamental) traders, liquidity traders,
and technical traders. These are shown in Exhibit 1.3. Each of the three
types is represented in TraderEx.[4]

Informational change about the value of a stock is the most important
reason for a security's valuation to change—when the fundamentals of a
company change, the company's value and stock price respond. Informed
traders are those who trade knowing that the current price level diverges
from the true, equilibrium value that you would observe in the market if
all participants were fully informed, and if there were no trading costs or

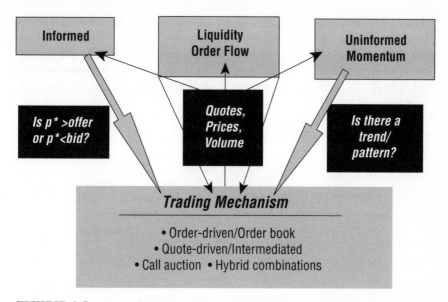

EXHIBIT 1.3   Types of Trades and Market Mechanisms in TraderEx

frictions. In TraderEx, when the P* valuation is greater or less than the stock's market price, informed orders are motivated.

An important area in empirical finance deals with the speed with which markets adjust to new information. In a hypothetical world with costless trading and complete, instantaneous information dissemination, price adjustments are instantaneous, one-shot events. In real-world markets, information-motivated orders arrive at the market sequentially, and price adjustments are noisy and noninstantaneous. Price shifts that reflect new information take place sequentially in TraderEx. This is shown in Exhibit 1.4 for a three-day simulation that we have run.

The contributed piece in Chapter 2 by Claudio Werder and René Weber displays price charts for several different stocks at the time of major news events (including, in one case, a rumor that turned out to be false). We suggest that you look at these charts now (particularly the intraday charts for Schering, Genentech, and Cott). As you do, you might reflect on two things: (1) the rapidity with which a stock's price can suddenly shoot to a new level; and (2) after a sharp jump, it appears that adjustments continue, but with price now following a far more wobbly path. Visually scanning charts like this does not constitute scientific analysis, but you may nevertheless find it instructive.

Informed participants are informed in TraderEx simply because they know the value of P*, and they act on this knowledge in the market by

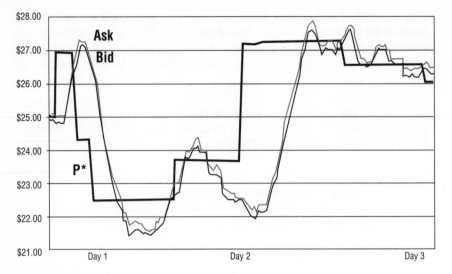

EXHIBIT 1.4 Graph of P* and Market Quotes, Demonstrating Lagged Information Assimilation (TraderEx Simulation)

buying or selling. The informed trader will send a buy order to market if P* is above the value at which shares can be bought (i.e., if it is above the market offer). Similarly, an informed trader will send a sell order to market if P* is below the value at which shares can be sold (i.e., if it is below the market bid). This conforms exactly with the pricing dynamics described with reference to Exhibit 1.2.

Operationally, when P* is above the offer or below the bid, the arrival rate of market orders to buy or to sell is increased from 50 percent to 70 percent of TraderEx's total order flow. When P* is between the bid and the offer, no informed orders are generated and market orders to buy and to sell arrive with equal probability. The imbalance between buy and sell market orders that occurs when P* is outside of the quotes pulls the market in the direction of P*. This is a key dynamic to be aware of. As you play TraderEx, keep asking yourself, "Where is P*?" If truth be known, P* typically is not between the bid and the offer (look again at Exhibit 1.4) and, like the children's book character Waldo, P* is very hard to find.

Informed orders are perfectly directionally correlated with each other. If one information-motivated order to buy arrives at the market, another will also arrive, and then a third, and a fourth, and so on until the market ask is pushed above P*. Of course, due to the random arrival of other orders, some sell orders will be intermingled with the informed buys. Similarly, if one information-motivated sell order arrives, other similarly motivated sell orders will also come in (perhaps laced with some buys) until the market bid is pushed below P*. This is in contrast to our second type of machine-generated orders, the liquidity-motivated orders. These orders are uncorrelated with each other. In the next section, we will see how the liquidity-motivated orders are generated by TraderEx.

In TraderEx, P* periodically updates from one value to another. Recall that the time span from one jump to the next is determined by a random draw that arrives according to a Poisson process. We have previously noted the following about the Poisson arrival process.

- It is memoryless (i.e., the probability of a new value arriving in the next moment of time remains constant as time passes).
- It is a simple process to work with—it has just one parameter, λ, that describes both its mean and variance.
- The rate at which information events can on expectation occur can be controlled by changing λ.

Concurrently, the magnitude of the information events, and thus market volatility, can be changed by changing the variance parameter of the lognormal returns distribution.

Liquidity Traders

We have seen that a one-sided flow of informed orders is triggered whenever the quotes do not bracket P*. If one informed buy order arrives, all other informed traders will send in buy orders until the market's offer rises above P* (which would cut off the flow of informed buy orders). Or, if one informed sell order were to arrive, all other informed traders will send in sell orders until the market's bid drops below P* (which would cut off the flow of informed sell orders). All information-motivated orders are market orders to buy or to sell. In the TraderEx simulation, no machine-generated information order comes in as a limit order.

The liquidity traders play a different role in our story. They come to the market because of their own idiosyncratic desires to trade. Orders from liquidity traders are two-sided, they can be either market orders or limit orders, and they arrive randomly.

The term *liquidity trading* is in the tradition of good old Keynesian economics. A key building block in the Keynesian model is the *liquidity preference function*, which describes people's demand to hold cash. This demand, when matched with the money supply, establishes the interest rate. Cash is the ultimate, perfectly liquid asset because it is the generally accepted medium of exchange. Keynes recognized two reasons for holding cash—a *transaction motive* (you need cash to buy goods and services, and you are paid in cash when you sell a good or service) and a *speculative motive* (you hold more cash if you think that interest rates will rise and bond prices fall, and you hold less cash if you think that interest rates will fall and bond prices rise).

Keynes's transaction motive leads to liquidity trading. To illustrate, consider a liquidity trader—let's call him Arlo—who suddenly becomes cash rich and buys some shares. Perhaps his Uncle Jester has just died and Arlo has been remembered in Uncle Jester's will. Across town, Sally, another liquidity trader, has to pay a bill for her son's college tuition, and she sells some shares. These cash flows and expenditures are unique to each individual. Arlo's and Sally's liquidity orders are totally independent of each other.

The liquidity orders in TraderEx are equally likely to be buy orders or sell orders, and the assignment for each newly generated liquidity order is done randomly and independently. Whatever motivates them, the important thing for us is that these orders are uncorrelated with each other. Recognizing this, let's expand the liquidity motive to include all reasons that are unique to an individual. Most importantly, let's include a trader's individual reassessment of share value. Each investor, having his own opinion about a security's value, is free to change that opinion for a reason that only he knows. Accordingly, a better term for the liquidity motive may be *idiosyncratic motive*. But we will stick with the former—*liquidity motive* is widely used, and also easier to say.

The computer-generated liquidity orders in TraderEx are produced by much the same process as the information orders. The differences are that liquidity orders may be limit or market orders, whereas informed orders are always market orders. Informed traders are impatient because they know that the market will soon adjust and erode their profit opportunities. The informed traders arrive only when P* is not within the market quotes, but liquidity traders can arrive at any time. For each liquidity order, its time of arrival, size, type (limit or market), and price are determined by a random draw from a relevant distribution. The price attached to each machine-generated liquidity order is set with the use of a distribution that we call the *double triangular*.

The double triangular distribution has two modes, one that is located with reference to the current market bid, and another located with reference to the current market ask. One double triangular distribution is used for the liquidity-driven buy orders and another, a mirror image of the first, is used for the liquidity-driven sell orders. The double triangular distribution for liquidity-driven sell orders is shown in Exhibit 1.5.

In this graph, price is on the vertical axis, and the probability of a price being selected for an incoming liquidity order is on the horizontal

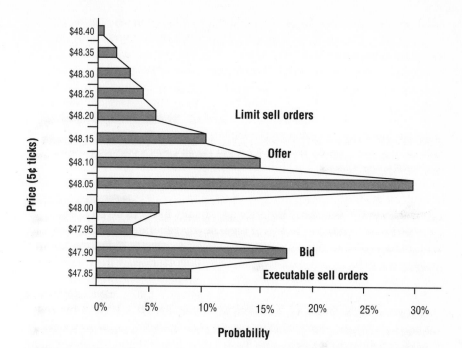

EXHIBIT 1.5 Double Triangular Distribution Used for Generating Liquidity-Motivated Sell Orders

axis. The top triangle has a maximum probability at $48.05, one tick below the market offer of $48.10, and the lower triangle has a maximum probability at the market bid of $47.90. If the price that is picked by the random draw is above the $47.90 bid, the order is placed on the book as a priced order to sell. For a sell order, the price is a *price limit* below which the order is not to be executed. For a buy order, the price is a price limit above which the order is not to be executed. These priced orders are simply referred to as *limit orders.*

If the price that is picked is at the $47.90 bid or below, the order is executable (at least partially) up to the amount available at the bid quote. If the limit sell price produced by the TraderEx software is below the bid, the order will execute down to that price as a market order. Any remaining units to sell are entered as a limit sell (an offer) at the limit price picked by TraderEx.

Because the market bid and offer are the location parameters for the double triangular distribution, the distribution shifts with the bid and the offer. The distribution itself has a neutral effect on prices. If informed orders pull the quotes up (or down), the double triangular rises (or falls).

Whatever level price might be at, the liquidity-motivated orders will not cause it to revert back to a previous level. Neither will they reinforce a trend to a new level.

The distribution, because of the relative size of the two triangles, maintains about a 70 percent/30 percent split in TraderEx between limit orders and market orders among the liquidity traders. This is roughly consistent with many real-world, order book markets. In TraderEx's quote-driven market structure without a limit order book, all orders are market orders, so liquidity-motivated orders are drawn only from the "executable" part of the double triangular.

In TraderEx, any drift that, by chance, is caused by liquidity trading is constrained by the information-motivated order flow. If a buy-sell imbalance from liquidity orders (without any P* change) causes the quotes to move up, informed orders to sell kick in once the bid quote rises above P*. Similarly, informed buy orders kick in whenever an order imbalance causes the offer to fall below P*. Accordingly, the informed orders keep the quotes loosely aligned with the fundamental determinant of share value, our informed order driver, P*. Alternatively stated, the informed orders cause price to mean revert to a previous value whenever a preponderance of liquidity motivated buy or sell orders has caused the quotes to move away from P*. *Mean* refers to an average, and *mean reversion* signifies that price reverts back to an equilibrium value (which has the properties of an average) if liquidity orders and/or technical trading have pushed it away.

Technical Trading

The third source of order flow is from technical traders. These players are prevalent in the market, and you might be one yourself. You could be a market technician using charting techniques, an algo trader, an arbitrageur, or a day trader who might be wearing one of these hats. We discuss technical analysis and algorithmic trading in Chapter 6. These activities are incorporated in TraderEx in a simplified fashion.

Our machine-resident technical traders use one simple rule, that of a momentum player: Buy if price starts to rise, and sell if price starts to fall. Specifically, the machine-resident momentum players operate according to the following algorithm: If a sequence of four or more buy-triggered (or sell-triggered) trades and/or upticks (down ticks) in the midquote occurs, the conditional probability is increased that the next machine-generated order will be a market order to buy (or sell).

Momentum trading is an essential component of TraderEx. Remember, any jump in P* that puts it above the offer (or below the bid), triggers a preponderance of machine-generated market orders to buy (or market orders to sell). These market orders cause prices to run up (or down) toward the new value of P*. Without uninformed momentum traders, it would be too easy for you to detect true P* shifts from the evolution of trade prices. If this pattern were not obscured in some way, you could profit too easily by buying or selling whenever price appears to be trending up or down. We do not want you to be a monopolist with respect to this strategy, and momentum trading can compete with you. It can also mislead you.

The momentum-driven machine orders make your life more complicated partly by jumping onto a run faster than you do. They can also cause very realistic uncertainty for you by reinforcing false momentum moves. Do you see price trending up? Perhaps four liquidity-motivated buy orders happened to have arrived simply by chance. The machine-generated momentum orders will then kick in and reinforce the trend, possibly tricking you into thinking that P* has jumped up when it hasn't. If you are not careful, your own orders can activate the machine-generated momentum orders. Or perhaps four liquidity-motivated sell orders in a row (and/or your own orders) have led to machine-generated momentum selling, which could trick you into thinking that P* has just dropped down when it hasn't. But you never know. Perhaps P* has changed. Even then, the machine-generated momentum orders can trick you by causing an otherwise justified price run to overshoot its mark, the new value of P*.

Both false runs and overshooting commonly cause price to rise too high or fall too low. Either way, price will then reverse course and revert back to P*. Consequently, by including machine-generated momentum orders, we have built patterns of reversals as well as runs into TraderEx. This makes it considerably more difficult for you to exploit any price move. You can never be sure if a run is real, or when and how it will end. The coexistence of positive and negative serial correlation in real-world markets (as well as in TraderEx) masks the existence of each and can prevent each from being arbitraged away.

Bringing the Sources of Order Flow Together

The three sources of order flow are a good characterization of the motives that any of us might have for sending an order to the market. We all act either because of news, because of an idiosyncratic motive (driven by our changing financial needs or reassessments of a stock's worth), or to exploit patterns in the data (that have been suggested by technical analysis, a trading algorithm, or an arbitrage pricing model). These three motives come together to produce a rich dynamic in the marketplace—together, they lead to substantial volume and accentuated intraday volatility. When you see prices jumping around in the market, you will want to know what is causing it. Is it news? Idiosyncratic factors? Technical trading?

As a retail investor, you might also consider what predominantly motivates you to trade. Do you have some special access to news? Do you have confidence in your own judgment (which you from time to time reassess)? Do you move funds into and out of the market in light of your cash flow needs? Do you think that you can pick up footprints in the data and, with sufficient accuracy, sense where price is heading? As retail customers in general and day traders in particular, we may at different times answer yes to all of these questions.

Some buy-side portfolio managers may be more easily classified according to how they invest and trade. A value fund, for instance, trading on the basis of news, would be classified as an informed trader. An indexer, trading because of cash inflows or redemptions and/or to keep its portfolio weights aligned with the market index it is tracking, would be classified as a liquidity trader. A hedge fund, trading because of patterns it has picked up in the data, would be classified as a technical trader.

All of us, either as retail customers or as employees of a fund, can shift between categories depending on the details of the specific situations that have brought us to the market. Whatever, it is more important to classify orders than people. Buy-side customers themselves do not, per se, even exist in the TraderEx software—only the distributions that spit out the orders that customers might submit. The only people in TraderEx are the market makers, and their only motive for trading is to earn a good return by enabling public customers to trade with immediacy at reasonable prices.

THE BID-ASK SPREAD

The bid-ask spread does not exist because of chance in real-world markets (and neither does it in TraderEx). Except for S&P 500 shares, the time-weighted bid-ask spread for shares in the S&P mid cap and small cap indexes in 2004 averaged 1.6 to 2.7 cents, indicating that spreads are generally wider than the minimum one-cent spread. Exhibit 1.6 is a table for market orders in the 2,000–4,999 shares category of orders from an SEC Division of Market Regulation document.

If the posted bids and offers are at least a tick or two away from each other, a spread exists between them. We discuss the spread in greater detail in Chapter 3; at this point, suffice it to say that the existence of the spread is attributable to the desirability of executing with certainty at a posted bid or offer. Because of the allure of certainty, a trader will submit

EXHIBIT 1.6 Memorandum: Comparative Analysis of Rule 11Ac1-5 Statistics by S&P Index, December 15, 2004

Market Orders (2,000–4,999 shares)	Number of Stocks		Stock Price ($)		Market Cap ($Billions)		Quoted Spread (Cents)		Effective Spread (Cents)	
	NYSE	NASDAQ	NYSE	NASDAQ	NYSE	NASDAQ	NYSE	NASDAQ	NYSE	NASDAQ
S&P 100	93	7	42.16	30.30	49.4	117.7	1.9	0.9	3.0	1.2
S&P 101–500	328	67	41.19	34.54	10.6	11.3	2.6	2.1	4.4	3.1
S&P Mid Cap 400	285	112	36.44	30.73	2.4	2.3	3.3	2.8	7.5	5.0
S&P Small Cap 600	318	270	27.53	24.32	0.7	0.7	4.1	4.3	11.7	8.8

Source: Securities and Exchange Commission, Division of Market Regulation

a market order to buy rather than post a limit buy order just a hair (or perhaps more) below the market ask. Similarly, he will submit a market order to sell rather than post a limit order to sell just a hair (or perhaps more) above the market bid.

A spread is maintained in the TraderEx simulation for the following reason. In the simulation software, informed participants and technical traders submit only market orders, and only the liquidity-motivated order flow puts limit orders on the book. As we have discussed, the liquidity-motivated orders are drawn from the double triangular distribution depicted in Exhibit 1.5, where the bid is $47.90 and the offer is $48.10. In this setting, with a five cent price increment, three price points or ticks are between the $47.90 bid and the $48.10 offer. The most probable price for an incoming limit order to sell is $48.05. This price, which in Exhibit 1.5 has a 30 percent chance of being picked, would improve on the best offer by one tick, and would thus reduce the spread. The probabilities of a limit order to sell being placed at $48.00 or $47.95 are just 6 and 3 percent, respectively, in Exhibit 1.5. Accordingly, there is only a low (9 percent) probability that the spread will narrow by more than one tick, and thus it will generally remain meaningful (more than one tick wide).

We have noted that the configuration of the double triangular distribution changes with the addition and elimination (either by execution or cancellation) of buy and sell limit orders. At times there is a small probability that a sell limit will be placed within one tick (five cents in our example) of a posted bid, or that a buy limit will be placed within one tick of a posted offer. When there is just one unpopulated tick between the bid and the offer, it is quite unlikely (generally less than a 10 percent chance) that a limit order will be placed that will narrow the spread. Why? With this tight a market and a five cent tick, you can trade with certainty at a price just five cents lower (if selling) or five cents higher (if buying). At these moments, shouldn't you just take the trade and run? From time to time, the market spread may equal the minimum tick size, but the important thing is that the spread remains meaningful because the probability that a spread-reducing limit order will be placed gets progressively smaller as the spread itself gets increasingly tight. The principle to keep in mind is simple: A bird in hand (e.g., selling at the bid) beats two in the bush (e.g., placing a sell limit order one tick greater than the bid). This principle applies both to real markets and to TraderEx.

THE LIQUIDITY DIMENSION

We have thus far classified orders according to the motives for placing them (information, liquidity, and technical). Orders can also be classified in a totally different way: whether they bring liquidity to a market or take liquidity away. Limit orders do the former, market orders the latter. Trading in general, and specifically the decision of whether to place a limit order or a market order, is all about operating effectively in an imperfect, illiquid environment. For a trader who receives a large order from his portfolio manager, trading is all about the search for liquidity.

Liquidity search involves two dimensions: geographic and temporal. The geographic dimension exists when trading is fragmented over more than one market (e.g., a national exchange such as the NYSE, a regional exchange such as the Boston Stock Exchange, an alternative trading venue such as ITG's Posit, and so forth). The temporal dimension exists when orders that could trade with each other arrive at different moments in a continuous trading environment (such as the NYSE). The order flow in TraderEx is not geographically fragmented—it is temporally fragmented. As you enter your orders into the simulation, think of how you are dividing your own efforts between being a liquidity supplier and a liquidity demander.

In light of the subject's subtleties and importance for portfolio management and trading, we deal with liquidity in its own chapter—Chapter 2. Suffice it here to say that this characteristic of stocks, portfolios, and markets has thus far received inadequate attention in the academic finance literature and in business school finance courses. The contributed piece by Michael Pagano in this chapter makes the point patently clear. Finance professors have devoted extensive attention to two attributes of financial assets and portfolios—risk and return. The third dimension of portfolio management, liquidity, has for the most part been ignored. How come? We address two reasons in particular in Chapter 2. First, liquidity is a slippery concept; it is hard to define and is not subject to straightforward measurement. Second, although in recent years academic research has focused on liquidity, it has historically been common practice in economic model building to assume that markets are perfectly liquid, frictionless environments. It is time that we bring liquidity in from the cold.

OVERVIEW OF TRADEREX

Because of the myriad difficulties of defining it with precision and measuring it with scientific accuracy, liquidity is a particularly difficult variable to come to grips with. But no analysis of a financial market can be complete unless we take the realities of illiquidity into account. In his contributed piece for this chapter, Richard Holowczak has set forth a challenge that faces finance professors and students alike. As he puts it, the problem is "how to bring to life concepts, theories, and analytics that in a classroom may seem arcane and too abstract, and which could prove difficult to apply." He continues with a discussion of how, to this end, a trading simulation may be used in an academic trading room.

Simulation is an excellent venue for discussing, studying, and learning about liquidity and the costs of trading in an illiquidity market. You can use the simulation to experiment with different strategies and apply them in different market structures. You can acquire risky positions, or you can tiptoe into the market. Either way, you lose only simulated dollars. But, then again, the dollars you might win are also simulated. Pretty soon you will find out more about yourself as a trader. Do you like it? Are you good at it? Are you fast at spotting opportunities and entering your orders? Are you getting better with practice? Do you still want to be a trader? We hope that all your answers are yes.

TraderEx is a stand-alone program. This means that your orders and quotes interact with those produced by the computer. The computer-driven orders and quotes are based on sequences of statistical events—order arrival times, P* changes, order size, order price, and so on. Each order and all other events are the result of a draw from one or more statistical distributions, and behind each draw lies a good economic story. The software has a single model for generating the machine orders that applies to each of its market structures. The structures, which we explain in further detail in Chapter 2 and then again later in the book, are *continuous order-driven* (a limit order book market), *periodic call auction* (a batched trading environment), and *quote-driven* (a dealer market). We also include a hybrid combination of the three.

The Ecology of TraderEx

A market is an ecological system. For the ecology to function, an ongoing balance must exist between different types of participants who meet and interact within it. To be resilient, a market must maintain an ecological equilibrium, or reestablish it quickly whenever an exogenous shock throws the market off balance. So, too, must a balance exist in TraderEx. Some participants must want to buy shares when others are looking to sell. Some participants must submit market orders and others must place limit orders. In TraderEx, the key to both balances (the one between buyers and sellers, and the one between limit order placers and market order placers) lies in the interaction between the information traders, the liquidity traders, and the technical traders. The displayed liquidity on the TraderEx screen is a result of this balance.

When trading for their own liquidity (aka idiosyncratic) reasons, be it cash flow needs or individual reassessments of share value, the liquidity traders' limit orders naturally populate both sides of the book. Because of our use of the double triangular distribution, a meaningful bid-ask spread exists on the book. The informationally motivated orders generate price changes following each new draw of P*, and they pull prices back to a previous level when liquidity trading and technical trading have pushed the quotes away from P*. In this regard, order arrival and information change have a self-correcting property with respect to P*. Moreover, the momentum orders cause false runs and overshooting. The false runs help to obscure the footprints of the information traders, and the overshooting provides compensation for limit order traders and market makers.

Overshooting compensates the limit order placers (in the order-driven market) and market makers (in the quote-driven market) for the following reason. When prices mean revert, volatility is accentuated. Mean reversion commonly occurs in relatively brief intervals of time (typically intraday), and consequently price volatility is generally accentuated in relatively brief intervals of time. Picture it this way: Price is driven down and then it bounces back up, or price is driven up and then it drops back down. These zigs and zags that occur during the day can largely offset each other and, in the absence of any major news event (change in P*), price at the close of the day can wind up fairly near to where it started out at the open. But, in the process, limit orders to sell that execute because price was pushed up enough for them to be lifted, and limit orders to buy that execute because price was pushed down enough for them to be hit, turn out to be good transactions. The limit order placers and market makers profit when price reverts back to a previous level. This is equivalent to a dealer profiting from transaction prices bouncing between a lower bid and a higher offer.

What causes mean reversion and the accentuation of intraday volatility? Not the information events per se. News means that price should change to a new level. It is the liquidity events and the technical trading that lay the groundwork for the volatility and the mean reversion. As we have seen, both of these drivers can push prices and quotes away from P*, the price that reflects the broad market's assessment of share value. But after liquidity events and momentum trading have pushed prices and quotes away from P*, the informed orders kick in and pull the prices and quotes back toward P*. Put it all together and you get mean reversion and accentuated volatility. Viewed more broadly, it is all part of the dynamic process by which prices are discovered in a marketplace. We pay particular attention to price discovery in a number of places in the book, especially in Chapter 6.

Mean reversion and accentuated volatility are products of the ecology of real-world markets and of the simulated market that we have constructed. They result from the interaction between the three motives for trading (information, liquidity, and technical factors). This interaction causes the quotes and transaction prices to move through time in complex ways. The prices and quotes do not follow random walks. They trend and reverse. They produce both positive and negative return autocorrelation. *Autocorrelation* means that a stock's return in one period (e.g., t) is correlated with that same stock's return in some other period (e.g., $t-1$ or $t-2$). The auto-correlation patterns are first degree (between returns that are contiguous) and of higher order (between returns that are separated by one or more intervening returns). Neither is consistent with a random walk model. This is the challenging environment of real-world markets and of TraderEx. It is useful to keep this thought in mind when you go to real-world markets to trade, or when you turn to your computer and launch TraderEx.

Canned versus Computer-Generated Prices and Quotes

Any computer-driven financial market simulation can be based on either (1) replays of historic (canned) data or (2) computer-generated data. With the canned data approach, quotes, orders, prices, and trades are taken from an historic transaction record, and the live participant trades against the historic values. The historic data approach is similar to back-testing an investment strategy, where you hypothetically follow a trading rule using market prices for a prior period of time. Many strategies, when implemented in real time, fail to live up to the expectations established by back-testing. A major reason is that when back-testing a hypothetical trading strategy with the data replay approach, your own orders cannot affect the record of past prices—the prices are what they were. With a canned data simulation, you can trade any quantity that you want without affecting the prices at which you trade. How realistic is that? In the real world, your orders can have a big effect on prices and quotes in the marketplace.

Canned data do have an advantage. You know that the stream of quotes and transaction prices that you are trading against reflect reality because they were produced by real-world dynamics. The transaction record used, however, is the product of the specific date, stock, and market that produced it. Perhaps the transaction record is for Wal-Mart (WMT) on September 9, 2005, a day that the stock opened at $45.65, traded in a range from $44.90 to $46.12 (a $1.22 or 2.7 percent hi-lo range), and closed at $45.89, which was three cents higher than its previous close, on volume of 10.8 million shares. Wal-Mart trades on the New York Stock Exchange, and on that date the stock experienced a specific level of volatility, a specific pattern of bid-ask spreads, a specific price trend, and so forth. You could not replay an experiment with a higher level of volatility, lower volume, or with any other parameter or market structure feature altered. Canned data are linked exclusively to the environment that generated them. Not so with the computer-generated data.

TraderEx generates its own market data to address the deficiencies of canned data. You can affect prices. You can rerun the TraderEx simulations to assess the impact of a parameter change, a strategy change, or a different market structure, while experimenting with just one thing at a time. This selective change of the environment is classic economics methodology—we are able to analyze one thing at a time while "holding all else constant," or *ceteris paribus*, for those who speak Latin.

The TraderEx Software

TraderEx reflects real-world markets but makes several simplifications. Most notably, the simulation is completely electronic—there are no phone calls or text messages, no opportunities to bluff others or to gain insights from others. We do not charge a commission to trade (you should be happy about that). Neither do we impose borrowing costs or other restrictions on going short. There are no fancy order types in TraderEx, just plain vanilla, unpriced market orders, and orders with limit prices on them. The software does not have stop orders or allow for all-or-none or fill-or-kill order conditions. It does not allow for negotiation between large participants, and it incorporates just two assets (one risky security and cash). There is no stream of external information (e.g. news stories) upon which you might base your expectations of future share value. There is a good reason for these features. With fewer complications and outside factors, you can focus on liquidity conditions, your tactical order placement decisions, and your profit performance.[5]

TraderEx generates, like the real world, its own order flow. In fact, it is a big number generator—a sequence of statistical events. We draw the numbers, interact them in various ways and, in return, get back transaction prices, quotes, and volumes that move around much as they do in real-world markets such as NASDAQ, the New York Stock Exchange, the electronic trading platforms of Europe, and the Alternative Trading Systems and Electronic Communication Networks in the United States.

To make trading mechanics come to life, we have, as discussed, assembled a set of distributions from which numbers are drawn to determine things such as the price and size of new orders, the frequency of order arrival, the frequency with which shifts in the stock's underlying (and unobservable) equilibrium price occur, and the magnitude of these shifts. We draw randomly from the various distributions but, because of how the orders are handled and turned into trades, the prices and quotes in TraderEx do not change randomly. If they did, the simulation would have little value for you or for us. Also, it would not be much fun.

You can place your orders whenever you choose and trade for whatever motive you wish. The machine orders are generated every x minutes (e.g., 5.5 minutes), where x is an exponentially distributed random variable. The size of a machine-generated order is determined by a random draw from a unimodal distribution that is skewed to the right (specifically, a beta distribution, if you really want to know). A given stream of orders is converted into a sequence of trades according to the rules of order execution that are appropriate for each of TraderEx's four different market environments: the continuous limit order book (order-driven), the periodic call auction (order-driven), the dealer intermediated (quote-driven), and a hybrid combination of the first three. We identify each of these market structures in greater detail in Chapter 2.

Four Requirements

To deliver its promise and to be truly engaging, a trading simulation must have four critical properties:

1. Prices are influenced by your actions.
2. You have some basis for anticipating future price movements.
3. You are able to replay a simulation run so as to observe the effect of a change of your strategy, of market structure, or of a market parameter.
4. You have a meaningful performance benchmark against which to assess how well you are doing and whether or not you are improving with experience.

Let's examine each of these essential properties. First, you can affect market prices. If you enter an order that betters the best bid or offer quote in the market, you may encourage a trade that would not otherwise have happened. If you enter a large buy order, you can push price up. If you enter a large sell order, you can push price down. These things happen all the time in the real world, and they do so in our simulation world as well.

Second, you can anticipate price changes. We have to give you something to go on other than guesswork. Prices and quotes in TraderEx do not simply move randomly. Trading strategies and order placement skills can be developed with TraderEx that would not be possible if the simulation's prices and quotes followed random walks. Trading is not just guessing. Patterns of runs and reversals coexist in real-world markets, and they do in TraderEx as well. Consequently, you should not determine when to act in our simulation simply by throwing darts at a time clock. Your orders should be timed, priced, and sized in relation to your anticipation of future market changes.

Third, you can replay simulation runs. You can replay the TraderEx simulation runs and observe the effect of a change of your strategy or parameter settings. If you have traded impatiently and have suffered the consequences, you are able to go back and see what would have happened if you had used a more patient strategy. Repeat a run and see what would have happened if you had been less aggressive, or had been operating under a different market environment. Each TraderEx run is based on a random number seed that is called a *scenario number*. There are 100 scenario numbers for you to pick from. Keeping the scenario number the same means that, all else equal, the random outcomes in the run would be repeated if you did nothing differently, and consequently you are able to see how your actions can change history. You will see how the outcome changes because you have done something different, changed one parameter setting, or changed the market structure in some specific way, with everything else remaining as before (the ceteris paribus condition).

The fourth and last requirement is that your performance can be assessed. You must have a meaningful performance benchmark that lets you know how you are doing and whether you are improving with experience. You can also use the benchmark to assess the relative success of different trading strategies that you might want to experiment with. For instance, how does trading patiently with limit orders compare with trading aggressively with market orders? One commonly used performance benchmark that works well in one context of our simulation is the volume-weighted average price of shares (VWAP) over the course of a trading day. If the average share has traded at a price of $32.10 and you have bought shares at an average price of $32.05, you have done well. Or, if you have sold shares at an average price of $32.15, you have done well. Note, however, that a direct comparison of an average purchase price or sale price with VWAP does not adjust for risk, and beating VWAP with a risky strategy may succeed only in unusual circumstances. In the market maker simulation, your end-of-day realized profit and loss (P&L) is the appropriate benchmark. You can be more aggressive in setting your quotes and then observe the impact on your P&L. Another important measure if you are playing the role of a dealer is the size of your inventory positions during a trading session. TraderEx tracks the maximum and average position sizes (both long and short) of the market makers, and allows you to see whether taking large positions pays off in terms of higher profits. We pick this discussion up again in Chapter 7.

What the Computer Does

A TraderEx simulation run is a sequence of discrete events over simulated time. TraderEx time passes more quickly than real time; a two-day simulation may take you an hour to complete. While TraderEx is running, the computer:

- Generates a flow of public orders.
- Establishes and updates the limit order book and, when appropriate, keeps and adjusts dealer bid and ask quotes.
- Sets transaction prices according to the market structure and trading rule setting.
- May give participants orders to execute.
- Maintains a screen that displays an order book, the transaction record, and the live participant's trade blotter.
- Captures performance data for on-line graphical display and subsequent analysis.

Here are some other basics that we have previously noted and that will be covered in more detail shortly:

- The live trader places orders whenever he chooses. The machine orders are generated every x minutes on average (e.g., five minutes), according to a Poisson process.
- The size of a machine-generated order is determined by a random draw from a beta distribution that produces orders between 1 and 99 units. In TraderEx's institutional trading setting, a unit can be thought of as 1,000 shares. The average order size is 25 units.
- In each of TraderEx's market structures—order-driven, quote-driven, and call auction—a given stream of orders is converted into a sequence of trades according to the requisite algorithms. The same order flow can give rise to different trade sequences and prices in different market structures.

TraderEx offers two alternatives for advancing time: *Go* and *Live*.

1. With the *Go* mode, you can advance the simulation from event to event by first clicking on the "GO" button, and then clicking on the advance arrow button "+>" to trigger the next event. This mode should be used while first gaining familiarity with the simulation.

2. In the *Live* mode, a time clock in the software advances the simulation automatically. To initiate the continuous running mode, click on the "LIVE" button, which toggles off the GO and > buttons, and begins to advance the clock automatically. The time clock can be set at one of three speeds: slow, medium, or fast (>, >>, or >>>). As you gain familiarity with TraderEx, accelerating the clock is a good way to intensify the game's challenge.

With two minutes remaining in the simulated trading day, you will receive an alert. The close of trading is also announced. The results of the simulation are displayed and are available for further analysis.

GETTING STARTED WITH TRADEREX

In this section of the chapter, we tell you how to get the simulation started; identify the alternative plays of the game that are available to you; and show you how to enter orders, interpret screen information, and assess your performance. Further details on each of the specific trading environments offered by TraderEx (continuous order-driven, periodic call, quote-driven, and hybrid combinations of the three generic structures) are given in Chapters 3, 4, and 5.

Running TraderEx

TraderEx is on the CD that is packaged with this book. The software installs from the CD and requires about four megabytes of hard disk space. After you install and start to run the TraderEx application, dialog screens will appear that present general information and prompt you to configure the market.

To begin, click on the TraderEx icon (reproduced in Exhibit 1.7) and the title window will open (see Exhibit 1.8).

After the program credits, you will set the game's configuration (see Exhibit 1.9).

The call auction is in the hybrid option ("Dealers+PLOB_Call"). There are three market structures, and two to four roles for the user in each. For the purpose of this illustration, we'll choose the Order-Driven Market and Proprietary Trader as your role. You cannot simultaneously choose any other option. As a proprietary trader, you start a run with zero shares and zero cash, and your objective is to end a run with zero shares and positive cash (your trading profit).

Now click on "Continue." Next, set the parameters or accept the default values of the simulation (see Exhibit 1.10).

EXHIBIT 1.7   TraderEx Icon to Start the Program

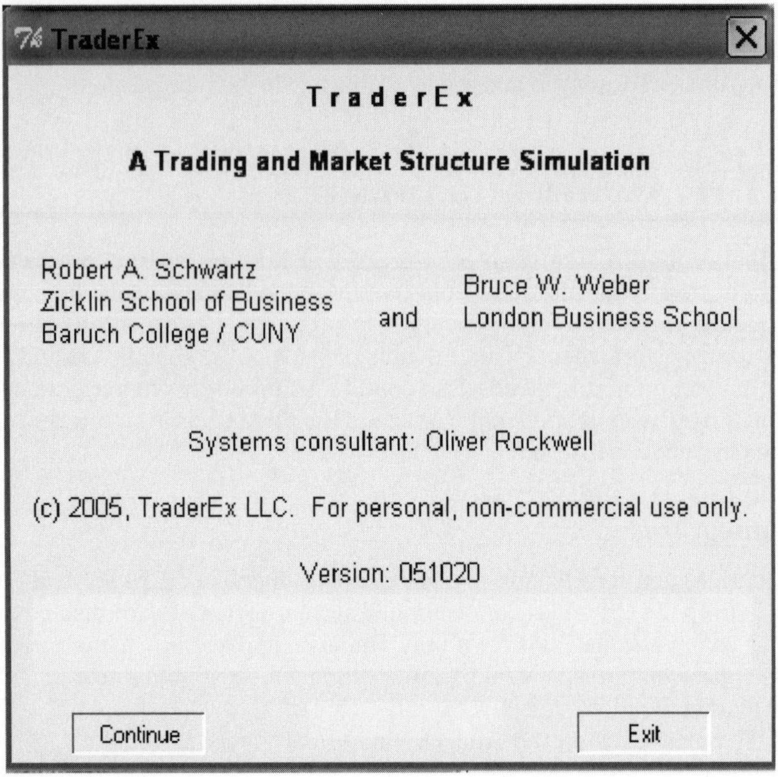

EXHIBIT 1.8   TraderEx Title Window

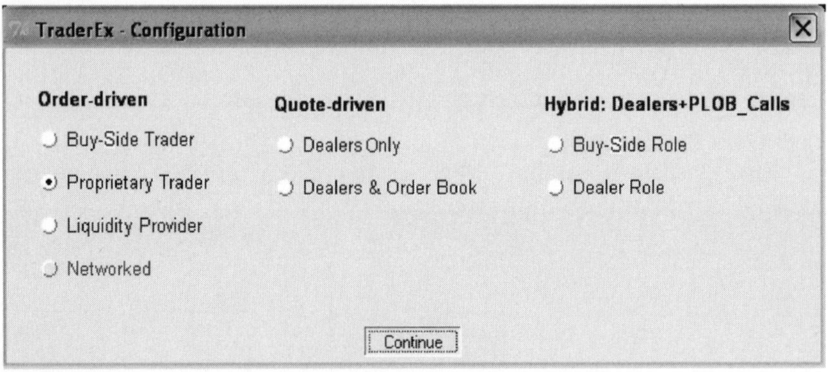

EXHIBIT 1.9   Configuration Window

> ⁊ ORDER-DRIVEN MARKET: CENTRAL LIMIT ORDER BOOK (CLOB) SIM . . .   [X]
>
> Orders Arrive Every 5.5   Minutes
> Limit Order Percentage 90   %
> Daily Returns Volatility = 3   %
> Initial Price = 14
> Simulation Will Run 1   Days
> Numbers Calls per Day (0 to 3) = 0
> Trading Day 9:30a.m-4:00p.m.
>
> Continue

EXHIBIT 1.10   Screen for Setting Parameters of Simulation

Click again on "Continue," accepting the defaults for this simulation. The fourth and final screen before the simulated market opens is the scenario number, which sets the random number seeds in the program's random number generators. The scenario can be any integer from 1 to 100. To run a simulation with the same market conditions, enter the same seed number. When the same seed is reentered, the random elements in the simulation will be identical (as long as you do not change any parameter settings). The only factor that will lead to different outcomes when the same seed and parameters are used is your own actions as a user (see Exhibit 1.11).

One more time, click on "Continue," accepting scenario number 1. It's now 9:30 A.M. and the market is open. After the random number seed has been entered, the simulation begins. You will now see the initial market screen after the 9:30 A.M. opening. Depending on the market structure chosen, the screen and instructions will vary (see Exhibit 1.12).

Even if you do nothing except advance time with the "+" button, the computer will generate public buy and sell orders and the market will move accordingly. As previously described in this chapter, these orders are statistically simulated from three sources: the informed trader, the liq-

> ⁊ **TraderEx - Entry**   [X]
>
> Order-Driven Walk-Book Pricing -- Enter Scenario # (1..100) 1
>
> Continue

EXHIBIT 1.11   Scenario Number Screen

TraderEx

DAY	TIME	SEED	TRDS	INDEX	VOL	HI	LO	LAST	VWAP
1	9:44	1	0	139.6	0			14.00	14.000

TICKER PRICE QTY TIME

QUOTE	13.90	14.00
	26	1

Hit BIDS OFFERS Take

#	TIME	SHARES	TYPE	PRICE

MARKET   ask bid etp wwap

OFFERS	
14.80	
14.70	
14.60	
14.50	41
14.40	23
14.30	26
14.20	
14.10	
14.00	1

BIDS	
26	13.90
13	13.80
13	13.70
	13.60
35	13.50
	13.40
17	13.30
	13.20
42	13.10
18	13.00
15	12.90

TOTAL 0 NA

[9:44] Market Order to BUY 1

VWAP = 14

NET POSITION	0
VWAP	14.000
AVG COST	NA
CASH	0.00
P&L	0.00

GO LIVE QUIT

EXHIBIT 1.12 Initial Market Screen

uidity trader, and the technical trader. Each will react to market conditions and to you as a trader. Remember, the quotes and transaction returns are not random—prices will form trends and reversals that you can anticipate during the day.

Now, let's walk through the simulation's main screen, which we glimpsed in Exhibit 1.10. The top line is straightforward (see Exhibit 1.13).

The next line across the top is a ticker with the last sale price, quantity (number of shares traded), and time of the trade. It will show the latest trades, moving from left to right, as the day progresses. Below and on the left is the central limit order book (CLOB). The top "QUOTE" area shows *best bid/offer*, with the bid for 26 shares at a price of $13.90 per share, and the offer of 1 unit at a price of $14.00. A unit is 1,000 shares. Below the inside bid quote are the other limit orders to buy ("BIDS"), and above the inside ask quote are the other limit orders to sell ("OFFERS"). Both the bids and the offers are arranged from the high price to the low price. The total bid or offer sizes that are entered at each price are shown next to the corresponding price.

Traders tend to focus their attention on the middle of the order book, where you find the best bid and offer. Some screens in real-world markets

EXHIBIT 1.13 Top Line of Simulation's Main Screen

Day	Time	Seed	Trades	Index	Vol, High, Low, Last	VWAP
Where we are in the simulated trading day		The seed number, previously entered as scenario number	How many trades have executed in the market	Simulated market "index" that is positively correlated with the stock's P*	Total shares traded, high, low, and last sale price	Volume-weighted average price of trades done so far

add a column to the right and to the left of the price ladder to show the *cumulative* bid and offer quantities. To avoid screen clutter, we have not done this, but the principle of the display is worth describing. Using just the bid side of the book just described, the cumulative quantities that can be sold to these buy orders are shown in Exhibit 1.14. In other words, the 26 to buy at $13.90, together with the 13 to buy at $13.80, means that 39 can be sold down to a price of $13.80. To sell more, you would have to accept a lower price.

Exhibits 1.15 and 1.16 show the market screen at 10:20 A.M. after more orders have arrived and five trades have occurred with a total volume of 38. The quotes have shifted up to $14.00 and $14.10. The VWAP for the five trades is $14.045. The two graphs in Exhibit 1.16 depict the market's behavior in the first 50 minutes of the trading session. The lower of the two graphs shows the "bid-ask bounce" as arriving market orders alternate between selling at the bid and buying at the offer.

EXHIBIT 1.14 Price Ladder for Bid Side of Order Book

Bids		Price	Offers
Cumulative			
		$14.00	
26	26	13.90	
39	13	13.80	
52	13	13.70	
52	0	13.60	
87	35	13.50	

Hit	BIDS	QUOTE 14.10 10	OFFERS	Take 14.20 40
		15.00	21	
		14.90	16	
		14.80		
		14.70	15	15
		14.60		
		14.50	51	10
		14.40		
		14.30	12	
		14.20	40	
10	10	14.10		
	7	14.00		
	26	13.90		
	13	13.80		
	13	13.70		
		13.60		
	35	13.50		
		13.40		
	17	13.30		
		13.20		
	42	13.10		

EXHIBIT 1.15   Market Screen at 10:20 A.M.—Quotes

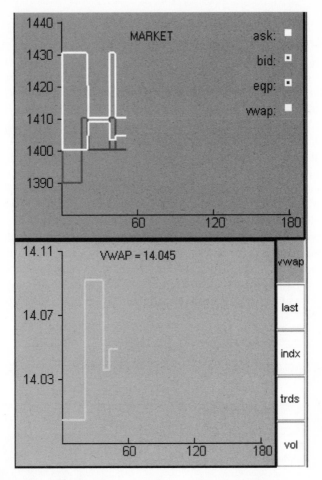

EXHIBIT 1.16 Market Screen at 10:20 A.M.—Graphs of Activity

The last two features are the charts on the right hand of the screen. The upper chart graphs bid and asked quotes and VWAP on the y-axis versus simulated time of day on the x-axis. By watching the bid-ask spread you could gauge market liquidity. The lower chart gives you several alternative graphs. These include market VWAP, the last sale price, the stock market index, number of trades, and volume (number of shares traded) in the market. You can toggle between them as you see fit. As a proprietary or "day" trader, you would most likely want to view the last trade price graph. The charts show only the most recent three hours of trading activity.

Entering Orders

Remember, you are a day trader, acting for your own account, hoping to end the day with a profit and no remaining position in the stock (i.e., being flat by the end of the day). By using market orders, you can "Take" offers and buy stock, or you can "Hit" bids and sell stock. Alternatively you can place limit orders in the order book. Buying and selling large sizes will move the market, so don't show your hand if your strategy is aggressive. You can make long and short trades and hold short positions (which means you have sold stock that you do not own in hopes of buying it back more cheaply).

To enter a market order, press the "Hit" or "Take" labels at the top of the order book, then enter the number of units in the box at the bottom— for example, 10 units (see Exhibit 1.17).

You can enter limit orders directly into the order book by clicking on the box next to the price limit that you want to set for your order. In the screens shown in Exhibits 1.18 and 1.19, the user enters a limit order to buy 10 at $14.10 by clicking the highlighted box, entering the quantity 10 at the bottom of the screen, and pushing the "Enter" key. The order to buy

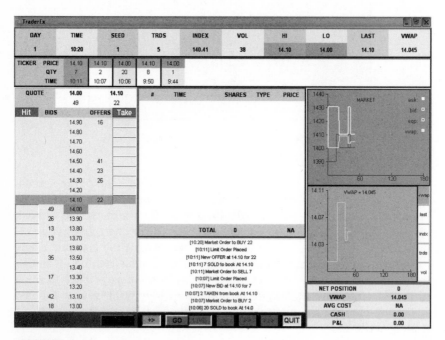

EXHIBIT 1.17 Full Market Screen

DAY	TIME	SEED
1	10:40	1

TICKER	PRICE	14.20	14.20	14.10
	QTY	2	8	4
	TIME	10:38	10:34	10:34

QUOTE		14.10	14.20
		--	12

Hit	BIDS		OFFERS	Take
		15.00	21	
		14.90	16	
		14.80		
		14.70		
		14.60		
		14.50	41	
		14.40	23	
		14.30	20	
		14.20	12	
		14.10		
	49	14.00		
	26	13.90		
	13	13.80		
	13	13.70		
		13.60		
	35	13.50		
		13.40		
	17	13.30		
		13.20		
	42	13.10		

buy market order size?	10

EXHIBIT 1.18 Placing an Order to Buy 10 Shares at $14.10

QUOTE		14.00		14.20	
		7		40	
Hit	**BIDS**		**OFFERS**	**Take**	
		15.00	21		
		14.90	16		
		14.80			
		14.70	15	15	
		14.60			
		14.50	51	10	
		14.40			
		14.30	12		
		14.20	40		
		14.10			
	7	14.00			
	26	13.90			
	13	13.80			
	13	13.70			
		13.60			
	35	13.50			
		13.40			
	17	13.30			
		13.20			
	42	13.10			

Size of buy limit order at 14.10   10

EXHIBIT 1.19 Limit Orders for $14.70 and $14.50 to sell are in the book. User is now entering a limit order to buy 10.

10 becomes the best bid in the market and narrows the quoted bid-ask spread.

Your open, unexecuted limit orders are displayed in the book's outside columns. In this example, the user has limit orders to sell 15 at $14.70 and to sell 10 at $14.50, which is added to the machine-generated order(s) to give the aggregate size of 51 in the book at $14.50. Limit orders can be modified by clicking on the price box with your order in it. The program asks you for the new limit order size, which can be larger or smaller than the current order, or zero if you want to cancel the order altogether.

Look again at the full screen in Exhibit 1.17. All transactions and executions are time stamped and logged in the bottom middle third of the screen. Only the last 10 trades are visible, and the list is not scrollable. You will also be warned here when the trading day is coming to a close.

The prices in the center of the order book, which appear in red and green on the computer screen, are the low and high prices of trades so far in the day. The top of the middle third of the screen is a log of your executed orders (see Exhibit 1.20). Listed are the order sequence number, time, side of the market, quantity, type (limit or market), and price. Only the last 10 are visible, and this, too, is not scrollable. At the bottom of this log is the total number of shares in your position and your average price from the beginning of the day.

In the example illustrated in Exhibits 1.18 and 1.19, the trader built up a long position of 50 in four trades, paying an average of $14.10 per share. The example here is profitable because 14 of the 50 have been sold at higher prices. The profit is shown in the performance table at

QUOTE	14.10		14.20		#	TIME		SHARES	TYPE	PRICE
	11		16		6	10:26	SELL	4	MK	14.10
Hit	BIDS	OFFERS	Take		5	10:26	SELL	10	LT	14.20
	15.00	21			4	10:06	BUY	28	LT	14.10
	14.90	16			3	9:53	BUY	4	LT	14.10
	14.80				2	9:51	BUY	8	LT	14.10
	14.70				1	9:50	BUY	10	LT	14.10
	14.60									
	14.50	41								
	14.40	23								
	14.30	18								
	14.20	16								
11	14.10									
66	14.00									
26	13.90						TOTAL	36		14.10

EXHIBIT 1.20 Log of Executed Orders

NET POSITION	36
VWAP	14.125
AVG COST	14.10
CASH	−506.50
P&L	1.00

EXHIBIT 1.21 Performance Table

the rightmost bottom of the screen (see Exhibit 1.21). The cash level (−506.50) reflects the net amount paid to purchase the 36 net position. The P&L is positive due to the 10 units being sold for 0.10 more than they were bought for. In general, the P&L is the value of the long position plus your cash level: $(36 \times \$14.10) - 506.6 = 1.0)$. This works because, remember, you started the session with zero shares and zero cash.

At the end of the simulation, TraderEx provides your final "Performance Measurement" scorecard. It captures the lower right-hand box at the time of the close. If, instead of acting as a day trader, you are handling a large order for a fund manager, a common benchmark is whether your average cost is lower than the VWAP for the day. In the example shown in Exhibit 1.22, you have successfully bought 116 at an average price of

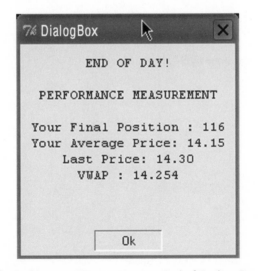

EXHIBIT 1.22 Performance Measurement at End of Trading Day

EXHIBIT 1.23 Buttons for Changing the Speed of the Simulation

$14.15, ten cents less than the VWAP of $14.254, so you did better than the average of the other traders this time out.

Introducing Time Pressure

You now know how to enter orders and interpret your performance measure. After you have gained some experience, you can put a little time pressure on yourself, using the buttons that are on the bottom of the computer screen (see Exhibit 1.23). So far, in *discrete events* mode, you have been able to control time by keeping the "GO" button on and using the "+>" button to trigger the next event.

You can use the *continuous time* mode by clicking the "LIVE" button, and the simulation will be updated automatically. You can set the speed to slow, medium, or fast with the ">", ">>," and ">>>" buttons. The faster the simulation, the more challenging you will find TraderEx to be. Be careful with the "QUIT" button; it ends the simulation and gives you the performance measures up to that point.

FROM THE CONTRIBUTORS

Richard D. Holowczak
Using Trading Simulations on an Academic Trading Floor:
Where the Rubber Meets the Road

Michael S. Pagano
Reflections of a Finance Professor

David Segel, The Mako Group
On-the-Job Training at Mako

Using Trading Simulations on an Academic Trading Floor: Where the Rubber Meets the Road

Richard D. Holowczak

The challenge that faces us and our students is how to bring to life concepts, theories, and analytics that in a classroom may seem arcane and too abstract, and which could prove difficult to apply. Here is an answer: Place the students in a setting where they are confronted with having to solve problems, make decisions, and see the results of the decisions they have made. It is this need that brings them to our trading floor.

Running an academic trading room presents its own challenges. As the director of the Wasserman Trading Floor, Subotnick Center, I have to ensure that we have the appropriate mix of data, software, hardware, and technical support so that realistic market environments can be created. Next, in cooperation with the faculty, we must structure the problems that the students work on.

An academic trading floor, by its very nature, is interdisciplinary. The primary academic fields that we interface with are finance, economics, accounting, and my own field, computer information systems. The floor has three major components: an information component (e.g., real-time and historical data sources, and news services), a methodology component (e.g., specialized software, spreadsheets, and other analytics), and a reality component (e.g., we can follow live news events as they unfold). This is where tools and techniques for problem solving meet specific problems. The problems do not necessarily fit into standard classroom categories. Issues regarding trading and investing transcend finance, economics, and information technology. At our center, we pay particular attention to the trading activity.

As this chapter makes very clear, trading is not investing. We can deal with each in our trading room, but let us here consider trading. We bring in a class of, say, 25 students, and sit each in front of a workstation. What do they see? Prices, quotes, and trades that are driven by a market. Where do these numbers come from? Three sources, as this chapter makes clear: live market data, canned data, and computer-generated data. Each has its strengths and weaknesses. We have found that computer-generated data such as what the TraderEx software provides has distinct advantages in the context of teaching market microstructure. A growing number of universities have established trading rooms containing computer hardware, software, and networking infrastructure similar to what a professional financial institution would possess. The overall aim of these facilities is to provide students with hands-on experience manipulating financial data in a fashion that complements and illustrates the concepts and theories that they are learning in the classroom.

There are three broad categories of exercises that typically take place on academic trading floors: those based on (1) historical data, (2) real time data retrieval and modeling, and (3) simulation. Professional financial market data and information services, such as those provided by Reuters, Bloomberg, Thomson Financial, and others, support retrieval of a broad range of historical financial data from equity, fixed income, foreign exchange, and derivatives markets. Because professionals rely on these data, they tend to be of high quality and can be imported directly into MS Excel or other tools for further study. While Web-based sources of financial data have made great strides in their offerings over the last five years, financial professionals still rely mainly on commercial services for their historical data needs.

Real-time data delivery is also a feature of professional financial market data and information services. With appropriate exchange agreements in place, it is possible to bring real-time data directly to the student's desktop in the academic trading room where they can further be manipulated within spreadsheets or built-in models and screens provided by the software vendor. Some examples of working with real-time data in support of finance curricula include (1) trading against live market prices, (2) arbitrage of various financial instruments between markets (e.g., such as a stock that trades in two different equity marketplaces), and (3) following live coverage of news events and their impact on the financial markets.[6] An example of the latter would be following the testimony of the U.S. Federal Reserve Chairman and observing how the Fed's statements affect the market in real time.

Back to the 25 students trading at their workstations. We have two ways they can trade. First, each student can trade against computer-generated order flow in a solitaire style game. Second, the TraderEx software in our trading room is networked and we can, for instance, sit 10 students in teams of two at five workstations, and have the student teams trade not only against computer-generated orders but also against each other's orders.

In this setting, what do they learn? Their experiences are multidimensional. For instance, they learn about market structure—as this book explains, order-driven, quote-driven, call auction, and hybrid combinations are all represented in the software. The students come to understand that prices and quotes depend not only on exogenous *information flows* but also on the dynamic interaction of endogenous *order flows*. They quickly appreciate the pressures generated by the rapid swings and shifts in the market, which come from the machine-generated order flow, and which are intensified in the networked setting where the students find themselves in stiff competition to get their orders filled at good prices and in a timely manner.

Our students are faced with a very precise, structured, irreversible environment in which, on an ongoing basis and on their own, they have to act and react to deliver performance. This is called pressure. They learn how to deal with pressure, survive, and perform in terms of the bottom line. They quickly find out how effectively they are operating, whether they enjoy it, and if they are cut out to be traders. In other words, the trading software is an effective screening device. Plus, this is all accomplished without putting real money on the line.

Achieving a successful experience requires proper preparation, execution, and control through all three phases of the training process—pretrading, trading, and post-trading. The pretrade phase is best handled in the classroom where key information about market structure, liquidity creation, and the basics of order handling are delivered. The second phase, which takes place on our trading floor, includes teaching the students how to use the simulation and giving them structured simulation exercises. We progress through this phase as follows: First we have them play the solitaire version in which they manually advance the clock; next we put the simulation on a time clock without the ability to pause; and lastly we move on to a networked play of the simulation. At the end, their trading results are captured and saved for the post-trading phase, which involves subsequent analysis and discussion. If time permits, the discussion can be further expanded to include, for instance, the handling of block orders, applications to market making, and key issues in market regulation.

One further thing: We invite the students to return to our trading floor on their own and to run the simulations as they wish. We are not surprised to see them take us up on our offer. The simulation is not just challenging—it is also fun.

Reflections of a Finance Professor

Michael S. Pagano

A finance professor faces the never-ending challenge of striking a proper balance between theory and practice. Finance is an applied field for students who want to establish successful professional careers. Accordingly, an educator must make the classroom experience insightful, relevant, and memorable. *Insightful* means blending classic finance theory with the latest developments in the field. *Relevant* means that the educational experience is connected to the realities of actual markets. *Memorable* means that the students will carry the knowledge with them and be able to use it effectively after they have entered the industry and are moving up the corporate ladder.

Recognizing this, I think of the materials generally presented in financial markets courses, investments courses, and portfolio theory courses. What do we do a first-rate job at? Telling students all about expected return and how it is related to risk. We all know that investors are risk-averse, must control risk, and have to be appropriately compensated for accepting risk and holding riskier portfolios. This calls for proper portfolio diversification. This is the import of the capital asset pricing model, the arbitrage pricing model, and the market model regression equation. Further extensions include value at risk (VAR) and hedging with derivatives to control risk. I could continue on. So our students graduate knowing a great deal about a risk/return world. There is only one trouble with this: The real world is not two-dimensional.

Three factors, not two, matter in the real world—risk, return, and . . . liquidity! An analysis of risk and return alone is comparable to analyzing just two dimensions of a three-dimensional object. Mistakes, errors, and misunderstandings are inevitable. Liquidity simply should not be ignored. Illiquidity's impact, however, cannot just be layered onto a risk/return relationship as if it was simply a third floor being added to a sturdy, two-story house. A three-dimensional efficient frontier is organically different from a two-dimensional frontier. Asset prices do not reflect only risk, and expected returns do not include only a risk premium—they also include an illiquidity premium.

What about order of magnitude? It might commonly be thought that risk is quantitatively more important than liquidity. Over relatively lengthy periods of time (e.g., a month, a year, or longer), it is indeed true that informational change is the main reason why prices change, and longer-run variance does more closely reflect change in the fundamental variables.

This is not the case, however, for short-run returns. It is in the short run that illiquidity-related trading costs have their sizable impact, as this book (see Chapter 2 in particular) makes clear. Consequently, volatility is elevated in short (e.g., intraday) periods.

Does the intraday volatility have an appreciable, adverse effect on long-run investment returns? Yes, indeed! For example, consider the contrast between a perfectly liquid, frictionless environment and a real-world market with one-way trading costs that can total 150 basis points (bps). In the case of a frictionless environment, suppose that, at a total cost of $1,000, you acquire $1,000 worth of shares and realize a 10 percent return after one year. At this point, you sell and put $1,100 in the bank. Approach a real-world market with $1,000 and you will incur a 150 bps cost when you buy, leaving you with $985 invested in the shares, and then see the shares rise 10 percent over the year. At this point you sell, again incur a 150 bps cost, and put $1,067.25 in the bank. Your gain? It is driven down by more than 32 percent to a net return of 6.73 percent. Without question, this translates into an expected return having to carry a relatively large illiquidity premium.

Recent academic research has finally recognized the importance of liquidity, but finance textbooks and most instruction still ignore this concept. It is easier to teach about a frictionless, perfect capital market because, in such a simplified world, only risk and return matter. A focus on liquidity, however, pulls us into an environment where definitions, modeling, and measurement are far more subtle and complex. Moreover, institutional realities (e.g., the structure of an equities market) that are totally not applicable in a frictionless world are of paramount importance in the real world where portfolio decisions, at a cost, must be translated into orders and trades. This can be intriguing material for the students, but it is not easily taught in the classroom.

Trading simulation software such as TraderEx provides an invaluable way of achieving a good balance between theory and practice. As a professor, I have found it extremely useful to describe key market structure concepts such as the functioning of a limit order book, liquidity provision, and the market impact of institutional order flow by combining theoretical discussions of these topics with the students' use of the trading simulation software. The hands-on simulation experience brings difficult concepts to life in the eyes and minds of the students.

Technology developments have had a powerful, positive, unintended consequence for finance professors in terms of both research and teaching. We now have enormous electronic databases that include tick-by-tick transaction prices, quotes, and volumes for listed stocks for major markets around the globe. These records have enabled us to see the footprints that illiquidity has left in the marketplace. It is now imperative for professional traders to be aware of these costs, and for buy-side trading desks to be focused on concepts involving transaction cost analysis and best execution.

Without question, the third dimension of portfolio analysis has now captured the attention of the industry. It is time that we bring liquidity into our undergraduate and MBA programs as well. We are gaining the knowledge and we have the tools to deliver it. This will pay substantial dividends in terms of a deeper, more relevant learning experience for our students, and they will remember it far longer after completion of their program.

On-the-Job Training at Mako

David Segel, The Mako Group

The Mako Group is one of Europe's foremost players in the trading world of exchange-listed derivatives, and we trade equity products and fixed income across the globe.[7] One reason for our long history of success is our ability to identify, train, and retain top trading talent. We are known in the industry as a place where some of the best traders come to realize their potential.

How do we find and train our candidates? What do we look for in a person's character, which suggests that he is a trading talent? What tools and methods do we employ to help our young traders succeed as quickly as possible? Here are our answers.

CHARACTERISTICS OF A STRONG CANDIDATE

The following six traits, ranging from discipline to entrepreneurial spirit, are what we primarily look for in a strong candidate.

1. *Discipline.* Discipline is the single most critical factor to success. It begins with academic discipline. The candidate's ability to absorb theoretical and practical information during the trading period is essential, as the academic program is challenging. The mental discipline to work long days with unwavering concentration will begin in the training days, but it will be required throughout the career of the trader. A trader will need the decision-making discipline to stick to a game plan while many, many forces attempt to disrupt or derail that plan. Most importantly, the emotional discipline to manage one's own fears, one's greed, and the associated ego, is paramount. And so, from the initial stages of interviewing prospective candidates, we are looking for signs of personal discipline or the lack thereof to help us best assess the candidate's potential as a trader.

2. *Humility.* If one could study the outside world's perception of the stereotypical successful trader versus the real personalities of top professionals, one would find a wide fissure. The world wants the success story to be macho, bullying, egoist, and insensitive. In reality, baseline humility and quiet confidence characterize the best of the best. Self-confidence is an important element, but it must be balanced by a humble spirit. Mako seeks candidates with an ability to

45

admit their mistakes. Those who can recognize their own weaknesses, and possess a nature of humbleness, will be well served by these traits to get through the most difficult moments, when egos threaten to sabotage success.

3. *History of success.* Every disclaimer we read says "Past performance is no guarantee of future success." But in fact, past performance can be a terrific indicator! In the case of identifying recruits, we look for a strong history of success in life challenges that have nothing to do with trading, but more to do with a demonstration that "this person can make things happen."

4. *Trading experience.* Previous experience trading the markets is not necessarily a plus. Eighty percent of our successful traders come to Mako with no professional trading experience. Our success rate among those who come in as such is extremely high, with almost 90 percent going on to become successful traders. Of the 20 percent that we hire from the trading community, a much higher percentage fail. They fail to adapt to new styles. They fail to adapt to what is frequently an environment of higher responsibility and pressure (our tie between performance and compensation is very rigid). Or they fail for other reasons. Only a small handful of our top traders have come from other trading firms, and they are by far the exception rather than the rule.

5. *A gift with numbers.* A good trader usually has an interest in all things quantitative. Concentration on the task at hand is critical in trading. Traders often focus on a set of numbers or relationships from 7 A.M. to 7 P.M. without so much as a break for coffee. Concentration is mentally and physically exhausting. If that trader does not have an innate interest in and ability to work with numbers, then this level of concentration is unsustainable—not to mention that he will never be competitive. A PhD in mathematics or engineering is helpful but by no means a requirement. The sums are not complicated. But innate quantitative interest and numeric ability are critical.

6. *Entrepreneurial spirit.* Mako looks for candidates who are always seeking value. We ask, "Is this someone who is going to take a risk to earn a return?" Actually, we find that the best traders are the ones who cannot sit at peace when there is opportunity within reach. Sometimes for fun we leave a $10 bill or a £5 note on the floor in the interviewing room in sight of the candidate, just to see how distracted they are by the "residual value opportunity." In this exercise it is interesting to find out if they are value seekers or not. We like candidates who have shown initiative from a young age to try experiments because they have a core need to make money. Did they deliver newspa-

pers or shovel snow for pocket money as youngsters? Did they set up a small business at university? Even if they failed, did they at least try?

MAKO TRADER TRAINING PROGRAM

At Mako, we view the process of learning to trade as similar to what an athlete or a musician experiences. The beginning stage of development is geared toward exposure, awareness, language, and mechanics. The second stage focuses on thoroughly engraining mechanics into practice. The third works to develop intuition and skill in the complex process of trade decision making.

As an expert trader, one expresses a market view by processing a large number of inputs and then taking decisive action. It becomes an intuitive expression of risk in the market, the value view to the trader. It is equivalent to a powerful performance of Puccini's "Nessun Dorma" by tenor José Carreras. It is like a game-winning fade-away jump shot for Philadelphia '76er Allen Iverson. It is sinking a 30-foot putt for golfer Tiger Woods. All are experts' expressions from their gut, intuitive reactions to their situation, all filled with creativity and decision making executed in the blink of an eye.

Training Program—Novice Stage (12 months)

Trainees in the exposure stage are schooled in four areas: the technicals, undertaking mock trading, gaining experience, and interacting with experts.

1. *Technicals.* A thorough knowledge of the technical aspects of our trading is critical. Over an 18-month period, we run a complete academic schedule with exams. We teach options theory, market practice, historical market events, trading strategies, risk management, systems and controls, and a variety of fundamental and technical concepts. This is designed to give the trader a solid foundation upon which to build the ability to make trading decisions.

2. *Mock trading.* Many of the more experienced traders in the market are products of the floor trading culture, where a powerful voice box and an extra long arm's reach both count as valuable assets. The open outcry environment is a terrific world in which to learn to trade. Inputs are limited; a trader only has available to him what he can see with his eyes or carry in his pockets. No telephone, no computer, no coach or manager or sounding board. Pressures are high, speed is

critical, mistakes are not quickly forgiven. And so we at Mako still teach every trainee pit trading skills, even if they will never trade in a pit. Trainees relish the opportunity to raise their voices a few afternoons a week and scramble with their peers for pretend orders in our simulated pit. They quickly learn the language and etiquette that the brokerage community expects them to use. Plus they learn trading lessons in a way that touches their competitive spirit, and this makes the lessons stick.

3. *Experience.* Spending time working in the market is key. Markets are curious places, with their own language, culture, etiquette, pace, and method. Immersion is critical to long-term success. We employ a Berlitz style of learning from an early stage. Trainees are thrown into market circumstances in support roles well before they have the language or practical skills to deliver quality work, but with help around them they learn this way and move more quickly through the early stages of trader training.

4. *Access to experts.* Working next to or in mentorship with expert traders is critical. Skills and success rub off. One can learn in isolation, but learning from experts practicing their skill every day is far better and faster. As an example, imagine learning to play competitive tennis just by hitting a ball against a concrete wall. Some of your skills will undoubtedly improve over time, but the progress will be slow and the diversity of experience will be limited. Play, however, with a professional, and your experience is different. At first the serve comes towards you at a frightening pace and you have no chance of returning it. But if the teacher is good, and your capacity to learn is intact, your pace and breadth of learning will increase exponentially. You will become a proficient tennis player in a much shorter period of time. It's the same with trading. So we create an environment in which every trainee has a daily opportunity to absorb experience from an expert.

Junior Trader Program—Mechanics Stage (9 months)

The next step is to learn to manage your own risk. Experienced traders at Mako will be responsible for making many significant risk and value decisions every day. They will do this in the context of a team environment, where their decisions will impact many people and many pieces of a portfolio. Before a trader can work at that level of responsibility, and in a fully integrated fashion, it is our belief that the trader needs some game-time action to experience real trading. So we have created an environment that operates in parallel to our production activity. It is live trading with real profit and loss, but it allows the trader to develop proficiency in steps, with a limit to the number of forces acting on his decisions at any given time.

We need to be clear about our objective in the first months of production experience as a trader. It is not to make money. It is to avoid losing money while learning and making mistakes. Mistakes are best made early when the stakes are small and the causes are clear. Too often traders start with too much risk from the beginning of their career and are taken out of the game with large losses that could have been controlled or limited to the realm of expensive lessons if their process had been more patient and controlled. We use the following restrictions to focus the junior trader:

- *Limit the scope.* Trade only one product or one name. If it is a stock, learn everything you can about that stock. Know its history. Learn its fundamentals. Understand who buys and sells it.
- *Limit the method.* We focus our junior traders on electronic markets and ask them to focus only on their system. No brokers, no alternate systems—nothing but the core activity. We can add complications later once they have mastered the core environment for their product.
- *Limit the exposure.* We ask our junior traders to start with the smallest tradable increment. Again, the first goal is not to make money; it's to learn from mistakes and to learn the environment. What's the point of doing this on a large risk profile? Greed and ego say, "Trade bigger!" but with some caution one can learn a huge number of lessons at reasonable cost incurred through trading losses.
- *Increase the experience.* A novice trader should trade as often as possible and as small as possible. Every trade is an opportunity to learn. Get over the intimidation about pulling the trigger by trading actively. Learn about the impact of fees and slippage by trading actively.
- *Keep a trading diary.* One terrific tool for novice traders is to keep a diary of each session's activity. What were the market's or the product's daily range and volume? How much did you trade? What was your biggest mistake? What was the best thing you did? All of this serves to create a discipline around the product—it allows the lessons learned to really set into the mental processor!
- *Deal with personal issues.* Fear, greed, and ego—how do they work in you? A trader must know what it feels like to buy sevens and then watch sixes, then fives, then threes trade. Fear of losing money, fear of failure, inability to admit you were wrong, all play their part in affecting the decision maker. And what happens when a trader experiences a profit? When you make a decision, enter a trade, and it goes your way, how do you react? "I'm clever!" or perhaps even "I'm smarter than the market!" are common responses. Human instinct

wants to realize that good decision by locking in a profit as quickly as possible, hence affirming the part of our psyche that wants to be right. This can destroy a trader's ability to make a sound judgment about the execution of the closing transaction. Sometimes greed creeps in and encourages you to get more out of a position, even if there is no more upside. Experience the human response early and learn about yourself as a trader before the stakes get higher.

Traders—Expression Stage (Learning Never Ends)

Once an individual has successfully accomplished all of the goals set out by the program in the preceding stages, he is ready to move on to a desk as a trader of Mako's core capital. Here this person will have the opportunity to work with a team of experts, and will be engaged in a real-time activity of pricing, trading, and risk managing a large inventory of integrated positions. All of the skills learned in the Exposure and Mechanics Stages of the program will be put to practice, and there will be large rewards to reap from the success of being an expert trader who expresses his or her market views through decisions every day.

The move into the realms of Mako's team of traders may mark the formal end of the training program, but as many expert traders will testify, one of the great satisfactions of this career choice is that, for traders, the learning never ends.

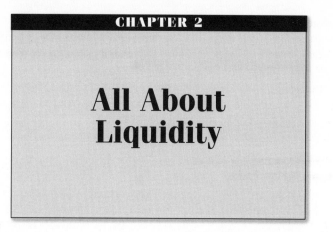

CHAPTER 2

All About Liquidity

S mart trading is all about coping effectively with trading costs along with intraday trending and accentuated price swings that characterize illiquid markets. In this chapter we explain what is involved. In so doing, we clarify that liquidity is elusive to define and not subject to straightforward measurement. We first consider the relationship between information and prices. In a perfectly liquid market, the two would be tightly linked. In actual markets they are not. We also establish liquidity's relationships to price and quantity discovery, price volatility, and market structure.

Traditional finance literature has devoted overwhelming attention to risk as a determinant of share prices, while liquidity, as a topic, has been short-changed (consider again Pagano's contribution to Chapter 1). Liquidity has a relevant relationship to risk—both are reflected in the volatility of short-period (e.g., intraday) price movements. Risk translates into volatility simply because information changes in unpredictable ways—sometimes it is good news and price rises, and sometimes the news is bad and price falls. Illiquidity translates into volatility in a more predictable way—transaction costs push prices up for buyer-initiated trades and down for seller-initiated ones, and accentuated price swings occur because of the difficulty of discovering market clearing prices in the presence of illiquidity.

As we will see, transaction costs that are attributable to illiquidity can have an order-of-magnitude, adverse impact on portfolio performance. Peter Bernstein has written an excellent book about investment risk, which he titled *Against the Gods: The Remarkable Story of Risk.*[1] The idea of betting "against the gods" makes sense because, with risk, you sometimes lose but you also sometimes win. If Bernstein were to write a comparable book about trading, we would suggest that he title it *Against the Devil: The Remarkable Story of Liquidity.* "Against the devil" is appropriate because, as an investor (or a company seeking to raise capital in the equity market), with illiquidity, you always lose.

FROM INFORMATION TO PRICES

Information is the input that drives investment decisions and trading, and security prices are a result of the process. In fully efficient markets, information would be reflected in prices with an accuracy that leaves no investor with an incentive to search for additional information or to trade. A fully efficient, frictionless world is a perfectly liquid environment. With perfect liquidity, shares can be purchased and sold instantaneously, at no added cost, at prices that correctly reflect share values. If information were fully reflected in prices, and if trading were seamless and costless, then security prices would follow a random walk (except for an upward drift that yielded a positive expected return on capital) and a stock's price would jump about randomly over time in response to the arrival of unanticipated information. However, when the realities of actual markets are taken into account, it is clear that trading is not frictionless and that share prices do not follow random walks. Understanding this is crucial to appreciating why trading is distinct from investing.

A Perfectly Liquid, Frictionless Environment

It is standard economic methodology to construct models that are based on simplifying assumptions, which of necessity are unrealistic. The capital asset pricing model (CAPM), a major pillar of modern portfolio theory, shows how share prices depend on the relationship between a stock's price movements and change in a broad market index. This model is based on three key assumptions:

- There are no taxes, no transaction costs, and no short-selling restrictions.
- Investors are fully informed and therefore have the same (homogeneous) expectations about what prices will be in the future.
- Unlimited amounts can be borrowed or lent at a constant, risk-free rate.

Viewed comprehensively, these assumptions may be rolled into one: The world is a perfectly liquid, frictionless environment.

In the perfectly liquid, frictionless environment, the information presented to all of us is in the form of the ultimate bottom line—we all know the risk and return characteristics for all stocks and for all port-folios. These characteristics are described by the distributions from which returns are drawn. A representative distribution is shown in Exhibit 2.1. The chart shows the distribution of daily returns for a stock with a mean return of 0 percent and a standard deviation of 1 percent. Two-thirds of the daily returns will be between –1 percent and +1 percent, while 95 percent of the time the daily return will be between –2 percent and +2 percent.

Investors in the perfectly liquid, frictionless world all know that actual returns are drawn randomly from the distribution shown in Exhibit 2.1. They also know how the return drawn for one stock is correlated with the return drawn for any other stock for any interval in time. These inter-stock correlations are *covariance terms.* In the frictionless world, investors also know that the distributions are normal, and that normal distributions are characterized by two parameters: their mean and variance. Consequently, all information in the frictionless world is summarized by the means and variances of returns distributions for individual stocks and portfolios, and by the covariances of returns across stocks and portfolios.

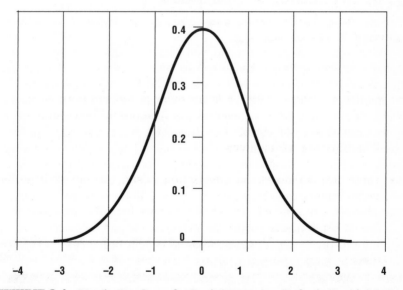

EXHIBIT 2.1 Distribution Curve for Stock Returns in a Perfectly Liquid, Frictionless Environment

This CAPM world is elegant in its simplicity. It provides important insights into several areas:

- The definition and measurement of risk.
- The risk reduction that can be achieved through portfolio diversification.
- The nature of risk and return relationships.
- The pricing relationships between a market portfolio (a basket of all stocks), the set of risky stocks that comprise that portfolio, and the risk-free asset.

In the environment that we have just described, each stock has an intrinsic value. The term *intrinsic value* means that a share's worth can be set with reference to one or more objective determinants. Accordingly, a stock's intrinsic value can be found by security analysts who do their homework forecasting revenues and earnings of the companies they cover.

In the CAPM environment, the worth of a stock is determined by just one thing: its beta—how that stock's return covaries with the return on the market portfolio. This can be explained as follows. Our starting point is that investors are all in perfect agreement about how a stock covaries with the market portfolio. Investors understand that higher covariance means higher risk, and that a higher expected return is the compensation for accepting higher risk. They also know that, if the risk is the same for two different stocks or portfolios, then the compensation will be the same.

What is it in this perfect world, you might ask, that leads two or more stocks with identical covariances to have identical expected returns? The answer is simple. Consider two stocks, A and B, whose covariance with the market portfolio is identical. If A has a higher expected return than B, which one would you (and everyone else) wish to hold? Stock A, of course. But as you (and everyone else) select A, what happens to the price of A and of B? A's price is driven up (and, accordingly, its expected return falls), and B's price drops (and, accordingly, its expected return rises). In the perfect world, these price changes would continue until the expected returns for A and B are equal, and thus neither dominates the other in the marketplace.

The prices that result from the expected returns for A and B being equal are intrinsic values. In the perfectly liquid, frictionless world, any deviation of a stock's price from its intrinsic value would be instantaneously eliminated by arbitrageurs either going long (if the stock's price is too low) or shorting the stock (if its price is too high).[2]

The world we live in, however, is not perfectly liquid, and stocks do not have intrinsic values. Without intrinsic values, share prices must be discovered in the marketplace as the buy and sell orders of a broad set of investors are brought together and turned into trades. That is why price determination and trading are complex processes. While we might all know this to be the case, we can get a sharper sense of what is involved by addressing a fairly simple question: Broadly speaking, what is the information set that underlies equity valuations?

Information

Let us look at what lies beneath the information depicted by returns distributions. *Raw* information pertains to market conditions and to the fundamental determinants of share value. To be useful, the raw information has to be collected, processed, and analyzed. The contributed piece by Claudio Werder and René Weber later in this chapter presents four different examples of major information events, three are real and one is a rumor. It is quite apparent from the discussion and accompanying price charts that, for these cases, prices did not adjust instantaneously to the news. When news occurs, sharp price responses follow, but following a jump, volatility can remain high and price may trend in one direction or the other (consider, for instance, Werder's and Weber's intraday charts for Genentech, Schering, and Cott).

Taking an aerial view, we can classify this information in two broad categories: market (trading) information and fundamental information that relates to the investment decision (the basic determinants of share value).

Market information includes knowledge of the current quotes, last transaction prices, and transaction volume. In addition, some traders take account of recent high and low prices, the daily opening price, the previous day's close, and short interest. It is also of value to have information on orders that have not yet executed, including knowledge of the limit order book, knowledge of orders held by traders in the crowd[3] (which are partially revealed), and statements of buying and selling interest by block, institutional, and other large traders (which are partially available on systems such as AutEx).

Fundamental information relating to the investment decision pertains to the determinants of future share value and includes six categories:

1. *Recent share price history*—knowledge of the historic values of the means, variances, and covariances of returns, and so on.
2. *Current financial information*—information concerning profits, current capital structure, earnings forecasts, and so on.

3. *Current strategy of management*—knowledge about the current strategic business and outlook, especially concerning growth.

4. *Current economic information*—information concerning the firm's product market, the firm's competitors, national and international economic conditions, and so on.

5. *Structural change*—knowledge of recent innovations, acquisitions, divestitures, discoveries, regulatory change, and so on.

6. *Organizational efficiency*—knowledge of corporate structure, cost structure, managerial ability, and so on.

The six categories of fundamental information pertain to the environment and to the firm whose security is being evaluated. We might view information even more broadly, however. The relevant set would also encompass attributes of the decision maker—the technical knowledge and experience that allow a good assessment of relevant facts. This information ranges from the decision maker's experience and skill at assessing intangibles, such as managerial ability, to formal knowledge of portfolio theory and the capital asset pricing model. Information of this type may be nothing more than enlightened intuition; nevertheless, it is a key input into decision making.

Through the buy and sell orders that participants send to the market, the full set of information is translated into price. *Price* is a monetary measure. Specifically, it is the exchange rate (e.g., in dollars, euros, or Swiss francs) at which shares can be bought or sold. If the transaction takes place at an exchange, it does so at an *official price*. In contrast, *value* reflects the worth of a share to a specific investor based on that individual's assessment of available information. Because of the complexity of information and the limitations of the tools available for analyzing it, investors generally differ in their private assessments of share value. In light of this, the term *value* can also be used to describe a consensus market assessment—a *consensus value* or *equilibrium value*. An equilibrium value, however, is not an intrinsic value, and security analysts do not undertake a treasure hunt to find a golden number that we might call an intrinsic value. Rather, share prices are set the way they are for most resources—in the marketplace, in relation to the forces of demand and supply.

There are some exceptions, however. Some prices are used for valuation purposes outside the market in which they are established. This is commonly referred to as *derivative pricing* or as *price basing*. Price basing is used, for instance, in relation to futures and options trading when a price determined in the derivatives market is used to set price in the related cash market. If value is completely linked to underlying fundamentals (e.g., if the value of an option depends entirely on the terms of the instrument and objectively measurable properties of the security that it is written on), then all investors have the same assessment of value and the worth of the security can be considered an *intrinsic value.*

Information can be classified in another way—it can be characterized as public information, inside information, or private information.

- *Public information*—widely disseminated information that is readily available to the public. Being readily available does not necessarily mean, however, that the information is provided freely. For instance, real-time data on market quotes and transaction prices and many historic databases must be paid for.
- *Inside information*—information possessed by only a select set of people who have a special position with regard to the information. Corporate officers and others with business ties to a company (such as an investment banker, lawyer, or proofreader) are commonly in possession of inside information.
- *Private information*—information that individuals may individually possess because of their own investigations and analyses.

Comprehensively viewed, the set of publicly available information is, in a word, enormous. Consequently, individuals see only parts of it and each participant typically assesses information in a way that, to some extent, is unique given his own vantage point. For this reason, private information plays a major role in the formulation of individual expectations. Nevertheless, tapping effectively into even a relatively specific information set can require considerable skill and expense, and an analyst who can do this successfully may earn handsome returns. An article in the *Wall Street Journal* on October 6, 2003 illustrates how.[4]

The *Journal* reported that between June and August 2003 certain large institutional investors, using two detailed pharmaceutical databases that cost subscribers between $25,000 and $50,000 a year, were able to determine that the drug company Schering-Plough was losing market share for its hepatitis C medicine to a competitor, Roche Holding AG.[5] The investing public got hints of the development in July, but full information was not available until August 22. During this period, Schering's share price peaked at $20.47 on June 18 and then drifted down, dipping below $17 as July turned into August. On August 21, the stock closed at $16.48. Strikingly, on August 22, the day when Schering confirmed the declining sales trend for its product, shares opened down $2.18 at $14.30. The *Journal*'s comment: "While nobody did anything wrong in this case—the investors weren't acting on inside information and the company violated no disclosure rules—it highlights an information chasm in the drug business that essentially punishes smaller investors." The underlying reality is that the large investors were acting on *private information*, and they were richly rewarded for their efforts. Undoubtedly, similar stories can be told many times over for many different industries.

Expectations

Given the current information set that they possess about a company, investors form expectations about a company's future returns, and they buy or sell shares based on these expectations. Consequently, expectations link current information to the market value of shares. Question: Do investors form identical expectations? If so, we say that they have *homogeneous expectations*. If not, we say that investors have *divergent expectations*.

Think of yourself and your friends. Think about what you read in the papers and hear on TV. Think of the discussions you and your friends have entered into at cocktail parties and other social events. Consider why some people are buying shares of Pfizer or Vodafone at the same time that others are selling. It is quite obvious, is it not, that investors disagree with each other's evaluations—that they have *divergent expectations*? This simple observation (with which, ironically, just about everyone will agree) is of major importance, both for your investment and trading decisions and because it has implications for the dynamic formation of quotes and transaction prices in the marketplace. When expectations are divergent, stocks cannot have intrinsic values and no stock analyst can determine a stock's price. Prices can be found only in the marketplace. It is as simple as that.

This reality aside, much formal analysis in financial economics assumes that different investors have the same expectations concerning security returns. Even though we may agree that the assumption of homogeneous expectations is unrealistic, models based on this assumption, such as CAPM, give much insight into how the market determines prices for various assets according to their risk and return characteristics, as we have just discussed.

But some academicians cite a reason for assuming homogeneous expectations that goes well beyond the need for model simplicity. To some, rational decision making implies the homogeneity of expectations. This is because decision making considers what a rational person would conclude given the facts, where the facts are the information set. A common academic symbol for the information set is the Greek letter omega (Ω). Presumably, what one rational person would conclude given omega, all rational people should conclude.

However, having considered the elements that comprise the information set, we may better understand why the assumption of homogeneous expectations is unrealistic. It is plausible for a group of investors to have homogeneous expectations only if they share the same information set and process omega in an identical way. Do they? Let's look again at the realities of the world that we live in.

Information sets are vast, complex, and a challenge to understand. Symbolically speaking, omega is an elephant. Different individuals see only parts of omega, and some investors produce private information. To an extent, we all resemble the six blind men who, upon touching different parts of the elephant, reach different conclusions about what they are in contact with. "A spear," says one, whose hand is on a tusk. "A rope," says another, who is holding the elephant's tail. "A fan," declares a third, whose hand is on the huge animal's ear. And so on, as shown in Exhibit 2.2.

Recognizing that investors can have divergent expectations paves the way for a further possibility. Individuals may also reassess their individual valuations based on what they come to know others are thinking. We refer to this as *adaptive valuations*. To illustrate: The news came out on January 3, 2006, that the U.S. Federal Reserve Board had indicated in the minutes of its December meeting that, being less concerned about inflation, the program of raising interest rates may be nearing an end. A bullish expectation based on this information would be that the market will rise on the promise of a monetary brake being relaxed. A bearish expectation could be that the market will fall because the Fed believes that further monetary tightening would be harmful to an economy that is dangerously

EXHIBIT 2.2 Six Blind Men Perceive an Elephant
Source: JainWorld.com.

fragile. Put yourself in the shoes of a bearish participant, and consider your reaction when, following the Fed's disclosure, a slew of new buy orders arrives on the market and prices, which to that point have been flat for the day, quickly pop and the Dow closes up 130 points for the day. Would you reconsider your own assessment of the Fed's decision in light of how others have reacted? If so, you have adaptive valuations.

Two economists, Shmuel Nitzan and Jacob Paroush, have shown that adaptive valuations reflect rational behavior when giving weight to other participants' decisions makes it more likely that a correct decision will be made.[6] James Surowiecki further elaborated on this and presented numerous examples in his popular book, *The Wisdom of Crowds*.[7] Curiously, the average opinion of a large number of people about something that is uncertain can be extremely accurate relative to each individually expressed opinion, even when nonexperts are part of the crowd. The "uncertain something" can range from the number of jelly beans in a large jar of beans, to the location of a submarine that had disappeared in the North Atlantic, to the value of a share of Yahoo! stock! Surowiecki puts it this way: "[W]hen our imperfect judgments are aggregated in the right way, our collective intelligence is often excellent."[8] In implicit recognition of this, many of us alter our views about the value of a stock when, either through direct interperson communication or by observing the behavior of the crowd in the marketplace, we learn the opinion of others. We return to this important point in Chapter 6.

The divergence of expectations among investors, along with the adaptive nature of evaluations, has major implications for the operations of a securities market. It explains why information change can lead to heavy trading. Namely, everyone does not react to new information identically and, as prices adjust to news, some choose to buy while others decide to sell. Further, as we have stressed, in an environment where expectations are divergent, share values cannot be determined at the desks of security analysts—they must be set in the marketplace where the buy and sell orders of a spectrum of participants are brought together and translated into trades. With divergent expectations and adaptive valuations, price discovery is complex, and the process works itself out over an extended period of time (we return to this thought later in the chapter and again in Chapter 6). In so doing, *price discovery accentuates price volatility.* A good grasp of this is essential when you are going into a market to trade.

Trading vs. Investing

Let's recap. Trading is a complex activity that is distinct and separable from investing. Investment decisions involve portfolio formation and stock selection with respect to longer-term risk and return relationships. Trading involves the implementation of investment decisions. It also involves buying and selling to exploit short-run price swings and arbitrage possibilities in an environment replete with illiquidity considerations—transaction costs, price discovery noise, and various other trading restrictions and blockages.

Some excellent investment managers would make poor traders, and vice versa. Successful trading requires special analytical skills, emotions, and attitudes. Good traders can sense a market, spot pricing discrepancies, and make lightning-fast decisions. The long run for an investment manager may be the better part of a year or more. The long run for a trader, as of 9:30 A.M., may be 12 noon or earlier. Trading involves strategy and tactics. You do not want to pay more than necessary for a purchase or accept less for a sale. At the same time, you do not want to miss a trade because you have bid too low or offered too high. Your optimal order placement decision in an illiquid market should depend on your demand to hold shares of a risky asset, your expectations of what the market-clearing price will be, and the design of the trading system that you are sending your orders to. None of this would be of any importance in a market that is perfectly liquid.

Trading well is important for participants regardless of their size. No one wants to pay the price of receiving poor executions, and all would like to reap the benefits of smart order timing. From sell-side broker/dealers to day traders, to hedge funds, arbitrageurs, and beyond, trading is the name of the game. But for one type of participant in particular, trading is also a formidable challenge—the buy-side traders who are looking to implement their portfolio managers' investment decisions. In his contributed piece to this chapter, Peter Jenkins considers this challenge in light of the buy-side trader's vision that he will always have, and from the point of view of the NYSE's current efforts, of which he is now a part. As Jenkins puts it:

> *Since moving to the NYSE, I continue to respect the challenges facing institutional traders who struggle to define and defend best execution while navigating the various order types and trading tools. In many ways, these are uncharted and choppy waters for institutional traders. The institutions must find ways to balance the regulatory and market events that impact their day-to-day trading activities while seeking both liquidity and the best strategy for trade execution so as to achieve best execution.*

As the big asset managers so well know, they have the largest need for liquidity.

DEFINING LIQUIDITY

We talk about liquidity and worry about being stuck holding illiquid positions. We know that three characteristics of assets and portfolios are relevant to a portfolio manager—return, risk, and liquidity—but most formal analyses and presentations in MBA finance courses focus only on the first two. *Return* is easily defined and measured. *Risk*, although more difficult to measure, is also an operational concept—it is typically measured by the variance or standard deviation of returns. But how might we define and measure liquidity?

The typical dictionary definition of a liquid asset is "one that is in cash or that is readily convertible into cash." This does not help much. "Readily" refers to the time required to convert into and out of cash, and to the dollar cost of the conversion. But how are time and cost measured, and what are reasonable values to look for? A better approach may be to focus on the attributes of liquidity, such as the depth, breadth, and resiliency of a market:

- *Depth and breadth:* A market has depth and breadth if orders exist at an array of prices in the close neighborhood above and below the price at which shares are currently trading, and if the best buy and sell orders exist, in total, in substantial volume (that is, if the sum of the orders at each price is sufficiently large).
- *Resiliency:* A market is resilient if temporary price changes due to temporary order imbalances quickly attract new orders to the market that restore reasonable share values. Trades are less apt to be made at inappropriate prices when a market is resilient.

Liquidity can also be measured by the tightness of bid-ask spreads (the difference between the lowest price at which anyone has stated a willingness to sell and the highest price at which anyone has stated a willingness to buy). The liquidity of a market may alternatively be proxied by the frequency with which an asset trades, and by the magnitude of an asset's short-period (e.g., intraday) price instability.

Each of the attributes just described can be measured. But how should the individual measurements be combined into a single index of liquidity? The set of attributes, viewed comprehensively, can lead to conflicting assessments (for example, a market may have depth and breadth but lack resiliency). Thus we do not have an unambiguous, operational definition of liquidity.

Nevertheless, a proxy such as an asset's average bid-ask spread has been used in statistical analyses. Accentuated short-period (e.g., intraday) volatility also reflects trading costs that are attributable to illiquidity and, for this reason, intraday volatility is a good inverse measure of liquidity. The effective spread [which, under simplified conditions, can be shown to equal $2 * \sqrt{cov(\Delta P_t, \Delta P_{t-1})}$] measures the combined influence of the quoted bid-ask spread and trade-to-trade volatility. Another good measure is market size and trading volume.

Illiquidity and Market Size

Large markets are said to be *deep*, and small markets are said to be *thin*. When you array a spectrum of securities by their market size, you find that liquidity and size go hand in hand. Accordingly, a stock's market size is a good proxy of the stock's liquidity. Common measures of size are market capitalization (the number of shares outstanding times the price per share), number of shareholders, and average daily trading volume.

It is important to recognize, however, that even if a large number of individuals have invested in a company (as is the case with many firms whose shares are traded in a major market center), the market for a company's stock may be thin. This is because, during any trading session, only a relatively small percentage of individuals may actually be seeking to trade. The problem can be particularly acute within a trading day as, at any specific moment in time, only a handful of individuals (if any) may be actively looking to buy or to sell shares.

Markets are thin because most investors seek to trade only when they are sufficiently dissatisfied with their portfolio holdings to incur the costs of a transaction. This is in contrast with the markets for most goods and services, where an individual must periodically go shopping in order to consume a resource. For instance, someone who drinks five bottles of beer a week must, on average, buy five bottles of beer a week.

Professional traders are well aware that an important influence on a stock's price behavior is its size, and the effect of thinness on the trading characteristics of individual securities has been well documented empirically. This would not be the case in the absence of transaction costs. In a frictionless environment, thinness would not matter. In the frictionless world, all stocks and all markets are perfectly liquid.

LIQUIDITY AND TRANSACTION COSTS

The cost of illiquidity is that, when a price concession has to be paid to execute an order quickly, buyers pay higher prices and sellers receive lower prices. In many respects, illiquidity and trading costs are two sides of the same coin. Trading costs include:

- Taxes and commissions.
- Order handling, clearance, and settlement costs.
- Trading halts, blockages, and other trading restrictions.
- The adverse price impact a big order from a large trader might have in a relatively thin market.
- The opportunity cost incurred when the market moves away from you before you have completed your trade.

In this section, we take a closer look at the trading costs side of the coin.

Transaction Costs

Transaction costs are classified as either *explicit costs* or *execution costs* (which are, by their nature, implicit). The explicit costs are visible and easily measured; they include, for example, commissions and taxes. Execution costs, by contrast, are not easily measured; they exist because orders may, as a result of their size and/or the sparsity of counterpart orders on the market, execute at relatively high prices (if they are buy orders) or at relatively low prices (if they are sell orders). *Slippage* and *implementation shortfall* are other terms used to describe the transaction costs incurred when buy and sell orders come to a market.

Trading costs can appreciably reduce your returns (look again at Pagano's contributed piece in Chapter 1). They also cause you to adjust your portfolios less frequently and, accordingly, to hold portfolios that would not be optimal in a perfectly liquid, frictionless environment. Pent-up demand increases the eagerness with which you and other investors seek to transact when you eventually do come to the market. The more eager you are to trade, the more likely you are to place a market order (demand liquidity) rather than a limit order (supply liquidity).

Moreover, because trading is costly and price discovery is a dynamic, uncertain process, you are apt to use a trading strategy when you come to the market to implement your investment decisions. You will want to think through decisions such as the kind of order to submit (e.g., limit order or market order), the price to place it at (if a limit order), and the time to submit the order (e.g., at the market open, at some point during the day, or at the market close).

Execution Costs

To understand execution costs, we first define the following terms:

- *Quotation*—a price at which someone is willing to buy or to sell shares and the number of shares that he wishes to trade. A quote can be either *firm* or *indicative*. If firm, the participant setting the quote is obliged to honor it if a counterpart arrives. If indicative, the quoting participant is not obliged. During normal business hours, quotes set by market makers and limit order placers are generally required to be firm.
- *Bid quotation*—the price at which someone is willing to buy shares. The highest posted bid on the market is the *best market bid*.
- *Ask quotation*—the price at which someone is willing to sell shares. The lowest posted ask on the market is the *best market ask*.
- *Market bid-ask spread*—the best (lowest) market ask minus the best (highest) market bid. The market spread is sometimes referred to as the inside spread or as the *BBO* (best bid and offer).
- *Individual bid-ask spread*—the difference between the bid and ask quote of an individual participant (typically a dealer) willing to both buy and sell shares (i.e., make a two-sided market).
- *Limit order*—an individual participant's priced order to buy or to sell a specific number of shares of a stock. The limit price on a buy limit order specifies the highest (maximum) price a buyer is willing to pay, and the limit price on a sell limit order specifies the lowest (minimum) price a seller is willing to receive. Limit orders that are posted on a market are *pre-positioned*. The pre-positioned orders to buy and to sell that are most aggressive establish the best market quotes and thus the market's bid-ask spread.
- *Market order*—an individual participant's unpriced order to buy or to sell a specific number of shares of a stock. In a plain vanilla, limit order book market, market orders execute against the pre-positioned limit orders. Market orders to buy are typically executed at the best (lowest) quoted ask, and market orders to sell are typically executed at the best (highest) quoted bid.

Next, it is helpful to distinguish between active and passive trading. In an exchange market with continuous trading, an execution is realized when two counterpart orders cross. This happens if one of the following three scenarios occurs:

1. One public trader first posts a limit order, and another public trader then submits a market order that executes against the limit order.

2. A market maker sets the quote, and a public market order executes against the quote.

3. Two or more public traders negotiate a trade. The negotiation may take place on the floor of the exchange, in the upstairs market, or via direct contact with each other.

In each case, one party to the trade may be viewed as the active trader or the instigator, and the other party as the passive trader or liquidity supplier. The one who is seeking to trade without delay is an active trader. Active traders are the public market order traders (cases 1 and 2) and the trader who initiates the negotiation process (case 3). Passive traders include the limit order trader (case 1), the market maker (case 2), and the trader who does not initiate the negotiation process (case 3). If you are an active trader, you will generally incur execution costs; these payments are typically positive returns for passive traders. However, if you are a passive trader, you run the risk of a delayed execution or of not executing at all.

We are now ready to identify three implicit execution costs. The major execution costs for a smaller, retail customer is the bid-ask spread and opportunity costs. A large institutional customer may also incur market impact costs.

1. *The bid-ask spread.* Because matched or crossed orders trigger transactions that eliminate the orders from the market, market bid-ask spreads are positive and, with discrete prices, must be at least as large as the smallest allowable price variation (currently one cent in the United States for most traded stocks). An active trader typically buys at the offer and sells at the bid, and the bid-ask spread is the cost of taking a round trip (buying and then selling, or selling short and then buying). Conventionally, half of the spread is taken to be the execution cost of either a purchase or a sale (a one-way trip).

2. *Opportunity cost.* Opportunity cost refers to the cost that may be incurred if the execution of an order is delayed (commonly in an attempt to achieve an execution at a better price), or if a trade is missed. A buyer incurs an opportunity cost if a stock's price rises during the delay, and a seller incurs an opportunity cost if a stock's price falls during the delay.

3. *Market impact.* Market impact refers to the additional cost (over and above the spread) that a trader may incur to have a large order execute quickly. It is the higher price that must be paid for a large purchase or the reduction in price that must be accepted for a large sale.

Exhibit 2.3 illustrates market impact in an order book market without hidden or iceberg orders. Market impact in this order book market would re-

QUOTE		26.10		26.20	
		4		12	
Hit	**BIDS**		**OFFERS**	**Take**	
		27.00	21		
		26.90	16		
		26.80			
		26.70			
		26.60			
		26.50	41		
		26.40	23		
		26.30	26		
		26.20	12		
	4	26.10			
	49	26.00			
	26	25.90			
	13	25.80			
	13	25.70			
		25.60			
	35	25.50			
		25.40			
	17	25.30			
		25.20			
	42	25.10			

EXHIBIT 2.3 Market Impact Illustration

sult from a market sell order larger than 4 units, or a buy order larger than 12 units. For instance, buying 30 immediately would entail purchasing 12 at 26.20 and the remaining 18 at 26.30, for an average purchase cost of 26.26, and market impact of 0.06 or 0.23 percent (23 basis points).

Market impact may also be thought of as a sweetener paid to induce the market to absorb the large order. Market impact also results when others, who learn that an order is in the offing or is being worked, front-run it (i.e., trade ahead of it to acquire a position quickly before price moves, and then quickly flip out of the position at a better price). It is not legal for a broker/dealer to front-run a customer order. However, it is legal to trade on the *expectation* (as distinct from the *knowledge*) that a customer might be seeking to buy or sell shares. Such expectations are common in an environment where large institutions break up their orders and present them to the market in smaller tranches over a period of time.

Transaction Costs and Portfolio Performance

Trading costs are commonly estimated for large, institutional trades. The Plexus Group analyzes trading decisions and trading costs for an institutional customer base that currently accounts for approximately 25 percent of worldwide exchange volume. Plexus Group was purchased by the Investment Technology Group (ITG) on January 3, 2006. Plexus has measured costs (including commissions) that average 1.57 percent (or 47¢ for a $30 stock). The breakdown, in basis points (bps), is shown in Exhibit 2.4.

Is roughly 150 basis points a large amount?[9] The cost of a round trip (buying and selling) is double, or 3.0 percent. To put this in perspective, Pagano, in his contributed piece in Chapter 1, uses the example of a portfolio manager with a one-year holding period who is considering acquiring shares of a company with an expected return of 10 percent per year. Pagano put it this way:

> In the case of a frictionless environment, suppose that, at a total cost of $1,000 dollars, you acquire $1,000 worth of shares and realize a 10 percent return after one year. At this point, you sell and put $1,100 in the bank. Approach a real world market with $1,000 and you will incur a 150 bps cost when you buy, leaving you with $985 invested in the shares, and then see the shares rise 10 percent over

EXHIBIT 2.4   Breakdown of Trading Costs

	In Basis Points*	In Cents
Commissions	17 bps	5¢
Market Impact	34 bps	10¢
Delay	77 bps	23¢
Missed Trades	29 bps	9¢
Total	157 bps	47¢

*One basis point is 1 percent of 1 percent.

Source: Plexus Group.

*the year. At this point you sell, again incur a 150 bps cost, and put
$1,067.25 in the bank. Your gain? It is driven down by more than
32 percent to a net return of 6.73 percent.*

We note that the percentage reduction in the risk premium for holding
the shares (the expected return minus the risk free rate) is even greater—
if the risk free rate is 3 percent, the risk premium is reduced from 7 percent to 3.73 percent, which is a 47 percent reduction!

The magnitude of this impact has led Wayne Wagner, chairman of the
Plexus Group,[10] to state that "total transaction cost is the largest cost
borne by investors over time, in most cases being a larger drag on performance than management and administrative fees. Yet these figures are
never disclosed, and often are dismissed by a manager as merely 'part of
the process.'"[11] We add the following to his statement: The magnitude of
these costs indicates why trading is an activity of major importance along
with investing.

The Plexus numbers are based on a large sample of trades. As broad
averages, they are intended to give a good picture of the magnitude of execution cost estimates. Execution cost measurements should be accepted
with caution, however. Particularly difficult has been measuring the execution costs of large trades and determining how these costs depend on
the size of a trade, the difficulty of a trade, and the market center in which
the trade is made. Capturing the market impact cost of a large order that
has been sliced into smaller pieces for sequential execution over an extended period of time is even more difficult. Matters can at times be further complicated if it is difficult to distinguish between active and passive
trades so as to obtain a targeted measure of execution costs for the active
traders. Execution costs are underestimated if active and passive orders
are not properly identified. We return to these issues in Chapter 7.

INTRADAY PRICE VOLATILITY, PRICE DISCOVERY, AND QUANTITY DISCOVERY

We next turn to three important attributes of an equity market that are
each liquidity-driven: the level of intraday price volatility, the accuracy of
price discovery, and the completeness of quantity discovery. We also discuss price and quantity discovery in further detail in Chapter 6. Technical
details concerning the measurement of returns and return variances, and
the effect of the interval length over which returns are measured on return
variances (one hour intervals, or one day intervals, etc.), are provided in
the Appendix at the end of the book.

Price Volatility

A number of financial economists have documented (and many practitioners no doubt sense) that, for a wide spectrum of stocks, markets, sample periods, and test designs, intraday price volatility is elevated. The elevation is particularly evident for the opening half-hour of trading. A recent study by Ozenbas, Schwartz, and Wood based on intraday data for the year 2000 for samples of New York Stock Exchange, NASDAQ, Euronext Paris, Deutsche Börse, and London Stock Exchange stocks found that volatility in the opening half-hour exceeded average volatility for all other half-hour periods (excluding the closing half-hour) by at least 75 percent in each of these five markets.[12] This elevation cannot be attributed to intraday patterns of news release, as controllable news releases generally do not occur in the opening 30 minutes of trading. Rather, it is better understood as a price discovery phenomenon. As such, the elevation is an attribute of an illiquid market.

Illiquidity and execution costs accentuate short-period volatility as transaction prices bounce between the higher values paid by eager buyers and the lower values received by eager sellers. The market impact of large buy and sell orders, whether executed all at once or submitted in pieces over a period of time, causes prices to bounce around. And very importantly, price discovery contributes to short-period volatility, as the market searches for but does not easily find equilibrium values.

Price fluctuations that characterize price discovery can be further destabilizing if they cause investors to lack confidence that a price level is reasonable. At times, sellers rush to market while buyers (out of either fear or cunning) hold back their orders, and price drops precipitously. At other times, buyers rush their orders to market while sellers (out of either fear or cunning) step aside, and price rises precipitously. When these buying and selling spurts happen, bouts of volatility result. Because this volatility accentuation is most apparent in short-run price movements, short-run volatility is a good inverse proxy for liquidity.

Price Discovery

The term *price discovery* identifies the process by which a market finds a new equilibrium after a shift in investor demand to hold shares. The task is inherently more difficult in more illiquid markets. Equilibrium prices are not visible. We can only guess what they may be. When trading is costly and a market is thin, elevated levels of intraday volatility are explained by transactions being made at prices that deviate from underlying, but unobservable, equilibrium values. Guessing is particularly difficult at the start of a trading day before orders are sent to a market and translated into trades. As we have noted, this likely accounts for the elevated volatility for the opening half-hour that was observed by Ozenbas, Schwartz, and Wood (2002).

Only in recent years has awareness of the price discovery function of a securities market emerged, and efficient price discovery still remains an essentially unarticulated objective. In the United States, the Securities and Exchange Commission (SEC) has not taken much account of price discovery in the equity markets, although the Commodities Futures Trading Commission (CFTC) has recognized price discovery as an important function of the futures markets. A reason for the difference in regulatory focus is that, for the equity markets, it has not been clear how to assess realized prices because base values against which a contrast can be made are not observable.

However, futures trading plays an important role in discovering prices for the cash market of the underlying asset that the futures contract is written on. This cash market price discovery role is particularly important for certain commodities that do not have well-organized cash markets. For instance, in the precious metals markets (e.g., gold, silver, and platinum), the futures price for the nearest futures contract (referred to as the delivery month) is typically used to set the spot price in the cash market for the physical underlying. This is true for many futures markets including agriculture, currency, and a variety of financial futures.

Price discovery would not be a critical function of the equity markets if participants were all in agreement about a security's value. Quite simply, if everyone individually were to evaluate the equity of Xyz.com at $50 a share, price discovery would be a no-brainer: Xyz.com shares would trade at $50, period, end of story. But what if individual share valuations differ? We discus this in further detail in Chapter 6, but at this point simply give you a taste of what is involved.

We use a simplified environment in Chapter 6 to show how quotes and prices can be found in the market when participants have different share valuations.[13] We take one stock (Xyz.com) and represent the difference of participant expectations by dividing them into two groups—one group is the bulls and the other is the bears. In our model, the bulls value Xyz.com shares at $55 and are the buyers; the bears value Xyz.com shares at $45 and are the sellers. Participants arrive sequentially in the market and each either posts a limit order to buy or to sell, or trades immediately (at bid or offer prices established by limit orders that have previously been placed). The larger the percentage of participants who are bulls, the closer the quotes and price will be pushed to $55. The larger the percentage who are bears, the closer the quotes and price will be pushed to $45.

Until trading begins, no one knows how the traders are divided between the bulls and the bears. The aggregate mood of the market is revealed only as orders arrive and are turned into trades. Consequently, price discovery is a dynamic, protracted process, and a good marketplace is needed to deliver acceptably good price discovery. In the late 1970s, William Batten, who at the time was CEO of the New York Stock Exchange, was speaking with a small group of academicians about the unique service that is provided by an exchange. After listening for a while he commented, "We produce the price." The comment was prescient. The insight is of major importance.

Quantity Discovery

The term *quantity discovery* refers to the ability of buyers and sellers to find each other and enter into trades that reflect the amounts that they really wish to trade. The simultaneous presence of one participant looking to buy shares at a price that another participant would be willing to sell at, without the two actually meeting and trading, is what we mean by incomplete quantity discovery.

With organized markets, quantity discovery is not an issue for smaller, retail customers. If you are in the market for only a couple of hundred shares, you can shoot your order to a limit order book or a dealer, trade with immediacy, and incur only explicit costs and spread costs. This is not the case if you are an institutional customer looking to trade, let us say, 300,000 shares of a stock with an average daily volume of 500,000 shares.

The problem a large trader faces is that revealing a big order can move prices before the order has executed fully. Front-running is the danger, and market impact is the cost. Big orders cannot simply be revealed fully on a limit order book or executed as market orders against the book or a dealer's quotes. Instead, they are held close to the chest, are worked carefully over time, and are commonly sliced and diced and brought to the market one tranche at a time.

One large trader alone working a big order does not necessarily represent incomplete quantity discovery. Two large traders doing so with one being a buyer and the other a seller does signal incomplete quantity discovery. When an active buyer and an active seller are together in the market at the same time, the market is said to be *two-sided*. In a perfectly liquid market, the two counterparties should be able to meet each other and trade. But, as we discuss further in Chapter 6, the evidence suggests, under a wide array of conditions (time of day, marketplace, trade size, and information environment), that markets are commonly two-sided and a sizable latent demand to trade exists. The bottom line is that quantity discovery is generally incomplete.

Much of what trading entails involves finding the other side. The more illiquid the market and/or the larger your order, the bigger the challenge is. Market architects are very aware of this; if you aren't already thinking about it, you should be, too.

THE ORIGINS OF LIQUIDITY

Where does liquidity come from? From buyers and sellers, of course. Ultimately, a market is liquid for sellers if some traders are seeking to buy shares, and a market is liquid for buyers if other traders are looking to sell shares.

Just how the orders of the various players are brought together and translated into trades depends on the structure of a market. The two generic market structures are *order-driven* and *quote-driven*. Order-driven markets are further classified as either *continuous trading* environments or *periodic call auctions*. In addition, some trades are negotiated. Let's take a quick look at how they operate. We will go into these market structures in greater depth in Chapters 3 through 5.

Continuous Order-Driven Markets

The only traders in a pure order-driven market are investors who are seeking to buy or sell shares for their own purposes. We refer to these participants as naturals. The two most basic order types used by naturals in a pure order-driven market are (1) *limit orders* (a maximum price limit is placed on a buy order and a minimum price limit is placed on a sell order) and (2) *market orders* (the instruction on a market order is simply to buy or to sell "at market").

The limit orders are entered into a *limit order book*. These orders establish the prices at which the market orders will execute. In the past, limit orders at the New York Stock Exchange were literally written down, by hand, in a book. This practice ended with the introduction of electronic order management, but the term *book* is still widely used. The first electronic display book was introduced at the NYSE in 1983 to facilitate the huge expected surge in trading of the seven new Baby Bell stocks following their divestiture from AT&T. Over the next several years, the electronic display book was introduced for more stocks until, by 1988, the electronic books were being used for 1,100 stocks in 361 workstations.

A market is referred to as *order-driven* precisely because the limit orders placed by some participants set the values at which others can trade by market order. In the order-driven market, the limit order placers are the liquidity suppliers, and the market order traders are the liquidity takers. Accordingly, liquidity builds as limit orders are entered in the book, and liquidity is drawn down as market orders trigger trades that eliminate limit orders from the book.

Some participants are motivated to be liquidity providers because, whenever a trade is made in the absence of news, the transaction price favors the limit order placer. Perhaps, for instance, the best bid set by a limit order placer seeking to buy is $50.00, and the best offer set by a limit order placer seeking to sell is $50.05. If a market order to buy arrives, it will execute at $50.05, or five cents more than the limit order buyer would pay if his limit order were to execute. Or, if a market sell order arrives, it will execute at $50.00, or five cents less than the limit order seller would receive if his limit order were to execute. What the limit order trader receives, the market order trader pays. But while the market order trader pays more for a purchase or receives less for a sale, he benefits from trading with certainty and immediacy.

Two conditions must be met for an order-driven market to function. First, some participants must be looking to buy at a time when others are looking to sell. Second, on both the buyer's side and the seller's side of the market, some participants must choose to place limit orders while others must select the market order strategy. These conditions are generally met for larger cap stocks. Relatively patient players place limit orders, hoping to transact at better prices, and relatively eager players submit market orders so that they may trade with speed and certainty.

For the effective creation of liquidity, intermediaries who operate as brokers are also needed in a pure order-driven market. A broker handles an order for a customer but, unlike a dealer or market maker, does not trade with the customers. Brokers typically handle the submission of customer orders although, with computerized trading, direct access by a customer is technically possible. Additionally, exchange personnel are required to operate the market, establish and enforce rules, and maintain the IT platform that the limit order book and various information systems run on.

Periodic Call Auctions

We have stated that an order-driven market can be structured in two ways: as a continuous market or as a periodic call auction. With a continuous environment, a trade is made at any moment in *continuous time* that the market is open and a buy order meets a sell order in price (as occurs when a market order executes against a limit order that has been placed on the book). Continuous order-driven markets are open for a *trading day* (e.g., 9:30 A.M. to 4:00 P.M. for the U.S. markets).[14] With continuous trading, limit orders that have been pre-positioned in the book enable buyers and sellers to meet in time. That is to say, suppose that your limit order to buy is submitted at 10:05 A.M. and that our order to sell at market comes in at 10:33. How do we find each other? With the book, your order is sitting there when our order arrives, and we have a trade.

In a call auction, trades are made at pre-announced moments in time (e.g., at the 9:30 A.M. open or at the 4:00 P.M. close). Orders entered for a call are held until the call, at which time they are batched together for a simultaneous execution, at a single price, in one big multiparty trade. (There are exceptions to this, however—see Berkeley's contributed piece in Chapter 4.)

A call is to continuous trading as a train is to a car. A commuter from the suburbs has the choice of traveling to the city by train or by car. With a car, the commuter has the freedom to leave home whenever he decides in continuous time. With a train, the commuter is pooled together with many other people according to a timetable that is set by the railroad. Similarly, a call, by pooling many orders together, focuses liquidity at predetermined points in time. This focused liquidity can sharpen the accuracy of price discovery and help control price volatility. It is a desirable venue to have along with continuous trading.

Quote-Driven Markets

To understand the quote driven environment, let's take one more look at the continuous, order-driven market. For a transaction to be made, a buy and sell order must meet each other in two ways: in price and in time. With regard to price, in the continuous order-driven market, a limit order placer sets a quotation price, and a transaction is realized if a market order customer accepts the price. With regard to time, the limit order placer waits patiently, with his order sitting on the book, for a market order placer to arrive. Consequently, it is the presence of a limit order book and the limit order placer's patience that enable a buyer and a seller to meet in time. This liquidity producing procedure, unfortunately, does not work effectively under all conditions.

If a market is thin and order arrival infrequent, and/or if some participants (e.g., institutional customers) have very large orders, and/or if a market is under particular stress (due, for instance, to a major news release), the order-driven market can break down. In these cases, structure beyond the limit order book is needed. Additional structure may be provided by intermediaries who are market makers (also known as dealers). Unlike brokers who only handle customer orders on an agency basis, market makers trade as principals with their customers.

In a pure quote-driven market, prices are set *only* by dealer quotes— hence the term *quote-driven*. The quote-driven market operates quite differently from the pure order-driven market where there are no market makers at all (we discuss this in considerably more detail in Chapter 5). Just as a limit order book enables buyers and sellers to meet in time in a continuous order-driven market, a market maker enables public customers to meet in time in a quote-driven system. The market maker does so by buying shares when public participants wish to sell, and by selling shares when public participants wish to buy. At any moment, a market maker's bid quote is lower than his offer (ask quote). The market maker attempts to profit by alternately buying shares from customers at the lower bid and selling to them at the higher offer.

By trading at their posted quotes, the market makers bring capital to the market that enables public customers to trade with immediacy. This does not mean, however, that the market makers are the fundamental source of liquidity. As is true for an order-driven market, the fundamental source of liquidity for public buyers is public sellers, and the fundamental source for public sellers is public buyers. Market makers simply help to transfer the ownership of shares from sellers to buyers by interceding in the trades. If you wish, think of it this way: A market maker supplies "immediate liquidity."

A market maker who has no shares (is neither long nor short) in a company is said to have a *flat position*. Picture a market maker starting a trading day with a flat position in Cisco. After buying shares to accommodate a seller, that market maker has a long position. To reliquify his position, the market maker then has to sell Cisco shares back to the market. Similarly, after selling shares to accommodate a buyer, that market maker has to reliquify by buying shares from the market. The reliquification of a position after buying from or selling to customers is known as *inventory control*. Controlling inventory, as we will see in Chapter 5, is a big part of a market maker's operations. You will have a chance to try this yourself with the TraderEx software that we introduced in Chapter 1.

Negotiated Trades

Liquidity can also be provided by two parties meeting each other directly and negotiating a trade. The negotiation can be between two NYSE floor traders handling customer orders on a not held (NH) basis, or between an institutional customer and an upstairs block positioner, or by two large traders otherwise meeting each other. It can be a direct person-to-person negotiation or an electronic negotiation. The alternative trading system (ATS) Liquidnet is a good example of an electronic negotiation environment—two customers can find each other on the Liquidnet screen and negotiate on both price and size. Pipeline, a more recent ATS that also brings large customers together electronically, accomplishes a similar goal and delivers price improvement but does not include an explicit negotiation process.

When trades are negotiated, it is less clear which of the contras is the active trader and which is passive, or which is demanding liquidity and which is the liquidity provider.

Hybrid Markets

Liquidity provision is handled differently in each of the structures that we have just looked at: the continuous order-driven market, the period call auction, the quote-driven market, and facilities that offer negotiated trades. In recent years, it has become more apparent that these structures are not alternatives but, rather, should be offered simultaneously in hybrid combinations. The hybrids give customers the flexibility they need to choose just how they will either supply liquidity themselves (and be compensated) or receive liquidity (and pay for it). Of course, combining alternative systems is a complex task. But only when markets strengthen their competitive positions by doing this do participants receive the liquidity that they may reasonably expect.

The continuous, order-driven electronic trading platforms in Europe include market makers on both contractual and voluntary bases. The NYSE opens and closes trading with a call auction, as do the European markets. Historically, NASDAQ and the London Stock Exchange were competitive market maker markets, but both have reengineered their systems to include the public display of customer limit orders—London with the introduction of the Stock Exchange Trading System (SETS) in 1997, and NASDAQ with the introduction of SuperMontage in 2002. Like the Börses in Continental Europe, both NASDAQ and London now run fully electronic opening and closing call auctions.

Most markets have long had hybrid structures. The New York Stock Exchange, for instance, has historically included a specialist who maintains a limit order book and who also participates in trading as a principal. Large trades for NYSE issues can be negotiated upstairs and brought to the Exchange's trading floor for execution. Upstairs market makers also provide dealer capital for NYSE block transactions.

In August 2004, the NYSE submitted a proposal to the SEC for a new market model, the NYSE Hybrid Market, which is being designed to integrate the best aspects of the auction market with automated trading by providing for subsecond automated executions when customers choose, while allowing for opportunities for negotiated price improvement over the published best bid and offer. In other words, the NYSE's new hybrid will combine what is known as a *slow market* (floor-based trading with human intermediaries) with what is known as a *fast market* (a high-speed, electronic trading platform). The motive for moving forcefully ahead in this direction is clearly articulated in the piece that John Thain has contributed to this chapter:

> *One of my first priorities upon arriving at the New York Stock Exchange was to meet with our customers, institutional customers among them. I wanted to know what they thought of the Exchange and what they wanted from us. I asked them, "What is it that you like and do not like about the New York Stock Exchange?"*
>
> *Some of our customers told me, "We want to trade in a different way than we are currently able to trade at the NYSE. We want to trade instantaneously, electronically, and anonymously."*
>
> *In response to our customers and our need to further strengthen our auction market model, we conceived the NYSE Hybrid Market.*

ILLIQUIDITY'S FOOTPRINTS IN THE TRANSACTION RECORDS

Illiquidity introduces systematic patterns in share price changes. As a consequence, prices do not follow random walks. But before we explore this further, let's return again to the perfectly liquid, totally efficient environment.

The Perfectly Liquid, Efficient Market and Random Walk

Random walk is a cool concept. In a nutshell, it means that where you take your next step is totally independent of all other steps that you have previously taken. That being the case, anyone following your path would have no ability whatsoever to predict where you might be going. You would be myopicly focusing only on the present. Your friend who is trying to guess your destination will find that the path you have thus far traced contains absolutely no useful information. It is as if your footprints did not exist.

The idea of a random walk can be applied to the stock market. Those of us with an interest in the equity markets like to follow prices. We like to predict where they might next be going. Is a stock heading up? Is it drifting down? Has it gone up too far or down too low? Is it about to reverse direction and revert back to an earlier value? Or, perhaps, is price only following a random walk? If our guess is correct, unless you are (or have been) a finance major in an undergraduate or MBA program, you probably think that the random walk idea is preposterous.

It is not. In fact, many financial economists believe that stock price movements are essentially free of any correlation pattern. For the most part, they believe that, aside from transaction prices bouncing between bid and offer quotes, it is not possible to predict where a stock's price might next be heading. Our colleagues would be correct if markets were fully efficient, frictionless, and perfectly liquid. Why is that?

Another cornerstone of modern portfolio theory (along with the capital asset pricing model) is the hypothesis that our equity markets are informationally efficient. This is known as the *efficient markets hypothesis* (EMH). As we said at the beginning of this chapter, information is the input that drives investment decisions and trading. Security prices are based on the information set. Informational efficiency means that security prices fully incorporate the entire information set. If this were not the case, some clever participant could grab hold of the information set and churn out some profitable trades. If someone could do this at some moment in time, then the price of a stock at that moment could not be reflecting the information set correctly. If this were to happen, the EMH would not hold.

So let's presume that a stock's price, at any moment in time, does properly reflect the full information set. What then would cause the stock's price to change? Any future price change cannot be attributed to the current information set. If it is, then the stock's price could not have been an appropriate reflection of the current information. For the EMH to hold, a stock's price can change only because of the advent of new information (news). The news would have to be totally unanticipated because any *anticipation* is part of the current information set. Now for the bottom line—if the news must be totally unanticipated, its effect on the stock's price cannot be predicted. Therefore, neither can any future price change. The stock's price must therefore follow a random walk.

Random walk tests were among the most important tests used to validate the EMH. For years, the EMH generally passed the tests and the EMH appeared to hold, at least in its weak form (namely, that all information in past stock prices and quotes is fully reflected).[15] The results were certainly sobering for any young buck poised to predict future price movements based on patterns that he saw in historical data. To this day, the EMH should keep us all acceptably humble. But, as we will see in Chapter 6, this does not mean that prices follow random walks, or that correlation patterns do not exist, or that technical analysis and algorithmic trading do not have valid roles to play.

With the advent of powerful computers and high-frequency data (complete, moment-to-moment records of transaction prices, quotes, and transaction volume), financial economists are increasingly finding that stock returns are not free of the correlation patterns that random walk theory says should not be there. And yet the theory seams to have solid, rational support via the EMH. What is the missing element? Missing is the recognition of one important reality—markets are not fully efficient, frictionless, and perfectly liquid. The next section describes how trading frictions and illiquidity can result in correlation patterns.

Intertemporal Correlation

The term *intertemporal* refers to events that occur in different time periods. For instance, if the price change for a stock in one period is correlated with the price change for that same stock in another period (e.g., one hour or one day later), the stock's returns are *intertemporally correlated*. When the return is for the same stock, this intertemporal correlation is referred to as *autocorrelation*, or as *serial correlation*.

Returns are positively autocorrelated when positive returns are more likely to be followed by other returns that are positive, and when negative returns are more likely to be followed by other returns that are negative. Therefore, if returns are *positively autocorrelated*, a series of price changes includes a larger number of *price continuations* (upticks followed by other upticks, or down ticks followed by other down ticks) than would be expected in a random sequence of price changes. If, on the other hand, returns are *negatively autocorrelated*, a series of price changes includes a larger number of *price reversals* (an uptick followed by a down tick, or a down tick followed by an uptick) than would be expected in a random sequence of price changes.

The intertemporal correlation need not be between sequentially adjacent returns. For instance, the return in one period may be correlated with the return two or more periods later. The correlation between sequentially adjacent returns is *serial correlation*, or *first order autocorrelation*. The correlation between nonadjacent returns is called *higher order autocorrelation*. The term *autocorrelation* simply means that the returns for an issue are autocorrelated, although not necessarily of first order.

The return on one stock in one period of time may also be correlated with the return on another stock (or stock index) in another period of time. This is *serial cross-correlation*. Serial cross-correlation exists when different stocks do not adjust simultaneously to common information change.

Positive Intertemporal Correlation

Four factors can cause the returns for a security to be positively autocorrelated: sequential information arrival, the limit order book, market maker intervention in trading, and noninstantaneous price discovery after change in investor demand.

1. *Sequential information arrival.* Thomas Copeland has shown that the sequential arrival of information (or, equivalently, the sequential adjustment of expectations) can cause a security's returns to be positively autocorrelated.[16]

2. *The limit order book.* If orders on the book are not quickly revised after informational change, new orders based on the information transact at prices set by existing limit orders. As a series of such transactions eliminates the older orders sequentially from the book, a security's transaction price rises or falls in increments to a new equilibrium value.

3. *Market maker intervention.* The affirmative obligation of stock exchange specialists leads these market makers to intervene in trading when transaction-to-transaction price changes would otherwise be unacceptably large. This can cause a security's price to adjust in increments to a new equilibrium value after the advent of news.

4. *Inaccurate price discovery.* Price discovery is inaccurate when new equilibrium values are not instantaneously achieved. Price discovery is inaccurate because investors do not instantaneously transmit their orders to the market; because orders left on the market are not continuously revised; and because, when they write their orders, investors do not know what the equilibrium prices are or will be. With inaccurate price determination, actual prices differ from equilibrium values. Some price changes are too small (they underadjust to news), and other price changes are too large (they overadjust to news). Ceteris paribus, if inaccurate price determination that involves partial adjustment (undershooting) predominates, returns will be positively autocorrelated.

Negative Intertemporal Correlation

Three factors may cause negative intertemporal correlation in security returns: the bid-ask spread, the temporary market impact exerted by large orders, and noninstantaneous price discovery after change in investor demand propensities.

1. *The bid-ask spread.* With a spread, orders to sell at market execute against the bid, and orders to buy at market execute against the ask. In the process, the transaction price moves between the bid and the ask. The bid and ask quotes themselves change over time with the arrival of

new orders and the elimination of old orders (that either execute or are withdrawn). Nevertheless, the bouncing of transaction prices between the quotes causes transaction-to-transaction price returns to be negatively autocorrelated. To see this, assume the quotes are fixed. Then, if at some moment in time the last transaction in a particular stock is at the bid, the next transaction that generates a nonzero return must be at the ask, and a positive return (price change) is recorded. If the quotes remain unchanged, the next nonzero return must be negative (when a market sell once again hits the bid). Thus price reversals occur as the transaction price moves back and forth between the bid and the ask. Even if the quotes change randomly over time, the price reversals attributed to the spread introduce negative intertemporal correlation in transaction price returns.

2. *Market impact effects.* The effective spread is generally greater for larger orders. Consider the arrival of a large sell order, for instance. If the book is relatively sparse, the transaction price will be depressed so that the order may be absorbed by the relatively thin market. In this case, the lower price itself attracts new buy orders to the market and price once again rises. Therefore, the initial price decrease is followed by a reversal (an increase). The reverse pattern would be caused by the arrival of a large buy order. Either way, the successive price changes are negatively autocorrelated.

3. *Inaccurate price discovery.* We have noted that, with inaccurate price discovery, actual prices wander about their equilibrium values. If inaccurate price determination that involves overreaction to news (overshooting) predominates, returns are negatively autocorrelated. Further, it can be shown that returns are negatively autocorrelated if an underlying equilibrium price changes randomly over time and transaction prices wander randomly about their equilibrium values.[17] This can be understood intuitively with the aid of the following visualization. Picture a man walking his dog on a leash across a field, with the dog racing randomly about the man, but never straying too far because of the leash. If the man follows a random path, the leash causes reversals in the dog's path, and thus the animal's movements are negatively autocorrelated.

Serial Cross-Correlation

The returns on two (or more) different securities are generally correlated with each other. This interstock correlation is referred to as *cross-correlation*. The returns for two different securities are *serially cross-correlated* if the correlated price adjustments do not occur simultaneously (that is, if they are nonsynchronous).

If all price adjustments were instantaneous for all securities (as would be the case in the perfectly liquid, frictionless market), the price adjustments across the different securities would be synchronous. However, the factors that we have discussed in relation to returns autocorrelation also cause price adjustment delays, which lead to nonsynchronous adjustments across stock, and consequently to serial cross-correlation.

The prices of some securities tend to adjust faster than others to changing market conditions. Some large, intensely watched issues may lead the market, and other smaller issues may lag behind. This gives rise to a pattern of serial cross-correlation where the price adjustments for securities such as IBM and Exxon precede the price adjustments for thinner issues such as Liquidity Inc. and Podunk Mines.

Serial cross-correlation patterns are no doubt diffuse, complex, and not readily subject to exploitation by a clever trader. The reason is twofold: The time lags involved are not stable, and imperfect price discovery may entail both overshooting and undershooting.[18]

DISCUSSION

Liquidity is indeed a difficult variable to deal with. Its very definition is multifaceted, and its empirical measurement elusive. How is the liquidity of individual assets related to the liquidity of a portfolio? To what extent is an asset's liquidity determined by its other attributes (sheer size, susceptibility to informational change, etc.) and by the characteristics of its investors (their size and reactions to informational change)? To what extent is liquidity determined by the characteristics of the marketplace where the asset is traded?

These are not simple questions to answer. Difficulties in defining, measuring, and analyzing liquidity largely explain why this attribute of financial assets and markets has not thus far been incorporated into formal stock evaluation models. Nevertheless, from brokerage firm operations to market center operations, the jobs that people perform and the institutional structures that they work within are deeply influenced by the realities of illiquidity, and by the fact that actual markets are not frictionless environments.

Recognizing that markets are not frictionless environments, we have revisited the efficient markets hypothesis. The EMH addresses the issue of informational efficiency (i.e., whether profitable trading strategies can be formulated on the basis of available information). The EMH has been widely tested by, among other things, searching for serial correlation patterns in stock returns. Historically, many test results have supported the hypothesis. Yet the trading costs and the complexities of price and quantity discovery that we have discussed are manifest in serial correlation. Why is it that these patterns are so difficult to detect? It is because positive and negative serial correlation coexist, and their coexistence makes their footprints in the transaction data extremely difficult to detect.

What might the presence of serial correlation suggest about the operational efficiency of a market? It suggests that markets could be made more operationally efficient by designing superior trading systems. To this end, technology has greatly expanded the possibilities. But securities markets are highly complex institutions and good, implementable economic answers regarding market design are not easily developed. Inefficiencies in the equity markets will without doubt endure for the foreseeable future. This means that we all will want to take account of illiquidity as investors, and to pay attention to transaction costs and the dynamics of price discovery as traders. Our most immediate goal is to control the transaction costs that erode portfolio performance. Further, if fortunate enough, we might also seek to enhance our returns by exploiting profitable trading opportunities that are sometimes presented.

Trading is the process by which portfolio decisions are implemented, and markets exist so that trades can be made. If you come into some funds and have some good investment ideas, you should be able to submit your buy orders to the market and get the shares. If you need to generate cash or have lowered your opinion about a stock, you should be able to submit your sell orders and dispose of the shares. But illiquidity and trading costs inhibit trading. At this point, we ask you to consider how each of the following affects the frequency with which you may send orders to the market and trade:

- High explicit trading costs (commissions and fees).
- High implicit costs (bid-ask spreads and market impact).
- Accentuated intraday volatility.
- Capital gains taxes.
- A feeling that our markets are not fair, that other participants will benefit at your expense.
- A feeling that prices adjust so quickly to news that you will never be able to buy profitably when there is good news, or will be unable to cut your losses by selling before the market has fully responded to bad news.

If our guess is correct and you are a buy-side customer, you have, with one exception, a negative response to all of them. The one exception is the accentuated volatility. If you think that you are able to capture it, go for it.

A final consideration about liquidity involves recognizing that markets are networks. The network comprises the participants who come together to trade. The larger a network, the greater the value it offers participants. Fax machines are a good example of a network: Each user's fax is more useful the more people have one, because there are more people to whom faxes can be sent and from whom faxes can be received. A large number of people using the same software also generates network value; we all benefit from the ability to pass files back and forth to each other in a standardized language and format. Similarly, an equity market is a network: As more orders converge in a marketplace, the orders provide more liquidity to each other and better price discovery for the broad market.

An adage in the securities industry reflects the positive force that a network exerts: "Order flow attracts order flow."[19] The equity market network does this because markets that attract more participants are more liquid. As such, they generally offer tighter spreads and produce more accurate price discovery. In the network, some participants will trade patiently and supply liquidity; others will trade aggressively and consume liquidity. The liquidity suppliers help to stabilize prices; the liquidity demanders can knock prices around. This is all part of how the ecology works—the suppliers and consumers of liquidity need each other.

Each of us, as a player, is a node in the network. As the number of nodes increases, a market becomes more liquid, and its performance characteristics improve.

We just listed several reasons not to be a player. For each of us individually, not trading because of any or all of these considerations may be a very rational response. Unfortunately, to the extent that these considerations have caused us, you, and/or anyone else to trade less frequently, the market can become less liquid for us all. Except for the fortunate few who are positioned to profit from it, illiquidity and the transaction costs and volatility that it causes are not, with one exception, our friend. The exception is that illiquidity sure does make trading a lot more exciting.

FROM THE CONTRIBUTORS

Peter Jenkins
Satisfying Institutional Traders' Quest for Liquidity

John A. Thain
Giving Customers Greater Choice in Trade Execution:
The NYSE Hybrid Market

Claudio Werder and René Weber
Market Reaction to New Information

Satisfying Institutional Traders' Quest for Liquidity

Peter Jenkins

Centralizing liquidity and providing strong price competition are paramount for granting institutional traders the opportunity to achieve best execution. In general terms, there are two categories of trades that institutional players are trying to execute. First, there are trades that can easily be handled by existing liquidity in the marketplace. Second, there are trades of such great magnitude (e.g., larger than 50 percent of a stock's average daily trading volume) that, when arriving in the marketplace, they significantly impact price. Institutional traders must constantly balance between two fundamentally different ways of achieving an execution that might be considered best execution: (1) having their orders internalized by a broker/dealer, and (2) routing their orders to the centralized marketplace. Either way, best execution is a difficult task to define (and no less achieve) given the complex market that institutional traders have to operate within.

A confluence of events, including the burst of the 1990s technology bubble and the extended bear market, has spawned a highly complex environment for today's institutional traders. Creating additional tension and challenge is the increased regulatory pressure, especially with regard to achieving best execution. In addition, there is ongoing management pressure to decrease costs, especially transaction costs, while maintaining payments for research and directed brokerage. Moreover, brokerage firms' margins have shrunk in the face of stagnating trading volume and lower volatility.

But that is not all. The implementation of decimal pricing in the U.S. marketplace has further challenged the market and market professionals. While decimals have produced tighter spreads, the stark reality has been a decrease in transparency and dealers having to trade on spreads that have collapsed. As a result, the over-the-counter market has reacted by moving toward a pure agency model, and trading venues are moving toward pure electronic systems. The New York Stock Exchange structure has remained fundamentally intact, but the average trade size has dramatically declined. Institutional traders had voiced their concerns about transparency and "pennying" (a competitor jumping ahead of an already posted offer with an order that is priced just one penny more aggressively), which prompted the marketplace to create new order types, new trading tools, and additional pools of liquidity. In addition to these initiatives, certain institutional traders have been demanding greater speed of execution as they gravitated toward new trading tools that provide anonymity and certainty of price. For the most part, however, large institutional traders continue to seek liquidity and price as their primary factor—speed of execution is only a secondary factor.

One of the most recent developments in the market has been the approval of the SEC's Regulation National Market System ("Reg. NMS"), which is scheduled for implementation in mid-2006. The primary features of Reg. NMS are the order protection rule and order access. The investment industry has debated, and continues to debate, whether Reg. NMS will create more competition among market centers, and whether this will increase the strength of the U.S. capital markets. What remains unknown is how the implementation of Reg. NMS will impact liquidity for institutional traders in the marketplace. Further compounding the Reg. NMS debate were the NYSE's announcement to merge with Archipelago, the merger of NASDAQ and Instinet, and the investments by several large broker-dealers in certain regional Exchanges. Again, the market will have to wait to see how all of these changes will impact liquidity within the marketplace.

Historically and going forward, the overriding theme has been this: *Greater customer choice is created by greater market competition.* As institutional traders continue to call for greater efficiencies and demand better ways to access liquidity, trade execution venues will continue to respond by offering these customers more choice in execution strategy and techniques. The NYSE has always been a key participant in the marketplace, providing a central source of price discovery and liquidity. Like other market participants, the NYSE is responding to the needs and demands of the institutional trader. It is doing so by building a Hybrid Market. The Hybrid Market will offer all customers in general, and institutional customers in particular, multiple methods to execute orders. The Hybrid Market will also provide more speed.

As one who was an institutional trader for over 20 years, I have had experience pursuing the trading strategy that appropriately satisfies the execution requirements of clients and portfolio managers while obtaining best execution. Since moving to the NYSE, I continue to respect the challenges facing institutional traders who struggle to define and defend best execution while navigating the various order types and trading tools. In many ways, these are uncharted and choppy waters for institutional traders. The institutions must find ways to balance the regulatory and market events that impact their day-to-day trading activities while seeking both liquidity and the best strategy for trade execution so as to achieve best execution. As our industry and markets continue to evolve, this careful balancing act will continue to challenge institutional traders as they strive to satisfy the requirements of their profession and, most importantly, to meet their fiduciary obligations to customers.

Giving Customers Greater Choice in Trade Execution: The NYSE Hybrid Market

John A. Thain

O ne of my first priorities upon arriving at the New York Stock Exchange was to meet with our customers, institutional customers among them. I wanted to know what they thought of the Exchange and what they wanted from us. I asked them, "What is it that you like and do not like about the New York Stock Exchange?"

Some of our customers told me, "We want to trade in a different way than we are currently able to trade at the NYSE. We want to trade instantaneously, electronically, and anonymously."

In response to our customers and our need to further strengthen our auction market model, we conceived the NYSE Hybrid Market.

In the simplest terms, the NYSE Hybrid Market is about choice—allowing our customers to choose how their orders are executed on the Exchange. It's also about creating a more flexible environment that better accommodates the increasingly diverse and complex trading strategies of our customers.

If our customers want speed, certainty, and anonymity for an order execution, they can choose the NYSE's automatic-execution service. If they want the opportunity for price improvement, they can choose the auction process. Or they can pursue new order types that seek to combine the best aspects of both auction and automation. Either way, our customers and their customers will receive the best possible price on their buy and sell orders, along with the superior liquidity, narrow bid/ask spreads, low trading costs, and low volatility that underscore the NYSE's commitment to providing the highest levels of market quality.

Our customers expect nothing less from the New York Stock Exchange. In fact, this initiative will enable the Exchange to become the first true hybrid equities market that offers the best of electronic trading and the auction market. This is strategically essential for our success and that of our customers. The Securities and Exchange Commission's adoption of Regulation NMS and the NYSE's effort to accommodate customer demand also underscore the impetus for creating the Hybrid Market.

At the Exchange, we understand that our customers can route and execute their trades elsewhere. That's competition. In addition, the competition for trading in NYSE-listed equities is more fierce than ever before. If we fail to give our customers what they want and someone else does, we know they will go elsewhere with their orders. With that in mind, the first objective of the Hybrid Market is to allow our institutional customers who want to trade electronically, instantaneously, and anonymously to do so.

The second objective of the Hybrid Market is to automate more of what we do. For example, we are adding technology that will markedly reduce the number of keystrokes specialist clerks will have to enter. The dramatic growth of orders and other electronic messages have made this a necessity. Automating non-value-added keystrokes and other previously manual tasks further improves efficiency and productivity, and allows us to handle higher volumes and remain competitive with other markets.

The third objective of the Hybrid Market—the most ambitious of the three—is to make sure that we retain those distinct capabilities and advantages that are special about our marketplace. One of those characteristics is price improvement, which is important to many customers in our market and something that most other markets do not provide. We want to retain the opportunity for price improvement for customers who want it, and to ensure that specialists and floor brokers have the tools to provide it.

Another important characteristic of our marketplace is lower volatility. The stocks that trade on the NYSE do, in fact, trade with a significantly lower volatility than stocks in a purely electronic marketplace. Statistics show that the stocks of companies moving from NASDAQ to the NYSE experienced on average a 50 percent decrease in intraday volatility.

In the Hybrid Market, we want the specialists and the floor brokers to be able to promptly add liquidity whenever there is an imbalance, and to interact with the marketplace as they do today. That's an important distinction of our market; it is important to our customers, and it is important for providing a fair and orderly market for all investors—both small and large.

We understand that it's vital to ensure our floor brokers' ability to represent their customers in two ways—verbally on the floor (as they have done for decades) as well as electronically. So, many of the innovations of the Hybrid Market are tools that allow brokers to continue to represent their customers in the new, more electronic environment. We are also providing specialists with the tools they need to continue to make fair and orderly markets.

It is always interesting to talk with our customers about exactly what they want their brokers to be doing. The general reaction is that all institutions want the market to be completely transparent at every price point except their own orders. We are trying to balance the need for transparency and the need for liquidity. At the same time, we are addressing the need for floor brokers to represent their customers in a way that adds value—knowing that many institutions really do not want their orders to be completely transparent and displayed in the marketplace.

The Hybrid Market platform is not an ECN. It is built largely on the NYSE's existing electronic order execution system, NYSE Direct+. Since its introduction in 2000, Direct+ has been electronically processing customer limit orders at the best bid or offer in subsecond speed. In 2005, more than 10 percent of all trade volume was executed on Direct+. We are, among other things, lifting various restrictions on Direct+ and allowing marketable limit orders and market orders to be executed on the expanded platform.

More tangibly, here is a snapshot of the many characteristics and benefits of the NYSE Hybrid Market:

- Specialists will continue to be catalysts for bringing buyers and sellers together in the auction, and will supplement liquidity to stabilize price movements. Floor brokers will participate both electronically and in person, using judgment to represent orders more effectively with new, advanced technology.
- Quotes will be instantaneously refreshed. The quotes will reflect the combined liquidity of the limit order book and the displayed electronic interest of the floor broker, crowd, and specialist. Limit orders will be published in real time. This structure will facilitate the ability of floor brokers and specialists to interact with supply and demand, as expressed by multiple orders that have been entered at multiple prices, along with individual, scaled orders (orders that have each been entered at multiple prices). The structure will also provide the opportunity for price improvement to incoming electronic orders.
- The investment management community will have the choice of auction representation and the opportunity for price improvement over the published bid and offer with new order types such as "NYSE Auction Limit Order" and "NYSE Auction Market Order."
- Investment management community customers who desire subsecond, automated trade execution will have access to the full breadth of the book and floor liquidity. Floor brokers' agency interest files, known as NYSE e-Quotes, will supplement liquidity beyond the published quote when customers choose to sweep NYSE liquidity. Unlike other markets' sweep procedures, liquidity outside the published quote will be price improved at the cleanup price, and liquidity takers will be price improved based on the brokers' agency interest on behalf of customers, as well as the specialists' electronic interest.
- Fair and orderly markets will be supported. A primary limitation placed on automated access to liquidity will be NYSE Liquidity Replenishment Points—predetermined points at which auction representation will

dampen volatility and lower trading costs, particularly in periods of market stress or order imbalances. The Hybrid Market's Liquidity Replenishment Points will deliver this.

- Best prices will be protected. Best-priced bids and offers in other markets will be immediately accessed unless customers are provided the same price on the NYSE. Incoming orders from competing market centers will be automatically executed at the displayed best price.
- NYSE Regulation will vigorously monitor the Hybrid Market to ensure market integrity and accountability. The rules-based Hybrid Market software will automatically address such issues as trading through better prices and trading ahead.

As our customers are already beginning to realize, there is much more to the NYSE Hybrid Market—including the most advanced trading technology and fastest order execution speed available today. Investors trading through NYSE member firms will gain faster access to liquidity and greater choice in trade execution. Customers will benefit from a brokers' judgment in both the auction and automated platform, and will also gain expanded, instantaneous access to specialist stabilizing capital outside the best bid or offer. Specialists will continue to add value by committing capital to dampen volatility, and will use enhanced technology to bring buyers and sellers together, improve prices, and serve as a point of accountability for the smooth functioning of the market.

The Hybrid Market represents the best union of auction and automation. It also combines the best of what's new and what has for many years served our customers well. The Hybrid Market will provide the highest level of market quality, superior and ready access to liquidity, the highest fill rates, and the lowest-cost trade execution. It will offer our customers the choice of speed via electronic order execution, and of price improvement via the auction. The Hybrid Market is the next-generation NYSE, an innovative trading platform that will support the future growth and success of the Exchange, our customers, and America's leadership in global financial markets.

Market Reaction to New Information

Claudio Werder and René Weber

A market can react strongly and share prices jump up or down as a reaction to new information. The information can be rumors, ad hoc news, global events, or just a profit warning or figures that are above or below consensus. We discuss here four examples, where these kinds of new information have had a strong impact on the share price.

RUMORS: PEPSICO TO TAKE OVER DANONE, JULY 2005

Share price increased by 27 percent in two weeks.

On Wednesday, July 6, 2005, the French magazine *Challenges*, in an advance copy of an edition to be published on Thursday, reported that PepsiCo Inc. had built up a stake of about 3 percent in Groupe Danone and was ready to spend €25 to €40 billion to acquire the French food producer (see Exhibit 2.5). It was said that the U.S.-based soft drink maker had already bought eight million shares at a price of between €66 and €72 per share, without naming its sources. Danone's market capitalization was €19 billion on July 6.

Danone told the press that it had not received any notification that PepsiCo was building a stake in the company and that any investor must declare themselves to the group once they own more than 0.5 percent of the share capital. After the closing bell on Tuesday, PepsiCo stated that it was untrue that it had built up a stake of about 3 percent in Danone and that it would make no further comment.

In early morning trading on July 7, Danone's shares were already up 5.8 percent to €77.05 and closed at €75.70. That morning, Danone revealed that it had not been approached by PepsiCo regarding a possible takeover or acquisition of a stake. On the back of certain comments mentioning a possible takeover price of €185 per share (massively unrealistic!), the price advanced further to €81.25 in Friday's trading. The stock was up 11.5 percent in just two days.

The following week was rather quiet and the stock traded between €78 and €79. On Tuesday, July 19, however, the rumors resurfaced and the stock jumped another 16.5 percent in just two days. It was mentioned that "according to people familiar with the situation," Danone was fortifying its defenses in a bid to remain independent. A bid would face fierce opposition from Danone's management and the French political establishment. A

HIGH 92.75 9/9/05,LOW 67.95 12/31/04,LAST 90.15 9/13/05

EXHIBIT 2.5 Danone Chart; January 1, 2000 to September 14, 2005
Source: Thomson Financial.

French legislator said the idea of French "national champions" such as Danone being acquired by foreigners was "scandalous" and added that the government would do "all we can" to oppose a bid.

Danone has been the subject of regular takeover talks for the past three years. Although considered by many to be an untouchable French corporate champion, the food group is one of the most widely held companies in France. Apart from PepsiCo, many other big food companies such as Coca-Cola, Kraft, Unilever, and Nestlé (as the white knight!) have been mentioned as potential buyers. However, the monopoly commission would most certainly block an acquisition by Nestlé, as a combination of Nestlé and Danone would bring clear market dominance in the European water market. The story of a takeover of Danone by PepsiCo makes sense when you look at Danone in terms of its product offering and geographical footprint. The water operations, in particular, would be of great interest to PepsiCo as the U.S. company is also active in that business. Regarding the dairy and biscuits business, the fit is much less obvious as these segments would be new to PepsiCo.

Driven by this rumor, Danone's stock price advanced 27 percent in just two weeks only to correct by dropping 10 percent the following week. This example shows that a rumor can have a strong impact on share prices, even if it does not become true! Due to the rumors, investors saw a possibility, a hint of what could happen if a takeover were to take place.

GEOPOLITICAL EVENTS: SEPTEMBER 11, 2001

Richemont (Cartier) dropped 28 percent, Tiffany dropped 24 percent in 10 days.

The terror attack in New York City on September 11, 2001, had a pervasive impact on equity markets. We next consider some of the effects that this event had on the equity market, especially on luxury goods shares, and we have chosen Tiffany (United States) and Richemont (Switzerland) as examples. In the United States, the stock exchange was closed for the full week and the Tiffany stock was therefore not traded during this time (see Exhibits 2.6 and 2.7).

The Swiss luxury goods company Richemont owns brands such as Cartier, Montblanc, JaegerLeCoultre, and Dunhill, and is therefore one of the world's leading luxury goods companies. Richemont's share price declined 11 percent from 36.25 Swiss francs (CHF) to CHF 32.40 after the terrorist attacks on 9/11. Moreover, the U.S. dollar (USD) weakened as well, and USD/CHF exchange rates fell from 1.68 on September 10 to 1.57 two weeks later. The Richemont stock consequently declined even further and after two weeks the share price had dropped to CHF 26 (–28 percent). The currency situation accordingly exacerbated the negative impact of 9/11 and shook confidence in the economy as a whole. As most luxury goods companies have their production capacities in Europe, their costs are in euros or Swiss francs (watches). However, a sizable share of their sales are generated in U.S. dollar–related regions (North America, Asia) and a lower USD therefore has a negative effect on their margin. Richemont's share price recovered slightly in October, but remained well below the pre-9/11 levels.

On the first day after reopening of the New York Stock Exchange, Tiffany closed at USD 21.96, which represented a 21 percent decline compared to the price on September 10. The drop was mainly driven by the events on 9/11 as exchange rates are not a major issue for Tiffany. The share price recovered much more quickly after 9/11 than

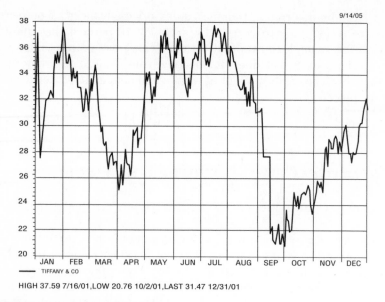

HIGH 37.59 7/16/01,LOW 20.76 10/2/01,LAST 31.47 12/31/01

EXHIBIT 2.6 Tiffany Chart, 2001

Source: Thomson Financial.

Richemont's and by the end of the year had regained levels seen prior to the terrorist attacks.

A geopolitical event usually can have an impact on the total market, but some sectors (in our example, the luxury goods industry) can be hurt even more. The market comes to detailed conclusions, and even inside a sector there can also be a difference, as one company experiences a more negative effect (in our example, Richemont) than another one.

AD HOC NEWS: A FINE LINE BETWEEN PLEASURE (GENENTECH) AND PAIN (SCHERING)

Schering declines 14.3 percent, Genentech rises 10.5 percent in one day.

On March 21, 2005, Schering AG and its partner Novartis published a summary of their CONFIRM1 clinical trial with the new anti-cancer drug

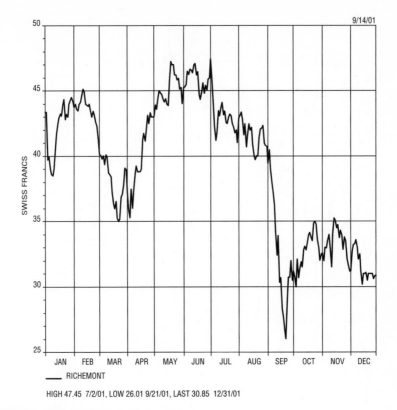

9/14/01

HIGH 47.45 7/2/01, LOW 26.01 9/21/01, LAST 30.85 12/31/01

EXHIBIT 2.7   Richemont Chart, 2001

Source: Thomson Financial.

PTK787 in patients with metastatic colorectal cancer (see Exhibits 2.8 and 2.9). Although some positive data were shown, the study's principal target, the so-called primary endpoint, was not met: PTK did NOT achieve statistical significance in extending progression-free survival of the treated patients.

This meant that the drug on which Schering had pinned high hopes would at best be delayed (12 to 18 months), if not definitely abandoned. Even conservative estimates had suggested that five years after launch PTK would generate sales of €600 million, or 12 percent of 2004 sales.

This delay was all the more painful given the fact that the Roche/ Genentech drug Avastin, which is based on the same active principle, had already been approved for the same indication and had been on the market since February 2004. Moreover, a few days earlier, on March 14,

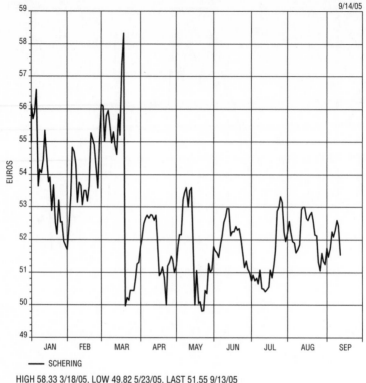

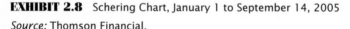
— SCHERING

HIGH 58.33 3/18/05, LOW 49.82 5/23/05, LAST 51.55 9/13/05

EXHIBIT 2.8   Schering Chart, January 1 to September 14, 2005
Source: Thomson Financial.

Genentech had announced that Avastin also prolonged patient survival in a certain type of lung cancer (nonsquamous NSCLC).

Following announcement of the bad news, the Schering stock dropped 14 percent in very brisk trading from €58.33 to €49.34 at closing on March 21. (See Exhibits 2.8 and 2.9.) By the end of September 2005 the share was trading within bandwidth of €50 to €53, although the European pharmaceuticals index had in the meantime risen some 18 percent. Its partner Novartis' share (PTK is being developed jointly) reacted minimally on March 21, 2005 and slipped just 0.9 percent, as the project is of lesser importance for the large multinational corporation.

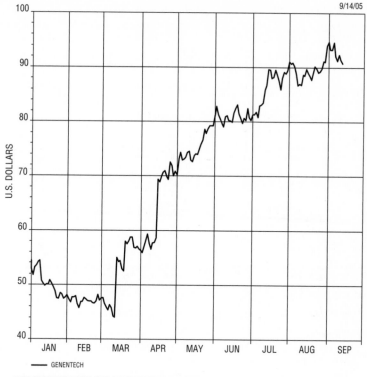

HIGH 94.74 9/1/05, LOW 44.08 3/11/05, LAST 90.80 9/13/05

EXHIBIT 2.9   Genentech Chart, January 1 to September 14, 2005
Source: Thomson Financial.

The Genentech stock closed up 25 percent at USD 55 on March 14 (publication of Avastin data). On March 21, it benefited from Schering's bad news with a 10 percent advance to USD 58. By the end of September, Genentech had climbed another 60 percent.

The intraday charts from March 21 show that Schering had its share price loss and Genentech its share price gain already in the opening (see Exhibits 2.10 and 2.11).

There are two lessons to be learned from this example. First, in the life sciences, sector stock prices can react very dramatically to product news. This is particularly true for leveraged biotech companies and

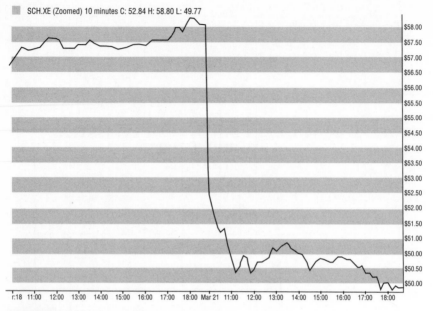

EXHIBIT 2.10   Schering Intraday, March 18–21, 2005

Source: © Infotec SA.

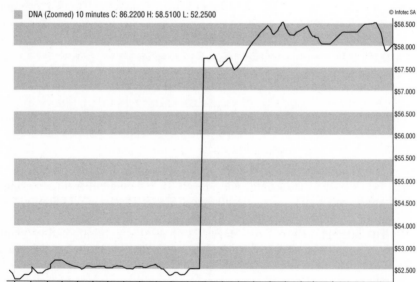

EXHIBIT 2.11   Genentech Intraday, March 18–21, 2005

Source: © Infotec SA.

mid-size companies. Second, news can also trigger a medium-term development if it is followed by a whole series of events in this direction, as was the case with Genentech, which delivered additional positive news for Avastin in the following months.

PROFIT WARNING: SOFT DRINK COMPANY ISSUES PROFIT WARNING, SEPTEMBER 2005

Cott decreases 17 percent in one day.

The Canadian company Cott, the world's largest maker of store-brand soft drinks, warned on Wednesday, September 21, 2005, that full-year earnings would be "substantially" less than expected and lowered its forecast for the year as a whole. It was the fourth profit warning issued within one year (see Exhibit 2.12). The company blamed weak U.S. soft drink volumes, a product shift toward lower-margin bottled water, and escalating raw material costs. The United States accounts for more than 70 percent of group turnover. Whereas the U.S. soft drink market generated just slight volume growth in the first half of 2005, bottled water continued to post double-digit growth. In terms of raw material prices, it has to be mentioned that packaging costs increased sharply, as the cost of their plastic bottles is susceptible to higher oil prices.

Cott cut its sales growth guidance to between 6 and 8 percent from its previous projection of between 8 and 10 percent for 2005. In terms of earnings per share (EPS), the company's revised 2005 indication was $1.06 to 1.11 Canadian (previous guidance $1.14 to $1.18 Cdn.). Some analysts already reduced their estimates prior to the announcement, which was reflected in the share price performance at the beginning of September 2005. But the profit warning led to a further share price decline of 16.7 percent to $22.07 Cdn. in just one day.

The company had already issued a profit warning on July 20, 2005, but at the time the effect was rather minor as the stock price had already been on the decline since February. It moved up strongly in August, but in September the stock price started to retreat again. The company's second quarter 2005 results showed an increase in sales of 6 percent (organic +3 percent) to USD 493 million, but earnings were down 15 percent to USD 25 million.

The intraday chart of Cott shows that the profit warning did not have

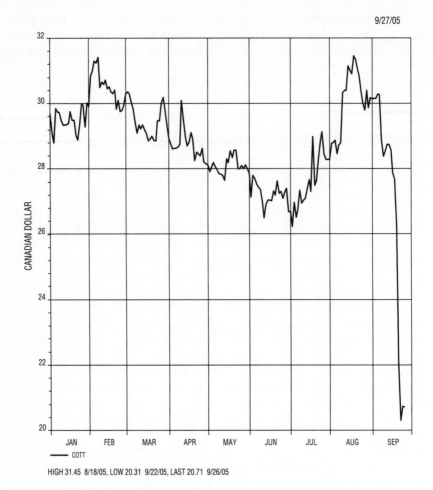

9/27/05

HIGH 31.45 8/18/05, LOW 20.31 9/22/05, LAST 20.71 9/26/05

EXHIBIT 2.12 Cott Corporation Chart, January 1 to September 23, 2005

Source: Thomson Financial.

an immediate impact and the share price came down over a two-day period (see Exhibit 2.13).

This profit warning shows how sensitively the market reacts to a
change in the earnings outlook. As it is not just the first profit warning, it
also raises the issue of confidence and trust, which is even more difficult
to regain.

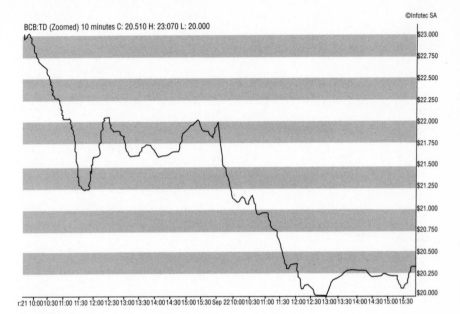

©Infotec SA

BCB:TD (Zoomed) 10 minutes C: 20.510 H: 23:070 L: 20.000

EXHIBIT 2.13 Cott Intraday, September 21–22, 2005
Source: © Infotec SA.

CHAPTER 3

How to Use Limit and Market Orders

S ome equity markets are referred to as *order-driven*, which means that the limit orders placed by some participants establish the prices at which other participants can trade by market order. To operate effectively in an order-driven environment, you must know how and when to submit limit orders and when, alternatively, to use market orders. You must know when to pay the spread as a cost of immediacy, and when to trade patiently and earn the spread as a liquidity provider. Additionally, a large trader (generally an institutional investor) must understand when and how to break a big order up into smaller pieces for submission over a succession of trades.

The participants in a pure order-driven market are the *naturals* (the natural buyers and sellers). There are no intermediaries who intervene to supply liquidity or immediacy in a pure order-driven market. We consider the role of dealers and other intermediaries in Chapter 5. In this chapter, we assume that all of the participants are naturals, and we ask you to view yourself as being a natural, too.

Markets are rarely pure, generic systems, however, and major market centers around the globe have hybrid structures. Trading at the NYSE is based on public limit order books and a trading floor that is populated by floor traders employed by exchange member firms. The books are managed by specialists who operate in the dual capacity of *brokers* (who handle customer orders) and *market makers* (who trade from their own capital and have an affirmative obligation to make fair and orderly markets). The other floor traders, working orders on a discretionary basis, effectively negotiate their trades. Upstairs market making is also an integral part of trading at the Big Board. NASDAQ and the London Stock Exchange, both of which were previously competitive market maker markets, have altered their systems to include customer limit orders (London in 1997 with the introduction of SETs, and NASDAQ in 2002 with the introduction of the NASDAQ Market Center, which at the time was called SuperMontage). The order-driven electronic trading platforms in Europe include market makers in their systems on both a registered, obligatory basis and a voluntary basis. Order-driven call auctions are used to open and close trading by NASDAQ, the NYSE, all major European exchanges, and many other markets around the world.

Since the 1977 launch of the Toronto Stock Exchange's Computer-Assisted Trading System (CATS), exchanges throughout Europe and the Far East have gravitated toward electronic order-driven platforms, which are widely considered an essential trading mechanism. In his contributed piece to this chapter, Jean-François Théodore describes the success his market (which today is named Euronext) has realized since instituting a fully electronic, continuous market in 1986 (at which time the Exchange was known as the Paris Bourse). Théodore elaborates on the use of various order types in the system, starting with the two predominant ones, market orders and limit orders. Further, he provides a clear explanation of not only why computerized order-driven markets were created, but why they actually "saw the light of day and grew." Théodore states:

> [I]nstitutional investors progressively became more familiar with the European investment universe. They found that the high price of liquidity resulting from the buy-and-sell spread of market makers could significantly reduce their financial performance. As most other European exchanges adopted the same European Market Model, based on a central limit order book (CLOB), a major part of the institutional order flow came back to the home exchanges of the listed companies.

Deutsche Börse's modern electronic market, Xetra®,[1] was instituted in 1997. In their contributed piece to the chapter, Rainer Riess and Uwe Schweickert, in a similar vein to Théodore, underscore the functionality of the electronic, order-driven continuous platform. They also show how continuous trading is effectively combined with periodic call auction trading in Xetra's hybrid market model. As a good complement to the ground that we cover in this chapter, Riess and Schweickert provide important information on the use of different order types that participants can choose with Xetra.

In recent years, electronic trading systems have made substantial inroads in the United States. One of the architects of these systems, Gerald Putnam, shows how Archipelago emerged as an electronic communication network (ECN) in 1997 following the introduction of the SEC's new Order Handling Rules. The facility attracted order flow by offering not just a limit order book but also order routing. As Putnam explains, "If an order could be executed at a better price outside of Archipelago's liquidity pool, it would be routed or preferenced to a NASDAQ market maker or even a competing ECN to find liquidity and to achieve best execution." Subsequently, Archipelago registered with the SEC as an exchange known as ArcaEx. Then on March 7, 2006, it merged with the New York Stock Exchange, and the NYSE Group (ticker symbol NYX) was formed. The market offers a rich variety of alternative order types but, as is typically the case for order-driven platforms, as Théodore points out, limit orders and market orders are at its core. In this chapter, we establish a basic understanding of how to use these two primary order types in continuous market trading.

THE ORDER BOOK AND THE MARKET

The SWX Swiss Exchange order book for Nestlé stock is shown in Exhibit 3.1. The SWX book arrays prices from high at the top to low at the bottom. Sell and buy order sizes are aggregated at each price. Deutsche Börse's Xetra order book for Beiersdorf AG, the maker of personal care Nivea products and Elastoplast brands, is shown in Exhibit 3.2. The Xetra order book shows the bids on the left side and the asks on the right. Like SWX, Xetra displays the aggregate order quantities at each price, but unlike SWX it also shows the number of live orders at each price. For instance, we see that two orders comprise the 92.00 bid for 350 shares.

Let's step back a moment and ask a key question about an order-driven market: Can the naturals supply liquidity to themselves? Of course they can. The natural buyers are the source of liquidity for the natural sellers (and vice versa), and those who place limit orders on the book provide immediacy to others who choose to trade by market order. But the order-driven ecology does not function well under all conditions.

A pure order-driven market can fail if it is too illiquid or under undue stress. You can get a sense of this from TraderEx. Trading can get pretty uncomfortable when TraderEx's parameter settings are changed so as to disturb the balance between informed orders and liquidity orders. Under the adverse conditions of informational change, you (and others) would find it very difficult to trade reasonably. If another security was available, you would probably want to turn to it. If TraderEx was a real market with sparse order flow and subject to substantial informational change, it would probably collapse or lose out to a quote-driven system. The TraderEx exercise that follows presents a picture of a very thin market (see Exhibit 3.3). What order would you care to place in it?

THE EQUITY TRADER COURSE

Member	O	B Size	Price		S Size	O	Member
			328.00		60		
			328.00		93		
			328.00		2,000		
			328.00		1,500		
			328.00		30		
			328.00		250		
			328.00		1,000		
			328.00		1,000		
			328.00		40		
			328.00		222		
		1,940	327.75				
		10	327.75				
		24	327.75				
		48	327.75				
		225	327.75				
		47	327.75				
		1,000	327.75				
		1,000	327.50				
		5,000	327.50				
		5,000	327.50				

EXHIBIT 3.1 SWX Order Book for Nestlé
Source: SWX Swiss Exchange.

MDAX – FFM – Order Market Overview

Window Trading View Columns

● Profile ○ Instr ○ InstrGrp   Exch: FFM

Instr	ISIN	Phase	BidCnt	BidQty	Bid	Ask	AskQty	AskCnt	LstPrc	LstQty	LstTime	NetChg	Volume	Auc
+ AMB2	DE0008400029	TRADE	1	68	59,92	60,09	166	2	60,01	36	15:07:06	+0,060	51.917	
+ ARL	DE0005408116	TRADE	1	500	27,88	27,93	700	1	27,96	27	15:07:02	-0,330	16.864	
+ AWD	DE0005085906	TRADE	2	1.100	27,80	27,97	350	2	27,80	1.000	15:01:56	-0,160	3.171	
- BEI	DE0005200000	TRADE	1	100	92,46	92,52	100	1	92,51	306	15:09:21	+0,110	9.891	
			1	100	92,45	92,96	297	2						
			1	223	92,39	93,00	200	1						
			1	10	92,30	93,18	400	1						
			1	200	92,25	93,20	342	1						
			1	400	92,23	93,25	1.000	1						
			1	400	92,15	93,40	231	3						
			2	350	92,00	93,44	400	1						
			1	500	91,95	93,45	200	1						
			1	100	91,65	93,49	3.336	1						
+ BOS	DE0005245500	TRADE	1	227	18,30	18,37	250	1	18,30	115	14:28:12	+0,130	6.538	
+ BOS3	DE0005245534	TRADE	1	500	19,10	19,12	78	1	19,12	32	15:08:17	+0,170	39.371	

EXHIBIT 3.2 Xetra® Order Book for Beiersdorf AG
Source: Xetra® is a registered trademark of Deutsche Börse AG.

TraderEx				
DAY		**TIME**		**SEED**
1		**10:20**		**6**

TICKER	PRICE	13.00	13.50	13.70
	QTY	8	44	28
	TIME	10:20	10:20	10:20

QUOTE	**13.00**	**14.40**
	2	13

Hit	BIDS		OFFERS	Take
		14.60	29	
		14.50		
		14.40	13	
		14.30		
		14.20		
		14.10		
		14.00		
		13.90		
		13.80		
		13.70		
		13.60		
		13.50		
		13.40		
		13.30		
		13.20		
		13.10		
	2	13.00		
	17	12.90		
		12.80		
	46	12.70		

EXHIBIT 3.3 Exercise: Very Thin Market with a Wide Bid-Ask Spread

Select "Proprietary Trader" mode, lower the "Limit Order Percentage" to 30 percent from 90 percent, and set "Seed" equal to 6. In the "GO" mode, advance to 10:19 A.M. At 10:20 a large order to sell 80 hits the bids from 13.70 down to 13.00, opening up a wide bid-ask spread. Click to advance time and you will see that the bid-ask spread remains wide due to the lack of machine-generated limit orders. With such a wide spread—over 10 percent—and so little displayed liquidity, the order-driven system will struggle to survive. Question: Under the 10:20 A.M. market conditions, what orders would you place in the market as a proprietary trader?

As we saw in Chapter 2, order-driven markets can be structured in two fundamentally different ways. With a *continuous market*, trading is generally a sequence of bilateral matches that occur whenever (in continuous time) two contra-side orders meet or cross in price. This continuous order-driven market is our focus in this chapter. In contrast, in a *call auction*, a larger set of orders is batched together for simultaneous execution, in a multilateral trade, at a specific point in time. At the time of a call, a market clearing price is determined and buy orders at this price and higher execute, as do sell orders at this price and lower. We turn to the call auction in Chapter 4.

Continuous markets and call auctions are generally united in hybrid combinations, with the calls being used at the beginning of each trading session to open the market and at the end of each session to close the market. Calls are also commonly used to restart the continuous market following any trading halt that may be triggered when a market is under stress, and in a few markets they are scheduled on a daily basis during a trading session (the German stock exchange, Deutsche Börse, does this). Calls are included along with continuous trading in the TraderEx sofware (in the hybrid market alternative).

ORDER TYPES

Order-driven markets typically allow for a variety of orders. For instance, stop-loss orders are instructions to buy if price rises above a given value, or to sell if price falls below a given value. Hidden orders (sometimes referred to as *iceberg orders*) allow for all or part of a large order to be entered into the computer of an electronic trading system without being disclosed to the market. The limit price of an order for one stock may also be *pegged* or linked to, and automatically change with, some other value, such as the price of another stock or the value of a market index. Special instructions can also be placed on orders: "all or none" (execute the order in full or not at all), "fill or kill" (execute the order immediately or not at all), and so forth.

The special orders provide participants with some useful tools, but to ensure consistent, transparent price determination, an exchange's matching algorithm can only discover trade prices and give standing to plain vanilla limit orders and market orders. And only plain vanilla limit and market orders are used in TraderEx. Truth be known, the heart of trading lies not with the fancy order types, but with the plain vanilla market and limit orders.

A *market order* is an unpriced instruction to buy or to sell at the best price established by limit orders and/or dealer quotes. Market orders are simple to understand. You see an opportunity to trade, you like it, and you go for it. With a market order in a continuous market, you trade right away and with certainty. Immediacy and certainty are what make the market order attractive. But you pay something for this—you buy at the ask and sell at the bid, and, in so doing, pay the spread.

A *limit order* specifies the highest (maximum) price that a participant would be willing to pay to acquire shares, or the lowest (minimum) price that he would be willing to receive to sell shares. In rapidly changing markets, traders will often use *marketable limit orders*, which means that at the time of placement the limit price to sell is at or below the bid, or the limit price to buy is at or above the ask quote. Even if you are willing to sell at the bid, you can protect yourself from executing at a lower price if the bid drops before your order reaches the market (or, if you are willing to buy at the offer, you can protect yourself from executing at a higher price if the offer rises before your order arrives). In general, though, the plain vanilla limit order is not marketable and is entered on the book. If you use a limit order and it executes, you have saved the spread—this is what makes the limit order strategy attractive. The wider the spread, the more attractive the limit order becomes. Schwartz and Weber (1997), using an earlier version of TraderEx in experimental lab tests performed with University of Pennsylvania students, found that the students submitted significantly more limit orders relative to market orders whenever the bid-ask spread widened in a simulation run.[2]

But there is no free lunch. It costs something to place a limit order, and the cost is not as visible as the bid-ask spread. Only when the cost is understood can you choose wisely between placing a limit order and submitting a market order. In brief, the cost of placing a limit order is twofold: (1) Your order may not execute within your trading window, and (2) it might execute because a better-informed trader knows, in light of new information, that your limit order is mispriced. We will return to these two costs shortly.[3]

Anyone submitting a market order, especially a large order, wants to know the total number of shares that can be executed "at market." To provide this information, the shares represented by different orders on both sides of the market have to be aggregated and the total disclosed to the market. The number of shares represented by your plain vanilla limit order will be added to the shares represented by all other plain vanilla limit orders at that price, and the total displayed to the market.

Aggregation is not possible for orders that have special conditions on them. Picture a situation where there are two buy limit orders at the best market bid of 52. One is a simple order to buy 400 shares at 52, and the other is an all-or-nothing order to buy 700 shares at 52. Together, the two orders total 1,100 shares, but 1,100 shares to buy at 52 *cannot* be shown on the book. If it were shown, other participants would have no way of knowing, for example, that a market order to sell 600 shares could not be executed fully against the 1,100 shares—the order is too small to meet the all-or-nothing condition on the 700-share order, and it is too large to execute fully against the 400-share order. For this reason, all-or-none and minimal fill conditions on limit orders prevent them from having "standing," and they cannot be displayed and treated the same way by the order book's matching algorithm.

Conditional orders must be handled outside of the matching model, typically in the order room of a brokerage house. At the New York Stock Exchange, specialists on the trading floor deal with conditional orders by taking them on their own books. One special order type can be placed in the book, however: the reserve or hidden (iceberg) order, where only part of the order's size is disclosed to the market, along with an indicator that the order does in fact contain a hidden or reserve size. Typically, once the displayed size executes, part or all of the remaining reserve size will be used to refresh the part of the order that is shown on the book.

A LOOK AT THE MARKET

A limit order book from TraderEx is displayed in Exhibit 3.4. The Exhibit shows limit orders to buy (the bids) at prices from $10.00 up to $10.90, and limit orders to sell (the offers) at prices from $11.90 down to $11.10. The numbers are the total number of shares placed at each price. For instance, the number "25" shown in the Bids column at $10.95 indicates that 25,000 shares are sought for purchase at a limit price of $10.90 (we take one unit to be 1,000 shares). These shares might be represented by one order for 25,000 shares, by two orders (perhaps one for 15,000 shares and a second for 10,000 shares), or by three orders or more. Similarly, the "21" shown in the Offers column at $11.10 indicates that 21,000 shares are

TraderEx		
DAY	**TIME**	**SEED**
1	**9:31**	**2**

TICKER	PRICE	
	QTY	
	TIME	

QUOTE	10.90	11.10
	25	21

Hit	BIDS		OFFERS	Take
		11.90	82	
		11.80	10	
		11.70	17	
		11.60	11	
		11.50	10	
		11.40		
		11.30		
		11.20	21	
		11.10	21	
		11.00		
	25	10.90		
		10.80		
		10.70		
		10.60		
	9	10.50		
	33	10.40		
		10.30		
		10.20		
	35	10.10		
	38	10.00		

EXHIBIT 3.4 Exercise: Opening Screen for Using Limit Orders

offered for sale at a limit price of $11.10. This number, too, may represent the total of one or more orders.

Limit orders sit on the book waiting for market orders to arrive. Market orders to buy execute against the limit orders to sell, and market orders to sell execute against the limit orders to buy. TraderEx follows the common industry practice of executing limit orders in a sequence that follows strict price and time priorities. *Price priority* means that the most aggressively priced limits (the highest-priced buys and the lowest-priced sells) execute first. *Time priority* means that if two or more orders are tied at the best price, the order that was placed first executes first. In other words, it's a first in, first out (FIFO) queue at a particular price. In actual markets, the price priority rule usually applies, but alternatives to the time priority rule are sometimes used. These include:

- Size priority: The largest order has priority.
- Pro rata execution: All orders are filled proportionally to their size.
- Random allocation: Orders are selected randomly to execute.

We use the strict time priority rule in TraderEx.

Now would be a good time to turn to your computer and open TraderEx as shown in Exhibit 3.4. Select the "Order-Driven" and "Proprietary Trader" mode, input $11 as the initial price, and select Seed = 2, keeping all other default values as they are. As you look at the order book, assume the following: You like the stock, and you would, if you had to, pay a price up to $11.50 for the shares (which is $0.40 above the offer). You have decided to build a long position of 100 units (100,000 shares) early in the trading day—by 11:30, say.

How might you go about getting those shares? Also think about the timing of your purchase. Even though your gains from trade would be considerable if you bought from the lowest offers, you would still rather pay less if possible.

Enter orders or let the computer advance for several trades so that you can get a sense of the market for the stock. Look at the last transaction price, the current quotes, and the current state of the limit order book. Think about what drives your trading strategy. Is patience rewarded? Or is hesitation costly here?

To formulate a good strategy, you need information. The full book of limit orders is shown on your TraderEx screen. This amount of transparency characterizes many of the electronic order book markets around the world, but different markets reveal different amounts of information. Those that display a lot of information are *transparent*, and those that display little are *opaque*. When trading only one unit, transparency is your friend. If you see that the book is big and deep (that the market is liquid), you can have some confidence that price will not run away from you before you get your 1,000 shares (unless, of course, news comes out, P* changes, and others quickly respond).

By way of contrast, think of the confidence (or lack thereof) with which you would make your trading decision if TraderEx displayed only the *top of the book*—the best (highest) bid and the best (lowest) offer. Also think about how you would feel if, instead of looking to pick up 1,000 shares, you wanted to buy 10,000 shares, 50,000 shares, or more. Would you be willing to place a huge order on the market and have it displayed to the other participants? Would you want others to know that you are in the market for 150,000 shares? Your answer should be a resounding no. While you are thinking about this, try the following question: Just how transparent should a market be? There is only one easy answer to this one—no market should be totally transparent or totally opaque. You like to see other people's orders but, particularly if you are a large institutional investor, you do not want others to know about the trades that you would like to make.

For the day's opening book displayed in Exhibit 3.4, no orders have been placed at eight of the prices. The absence of orders at price points above the offer and below the bid are gaps in the book that can occur by chance. These gaps are sometimes referred to as *air pockets*. In contrast, the absence of an order at $11.00 may not be a matter of chance. This value is within the bid-ask spread that is defined by the lowest offer of $11.10 and the highest bid of $10.90. With this particular book, a market order to buy will execute at $11.10 (the best, most aggressive offer), and a market order to sell will execute at $10.90 (the best, most aggressive bid). We consider why the spread exists later in the chapter.

Remember, the book depicted here is a *snapshot* of orders that exist at a moment in time. As time passes, new limit orders arrive and existing limit orders are cancelled or turned into trades by the arrival of market orders. It is helpful to categorize the events that cause these things to happen. We have two primary types of events—liquidity and information. Along with technical trading, they account for the liquidity-motivated and information-motivated machine-generated order flow in the TraderEx simulation.

Recall that, in our simulation, information traders and technical traders enter only market orders, and that only our liquidity traders enter limit orders. You, on the other hand, are free to enter limit or market orders for whatever reason you choose. Do you think that the spread is unduly wide and will soon narrow? If so, place a limit order. Do you believe that the market is excessively volatile? If so, try to capture that volatility by placing some limit orders. Are you worried that the market is about to move away from you? If so, place a market order. Does operating in this manner classify you as a technical trader? It sure does. After all, what do you have to go on in the simplified environment of TraderEx but the dynamic behavior of quotes and prices in the market?

Suppose that after reflecting on the situation depicted in Exhibit 3.4, your instinct and willingness to experiment and take risk lead you to enter a 20-unit limit order to buy at $10.80. If market orders to sell come in and eliminate the 25,000 shares that are ahead of you (shares that have time priority), then your 20,000 share limit order is next to execute. Of course, in the interim, a more aggressively priced limit buy could jump ahead of you (perhaps at $11.00). If it does, it has priority (because of the price priority rule). Nevertheless, you enter your limit order at $10.80 and hope for the best. Yet, the more you think about the uncertainty of receiving an execution, the more attractive buying with immediacy and certainty at $11.10 may become—especially if you are valuing shares at $12 (note that we are using dime ticks, not nickels). As we explain in the next section, we refer to your $12 valuation as your *reservation price*. It is an important and useful concept.

A RESERVATION PRICE

Suppose that you are coming to the market to buy 1,000 shares (one unit). The market is currently $10.90 bid, $11.10 offer, and you would be willing to buy shares up to a price of $12 if you had to. (To keep life simple, let's say there are no commissions involved.) The $12 price is your assessment of share value. It is your statement that you will benefit from any trade that gets you the shares at a price below $12 and, of course, the cheaper the better. At $12 you would be indifferent, and you certainly would not go above your assessment of $12 a share. Anything higher than $12, you would walk away from the trade.

Economists have a term for this value assessment. We call it your *reservation price*. When you are buying, your reservation price is the highest (maximum) amount that you would be willing to pay for the shares; anything higher and you do not want them. When you are selling, your reservation price is the lowest (minimum) amount that you would be willing to receive for the shares; anything lower and you hang on to them.

Economists use the concept of a reservation price to measure the gains from trading. We define one unit to be 1,000 shares; if you succeed in picking up one unit at the $11.10 offer when your reservation price is $12, we assess your gains from trading as $0.90 a share ($12 minus $11.10), or as $900 in total ($0.90 times 1,000 shares). If the bid of $10.90 is your quote and your limit order executes, your gains from trading are assessed at $1.10 a share ($12 minus $10.90), or as $1,100 in total ($1.10 times 1,000 shares).

Each investor sets his own reservation price for a stock. Your reservation price depends on your risk tolerance and your assessment of share value. Your reservation price changes with the arrival of new information (news), your reassessment of existing information, and changes in your risk tolerance and cash position.

You might wonder how a reservation price relates to the P* variable that we introduced in Chapter 1. These are two different concepts. P* drives what we call *information trading* in TraderEx. If P* is above the offer, more buy orders arrive at the market. If P* is below the bid, more sell orders arrive. This does not imply that P* is the reservation price of our machine-resident information traders. Share valuations can differ among participants and, as they do, reservation prices differ as well. But there is only one P*. As noted in Chapter 1, P* is an equilibrium value that would be found if all information-motivated orders were batched together and cleared at a single price in a big multilateral trade according to call auction principles.

You might also question the difference between a reservation price and a limit order price. Your reservation price is a value that you will not go beyond. You set your limit price in accordance with your trading strategy. It is a value that you *choose* not to go beyond because you believe that a better price may be attained. In continuous market trading, do not put your reservation prices on your limit orders. Your limit buys should be priced lower than your reservation price, and your limit sells should be priced higher, depending on your expectation of the price at which you might be able to execute. For instance, if your reservation price is $12, if shares are currently trading in the neighborhood of the $10.90 bid and $11.10 offer, and if you think it likely that price will swing down to $10.70, you might do well to wait in hopes of buying at this lower price. Similarly, someone else who values shares at $10.50, sees the current quotes, and expects that price will likely pop up, might do well to wait in hopes of selling at a higher price.

This should clarify that a reservation price, the value P*, and a limit price are three distinct entities.

COST OF PLACING A LIMIT ORDER

Let's go back into TraderEx. Enter the "Order-Driven / Proprietary Trader" mode, input $11 as the initial price, and select Seed = 3, keeping the default values as they otherwise are. After the first trade at $11, enter a limit order to buy 20 at $10.80 (see Exhibit 3.5). Click on the "+>" key to

TraderEx		
DAY	**TIME**	**SEED**
1	**9:43**	**3**

TICKER	PRICE	11.00
	QTY	3
	TIME	9:43

QUOTE	**10.90**	**11.40**
	16	22

Hit	BIDS		OFFERS	Take
		12.00		
		11.90	24	
		11.80	33	
		11.70	59	
		11.60		
		11.50	7	
		11.40	22	
		11.30		
		11.20		
		11.10		
		11.00		
	16	10.90		
20	20	10.80		
	14	10.70		
	18	10.60		
	19	10.50		
		10.40		
	41	10.30		
		10.20		
	42	10.10		

EXHIBIT 3.5 Placing a Limit Order for 20 Shares at $10.80

advance time, and watch the screen. The first thing that happens (9:55) is that a limit order to buy 51 at $11 arrives, jumping in front of you in the book—drat! You're not the only one who likes the stock today. Next, a few market sell orders come in, and one buy shows up. The 51 units at $11 get whittled down to 8 and then to nothing at 10:16, when the bid drops to $10.90. At 10:19 a market order to sell 45 hits the 35 bid at $10.90 and then your 20 at $10.80 executes. Bingo! Congratulations, you have made a trade! You are now the proud owner of 20,000 shares. You have succeeded in buying the 20 units at $10.80, or $0.20 less per share than you would have paid if you had bought with a market order. Perhaps limit orders are a good way to go after all.

But is the news really good? Not necessarily. The answer depends on what motivated the market sell orders. If liquidity-motivated orders banged price down and gave you the execution, you should be pleased. When the liquidity-driven imbalance is over, price will likely mean revert back to its previous level and you will have made a little profit. But what if the market sell orders came in because of information change? What if, in the TraderEx environment, P* has dropped below the bid and triggered the arrival of the informed sell orders? This would not be good. Before we move on, advance the simulation to 10:21 (see Exhibit 3.6). The market of-fer is now 10.70. Although the offer is only good for six units, you are be-ginning to feel that you may have overpaid.

Of course, you would not have been pleased if you had bought at mar-ket for more than $11 earlier in the day. Either way, you now own 20 units (20,000 shares) that are trading below the price at which you bought them. But because you bought them at your limit order price, you are still better off to the tune of $0.20 a share. At this point, it appears that the limit order strategy might still have been better than the market order strategy after all.

Wait, not so fast. Strategies are decided *ex ante*, before an action is taken and results observed. *Ex post*, or after the fact, one has the benefit of hindsight. After the fact, the shares were purchased, price fell, value was lost, but less value was lost because the limit order price was $0.20 a share below the market order price. Ex post, the limit order strategy was the better of the two. Of course, it would have been even better to have not bought at all.

But ex ante is a different matter. Let's change the story a bit. You are watching the screen, waiting, and the flow of incoming orders is domi-nated by buys. Price rises. A thought crosses your mind: What if the buys are coming in because P* has risen? Now the market is at $11.10 bid, $11.20 offered, and you have lost the opportunity to buy shares at the lower price. The ex post assessment now favors the market order strat-egy—if you had bought at market at $11.10, you could have flipped the

TraderEx			
DAY	TIME		SEED
1	10:21		3

TICKER	PRICE	10.70	10.80	10.90
	QTY	14	20	8
	TIME	10:21	10:19	10:19

QUOTE	10.60	10.80
	18	6

Hit	BIDS		OFFERS	Take
		11.60		
		11.50	29	
		11.40	22	
		11.30		
		11.20	5	
		11.10	92	
		11.00	9	
		10.90		
		10.80	6	
		10.70		
	18	10.60		
	19	10.50		
		10.40		
	41	10.30		
		10.20		
	42	10.10		
	21	10.00		
		9.90		
	44	9.80		
	27	9.70		

EXHIBIT 3.6 Market Price Drops after Purchase of Shares

shares at $11.20 for a profit of $0.10 a share. But you placed a limit order instead, and the order still remains sitting, unexecuted, on the book. And for the remainder of the day, price will likely not come back down.

The possibility of information change occurring while a limit order is on the book introduces two kinds of risk (cost). The first is the risk of trading with a better-informed participant—you get the shares, but now they are worth less than you paid for them. This is sometimes referred to as the risk of being "bagged." The second risk (cost) is the risk of not executing. You wind up not buying the shares even though your valuation (reservation price) is $12. With informational change we have a "tails you lose, heads the other guy wins" situation. The news is bearish, price falls, your limit order executes, and the quotes fall further. Oops, tails—you lose, and you suffer ex post regret. But if the news is bullish, price rises and the order does not execute. Too bad, heads—the other guy wins, and, again as a limit order placer, you suffer ex post regret. At this point you might ask, why would anyone ever submit a limit order in the first place?

COMPENSATION FOR PLACING A LIMIT ORDER

Exchange execution fees are rarely charged for placing limit orders. Many ECNs today rebate two to three tenths of a cent per share to limit orders that execute, while charging three to four cents per share to market orders that remove liquidity. These are small amounts compared to the price changes that can occur. The major compensation for placing these orders must come from the pricing dynamics of the continuous order-driven market. After being driven in one direction, price will, at times, reverse direction and revert back toward a previous level. This pricing dynamic is called *mean reversion*, a concept introduced in Chapter 1. Any variable is said to mean revert if, after having been pushed away from its mean (average), it tends to revert back toward its mean.

For example, as before, given quotes of $10.90 bid, $11.10 offer, you have entered a limit order at $10.80. Once again, more sells than buys show up and, after a while, your order executes. Perhaps price and the quotes continue to fall a bit more, but this time P* has not changed, the market strengthens, and the quotes revert back toward their previous values of $10.90 bid, $11.10 offer. This time, rather than having bought at the $11.10 offer, you acquired the shares at $10.80 and the stock has resumed trading at its previous level. This leaves you between $0.10 and $0.30 per share better off. Profit possibilities like this can compensate for the two risks involved in limit order trading: the risk of trading with a better-informed customer (being bagged), and the risk of not executing.

Informational change could have caused the price move in the earlier example. News implies that price should change to a new level and, once it gets there, there is no tendency for price to return to where it had been. But the price move in the current example was caused by a temporary liquidity imbalance and, after the temporary imbalance corrected itself, price reverted back to its previous level. When price mean reverts, price volatility is accentuated.

Mean reversion generally (but not necessarily) works itself out in relatively brief intervals of time, typically intraday, and consequently price volatility is accentuated for relatively brief intervals of time. Think of it this way: Price is driven down and then it bounces back up, or price is driven up and then it drops back down. These zigs and zags that occur during the day can largely offset each other and, in the absence of any appreciable news event, price at the close of the day can wind up fairly near to where it was at the open, even though the high-low range for the day can be substantial.

In summary, a liquidity event that causes a price decline could result in a limit buy order executing, or a liquidity event that causes a price increase could result in a limit sell order executing. After being driven down (or up), price tends to revert back up (or down). You, as a limit order trader, profit as price mean reverts after your order has executed. Sufficient mean reversion can offset the bagging and nonexecution costs generated by the information events.

One more thing: Mean reversion and accentuated short-period price volatility are essentially the same thing. They provide the essential compensation for limit order placers to supply liquidity.

SHOULD YOU SUBMIT A LIMIT ORDER OR A MARKET ORDER?

Having pondered the costs and the benefits of placing a limit order, what do you want to do with your 20-unit (20,000 shares) order? Is the compensation that you might get for placing a limit order sufficient in light of the costs? More details are needed before we can answer this. Let's first consider how a population of participants may naturally separate into two groups—one that goes the limit order route and another that elects to trade by market order. You might then consider which of the two groups you would best fit into with your 20-unit order.

Everyone who places a limit order risks information changing while his order is sitting on the book. It's been called the "sitting duck" problem. Your limit order is sitting there, waiting to be shot at if an adverse news event suddenly occurs. Every limit order placer faces the dual risks of being bagged and of not executing. What differs from investor to investor is the importance of the nonexecution risk. An investor who is relatively content with his share holdings will not lose much if a limit order to buy or sell some shares does not execute. But an investor who strongly wants to adjust his share holdings will be very sensitive to the possibility of the limit order not executing. For a spectrum of participants, those who are the most content with their current holdings will place limit orders (to profit from the accentuated volatility), and those who are the most eager to change their current holdings will place market orders (to get immediacy and to avoid the risk of not executing).

The market can reach a balance between limit order traders and market order traders. We have seen that the compensation for placing a limit order is mean reversion and the associated accentuation of short-period volatility. We also know that liquidity events have bigger price impacts when the book is thinner. That is, there is an inverse relationship between the depth of the book and short-period volatility accentuation. When the book is very thin, the compensation for placing a limit order is high and more participants will place limit orders. As the book fills, the volatility accentuation dampens, the compensation for placing a limit order decreases, and fewer limit orders will be in the book. When volatility reaches a level that is just sufficient to compensate the marginal limit order placer, the depth of the book and the accentuated short-period volatility are in balance. At this point, the limit order traders and the market order traders are supporting each other appropriately, and the market is in ecological balance.

Coming at this from the other end of the spectrum, if the book is very thick and volatility accentuation low, the compensation for placing a limit order is meager and few participants will submit them. As long as market orders predominate, the book thins, volatility accentuation increases, and the compensation for placing a limit order rises. When volatility reaches a level that just compensates the marginal limit order placer, the depth of the book and the accentuated volatility are in equilibrium and, once again, the market is in ecological balance.

So, do you wish to place a limit order or a market order? Your answer should depend on how many orders are on the book, the size of the bid-ask spread, and your assessment of the probability that the limit order you might place will execute. But another detail is needed: Your answer should also depend on your own eagerness to trade. The concept of a reservation price is useful here. The higher your reservation price (all else the same), the more eager you should be to execute as a market order buyer.

Remember, your reservation price for the stock is $12. If you buy by market order at $11.10, your gain from trading is $0.90 a share ($12 minus $11.10), or $900 total ($0.90 times 1,000 shares). If your limit order at $10.80 executes, your gain from trading is $1.20 a share ($12 minus $10.80), or $1,200 total ($1.20 times 1,000 shares). Are you willing to give up a certain gain of $900 for the uncertain possibility of gaining $1,200? Given your reservation price, the answer depends on the probability of your limit order executing because of a liquidity event.

In making your decision, you should choose the alternative that gives you the highest expected gain from trading. In assessing the payoffs in a risky situation, it is well established in economic theory that the *utility* of dollar gains and losses should be assessed, rather than the raw dollar amounts. That might suggest that in making your trading decision, the utility of the trading gain should be assessed, rather than the raw trading gain itself. But this is not the case, for one reason: Your reservation price already reflects your aversion to risk.[4] You need only consider the raw dollar amounts.

For the market order route, the expected gain is the $900 you can get with certainty. For the limit order route, the expected gain is the $1,200 you get if your limit order executes, times the probability of it executing because of a liquidity event. We can define a *breakeven probability* (P_{BE}) as the probability value that equates the two expected gains. The expected gains are equal when

$$\$900 = P_{BE} \times \$1,200$$

Thus the breakeven probability is

$$P_{BE} = \frac{\$900}{\$1,200} = 75\%$$

If you believe that the *actual probability* of getting an execution is higher than 75 percent, submit a limit order. If you think that the actual probability is lower than 75 percent, submit a market order.

The higher your reservation price, the higher is your breakeven probability, and the more apt you should be to place a market order. This is intuitively reasonable. As your reservation price gets higher, the differential gain between the limit order and the market order executions becomes less consequential. For instance, if your reservation price is $13.00, your gains from trading by market order are $1,900 in total, and your gains from trading by limit order are $2,200 in total, then your breakeven probability is 86.3 percent.

With a breakeven probability of 86.3 percent instead of 75 percent, you will be more apt to place a market order. This follows from your reservation price being $13 rather than $12.

If you do go the limit order route, you have to decide the price at which to place your order. Using the analytic framework that we have developed, you should select the price point that maximizes your *expected gain* from trading. Your expected gain per share is the actual probability that your limit order executes (P_A) times the gain per share that you get if it does:

$$\text{Expected Gain} = P_A \times (\text{Reservation Price} - \text{Limit Price})$$

Continue to let $12 be your reservation price. The market is as shown in Exhibit 3.4 with an $11.10 offer and a $10.90 bid. Consider four price points for buying, $11, $10.90, $10.80, and $10.70, with associated probabilities of execution of 0.90, 0.85, 0.80, and 0.70 respectively. You have price priority and become the high bidder at $11, and hence P_A is highest at this price point. But $10.90 is the existing market bid and the 25 units that are already there would have *time priority* over your order at this price point; accordingly, P_A at $10.90 has the considerably lower value of 0.85. At $10.80, you also lose *price priority*; with 25 units ahead of you, the actual probability of your order executing would have the yet lower value of 0.80. Putting this all together we have:

Expected Gain at $11.00 = .90 × ($12.00 − $11.00) = $0.87

Expected Gain at $10.90 = .85 × ($12.00 − $10.90) = $0.935

Expected Gain at $10.80 = .80 × ($12.00 − $10.80) = $0.96

Expected Gain at $10.70 = .70 × ($12.00 − $10.70) = $0.91

We now have an answer (see Exhibit 3.7). Your maximum expected gain is the $960 that you get at the $10.80 price point. Since this is greater than the $900 you would gain from trading by market order at $11.10, you should enter a limit order to buy shares at $10.80.

In Chapter 1 we made reference to Malcolm Gladwell's book *Blink*, noting a difference between how investment decisions and trading decisions are made. With investment decisions, time is taken to make so-called "rational" choices. In contrast, trading decisions are typically made

EXHIBIT 3.7 Limit Prices, Buy Order Execution Probabilities, and
Expected Gain from a Trade

Trade Price	Probability	Expected Gain per Share	Expected Gain per Unit
$11.10	1.00	0.90	$900.00
$11.00	0.90	0.90	$900.00
$10.90	0.85	0.94	$935.00
$10.80	0.80	0.96	$960.00
$10.70	0.70	0.91	$910.00
$10.60	0.53	0.74	$742.00

quickly on the basis of instinct and fast reflexes. But we have just developed a rational approach to making a trading decision. Is this inconsistent with our earlier statement?

It is not. We do not mean to imply that everyone knows enough about execution probabilities to be able to make these calculations and to reduce the trading decision to a simple algorithm (although we do discuss algorithmic trading in Chapter 6). Rather, our example is intended to give you a framework for *visualizing* your trading decisions and then, with practice, making your decisions faster and with greater accuracy. But do not expect to get it right on every order and every trade. Professionals know that they cannot do this. The trick is to be right more often than you are wrong so that, over many trades, you come out ahead.

Exhibits 3.8 through 3.11 recap the process for a limit order pricing

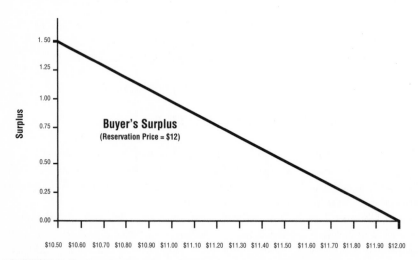

EXHIBIT 3.8 Surplus per Share for Buyer with Reservation Price of $12

decision for a buyer. An identical analysis could be carried out for a sell limit order, with the seller's surplus increasing as the price received from a sale rises, and the probability of realizing an execution falling as the price of the sell limit is raised. Exhibit 3.8 shows the buyer's surplus decreasing as the purchase price approaches the $12 reservation price.

Exhibit 3.9 shows a trader's assessment of the probability of a buy order executing at different limit order prices in a particular time frame (e.g., within three hours). A limit order to buy at the offer price of $11.10 executes with certainty; it is, in fact, a *marketable limit order*. Note that the probability jumps twice, first for orders placed at $11.00, one tick ahead of the bid quote, and then at the offer quote, $11.10. The jump at $11.00 is from gaining price and time priority over all other buy limit orders, while the jump at the $11.10 offer is due to the order executing with certainty.

Multiplying the surplus from buying by the probability of an order executing over the range of limit prices from $10.60 to $11.30 gives the buyer's expected surplus. In Exhibit 3.10, we see a case where a limit order one tick below the $10.90 bid at $10.80 maximizes the expect surplus for the buyer.

All else equal, the probabilities of order execution decrease as the book gets thicker and increase as the book gets thinner. Assume that the book gets thicker and that the assessed probabilities of your order executing fall 10 percent (e.g., 80 percent reduced to 72 percent) for all price points below the $11.10 offer price. This is depicted in Exhibit 3.11.

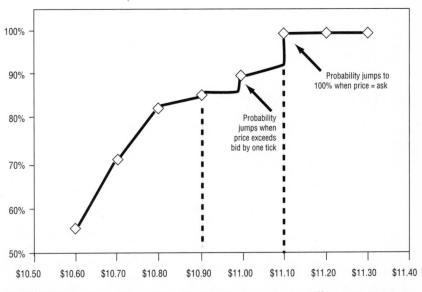

EXHIBIT 3.9 Probability of Buy Limit Order Executing at Different Limit Prices

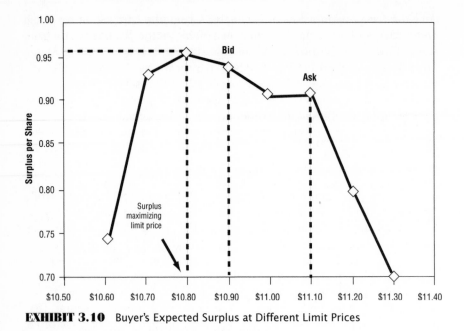

EXHIBIT 3.10   Buyer's Expected Surplus at Different Limit Prices

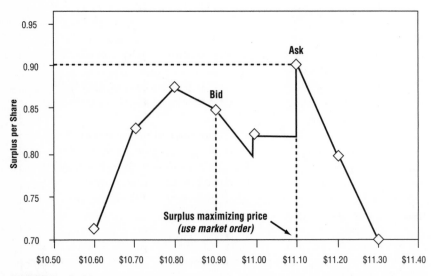

EXHIBIT 3.11   Buyer's Expected Surplus with Lower Probabilities of Limit Order Execution

Lowering the probabilities of buy orders executing in the order book leads traders to use market orders more often. In this illustration, the surplus maximizing buy order price is at the ask quote, indicating that a market order to buy is now the optimal order.

THE BID-ASK SPREAD

Having discussed the costs and benefits of trading with limit orders, let's return to the question of why there are bid-ask spreads in order-driven markets. The answer is simple for dealer markets. As we discuss further in Chapter 5, a spread between each individual dealer's bid and offer is an important revenue source for a dealer. When the quotes of multiple dealers are aggregated, the individual dealer spreads endure and the lowest quoted ask on the market remains discretely above the highest quoted bid on the market.

The dealer buys and sells shares to accommodate public sellers and buyers, and is compensated by the spread for doing this. An order-driven environment operates differently. Public customers (the naturals) who place limit orders buy because they really want the shares, sell because they really do not want the shares, and are *not* primarily looking to profit from the spread. Nevertheless, they place their limit orders on the book and they do so at different prices. If a sizable number of naturals are in the market, why don't their orders get placed at virtually every price point in the neighborhood where the stock is trading?[5] Wouldn't the book simply fill up and the spread disappear?

We provided a quick, intuitive explanation of why this would not happen in Chapter 2. We said that, because of the allure of certainty, no trader will post a limit buy order only a hair or so below a market ask, and no trader will post a limit sell order only a hair or so above a market bid. Let's expand on this thought.

There is a simple reason and a more intricate reason why spreads exist. First, the simple reason. If a buy and a sell order meet in price, a trade occurs and, as the orders execute, they disappear from the book. Therefore, for buy and sell orders to be sitting on the book, they must be at different prices. The minimum allowable price difference between the differentially priced orders is commonly referred to as the *minimum price variation* or *tick size*. For the book displayed in Exhibit 3.3, the minimum price variation is 10 cents. For the U.S. markets, a one-cent tick size is generally used. With a one-cent minimum allowable price variation, if the bid is $10.90, the lowest offer that can sit unexecuted on the book is $10.91. Consequently, a spread of at least one cent must exist.

Now for the more challenging question. What, other than the chance event that an order did not arrive at a price, might account for a spread that is larger than the minimum allowable price variation? To get an answer, let's again consider a participant's decision of whether to submit a limit order or a market order. If you recall, we started with the following situation:

- Your reservation price is $12.
- If you buy 1,000 shares by market order at $11.10, your gain from trading is $0.90 per share, or $900 total.
- If you place a limit order at $10.90 and it executes, your gain from trading is $1.10 per share, or $1,100 total.
- Your breakeven probability is 900/1,100 or 81.8 percent.

Now place your buy limit order one tick higher at $11.00:

- Your gain from trading if it executes is $1.00 per share, or $1,000 total.
- Your breakeven probability is 90.0 percent.

Now switch over to a one-cent minimum price variation and place your buy limit order at $11.09, one penny tick below the offer:

- Your gain from trading if it executes is $0.91 per share, or $910 total.
- Your breakeven probability is 98.9 percent.

Let's drive this further. Make the minimum price variation infinitesimal and place your buy limit infinitesimally close to the $11.10 offer:

- Your gain from trading if it executes is infinitesimally less than $0.90 per share, or $900 total.
- Your breakeven probability is infinitesimally less than 100.0 percent.

Clearly, if it executes, your gain from buying by limit order decreases as you raise its price. But putting a higher price on your limit order must also increase the probability of it executing: Fewer competing buy orders will be placed ahead of you on the book, and the higher price makes it more attractive for a potential seller to enter a market order rather than place a limit order on the offer side of the book. The key question is whether the *actual probability* of realizing an execution can remain higher than the breakeven probability as you raise the price of your limit order. In our numerical example, the *breakeven probability* is 81.8 percent, 90.0 percent, 98.9 percent, and infinitesimally close to 100.0 percent for limit orders placed at $10.90, $11.00, $11.09, and infinitesimally close to $11.10, respectively. Could the *actual probability* of a limit order executing be infinitesimally close to 100.0 percent for a limit buy placed infinitesimally close to a limit sell? The answer is not obvious. Let's think about this some more.

The key insight here is that there is a nontrivial probability difference between executing with certainty and taking the chance of getting a better price. As long as your buy order has not executed, it may never execute within your trading horizon because of the arrival of bullish news. In the terminology of TraderEx, your order may not execute because P* has jumped. Picture the trader who has placed a limit buy at $11.09. If the order executes because of a liquidity event, the trader saves one penny per share. But what if P* jumps up? (Half the time when it jumps, it jumps up.) The trader would have profited from that jump if he had submitted a market order, but loses out if the limit order route is chosen. Similarly, a trader who has a limit sell order on the book when P* jumps down loses out from having chosen the limit order rather than the market order route. Again, our question: Could the actual probability of a limit order executing be infinitesimally close to 100.0 percent for a limit buy placed infinitesimally close to a limit sell? Our answer: No, it cannot. There is always a probability jump at the offer (for a buy limit order) and at the bid (for a sell limit order). With this in mind, would you be tempted to place a limit order at $11.09? at $11.0999?

How close would anyone place a limit order to a contra-side order that is already on the book? The answer depends on the trader's reservation price. If your reservation price is close to the $11.10 offer, the gain from trading by market order is low and you do not lose much from taking the limit order route if your limit order does not execute. Consider this situation:

- Your reservation price is $11.15.
- If you buy 1,000 shares by market order at $11.10, your gain from trading is $0.05 per share, or $50 total.
- If you place a limit order at $10.95 and it executes, your gain from trading is $0.20 per share, or $200 total.
- The breakeven probability is 25.0 percent.

This shows that, with a low reservation price, your gain from a trade may be slim, but you might still put in a limit order (remember, we have simplified matters by ignoring commissions). This example reinforces what we said previously, that the more content you are with your current holdings (i.e., the less eager you are to trade), the more likely it is that you will place a limit order rather than a market order. In this last example, the breakeven execution probability is only 25.0 percent (remember, in the original example with a reservation price of $12, the breakeven execution probability is 81.8 percent).

With the lower reservation price ($11.15), suppose that you do submit a limit order. Will you be tempted to place your limit order close to the $11.10 offer? Here is the scoop on this one:

- Your reservation price for the stock is $11.15.
- If you buy 1,000 shares by market order at $11.10, your gain from trading is $0.05 per share, or $50 total.
- If you place a limit order at $11.09 and it executes, your gain from trading is $0.06 per share, or $60 total.
- The breakeven probability is 83.3 percent.

Once again, the breakeven probability is high and thus the market order strategy will, most likely be more attractive.

We are now very close to our answer. Maybe someone out there nevertheless chose to place a limit buy one penny below the already posted offer at $11.15 Certainly, penny spreads are commonly observed for active NASDAQ and NYSE stocks. However, these quotes are generally for only a small number of shares, and they typically sit on the books for very short periods (a minute or so). Algorithmic traders and basket traders will place limit orders within a penny of a counterpart quote for a large number of stocks, let some of them execute, and than quickly cancel or reprice the rest. This does not happen in TraderEx (we have only one risky asset). When TraderEx is played with a penny tick size, we do not expect to observe many penny spreads.

Cohen, Maier, Schwartz, and Whitcomb (CMSW) have pursued the issue further.[6] To explain the existence of a nontrivial spread in a pure order-driven market, CMSW shrink the tick size way further and ask whether an infinitesimal minimum price variation can result in an infinitesimal spread. They then show that, even if price is a continuous variable, no limit buy will ever be placed infinitesimally close to an established offer and, similarly, no limit sell will ever be placed infinitesimally close to an established bid. CMSW do this by showing that, as the limit order is placed ever closer to a counterpart quote, the differential gain of trading by limit order rather than market order goes to zero, while the probability of the limit order executing rises, but not to unity. We repeat: The execution probability for a limit order placed infinitesimally close to a counterpart quote remains discretely less than one. As already discussed, the reason for this is that a posted offer that is not accepted may cease to be available (it could be cancelled or hit by someone else's buy order), and the opportunity to trade at that price may not arise again. Simply stated, the difference between being extremely close to making a transaction and actually consummating the trade is not infinitesimal.[7] Fishermen tell stories about the one that got away; traders do, too.

As the gain from a limit order that executes approaches the gain from the market order, the breakeven probability goes to unity. Consequently, with a finite probability of not executing, the actual probability of execution must be less than the breakeven probability for any limit buy order in the immediate neighborhood of a posted offer (or for any limit sell order in the immediate neighborhood of a posted bid). Therefore, within the immediate neighborhood of a counterpart quote, the market order strategy must dominate the limit order strategy for each and every trader. The spread, therefore, cannot be infinitesimal and must therefore be nontrivial. Consequently, a meaningful spread must exist in an order-driven market.

The CMSW paper offers the following imagery to shed an intuitive light on their finding. The allure of trading with certainty by market order at a previously posted sell exerts a gravitational pull on any incoming buy order. A new buy is attracted to the offer, is submitted as a market order, and a trade is triggered. The allure of a previously posted bid exerts the same *gravitational pull* on an incoming sell order. Accordingly, any new limit order will be priced far enough away from the counterpart quote to lie outside the gravitational pull of the counterpart quote. Thus a new limit buy will not be placed "too close" to an already posted offer, and a new limit sell will not be placed "too close" to an already posted bid. Thus there will always be a spread between the best bid and offer.

Spreads that are wider than the minimum tick size are common, especially with penny pricing. For any individual stock, the size of the spread depends on the strength of the gravitational pull. The gravitational pull is stronger for stocks that are higher priced, that are more price volatile (more subject to informational change), that trade less frequently, and that in other respects are less liquid. Stocks that fall into these categories are expected to have wider spreads. The gravitational pull is also stronger for larger orders because larger orders arrive at the market less frequently. Consequently, the spread between large buy and large sell orders on the book is generally relatively wide.

Each stock has an *equilibrium size of spread* that depends on the variables we have just mentioned (price, volatility, frequency of informational change, trading frequency, etc.). As trading progress, the spread can widen with the arrival of market orders and narrow with the arrival of limit orders. When the spread is wider than its equilibrium value, it is more apt to narrow; when it is narrower, it is more apt to widen. Exercise #1 in the final section of this chapter is germane to this point. We ask you to change various parameter settings in TraderEx and to assess their impact on the average size of the spread in your simulation runs. You might also test how cleverly you can switch between market orders and limit orders when you sense that the spread is relatively tight or excessively wide, given your TraderEx parameter settings.

HANDLING A LARGE ORDER

Thus far, we have asked you to consider yourself participating in the market to buy or sell 1,000 shares. What if your order size is increased to 50,000 shares? to 500,000? How would this affect your thinking and your analysis of alternatives as you go to the market to trade? Perhaps you would place a 1,000 share order on the book. But a 50,000 share order? Would you, in Exhibit 3.4 for instance, be willing to enter the number "500" where a "0" now stands at $10.80? That sure would annihilate the air pocket at $10.80! Nothing else exposed on the book is anywhere near that size! Other participants would definitely sit up and take notice. Would you benefit from having this enormous limit order to buy sitting visibly on the book?

First of all, you would be making it a lot more attractive for sellers to place limit orders instead of hitting the limit buys with their market orders to sell. Why? Because your 500,000 share order, as long as it is sitting there, acts as a barrier (a backstop) to price dropping lower. The barrier increases the probability of a seller's limit order executing, and thus gives that contra-side participant a good opportunity to try to get a higher price.

What should you do if you are in the market for 500,000 shares, or 5,000,000 shares, for that matter? A number of alternatives are available to the big traders. They can engage the services of a broker/dealer to search for the other side and/or to commit dealer capital to the trade. They can use a crossing network or a price discovery call auction (we discuss these in Chapter 4). Big institutional investors can send their orders to an ECN such as Archipelago, or to one of the new alternative trading systems such as LiquidNet or Pipeline.[8] Our simulation offers some of this. In the TraderEx hybrid model, you can trade with a dealer, you can send an order to the TraderEx call auction, and the TraderEx limit order platform itself resembles the trading engine of NASDAQ's INET or an Archipelago.

You have further options in real markets and in TraderEx. One possibility in TraderEx's pure order-driven model is to split the order into smaller pieces, and to enter the pieces at multiple price points. Each piece would be less visible on the book but, beyond this, not much would be accomplished if your entire order is very large. You would still be increasing depth on the buy side of the book and, in so doing, would be making it more tempting for sellers to place limit orders instead of market orders.

A more promising route to take when playing TraderEx would be to send only a part of the order (perhaps 1,000 to 5,000 shares) to the market at a time and to hold on to the rest (keep the shares "in your pocket"). You would then work the remainder of the order in a series of trades over an extended period of time. This practice is common in today's marketplace—large institutional participants do this regularly. The practice is widely referred to as *slicing and dicing*. We suggest that you do this when playing the role of a large participant in TraderEx.

AN OPTION TRADER'S VIEW OF LIMIT ORDERS

In an order-driven market, limit orders take on some properties of options that provide useful insights for trading decisions. An option is the right but not the obligation to do something. Someone extends the option (and is compensated for doing so) and somebody else receives the option (and pays something for it). A standardized, exchange-traded option is the right either to buy or to sell shares under certain specified conditions. The right to buy shares is a *call option*, and the right to sell shares is a *put option*. The person who extends the call or put "writes the option," and the person who acquires the call or put "buys the option." The price paid for the option is the *premium*.

An exchange-traded option specifies the stock the option is written on (the *underlying asset*), the time to expiration (the length of time the option is good for), and a *strike price* (the price at which the option can be exercised). For instance, the option might be a three-month exchange-traded call on Xyz.com with a strike price of $10.50. If the underlying, Xyz.com, is currently trading at $11.00, the premium for the call might be $0.61. Say you buy the option. If, in three months, Xyz.com is trading at $11.71, you will exercise the option (buy the shares) at the strike price of $10.50, sell the shares received from the option at $11.71 and, after subtracting the $0.61 you have paid for the right to do this, you walk away with a profit of $0.60 a share. On the other hand, if the option expires with the stock trading below $10.50, you will have paid $0.61 for something that has wound up being worthless.

An option is said to be *in the money* if exercising it would be the preferred action. If exercising the option would not be the preferred action, the option is *out of the money*. A call option is in the money if the price of the underlying is above the strike price and out of the money if the price of the underlying is below the strike price. The opposite is true for a put option: A put is in the money if the price of the underlying is below the strike price, and out of the money if the price of the underlying is higher. For both puts and calls, the option is *at the money* if the price of the underlying equals the strike price on the option. At the expiration date, in-the-money options are exercised and out-of-the-money options simply expire.[9]

The writer of a standardized option receives the premium for writing it, and hopes that the option will expire out of the money and will therefore not be exercised. If the option is exercised, the writer will still profit (but not by as much) if the difference between the price of the underlying and the option's strike price is less than the premium the writer has received. The buyer of the option hopes for the opposite. For a call option, the buyer comes out ahead if the price of the underlying exceeds the option's strike price by more than the premium paid for the right to buy the shares; for a put, the buyer comes out ahead if the price of the stock is less than the strike price of the option by an amount greater than the premium paid for the right to sell the shares. For both the call and the put, options trading is a zero-sum game: What the buyer gains the writer loses, and vice versa.

Words are one way to describe an option; a payoff diagram is another. Exhibit 3.12 shows the relationship at expiration between the payoff that you will get per share (on the vertical axis) and the price of the underlying at expiration (on the horizontal axis) if you buy an exchange-traded call (Panel A) or put (Panel B). Both diagrams show the following. When the option is out of the money or at the money, your payout is negative, and the loss is a constant amount—the premium that you paid for the option. When the option is in the money, your payout increases dollar for dollar as the price of the underlying rises (for a call) or falls (for a put).

Option is a remarkably broad concept, and option pricing theory has wide applicability. We can apply it here to the use of limit orders. By placing a 1,000 share buy order at $11.00, you are extending the right to anyone in the market to sell you 1,000 shares at $11.00. In effect, you have written a put option that resembles the exchange-traded puts we have just discussed. Of course there is no contractual expiry (expiration) point for the option—you can withdraw it whenever you want. Nevertheless, while your order is on the book, it is a live option that can be hit by anyone who wishes to sell you the shares. Your $11.00 limit price is the strike price of the option that you have effectively written—the price at which others can sell the shares to you if they so choose.

Similarly, if you place a 1,000 share sell order at, say, $11.00, you are extending the right to anyone in the market to buy 1,000 shares from you at $11.00. Implicitly, you have written a call option. As long as your option remains on the book, it is a live option that can be hit by anyone who wishes to buy the shares. The $11.00 price it is placed at is your option's strike price.

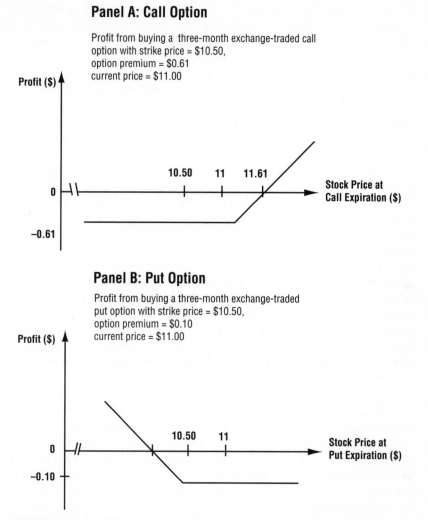

Panel A: Call Option

Profit from buying a three-month exchange-traded call
option with strike price = $10.50,
option premium = $0.61
current price = $11.00

Panel B: Put Option

Profit from buying a three-month exchange-traded
put option with strike price = $10.50,
option premium = $0.10
current price = $11.00

EXHIBIT 3.12a and b Option Payoff Diagrams for Exchange-Traded Call and Put Options

What about the premium, you might ask? This is not so obvious. You have simply placed a limit order, and nobody has paid you to do it. How do you get compensated for having written the option? Unlike the exchange-traded option, the premium is implicit. You receive payment when a liquidity imbalance causes your limit order to execute (i.e., the option is exercised), and the price of the underlying mean reverts back toward a previous level. We will return to this in a moment.

The option characteristics of a posted quote were first identified and analyzed by two financial economists, Thomas Copeland and Daniel Galai.[10] These researchers focused on dealer quotes, however, not on public limit orders. Copeland and Galai recognized that, by posting a bid, a dealer is effectively writing a put option to public sellers and that, by posting an offer, the dealer is effectively writing a call option to public buyers. But no explicit premium is charged. The put and call options are not exactly free, however, because the offer is higher than the bid (the market maker seeks to profit from the spread). Copeland and Galai did not stop at simply conceptualizing a dealer's quotes as being options—they continued on to use option pricing theory to solve for the optimal quotes for the dealer to post.

Students of the market (both practitioners and academicians) have subsequently recognized that an investor who places a limit order similarly extends a free option to others who might then execute against it by submitting a market order. The options way of looking at limit orders is conceptually useful. We have just noted that the compensation for placing the option is implicit in the dynamic behavior of security prices (namely, prices can mean revert). But what does it cost you to offer a put or a call option to market order traders? Based on our previous discussion, we know that the cost comes from the "heads they win, tails you lose" situation that you are in whenever information changes. Let's restate this thought using option terminology and P*, the driver of informed order flow in TraderEx.

One of two things can happen if you have placed a buy limit at $11.00 and P* changes. First, P* jumps down, informed order flow is triggered, and the put option that you have extended to the market is in the money and executes. If, after you learn the new information, your own reservation price drops below $11.00, you lose. Second, P* jumps up, and the informed order flow drives up the price of those shares that you really want. Now your option is out of the money and remains unexecuted. This time, the other guy has won.

Copeland and Galai, in dealing with the cost of information change, did not include the nonexecution cost (heads, the other guy wins) but focused only on the bagging cost (tails, you lose). This simplification is reasonable for Copeland and Galai because they were modeling the placement of dealer quotes by the market makers who are not looking to buy or to sell shares for their own investment purposes. We can retain this simplification by assuming that your desire to change your share holdings is weak enough for us to ignore your opportunity cost of not making a trade. When your primary motive for placing limit orders is to benefit from the liquidity events (i.e., to capture the accentuated volatility), you are in effect operating like a market maker.

Working in the order-driven context, Beiner and Schwartz have more recently considered the option value of a limit order from a different perspective. Rather than analyzing the option that your limit order *extends to others*, Beiner and Schwartz assessed the option *that you obtain* when you enter a limit order.[11] The Copeland-Galai analysis underscores the bagging cost of placing a limit order; the Beiner-Schwartz analysis recognizes this same cost, but highlights the benefit differently. By placing a limit order, you have positioned yourself to profit from a liquidity event if and when a favorable one occurs.

With a continuous, limit order book trading environment, you cannot wait for a liquidity imbalance to develop and then shoot your order into the market to take advantage of it. Others have likely pre-positioned their orders on the book so as to be there when an imbalance occurs, and you must also preposition your order. To capture mean-reversion volatility, you must place your limit order on the book and wait for the market orders to arrive. Pre-positioning your order is the only way to profit if and when a favorable liquidity event occurs.

Your option to buy is exercised upon the arrival of a counterpart market order. If the counterpart order is liquidity driven, you win. If it is information driven, you lose. The loss that you sustain from the information event is the premium that you implicitly pay for the right to profit if and when a favorable liquidity event occurs.

Exhibit 3.13 shows the payoff diagram for the option you own (by placing your limit order), where the option gives you the right to buy one share (for simplicity) when your reservation price for the underlying is $50. Assume (also for simplicity) that your put option (your limit order to buy) either executes or expires upon the next event. Because limit orders execute at their price limits in a continuous market, you have specified a limit price (P_{Lim}) that is a nice, discrete distance below your reservation price of $50. In Exhibit 3.13, we have set P_{Lim} at $47. Let the next event be a transaction that is triggered by a market order submitted by a contra-side liquidity trader. In Exhibit 3.13, P_T is the value to which the next (liquidity) event drives the transaction price.

Exhibit 3.13 shows that your payout is zero if the next transaction is at a price above $47 (your limit order does not execute), and that your payout is $3 if the next transaction is at a price of $47 or below and your limit order does execute. This diagram looks a bit different than the one shown in Exhibit 3.12 for a standard put option, but in spirit it is quite similar.[12] Because the cost of obtaining the limit order option is not explicit, your gain when the option expires out of the money is zero, not a negative amount. Because, in the continuous market, limit orders execute at their limit prices, your gain does not increase dollar for dollar as the transaction price caused by the liquidity event decreases below $47. Rather, your

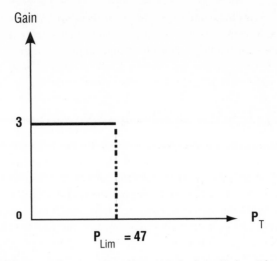

EXHIBIT 3.13 Gain from a One-Share Limit Buy Order When a Liquidity Event Occurs

gain remains constant at \$3. We will see in Chapter 4 that this is not the case for a limit buy order placed in a call auction.

Let's bring news events back into the picture. The arrival of bearish news can also cause your limit order to execute before you have received the information and are able to withdraw your order. Exhibit 3.14 shows the payout for your limit buy at \$47 when this happens.

In this table, P_1^R is your revised reservation price after you have received the news (that is, just after the information event occurs), and P_T is the value to which the information event drives the transaction price. If an information event occurs without driving P_T to \$47 or below, your payout is zero. This is the case when the information event is (1) the advent of bullish news or (2) the advent of bearish news that does not drive P_T to \$47 or below. If an information event does drive P_T below the price limit, the order executes. You will profit if the information event is the advent of

EXHIBIT 3.14 Payoff from a One-Share Limit Buy Order When an Informational Event Occurs

	$P_T < 47$	$P_T = 47$	$P_T > 47$
$P_1^R > 47$	$P_1^R - 47 > 0$	$P_1^R - 47 > 0$	0
$P_1^R = 47$	0	0	0
$P_1^R < 47$	$P_1^R - 47 < 0$	$P_1^R - 47 < 0$	0

bearish news that does not drive your reservation price, P_1^R, below P_{Lim}. But if the bearish information event does drive your reservation price below P_{Lim}, you lose.

THE BIG PICTURE

This is a good time to back up and reconsider some of the ground that we have traveled. If you are eagerly looking to execute your order for a reasonably liquid stock, you should probably use a market order as your default order placement tactic. However, you should submit a limit order if, given the stock's current price, you are relatively content with your share holdings but would be willing to buy more shares at a lower price, or would be willing to hold fewer shares at a higher price. You can enhance your portfolio returns this way to the extent that the market exhibits accentuated volatility caused by price-moving liquidity events. If your share holdings are in reasonable balance, you might in fact place two orders at the same time—a limit order to buy if price dips down, and a limit order to sell if price spikes up. Under conditions of pronounced intraday mean reversion, simultaneously placing a limit order to buy and a limit order to sell is a way to capture the volatility accentuation that mean reversion implies. When operating in this manner, you in certain respects resemble a securities dealer. You could also be standing in the shoes of an algorithmic trader (see Chapter 6).

Placing limit orders requires some thought beyond submitting market orders. Should I place one? If so, at what price should I place it? For how long should I keep it on the book if it does not execute—a minute, an hour, a day? We have assessed the benefit (profiting from mean reversion) and costs (being bagged or not getting an execution) of placing a limit order. We have done so from three different perspectives. First, in terms of the order itself; second, in terms of the option that you have effectively extended to others by placing a limit order; and third, in terms of the option that you have effectively obtained by placing your limit order on the book. Each view presents the benefit and costs in a slightly different way. Each provides a slightly different sense of what is involved in limit order trading.

The option properties of limit orders are particularly interesting. When you place a limit order, the implicit terms of the "option" you have thereby created are a bit different than the terms of a standardized, exchange-traded option, but the two are comparable. The payout diagrams are also a bit different but, nevertheless, compatible. Of particular interest is one further point: Regular options and limit orders both derive their value from the volatility of the underlying stock. For regular options, value comes predominantly from volatility that reflects informational change; for limit orders, value comes from the mean-reverting volatility caused by liquidity events during your trading window. Again, the details may differ, but the underlying principle is the same.

Key to our structured discussion of limit orders is the probability of a limit order executing, and how this probability depends on the price at which the order is placed. If execution probabilities are known with scientific precision (and if you are able to state your reservation price for the stock), your optimal limit order strategy can be readily determined. The problem is in knowing the execution probabilities. This is where experience comes in. As a successful trader, you get a feel for the market. You sense when and why prices are moving to a new level or are swinging around and will revert back to a previous level. You know when to grab hold of a price and when to be patient. You develop a sensitivity to market timing. We pursue these thoughts further in Chapter 6 in our consideration of four topics: price discovery, quantity discovery, technical analysis, and algorithmic trading. But first, let's move on to consider how market and limit orders are handled in the other kind of order-driven market—the call auction.

FROM THE CONTRIBUTORS

Gerald Putnam
The Emergence and Growth of an Electronic
Order-Driven Market

Rainer Riess and Uwe Schweickert
The Use of Limit and Market Orders

Jean-François Théodore
Order-Driven Markets: The Route to Best Execution

The Emergence and Growth of an Electronic Order-Driven Market

Gerald Putnam

In 1997, Archipelago was launched as one of four qualified electronic communications networks (ECNs) approved by the Securities and Exchange Commission (SEC). Like the other ECNs, Archipelago was a fully electronic, order-driven market. Though the granddaddy of ECNs, Instinet, had been in existence for many years, the inclusion of ECN quotes in the National Market System and the ability for all investors to have the power to publicly post their trading interest using limit orders was the result of the SEC's implementation of its Order Handling Rules in 1997. A retail investor could now drive the price of Microsoft or Intel simply by sending a limit order, through his broker, to an ECN like Archipelago. The intense price competition that was created as a result of these rules has led to more competition, tighter spreads, and better executions for investors.

With only a handful of clients and little liquidity, Archipelago accepted only two order types and provided a platform for clients to anonymously post their limit orders for display in the over-the-counter (OTC) or NASDAQ-listed marketplace. Prior to that time, the ability to drive the inside price was the domain of the NASDAQ market makers and their quote-driven market structure. Needless to say, in most cases, an order-driven market is only as successful as the orders driven to it. Until you get to the point where there are orders resident in the system, available to match with other incoming orders, an order-driven market has limited liquidity, unless, of course, you also provide a way for participants to tap into the liquidity resident in other markets.

Since we knew that the Archipelago ECN would initially have only a handful of customers and little posted liquidity in the NASDAQ stocks it traded, it was created with what is today known as a smart router or best execution model. If an order could be executed at a better price outside of Archipelago's liquidity pool, it would be routed or preferenced to a NASDAQ market maker or even a competing ECN to find liquidity and to achieve best execution.

As an open liquidity pool, Archipelago began by routing almost all of its orders to other market participants, but all of the time we firmly believed that eventually the orders entering our system would begin to interact and that, ultimately, we could build a deep and rich limit order book that would result in abundant internal liquidity. After all, if a limit order was not marketable at the time it was entered, it would be posted

144

to Archipelago's order book to await execution. At some point, the limit orders residing in the book would begin bumping up against other limit or market orders entering the system. At that tipping point, certain stocks could become "electronic naturals," or stocks that need no help from an intermediary because buyers and sellers could come together directly.

Eventually, that is exactly what occurred. The limit order book grew with orders priced and displayed at multiple price levels. An investor could see not only the best bid and offer on Archipelago but what was available to buy or sell one, two, or five pennies away. The dynamics of the order-driven market were such that books were building on Island, on Instinet, and other new ECNs that had entered into the business. These orders were accessible quickly and easily simply by submitting an order to Archipelago or one of the other ECNs that had sprung up and were modeled after our open, best execution model. The OTC market had evolved from a dealer market to a mature, more diverse, and interconnected marketplace, all because of the power of limit orders.

As competition thrived, the ability for these order-driven markets to create new tools for the trading community became more and more critical. Simple market and limit orders could not meet the demands of all market participants. The need for more diverse and complex order types arose—order types that could limit the market impact of a large institutional order, conceal within the order the top price a mutual fund would be willing to pay for a stock, or offer the ability to place an order that could adjust to the rapidly changing price fluctuations in active stocks. Though they would never replace the frequency of market or limit orders, these sophisticated order types did give traders new ways to fine-tune limit orders and to develop new strategies in the electronic universe.

Today, the Archipelago Exchange (ArcaEx) has approximately 20 order types meeting the needs of a variety of trading participants. Undoubtedly some of the most frequently used orders are those that electronically attempt to work an order, on behalf of a client, the way an upstairs trader or floor broker might. One of the most frequently used order types is the reserve order. A reserve order is more sophisticated than a regular limit order since it has a displayed price and size along with an undisplayed size component. As orders come into the order book, they can potentially interact not only with the displayed portion of the reserve order but with the undisplayed portion if the incoming order has a larger size component. Additionally, a reserve order will automatically replenish the displayed order size as executions occur so the order is always in the market until it is fully executed or cancelled.

Another example of a working order is a discretionary order with two price components—a display price and a discretionary price. The order is displayed at the specified price, not the discretionary price. However, if a bid or offer appears at or within the discretionary price range, the order will be matched internally or proactively routed externally at the quoted price.

An additional order type on many electronic platforms is a pegged order, which is designed to automatically adjust to price fluctuations in a given stock. A pegged order will track the national best bid or offer and automatically adjust the price of an order as the price moves. It is important to note that whenever the price is changed on a pegged order, the time stamp is also changed so the order would have a lower priority than a limit order already resident on the book at that price.

As electronic trading grew in popularity, a number of order types came on board that were designed to meet the growing needs of traders demanding all-electronic fills and immediacy. This need was met through order types like the "immediate or cancel" (IOC), which is a market or limit order that is executed in whole or in part as the order is received without routing the order to another market. The portion that is not executed is immediately cancelled.

Another all-electronic order type that gained almost immediate popularity in the order-driven market is the post-no-preference (PNP) order. This is a limit order to buy or sell that is only executed in whole or in part on the receiving market. Any residual size would be posted in the order book without routing any portion of the order to another market center. And if you want to cancel your PNP order, it can be done immediately. With both the IOC and the PNP order types, traders can access not only the displayed liquidity, but also the hidden liquidity attached to reserve and discretionary orders.

The benefits of probing all-electronic liquidity include fast, anonymous market access and control over your order. Archipelago even designed a Now Order®, which was a limit order that could only be executed in whole or in part by one or more all-electronic venues for immediate execution, if the order could not be executed internally. These orders would be immediately canceled if they would require being routed to a manual marketplace or could not be executed all-electronically at the prevailing best quoted price or better.

As the equity marketplace has evolved, the order-driven markets have matured as well. The Archipelago ECN has graduated and is now the Archipelago Exchange or ArcaEx. Though it operates much like the ECN did, ArcaEx provides a place for all-electronic intermediaries or market makers that provide liquidity alongside other market participants.

NASDAQ created SuperMontage, a system that operates much like the early ECNs, and manual exchanges are creating more electronic trading platforms and order-driven venues.

Tomorrow the limit and market orders of today, along with the more sophisticated order types that have followed, will be joined by orders that span across equities, options, or other derivatives. Already, in Europe, enterprising initiatives at the Deutsche Börse, Euronext, and the London Stock Exchange are bringing different products and services together under one roof. In response to clear customer demand, competitors overseas are creating "one-stop shopping." In Asia, too, exchanges combine equities and derivatives. This trend is migrating to the United States and, in the not too distant future, U.S. exchanges will provide multiproduct, single-platform functionality. The tools that are being offered will continue to meet the demand for innovation and the advancement of the financial markets.

The Use of Limit and Market Orders

Rainer Riess and Uwe Schweickert

Electronic order book trading has evolved as best of breed for structuring public equity markets around the world. European exchanges have been in the driver's seat for that development in the 1990s with the successful introduction of electronic order-driven trading systems. Deutsche Börse AG introduced Xetra—the Exchange Electronic Trading System—for the German market in 1997. Xetra is a hybrid trading system with an order-driven market design at its core, and a combination of market making elements that provide additional liquidity where and when necessary.

The Xetra system provides continuous trading and call auction trading. Continuous trading is organized on the basis of a central open limit order book (CLOB). Limit orders are displayed to market participants by their price and size. Call auctions are used for market opening, closing, and a midday intraday auction together with continuous trading. Order matching is fully electronic and follows strict price and time priority across all market models. All market models offer transparency and fairness.

With Xetra, participants can choose between different order types— market order, limit order, iceberg order, and market-to-limit order. Iceberg orders are limit orders that are only visible with their *peak size* in continuous trading. The remainder is hidden until the peak size is fully executed at its limit. It then fills up again with new time priority until the total order size is matched. Iceberg orders provide for hidden liquidity in continuous order book trading, and are especially valuable for trading mid- to large-size orders, particularly for less liquid stocks. Market-to-limit orders are a combination of plain vanilla market and limit order. Incoming market-to-limit orders are matched against the best bid (offer) for sell (buy) orders. If the order is not fully executed with its total size at that inside market price, the remaining part takes on the matching price as a limit and sits in the book as the new best bid (offer) for a buy (sell) order. Additionally, market participants can add several restrictions to their orders, such as "stop-loss" or "opening auction only."

The main decision problem that traders face when choosing between submitting a limit or a market order is driven by the need for immediacy in order execution. Limit orders, if not marketable at order arrival, are patient orders supplying liquidity to the book. Market orders are always aggressive orders that demand liquidity. The discussion in this chapter has focused on the different motives as well as the costs and benefits associated with that decision problem. Relevant decision parameters include the liquidity of the stock, the relative order size to be executed in the market, and whether traders are liquidity or information motivated. So how do traders choose between limit and market orders in real markets?

Trading German blue chip stocks of the DAX-30 index on Xetra is quite similar to the market design of the TraderEx simulation. Therefore, Xetra market data provide valuable empirical insight in real market operations for one of Europe's most important electronic marketplaces. Using a sample that includes all executed orders in DAX-30 trading on Xetra for June 2005, we find that iceberg, limit, and market orders differ significantly in size and use on expiration days. Iceberg orders average 12 to 14 times larger than the more standard orders. Market orders which were 7 percent of executed volume jump to 43 percent of executed volume on expiration days. There was a *triple witching day*[13] on June 17, 2005, and we provide a data comparison between the days in June without the triple witching day (Exhibits 3.15 through 3.17) and the triple witching day only (Exhibits 3.18 and 3.19). The data highlight the differences in market participants' trading behavior between regular versus *special* trading days. Exhibits 3.15 through 3.19 provide the market shares and relative average order size of order types with respect to trading phases distinguished by opening, closing, and intraday call auctions, and continuous trading.

Exhibits 3.15 and 3.16 show that limit order trading dominates total trading activity on regular trading days with 90.7 percent by number of executed orders and 85.0 percent by executed order volume. Limit orders are typically preferred over market orders during continuous trading in high liquid shares, as is the case for the German blue chip stocks. The picture changes in call auction trading—now limit and market orders are almost equally distributed both by number of orders as well as by order volume. The closing auction is the most used auction on Xetra, with about 7.7 percent market share in executed volume. Iceberg orders as a special limit order type have relatively low importance by number of executed orders (0.7

EXHIBIT 3.15 Number of Executed Orders, June 2005, Excluding June 17

Xetra®, DAX®, June 2005	Iceberg	Limit	Market
Continuous Trading	00.7%	88.8%	06.4%
Intraday Auction	00.0%	00.1%	00.1%
Closing Auction	00.0%	01.3%	01.2%
Opening Auction	00.0%	00.5%	00.8%
Totals	**00.7%**	**90.7%**	**08.5%**

Source: Xetra® and DAX® are registered trademarks of Deutsche Börse AG.

EXHIBIT 3.16 Executed €-Volume (Percent), June 2005, Excluding June 17

Xetra®, DAX®, June 2005	Iceberg	Limit	Market
Continuous Trading	08.1%	80.5%	02.5%
Intraday Auction	00.0%	00.1%	00.1%
Closing Auction	00.0%	04.0%	03.7%
Opening Auction	00.0%	00.4%	00.4%
Totals	**08.1%**	**85.0%**	**06.7%**

Source: Xetra® and DAX® are registered trademarks of Deutsche Börse AG.

percent). Nevertheless, they account for 8.2 percent of total executed order volume and add to total limit order usage.

Exhibit 3.17 describes the average executed order size relative to the total average executed order size on Xetra (total average = 1). We can see that market orders are below average order size with 0.8, and that limit orders are only slightly larger in size with 0.9. Market orders are smallest in continuous trading and largest in closing call auctions. Limit orders are close to total average in continuous trading and more than double the average size of market orders. In closing auction trading, limit and market orders are comparable in average execution size. As one would expect, iceberg orders are 12.4 times larger than the average order execution.

What can we learn from this data for regular trading days? Traders seem to prefer patient orders in a first step. But this is an oversimplification—88.8 percent of orders executed in continuous trading cannot be patient limit orders. Overall, we expect an equal distribution of patient and aggressive orders at least by executed volume. Therefore, we must assume that traders also use limit orders as marketable limit orders that execute immediately in the market. This means that the order limit also

EXHIBIT 3.17 Relative Average Executed Order Size, June 2005, Excluding June 17

Xetra®, DAX®, June 2005	Iceberg	Limit	Market	Market-to-Limit
Continuous Trading	12.4	0.9	0.4	0.2
Intraday Auction	11.5	0.8	1.2	0.6
Closing Auction	14.1	3.0	3.0	2.1
Opening Auction	17.1	0.9	0.5	0.7
Overall Average	**12.4**	**0.9**	**0.8**	**1.2**

Source: Xetra® and DAX® are registered trademarks of Deutsche Börse AG.

serves as insurance against unexpected price movements between the time of an investment decision and order arrival in the book. Traders may protect their trading interests (e.g., on the basis of their reservation price) against adverse price movements. They have the advantage of a market order in terms of immediacy but are protected on a certain price level against order execution. This behavior is reasonable in purely order-driven markets where price formation takes place on the basis of demand and supply without any further intermediation, and it shows that there is not as obvious a distinction between patient and aggressive trading as one may expect.

Pure market orders are relatively attractive in call auction trading. This is the case because auction trading pools the liquidity over a certain time interval before price determination takes place in a partially closed order book. This means that in contrast to continuous trading, orders are not displayed by price and size during the auction's call phase. Instead, Xetra displays an indicative auction price and size on the basis of most executable volume if the book is crossed and the best bid offer if the book is not crossed. Therefore, market order trading in call auctions is less costly compared to continuous trading. In addition, call auction trading provides for benchmark prices, especially in closing auctions where the end-of-day price is of special significance to market participants. These reasons make market order trading in call auctions attractive to traders, as they can participate in the auction price and volume with certainty at comparably low costs. Traders do post market orders in auctions with higher average order size.

Let us look at the differences in trading behavior on a special trading day, the triple witching day on June 17. Exhibits 3.18 and 3.19 show the market shares of executed order volume and the relative average order size on that special day. We observe that market order trading jumps to 43.3 percent by executed volume with a significantly larger average executed order size of 9.5. This phenomenon is mainly driven by

EXHIBIT 3.18 Executed €-Volume (Percent), June 17, 2005

Xetra®, DAX®, June 17, 2005	Iceberg	Limit	Market
Continuous Trading	04.1%	42.0%	01.0%
Intraday Auction	00.2%	06.2%	36.6%
Closing Auction	00.0%	04.1%	05.5%
Opening Auction	00.0%	00.1%	00.1%
Totals	**04.3%**	**52.4%**	**43.2%**

Source: Xetra® and DAX® are registered trademarks of Deutsche Börse AG.

EXHIBIT 3.19 Relative Average Executed Order Size, June 17, 2005

Xetra®, DAX®, June 17, 2005	Iceberg	Limit	Market
Continuous Trading	14.0	1.0	0.4
Intraday Auction	22.6	7.1	68.8
Closing Auction	9.9	6.1	5.5
Opening Auction	18.6	0.8	0.5
Overall Average	**14.2**	**1.2**	**9.5**

Source: Xetra® and DAX® are registered trademarks of Deutsche Börse AG.

the intraday auction on the triple witching day, where the settlement prices of expiring derivatives are determined on Xetra. Traders engaged in the respective financial derivatives need to participate in that settlement price in order to even up their positions. From a trader's perspective, the price level itself is less important than the need to participate in the benchmark price with executed volume—immediacy and certainty in benchmark price participation is the main driver for market order usage. Therefore, the intraday auction is dominated by large market order submissions that in turn attract other market participants to profit from the trading pattern on a triple witching day.

To sum up, limit order trading dominates order-driven markets in continuous trading. Market orders are attractive in call auction trading as they ensure price and volume participation with certainty. The classic dichotomy in order book trading between passive and aggressive order types is not that obvious—order limits often serve as insurance levels against adverse price movements rather than as restrictive price limits. Iceberg orders are typically used as passive orders. This special limit order type, together with the option for hidden liquidity, has been well adopted by traders. It attracts large order sizes to electronic order books during continuous trading.

What does this mean for future trends in market design? We have observed a strong increase of liquidity in continuous electronic order book trading over the past years. This has been promoted by market structure innovations such as the introduction of central counterparty clearing services in the German market in 2003. We have discussed empirical evidence of strong hidden liquidity by iceberg orders for large order sizes, and traders' behavior that blurs the dichotomy between passive and aggressive orders. Bringing these parts together can help to address one of the last remaining open issues in the order book trading market model—from a marketplace operator's perspective, how to effectively combine the already efficient price discovery process with quantity (size) discovery, in the continuous trading of large orders.

The most promising way to integrate block trading into continuous order book trading would be to follow the trend toward hidden liquidity and to introduce an innovative hybrid order that is available for both passive and aggressive trading. We are thinking of a volume order that integrates the benefits of order book trading with the ability to execute block orders at lowest trading costs. This would be to the benefit of all market participants. For further discussion, see Martin Reck's contributed piece in Chapter 5.

Order-Driven Markets:
The Route to Best Execution

Jean-François Théodore

The great merit of this chapter is clarity: The rules of the game in an order-driven market are made to appear extremely simple and obvious. So obvious that one could think that order-driven markets have always existed as a state of nature. But the generalization of this market structure results from a history where competition between trading venues has played a major role.

Electronic order-driven markets were born in the middle of the 1980s. The CATS system of the Toronto Stock Exchange was the precursor. In 1986, following this example, the Paris Bourse was then the first in Europe to implement a similar system, based on the CATS system. The latter was subsequently improved and became the Cotation Assisté de Continu (CAC) system. The Nouveau Systeme de Cotation (NSC system) is the latest generation in this development. It is much more powerful and reliable than the first systems. The NSC system enabled Euronext to become the first pan-European stock exchange: After Paris, the migration of Amsterdam and Brussels to the new system was implemented in 2001, followed by Lisbon in 2003. But its philosophy remained unchanged.

Technique explains why order-driven markets could be created, but not why they actually saw the light of day and grew. We need to put ourselves back in the context of the 1980s, when major institutional investors around the world—and especially U.S. pension funds—were growing so rapidly that they had to diversify their assets globally. Europe was the first target and the first beneficiary of this trend. Unfortunately, Europe was and still is a complex continent: It was fragmented into small countries (as compared to the United Sates), with a national exchange in each of them. Typical U.S. investors found that it was really simpler to have one single wholesale contact in Europe and be able to make prices for the whole range of European blue chips. They turned to the European market makers, most of whom were located in London.

But institutional investors progressively became more familiar with the European investment universe. They found that the high price of liquidity resulting from the buy-and-sell spread of market makers could significantly reduce their financial performance. As most other European exchanges adopted the same European Market Model, based on a central limit order book (CLOB), a major part of the institutional order flow came back to the home exchanges of the listed companies.

Euronext N.V. was formed on September 22, 2000, when the exchanges of Amsterdam, Brussels, and Paris merged. The Euronext group expanded at the beginning of 2002 with the acquisition of the London International Financial Futures and Options Exchange (LIFFE) and the merger with the Portuguese exchange Bolsa de Valores de Lisboa e Porto (BVLP). Today, Euronext is Europe's leading cross-border exchange, integrating trading operations on regulated and nonregulated markets for cash products and derivatives. In 2004, the turnover on the Euronext Cash Market via the central order book amounted to more than €1,500 billion, and in total more than 141 million trades were executed. In 2005, the platform reached a new peak with 14 million trades registered in September. For seven major European CLOBs, monthly averages for the value of shares traded in US dollars from January to July 2005, as reported by the World Federation of Exchanges, are shown in Exhibit 3.20.

Dedicated trading screens were originally installed by the exchange on members' premises and connected to the central system by specialized lines. Only specialized "CAC-men" could enter orders in the system. The next step was to create an "open architecture" for the trading system. The trading architecture was now a network of computers, the central computers of the exchange being connected with members' computers. These latter could receive orders directly from their own clients' computers. Agency brokers remain legally responsible for ensuring that the orders they transmit are consistent with a fair and orderly market, but they are no longer necessarily the initiators of such orders. Direct market access by investors now accounts for a significant share of trading volumes.

The open architecture also enables the network of trading terminals to be extended geographically, and it is a key driver of the success of a

EXHIBIT 3.20 Share Trading in Main CLOBs in Europe (Monthly Averages from January to July 2005)

	Value of Share Trading (USD Billion)
Spanish Exchanges	91.6
Borsa Italiana	101.1
Deutsche Börse	111.4
Euronext	183.1
London Stock Exchange	152.7
OMX Exchanges	53.7
Swiss Exchange	53.6

Source: World Federation of Exchanges.

multicenter market like Euronext. For instance, more than one-third of shares listed in Brussels are traded cross-border—that is, by Euronext members located outside Belgium.

Simultaneously, the reliability of the central trading system had to be reinforced in order to be resilient to a tremendous increase in trading volumes. Electronic trading systems have to be available to clients 100 percent of the time during the trading session. They also have to be sufficiently powerful to ensure immediacy of order execution. To give an idea of the performance of the latest generation of trading systems, 99 percent of executable orders are executed within less than half a second in Euronext systems, even when market volumes are exceptional.

This chapter also mentions that transparency is key to the smooth functioning of an order-driven market. As far as Euronext is concerned, market data disseminated to members include all disclosed buy orders and sell orders (price and size). Market data disseminated publicly include the accumulated disclosed volumes and prices at the best bid and the best ask of the order book.

Electronic order-driven markets were beneficial to clients not only for their efficiency but also for their costs. Average explicit costs decrease when the number of trades increases. Euronext lowered its fees by one-third in the last four years. Implicit costs can be measured by the quoted and effective spreads. For instance, spreads in Amsterdam were reduced by one-third after the migration of the exchange to the NSC trading system.

It is astonishing to compare the multiplicity of the effects of the new way of trading equities to the simplicity of this elementary algorithm: Just match limit orders and market orders according to a price and time priority. The authors of the chapter are right when they explain that these two types of orders are the predominant ingredients of an order-driven market. Limit orders are, by far, the most frequently used orders, and their relative frequency increases with order size. Market orders are executed at the best price determined by the trading system; above the quantity available in the order book at that price, the remaining unexecuted portion of the order is added to the order book. Market orders are relatively frequent for small order sizes (less than 5,000). At-best orders are also used by traders, especially for small sizes; these orders are executed fully, or as fully as possible, at any price against all orders on the opposite side. Hidden (iceberg) orders, which are described in this chapter, are also commonly used. Other types of orders are far less frequently used than the plain vanilla ones.

A key feature of central order books is to allow for a convergence of retail and institutional trades onto a central matching engine. The breakdown of order sizes on Euronext is roughly one-quarter under €5,000, one-quarter from €5,000 to €20,000, one-quarter from €20,000 to €60,000, and one-quarter above €60,000. Retail orders, which are generally more often market orders or at-best orders, are thus often matched against institutional orders, providing the system with liquidity.

This feature is a further advantage of the CLOBs: A market participant can be sure that he will have access to all other market participants, and that a rigorous price-time priority drives order matching. Thus, CLOBs are quite coherent with the best execution requirement defined by the new European Markets in Financial Instruments Directive (MiFID). In the future, they will remain at the heart of the architecture of European markets.

EXERCISES

1. Run the simulation for one day as a Proprietary Trader, and return to a zero position by the end of the day. Note moments during the day when the spread is particularly narrow or wide.
   - What could explain the phenomenon of the spread narrowing and widening in the order book market?
   - How does the size of the spread affect your trading decisions?
   - Were you able to return to a flat position and make a profit? What were the main factors that affected your profits?

2. Run the simulation and try to accumulate a net position of +500 units by the end of the day. As a goal, try to keep the average purchase cost below VWAP. Try to use both limit orders and market orders.
   - Did you buy all 500 units? Were you able to beat VWAP?
   - What influenced your performance relative to VWAP? Would you trade differently in a rerunning of the simulation?
   - What are the advantages and disadvantages of the two order types, limit and market?
   - Rerun the simulation with same random number seed and accumulate a net position of –500 by the end of the day. Try to keep your average selling price above VWAP. How does selling a large quantity compare to buying for this particular market setting?

3. The software has the ability to capture data in a file for post-simulation trade analysis. After completing the trading day specified in Exercise 2, follow the instructions in the software to open the file in Excel or another spreadsheet package.
   - Graph the evolution of prices in a trading day. Show the bid, ask, and last trade price.
   - Add the P* value to the graph, and discuss how the market prices interacted with the P* value and its changes.
   - In another graph, show how VWAP evolved over the course of the trading day, and plot the points in time when your orders executed. Which of your trades were most profitable and which were least profitable? How would your performance have changed if you had traded your order to buy 500 units evenly over the trading day? Or all at or close to the open? Or all at or close to the close?

4. Post-Simulation Run Analysis
   - Run the simulation and assess whether prices follow a random walk using the output file created during the run. What assessment technique did you use? What did you find?
   - In the context of the efficient markets hypothesis, do you think that the dynamic behavior of prices in TraderEx is weak form efficient? That is, are there systematic non-random patterns in prices, or are price increases and decreases equally likely?

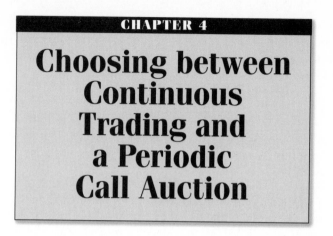

CHAPTER 4

Choosing between Continuous Trading and a Periodic Call Auction

A s we saw in the previous chapter, an order-driven market can be structured in two different ways. With a *continuous market*, a trade can be made at any moment in continuous time that a buy order and a sell order meet with compatible prices. With a *call auction*, orders are batched together periodically for a simultaneous, many-to-many execution. At the time of a call, a market clearing price is determined. Buy orders with limit prices at this price and higher execute, as do sell orders at this price and lower.

If you are familiar with skiing, you will appreciate the difference between alpine downhill and snow boarding. While the two ways of getting down a mountain have much in common, each requires a different technique. So, too, do call and continuous trading. As we will see, limit orders and market orders are handled differently in call and continuous trading and, accordingly, they should be submitted differently. If you were to enter your orders in a call auction as you would in a continuous market, you could get suboptimal results (and, by analogy, wind up in a snowbank).

Most people are more familiar with continuous markets than with call auctions. Accordingly, we devote a good part of this chapter to clarifying just how a call auction operates and how it is best used.

HOW IS A CALL AUCTION USED?

Fully electronic call auctions are the standard procedure used for opening and closing equity markets around the world. Market openings are particu-

161

larly important because prices must be *discovered* when trading resumes after the overnight close. Currently, the NYSE opens with a call that is not fully electronic, and the Big Board closes with a batched auction that has call auction features but also is not fully electronic.

Market-on-close (MOC) and limit-on-close (LOC) orders are popular order types used to participate in the closing NYSE trade. All MOC orders must be received at the NYSE by 3:40 P.M. (20 minutes before the close), unless they are entered to offset a published imbalance. For instance, after a published buy imbalance at 3:45 P.M., only MOC orders to sell are accepted.

Until 2004, NASDAQ had no formal opening or closing procedure at all. At the start of a trading day, market makers would log on to NASDAQ's servers and, at the end of the day, they would simply log off. This changed in March 2004 when NASDAQ introduced a fully electronic call auction to close its market, and again in November 2004 when NASDAQ started opening its markets with an electronic call that is a slightly modified version of its closing procedure. The contributed piece by Frank Hatheway in this chapter contains an excellent discussion of NASDAQ's experience with these innovations.

Closing calls were introduced by the Europe bourses and by NASDAQ in response to customer demands to enhance price determination at the close because of the multiple uses to which closing prices are put, including establishing net asset values for mutual fund purchases and redemptions, marking-to-market of trading positions, calculating margins, and determining settlement amounts in the derivative markets. Derivatives trading and payments at expiration, particularly in individual equity options, can be adversely affected by a relatively small number of orders causing price dislocations in the cash market for the underlying security. Indexers have their own needs to trade with precision at the closing prices used to compute the index values that they are seeking to track. The difficulty of doing this is particularly acute on days when firms are being added to and deleted from an index. Reliable and accessible closing prices are important for derivatives traders and for indexers seeking to track their index benchmarks with minimal error.

CALL AUCTIONS AND MARKET STRUCTURE

Over 100 years ago, the New York Stock Exchange was a call market (nonelectronic, of course). In some respects, the nonelectronic call was a fine system for participants on the exchange floor, but it had serious deficiencies for anybody away from the floor. Investors not physically present had little knowledge of and information about what was happening (the calls offered no transparency), and access to trading was limited because shares of a stock could be exchanged only periodically when the market for the stock was "called." On May 8, 1869, the call procedure was abandoned when the NYSE merged with a competing exchange, the Open Board of Brokers, and became a continuous trading environment.

Outside the United States, floor-based call trading continued to flourish at continental European exchanges up to the 1980s. The Tel Aviv Stock Exchange (TASE) ran a floor-based call market through the mid-1980s and the Paris Bourse had its *à la criée* call market until the 1986 introduction of its electronic market, CAC (an acronym that stands for *Cotation Assisté en Continu*). These nonelectronic call auctions did not survive. With growing competition among exchanges and the introduction of electronic trading platforms, continuous trading had become increasingly dominant. This went hand in hand with extended trading hours. With both developments, volume at the calls grew thinner and their importance evaporated.

But in recent years, tremendous advances in information technology and a slew of other developments in the industry have paved the way for the call's reemergence. With an electronic limit order book and electronic connectivity, participants from anywhere around the globe can see a call auction as it forms, and users can enter their orders with electronic speed.

While information technology can be used advantageously in continuous trading, it is essential for efficient call auction trading. Moreover, the call auction is an extremely good environment for the application of information technology (IT). In a continuous market, IT speeds up the rate at which orders can be submitted, displayed, and turned into trades and, as a result, the importance of nanoseconds is accentuated. The contributed piece in this chapter by James Ross contrasts the use of the time clock in call and continuous trading. As Ross explains, the very nature of competition between order placers in an electronic, continuous trading environment can temporally fracture the order flow. When this happens, it produces two very undesirable results—heightened trading costs and accentuated volatility.

In an electronic call environment, IT is used to sort and cumulate orders, to work out contingencies and special orders, to find indicative clearing prices while the market is forming, and to set final clearing prices at the end of the process when the book is frozen and executions identified. In a call auction, the computer is used to do one thing in particular that it was created to do—compute (and also keep market participants informed in real time as the book builds).

In principle, a call auction is the ideal way to find equilibrium prices at specific points in time. Continuous trading, on the other hand, is preferable if your motives for trading require immediacy, or if you are relatively content with your current share holdings and are using limit orders to capture volatility (and, in so doing, are a liquidity provider). Accordingly, in most exchanges, call auctions and the continuous market are combined to form a more optimal structure for all kinds of users. With this hybrid market structure, you can select among alternative trading venues depending on the size of your order, the liquidity of the stock you are trading, your motive for trading, and your desire or lack thereof to trade quickly.

The inclusion of electronic call auctions adds good market structure for a number of reasons:

- Order batching augments liquidity provision by focusing buy and sell orders at specific points in time. This is appealing for small cap stocks that have relatively sparse order flow, and for large cap stocks that receive a disproportionate amount of "lumpy" institutional order flow.
- For the broad market, electronic call auctions can reduce price volatility, unreliable pricing, unequal access to the market, and various forms of manipulation and abuse.[1]
- For all stocks, commissions in a call may be lower due to the greater ease of handling orders and of clearing trades in the call auction environment.
- A call auction is a price discovery mechanism. As such, it has a particularly important role to play at market openings.

The order book for an electronic call is usually open so that participants can see the array of bids and offers that have been anonymously posted. As a market forms, public participants typically receive the best bid and ask prices (for instance, the five best bids and offers) along with size (the total number of shares at each price). Regarding our simulation software, TraderEx's auction is fully transparent—the cumulated orders to buy and to sell are displayed, at each price, for a wide array of prices. Exhibits 4.1 and 4.2 show two TraderEx call auction screens, one at 9:31 (before any crossing orders have arrived) and one at 9:37 (after the book has further built). The 9:31 screen has no overlapping bids or offers, and would not lead to a trade if the call were to execute at that time. Six minutes later many additional orders have arrived and the indicated price and volume are $48.50 and 455 units (455,000 shares). The price chosen maximizes the number of matched units (455 units). There is a sell-buy imbalance of 36 units at $48.50, meaning that 36 of the 491 units on the bid will not be matched.

If you want to enter an order in a TraderEx call, when should you do so? The more the book builds, the more confidence you will have in the price that is being discovered, and the better you will be able to judge how

🎰 TraderEx		
DAY	**TIME**	**SEED**
1	9:31:00	10

TICKER	PRICE	
	QTY	
	TIME	

MARKET	**indicative**	**48.00**
CALL	**imbalance**	**0**

BIDS		OFFERS	
	48.90	171	
	48.80	125	
	48.70	91	
	48.60	91	
	48.50	49	
	48.40	49	
	48.30	49	
	48.20	22	
	48.10	22	
	48.00		
20	47.90		
49	47.80		
66	47.70		
66	47.60		
88	47.50		
117	47.40		
117	47.30		
117	47.20		
117	47.10		
155	47.00		

EXHIBIT 4.1 Opening Screen of a TraderEx Call Auction. No buy or sell orders exist yet at the indicative clearing price of 48.

7⅚ TraderEx		
DAY	**TIME**	**SEED**
1	9:37:00	10

TICKER	PRICE	
	QTY	
	TIME	

MARKET	indicative	**48.50**
CALL	imbalance	**-36**

	BIDS		OFFERS	
	93	49.40	1024	
	136	49.30	868	
	136	49.20	771	
	136	49.10	671	
	204	49.00	662	
	281	48.90	603	
	281	48.80	548	
	281	48.70	497	
	337	48.60	497	
	491	**48.50**	455	
	602	48.40	422	
	683	48.30	360	
	804	48.20	264	
	858	48.10	264	
	907	48.00	222	
	1033	47.90	203	
	1153	47.80	168	
	1237	47.70	168	
	1285	47.60	115	
	1307	47.50	78	

EXHIBIT 4.2 A Subsequent Screen of the TraderEx Call Auction before the Call Executes

aggressively to tap the liquidity that is on the book. This is particularly important to you if you have a large order to work. Accordingly, you might best wait until the last screen is shown and then enter your order just before the book is frozen, the price is set, and executions identified. In other words, you would like to have a *last-mover advantage*. But be careful, this is risky in TraderEx. The call is held at a randomly selected time, and thus you never know when you are looking at the last screen. There might not be a book at 9:38. If you wait for it, you can lose out entirely. Making the time of the call uncertain is our way of inducing you to get your call auction order onto the book in a more timely fashion. If an actual system doesn't include some inducement such as this, its book might never build.

One feature of call auction trading that has been thought by some to be a drawback is that the facility does not provide transactional immediacy—you have to wait for it to happen. This limitation ceases to be a deficiency when call and continuous trading are combined in a hybrid market structure. Even with a continuous-only market model, it is worth noting that customers who place limit orders are not looking for immediate executions. And, as we saw in the previous chapter, immediacy is not a free lunch (bid-ask spreads and market impact costs are incurred). Many institutional participants are more concerned with anonymity and keeping trading costs low, and do not wish to pay the price of immediacy.

Think about this when you enter your orders in TraderEx. Under what conditions would you seek to trade quickly by market order in the continuous market, and when might you patiently wait to trade in the call? If you know that a call is coming, would you be more or less apt to enter a limit order in the continuous market, knowing that if it fails to execute, you can roll your order into the call?

BOOKBUILDING

To deliver its promise of being a highly efficient trading environment, a call must attract sufficient volume. To accomplish this, participants must be given incentives to enter their orders early in the precall, order entry period. The early stages of bookbuilding cannot be taken for granted. This is especially true for an auction that opens the market at the start of a trading day, a time when participants are particularly nervous about having any influence on price discovery. Bookbuilding is similar to quantity discovery (getting orders out of participants' pockets and turning them into trades). We discuss price and quantity discovery in further detail in Chapter 6.

Picture yourself viewing the book in the early stages of the precall, order entry period. You will not see many orders at this point. Consider again the screen shown in Exhibit 4.1. There are a few buy orders at relatively low prices, some sell orders at relatively high prices, and no matched orders at the first indicated clearing price. How eager would you be to enter an order now? You might like first to see how the book builds with the arrival of more orders. With more orders in the book, you will have a better sense of the leanings and mood of the market (*color*, it is often called), and will have a more precise idea of where the stock will likely open. Chances are, you will wait, which is what many traders do. The book generally does not start to build seriously until about 3 to 10 minutes before the time of the call.

Large institutional customers in particular are reluctant to post orders in an opening call that would reveal their trading intentions and which, because of their size, could affect the clearing price that is set at the call. The big players want to be price takers, not price setters. The orders of the big players may have an important role to play with respect to price discovery, but no individual participant wants to be responsible for price discovery. If you are a large player approaching an opening call, chances are good that you will try to assume a low profile. You will wait, put in small orders, and be careful not to leave your footprints on the book.

With any trading environment, one must be concerned about the possibility of market manipulation. The larger the number of participants in a call, the more difficult, the more risky, and the more expensive any planned technical manipulation is. In fact, a transparent, well-attended call is a good defense against market manipulation. Nevertheless, in the early stages of bookbuilding, an aggressively priced buy order may, by signaling bullish information, lead other participants to raise their prices and thereby produce a higher clearing price. An aggressively priced sell order may have just the opposite effect. Accordingly, a large seller could bluff buyers into the market by initially entering an aggressive buy order, which he then cancels and replaces with a sell order just before the call takes place. A large buyer could sucker the market by doing just the opposite. But manipulating a market violates trading rules, and order entry and cancellations in a call can be easily monitored. The big players would be well advised not to play this game in an electronic and therefore easily monitored call.

There is another trading game, however, that is neither illegal nor easy to defuse. It involves big investors, on opposite sides of the market, playing a waiting game. Chakraborty, Pagano, and Schwartz[2] have shown how this waiting game can be played, and how it creates a problem for order revelation and bookbuilding. Picture two large players, one a buyer and the other a seller, who, along with other participants, could meet, provide liquidity to each other, and trade in a call auction. Both of the large players know that they will individually get a good execution if they enter their orders together. But each also knows that if one of them enters the call while the other waits for a subsequent round of trading, the one who enters will receive an inferior execution and the one who waits can achieve a better execution. This is a last-mover advantage. Consequently, both of these large participants hold their orders back. When they do, the outcome is worse for both of them. In all likelihood, their orders will not meet again, the buyer will eventually pay a higher price, the seller will eventually receive a lower price, and the bookbuilding is incomplete. We have just described an economic model that is sometimes referred to in game theoretic terms as *prisoners' dilemma*. We explain this in further detail in Chapter 6.

Understanding the bookbuilding process could enable market architects to develop trading procedures that would help defuse the problem. As we have noted, bookbuilding is more difficult at the start of the trading day when price discovery and the lack of a recent reference price are more of an issue. Opening calls generally attract retail order flow, but large institutional customers tend to hold back (the institutions participate more heavily in closing calls). There are, however, several possibilities for encouraging early order placement and facilitating bookbuilding. Time priorities are generally used to this end, and commission rates can be reduced for early order entry. The time of the call may be randomized to induce earlier order entry (as we have noted, TraderEx uses this technique). The inclusion of retail customers who are less concerned that their orders will have any meaningful impact on the clearing price also helps to build the book and draw more institutional customers to the facility.

Lastly, a market maker intermediary could be included in the call to *animate* the process. In an animator role, the market maker would seed bookbuilding by entering orders early in the process. The market maker could then possibly withdraw these orders if sufficient public order flow comes in. For instance, a market maker might get things started by posting a moderately aggressive order to buy 1,000 shares. The buy order would then attract sell orders, and the arriving sell orders could in turn attract more buy orders, and so on in a virtuous circle. If the buy orders arrive, the animator will have done his job and can pull back or withdraw entirely from participating in the market. However, if the public buy orders do not arrive, the animator will have to be a buyer at the call. Thus the animator may acquire a long or a short position as a dealer. Recognize, however, that the market maker's principal objective as animator is not to supply liquidity to the market, but to animate bookbuilding so that the public can successfully provide liquidity to itself.

ORDER HANDLING DIFFERENCES

Orders are processed differently in call auctions than in continuous trading. The time clock itself is used differently, as James Ross clarifies in his contributed piece. With a call auction, trades are made at specific points in time rather than whenever, in continuous time, a buy and a sell order happen to cross. To accomplish this, orders submitted to a call auction that could otherwise have been matched and executed are held for a multilateral clearing. The clearings are generally held at predetermined points in time (at the open, at the close, and/or at set times during the trading day).

At the time of a call, the batched orders are matched and a single clearing price established. The single clearing price reflects the full set of orders submitted to the call. Buy orders at and above the clearing price execute, as do sell orders at and below the clearing price. Because all executed orders clear at the same price, there is no bid-ask spread in call auction trading. Very importantly, with single price clearing, buy orders priced above the single clearing value and sell orders priced below it receive price improvement. Price improvement means that an order is executed at a better price than the one at which it had been placed. For instance, a buy order with a limit price of $52.10 would be filled at $51.50 if $51.50 is the market clearing price established at the call. Alfred Berkeley's contributed piece in this chapter gives strong emphasis to this property of call auction trading.

Many variations in auction design exist. Calls can be held "on request" instead of at predetermined, regular intervals. Multiple prices, or discriminatory pricing, in a call is possible and can be beneficial. The amount of precall pricing information to reveal is a decision variable. Traders may be free to change their orders/quotes until the last moment, or restrictions of various kinds may be imposed, and so forth. Taking an aerial view, we identify four basic types of call auctions (with several variations in between).

1. *Price Scan Auction.* In a price scan auction, a sequence of prices is "called out" until a value is found that best balances the buy and sell orders. The NYSE call auction opening best fits into this category. The Exchange specialists periodically announce indicated opening price ranges; floor traders respond with their orders and, as they do, the specialists adjust their indicated opening prices. Facing growing volumes, the NYSE introduced the Opening Automatic Reporting System (OARS) in 1980 to electronically store and tabulate pre-opening orders for specialists. The Paris Stock Exchange's market, before the Bourse introduced electronic trading in 1986, was a classic price scan

call auction. When the market for a stock was called, an auctioneer would cry out one price after another, scanning the range of possibilities, until an acceptable balance was found between the buy and sell orders. *Tâtonnement,* or trial-and-error, was the term used by French economist Leon Walras to describe how equilibrium auction prices can be found by repeated experiment.

2. *Sealed Bid Auction.* In a sealed bid auction, participants submit their orders in sealed envelopes that are not opened until the time of the auction. These auctions are totally "closed book" (nontransparent) during the pre-open phase and, consequently, you do not know what orders the others are submitting (and others do not know what you are doing). The term may also be applied when orders are submitted electronically or by other means if pretrade orders and indicated clearing prices are not revealed to participants. The primary market for new U.S. Treasury debt securities is a good example of a sealed bid auction. Primary dealers bid competitively for new bonds, notes, and bills, without disclosure to other participants. Officials go down the list of competitive bids, accepting the highest bid prices until all the securities have been awarded. All lower bids are rejected.

3. *Crossing Network.* A crossing network is a batched trading environment that does not, itself, discover price. Buy and sell orders in a crossing network are matched in a multilateral trade at a reference price that is set elsewhere. Generally, the value used at a cross is either the last transaction price or the midpoint of the bid-ask spread set in a major market center. In the United States, ITG's intraday Posit crosses and Instinet's after-hours cross are good examples of this facility. Currently, NASDAQ is planning to introduce several intraday crossings. Orders submitted to a crossing network can be priced, meaning that a price limit is specified above which a buy order will not be in the cross, or below which a sell order will not be in. When the matching occurs, buy orders priced at and above the reference price execute against sell orders priced at and below the reference price. Because the reference price is set elsewhere, the total number of orders that execute in a crossing network is generally not maximized.

4. *Open Limit Order Book Auction.* With an open limit order book, posted orders are displayed to the public in the precall order entry period. As the time of the call approaches, the procedure also identifies and updates an indicated clearing price that, at each instant, is the value that would be set in the call if the call were to be held at that instant. At the time of the call, the book is frozen and the indicated clearing price becomes the actual clearing price. The point of time

when the matching algorithm is applied to the order book may be set in advance or determined randomly within a period of time, as it is in TraderEx. In an electronic trading environment, the auction can be designed with various degrees of pre-auction transparency that allow traders to react to an indicated clearing price that is displayed as the market forms.

The intriguing contributed piece by Alfred Berkeley in this chapter characterizes a call auction from a different perspective. Rather than focusing on how orders are handled (e.g., brought together for a multilateral trade at a single price at a predetermined point in time), Berkeley focuses on what a call delivers—namely, as we have noted, a call offers price improvement for pre-positioned limit orders, something that a standard continuous market cannot do.[3] The desirability of giving price improvement to pre-positioned limit orders is clear—it encourages liquidity creation. Berkeley's firm, Pipeline, does exactly this. Even though Pipeline's trading platform generally makes bilateral matches, the system is, in Berkeley's view, a call auction. The perspective shows how robust the concept of a call auction really is.

The fourth category of calls, the open limit order book call, is the most important in equity markets on both sides of the Atlantic. Its fundamental operations can be depicted with the aid of Exhibits 4.3 through 4.6. Each of these exhibits shows share price on the vertical axis, and the number of orders on the horizontal axis. In practice, the number of shares sought for purchase or offered for sale would be displayed on the horizontal axis, but our discussion is simplified by assuming that all orders are for the same number of shares (e.g., one round lot). We have also, for simplicity, taken the minimum price variation to be the ridiculously large amount of $1.

Exhibit 4.3 displays the individual buy and sell orders. The horizontal axis gives the total number of orders (buys plus sells) that have been placed at each price. At each price, the orders are arrayed according to the sequence in which they have arrived so that time priority may be preserved. At the price of 52, just one sell order has been placed. At 51, a sell order arrived first, and then a buy order. At 50, two buy orders arrived followed by one sell order, and so on.

Exhibits 4.4 and 4.5 show how the individual buy and sell orders are aggregated. The buy orders only (both individual and aggregated) are shown in Exhibit 4.4. Because the price limit on a buy order is the highest price at which the order is to be executed, the buy orders are cumulated from the highest price (in this case 51) down to the lowest (47). At 51, there is just one order to buy. Two additional buy orders have been entered at 50 and thus, at 50, there is a total of three buy orders. At yet

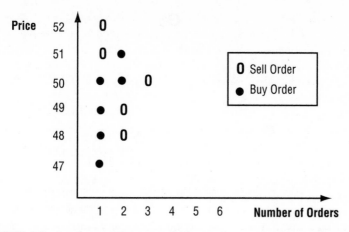

EXHIBIT 4.3 Batching of Customer Orders

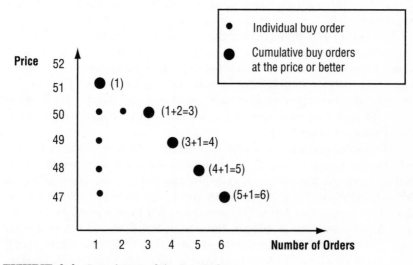

EXHIBIT 4.4 Cumulation of the Buy Orders

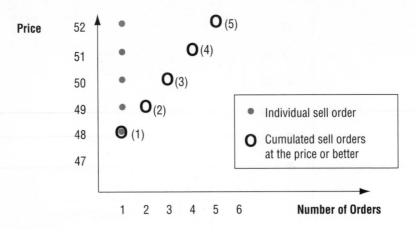

EXHIBIT 4.5 Cumulation of the Sell Orders

lower prices, one order has been placed at each of the prices, 49, 48, and 47, and the cumulative number of orders at these prices is four, five, and six, respectively.

The sell orders only (both individual and aggregated) are shown in Exhibit 4.5, and they are also cumulated. Because the price limit on a sell order is the lowest price at which the order is to be executed, the sell orders are cumulated from the lowest price (48) up to the highest price (52). There is only one sell order at each of the prices, and the cumulative number of sell orders increases by one order as we move from the single order at 48 to the five orders at 52.

The cumulative buy and sell orders are matched in Exhibit 4.6 to determine the clearing price at which they execute, and the specific orders that execute. At the intersection of the two curves, the price is 50 and the number of orders is three. Thus, three buy orders execute (the one placed at 51 and the two at 50) and three sell orders execute (the one placed at 48, the one at 49, and the one at 50). Three is the maximum number of orders that can execute: at the higher price of 51 there is only one buy order, and at the lower price of 49 there are only two sell orders. For this reason, the clearing price in a call auction is typically identified as the value that maximizes the number of shares that execute (and, in the special case that we have been considering, the number of orders that execute).

Because of the price priority rule, the most aggressive buy orders are matched with the most aggressive sell orders. If several orders have

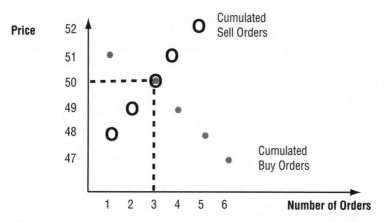

EXHIBIT 4.6 Matching of Cumulated Buy and Sell Orders

the same price limits, the order that was submitted first is executed first (time priority). In the example shown in Exhibit 4.6, three of the executed orders receive price improvement (the buy at 51, the sell at 49, and the sell at 48). The less aggressive orders (the buys at 49, 48, and 47, and the sells at 51 and 52) remain unexecuted. The unexecuted orders will stay in the central order book and may be rolled into the continuous market, held for the next call, or cancelled, depending on the wishes of the investors.

In Exhibit 4.6, at the market-clearing price of 50, the cumulated sell orders match the cumulated buy orders exactly. What happens if no price exists that gives an exact match? For instance, what would happen if three buy orders rather than two had been entered at 50 for a cumulated total of four? For the case at hand, the decision rule would still pick 50 to be the price (this value would continue to maximize the number of orders that execute), but with only three sell orders at 50, only three of the four buy orders could be executed. Consequently, a further decision rule is needed to specify which three of the four orders to pick. The rule commonly used is the time priority rule: Orders execute according to the sequence in which they were placed, with the first to arrive being the first to execute. Time priority in call auction trading gives you an incentive to place your orders earlier in the precall, order entry period. Other rules for rationing in a call auction when the buy amount exceeds the sell amount (or vice versa) are size priority, or pro rata. *Pro rata* means that each order on the larger side of the market is partially and proportionately filled.

Further situations can be described that require more complex rules of order execution. For instance, two different prices may result in the same maximum number of shares that would trade. You might notice this from time to time in the TraderEx call auctions. In these cases, TraderEx selects the price that minimizes the buy-sell imbalance. If more than one price has the same trade volume and imbalance level, the one closest to the prior trade is used. As is typically the case, the rules required for an actual operating system are considerably more complicated than those we need to consider to achieve a basic understanding of the system. We describe further rules in the Appendix to this chapter.

NASDAQ'S CROSSES

The NASDAQ Stock Market runs opening and closing procedures that are referred to as *crosses*. The NASDAQ crosses are open limit order book auctions with design features that are both distinctive and interesting. Let us focus on the closing cross (there are minor differences between it and the opening cross).[4]

NASDAQ's Closing Cross includes new types of orders; new order handling, display, and price determination procedures; and safeguards against unduly large price changes. But its fundamental functionality is straightforward. The key to NASDAQ's Closing Cross is the interaction of its continuous market with three types of orders specific to the close:

1. Market-on-close (MOC) orders
2. Limit-on-close (LOC) orders
3. Imbalance orders (IO)

The MOC and LOC orders are standard market and limit orders, except that they are to be executed in Closing Cross only. These on-close orders can be entered or cancelled at any time from the market's 9:30 A.M. opening until 3:50 P.M., 10 minutes before the market's close.

At 3:30 P.M., the facility starts accepting imbalance orders. As the name implies, imbalance orders are designed to reduce any imbalances that may exist between the market orders and limit orders that have been entered for the cross. All imbalance orders must be limit orders and therefore priced. An IO sell is executable only if it is priced at or above the 4:00 P.M. NASDAQ offer, and an IO buy is executable only if it is priced at or below the 4:00 P.M. NASDAQ bid. Because they are prevented from being priced aggressively, IO orders will never trade against each other. Rather, IO sells will execute against any buy imbalance (that drives price up), and

IO buys will execute against any sell imbalance (that drives price down). In effect, IO orders absorb imbalances, and in any given NASDAQ cross, IO orders on only one side of the market (only buy or only sell) can execute. IO orders can be entered until the time of the cross but, like MOC and LOC orders, cannot be cancelled after 3:50 P.M.

Transparency is critical for the cross to work. The driving force behind good price discovery at the close is for participants to see any buy or sell imbalances, and to benefit from an imbalance by entering an order that offsets it. Between 3:50 P.M. and 4:00 P.M., NASDAQ disseminates information about imbalances, indicative clearing prices, and the number of on-close and IO shares that the market is able to match at an indicative clearing price as the close approaches. The frequency of information dissemination increases from every 30 seconds (starting at 3:50) to every 15 seconds (at 3:55), to every 5 seconds (at 3:59).

At 4:00 P.M., no further orders are accepted, and the determination of the closing prices begins. At the cross, the MOC, LOC, and IO orders are brought together, along with limit orders and quotes from the NASDAQ Market Center. A fairly complex algorithm is then used to determine the clearing price and the specific orders that trade. The first criterion used for selecting the clearing price is to maximize the number of shares that will trade at the cross. If two or more prices result in an identical maximum number of shares that will trade, the algorithm for selecting a clearing price includes additional criteria: First, minimize the LOC imbalance and then, if a unique price still cannot be found, minimize the distance from the final midquote value in NASDAQ's electronic platform, the NASDAQ Market Center (initially referred to as SuperMontage).

Time and price priorities are used to determine the specific orders that execute given the clearing price. In the determination, MOC orders receive the highest priority, which makes them highly likely to execute, although their certainty of execution is not guaranteed. In general, LOC buy orders at the clearing price and higher execute, as do LOC sell orders at the clearing price and lower. All of the executed orders for a stock clear at a single price. The NASDAQ computer sets the closing price stock-by-stock and reports all of the orders that execute for a stock as a single print. Generally, the reports are completed within four seconds of the 4:00 P.M. cross, and NASDAQ Official Closing Prices are disseminated at 4:01:30 P.M. Because of the transparency of the system, the pooling of all orders for a stock, and the inclusion of imbalance-only orders, these single-price auctions generate values that are less subject to price dislocations and are more in tune with the broad market's demand to hold shares.

Thus far, NASDAQ has been pleased with the success of its two crosses. In September 2005, volume in the opening cross averaged 22.9 million shares, and in the closing cross averaged 16.4 million shares. Further, as we have noted, the introduction of several NASDAQ intraday crossing networks is now in the planning stage.

HOW TO SUBMIT AN ORDER TO A CALL AUCTION

We saw in the previous chapter that, for the continuous market, limit orders set the prices at which market orders execute, and limit orders sitting on the book provide immediacy to the market orders (i.e., the market orders execute upon arrival). So if you are willing to wait patiently for an execution in a continuous market, place a limit order and be a passive liquidity provider. Or, if you want immediacy and are willing to pay its price, be an aggressive liquidity demander by submitting a market order.

These distinctions disappear in call auction trading. In a call auction, all participants wait until the next call for their orders to execute. Consequently, market orders in a call auction do not receive immediacy as they do in continuous trading. Further, in the call environment, market orders are nothing more than extremely aggressively priced limit orders. Specifically, a market order to buy effectively has a price limit of infinity, and a market order to sell effectively has a price limit of zero. We will get back to this in a moment.

There are more differences. The distinction in continuous trading between limit order placers who supply liquidity and market order placers who remove liquidity does not apply to call auction trading. In a call auction, all participants supply liquidity to each other. However, with an open book call, those participants who place their orders early in the pre–call, order entry period are key to the bookbuilding process. In a call auction, it is the early order placers who are the catalysts for liquidity supply.

What should your limit price be when you submit a limit order to a call auction? To answer this on a conceptual level, let's again invoke the concept of a *reservation price* that we introduced in Chapter 3. In that chapter, we took your assessment of a stock's value to be $12 a share, and referred to the $12 valuation as your *reservation price*. Your share valuation depends primarily on your assessment of the company, not on the trading facility that you send your order to, so let us continue to let $12 be your reservation price. Assume the stock is currently trading in the neighborhood of $11.10. At this price level you are a buyer, and your order is small enough that market impact costs are not a factor. What price should you put on your order in the call? We address this question in each of three contexts: (1) the call auction is the only trading mechanism, (2) the market structure offers an opening call that is followed by continuous trading, and (3) the market structure offers continuous trading that is followed by a closing call.

Call Auctions Are the Only Game in Town

Let's assume a 10-cent price increment and try some values. If you put a price of $11.10 on your order and the clearing price at the call is $11.10 or less, your order executes. Excellent. You are willing to pay $12, but wind up paying only $11.10, and accordingly receive a surplus of $0.90 a share ($12 minus $11.10). But what if the clearing price turns out to be $11.20? Rats! Your limit was $11.10, so no execution! You would have received a surplus of $0.80 a share, but instead you receive nothing. With hindsight, $11.20 would have been a better price to put on your order. Why? If the clearing price turned out to be $11.10, you would have executed at $11.10 and still have received the surplus of $0.90, and if the clearing price turned out to be $11.20, you would have traded and received a surplus of $0.80 instead of zero. The point is you give up nothing by putting the higher $11.20 price on your order. (See Exhibit 4.7.)

Let's extend the logic. Suppose that you place your order at $11.20 and the clearing price at the call turns out to be $11.30. Rats again! It's the same unfortunate situation. At $11.30 you would have realized a surplus of $0.70 a share, but instead you receive nothing. We could ask the same question about a limit price of $11.40, of $11.50, and so on, and still come up with the same answer. The point is, if you would receive a positive surplus (reservation price minus limit price) from a transaction, you want to make that trade in the absence of any alternative way to trade.

Understanding this, we can reword the question. What price should you put on your order to ensure that:

- Your order will execute if the surplus that you would realize from buying at the clearing price is positive?
- Your order will not execute if the surplus that you would realize from buying at the clearing price is negative?

These two conditions are both met if and only if your limit price equals your reservation price. Consequently, your reservation price should be your limit price. William Vickrey, winner of the Nobel prize in 1996, demonstrated that some auction designs similarly lead participants to truth-revealing strategies—that is, to bids that are identical to the bidders' reservation prices.[5]

Now back to market orders. The higher your reservation price for the stock, the higher the limit price you will put on the order that you send to the call auction. As you become increasingly aggressive, you

TraderEx		
DAY	TIME	SEED
1	11:49:04	1

TICKER	PRICE	11.50	11.50	11.50
	QTY	30	30	11
	TIME	11:41	11:41	11:41

MARKET	indicative	11.40
CALL	imbalance	-34

BIDS		OFFERS	
		12.30	557
		12.20	493
		12.10	493
	19	12.00	477
	19	11.90	477
	19	11.80	433
	19	11.70	433
	19	11.60	334
	157	11.50	334
	320	11.40	286
	511	11.30	232
	671	11.20	90
	707	11.10	
	751	11.00	
	788	10.90	
	813	10.80	
	813	10.70	
	813	10.60	
	886	10.50	
	909	10.40	

Size of buy limit at 11.70	20

EXHIBIT 4.7a Call Auction Entry to Buy 20 with a Limit Price of $11.70

TraderEx			
DAY	**TIME**		**SEED**
1	11:51:04		1

TICKER	PRICE	11.50	11.50	11.50
	QTY	30	30	11
	TIME	11:41	11:41	11:41

MARKET	indicative	11.40
CALL	imbalance	-54

	BIDS		OFFERS	
		12.30	591	
		12.20	506	
		12.10	506	
	19	12.00	490	
	19	11.90	490	
	19	11.80	433	
20	39	11.70	433	
20	39	11.60	334	
20	177	11.50	334	
20	340	**11.40**	286	
20	531	11.30	232	
20	691	11.20	90	
20	741	11.10		
20	785	11.00		
20	822	10.90		
20	858	10.80		
20	858	10.70		
20	858	10.60		
20	931	10.50		
20	954	10.40		

EXHIBIT 4.7b　Call Auction Entry at $11.70 Results in Execution at $11.40

TraderEx				
DAY		**TIME**		**SEED**
1		**11:51**		**1**

TICKER	PRICE	11.40	11.50	11.50
	QTY	286	30	30
	TIME	11:51	11:41	11:41

QUOTE	**11.40**	**11.70**
	48	51

Hit	BIDS		OFFERS	Take
		12.20		
		12.10	8	
		12.00		
		11.90	57	
		11.80		
		11.70	51	
		11.60		
		11.50		
	48	11.40		
	48	11.30		
	67	11.20		
	5	11.10		
	21	11.00		
	37	10.90		
	36	10.80		

EXHIBIT 4.7c   After Call Auction executes with 286 trading at 11.40, the market rolls over to continuous trading as shown.

might think of submitting a market order and accepting whatever clearing price the call produces. This is an unnecessary and ill-advised strategy. All participants should have some finite reservation price (no matter how high it might be), and this price should be specified as a price limit to protect against a weird event occurring (such as the sell side of the book getting cleared out by a huge buy imbalance). A price limit protects you against this risk. Nevertheless, some participants who are accustomed to placing market orders in the continuous trading environment might still choose to send unpriced market orders to the call. In effect, that market order placer is saying, "Whatever the price in the call might be, I want my order to execute—\$20, \$200, \$2,000, or more, I want it to execute."[6] It is in this sense that, in a call auction, a market order to buy is a limit order with a price set at infinity (your demand is completely inelastic, if you remember your microeconomics). Similarly, a market order to sell submitted to a call is a limit sell order with a price set at zero.

Opening Call Followed by Continuous Trading

We have thus far been looking at call-only limit orders. The situation is more complex when we introduce the possibility of rolling an unexecuted order from the call into the continuous market. You can now modify your limit price in the call to take account of the possibility of realizing a superior transaction in the continuous market. This is the tactical question: "Should you buy shares of ABC.com at \$11.90 in the call, or try for a better price in the continuous market? Recall that, because of the possibility of price improvement in call auctions, you'll place a higher limit price on a buy order (and a lower limit price to sell) than you would in a continuous order book market. To answer the question that we just posed, let's ask a few more questions.

> **Q1:** Would you rather buy ABC.com at \$12.00 in the call auction, or not have your order execute at all?
>
> **A1: Indifferent.** \$12.00 is your reservation price. The surplus you would receive is zero, which is what you get when you do not execute at all.
>
> **Q2:** Would you rather buy ABC.com at \$11.90 in the call, or at \$11.90 in the continuous market when there is a 0.99 probability that your order will execute in the continuous market?
>
> **A2: Go into the call at \$11.90.** Putting \$11.90 on the buy order you submit to the call means that you will indeed buy if the clearing price is \$11.90 or less. It would not be wise to forgo the \$0.10 surplus in the

call for a $0.10 surplus in the continuous market given that you have a .01 probability of not realizing it (if your order does not execute in the continuous market you get nothing). If you try for an execution in the continuous market it must, therefore, be at a better price (e.g., $11.80). In the three questions that follow, we contrast an execution in the call with an execution in the continuous market at a price that is one tick less aggressive.

Q3: Would you rather buy ABC.com at $11.90 in the call, or at $11.80 in the continuous market when there is a 0.90 probability that your order will execute in the continuous market?

A3: Don't go into the call at $11.90. Accepting an execution at $11.90 in the call when there is a high (0.90) probability of executing at $11.80 in the continuous market would not be a good decision. To prevent an execution at $11.90 in the call, put an $11.80 limit on your order.

Q4: Would you rather buy ABC.com at $11.90 in the call, or at $11.80 in the continuous market when there is a 0.10 probability that your order will execute in the continuous market?

A4: Go into the call at $11.90. With only a 0.10 percent probability of executing at $11.80, you should enter the call with the possibility of buying at $11.90. Thus your limit price now should be $11.90.

Q5: Would you rather buy ABC.com at $11.90 in the call, or at $11.80 in the continuous market if the probability of your order executing in the continuous market is 0.50?

A5: Hmmm. This is less obvious because 0.50 is not an extreme probability. More structure is required to answer the question.

To proceed, first recall that your goal is to maximize the expected value of your surplus. Next, consider your options:

(A) Price your order in the call at $11.90. If the clearing price is $11.90, your order executes, and you realize a surplus of $0.10.

(B) Price your order in the call at $11.80. If the clearing price is $11.90, your order does not execute. You have effectively prevented a call execution at $11.90 for a 0.50 probability of executing at $11.80 if the clearing price in the call is higher than $11.80. This option gives you an expected surplus of $0.20 \times 0.50 = 0.10$.

Conclusion: The two options generate equivalent surpluses, and you should be indifferent between them.

We can use the structure presented with respect to Q5 to show exactly why the answers to questions 2 through 5 are, respectively, "yes," "no," "yes," and "hmmm." For each of the questions, here is how the surplus you would receive in the call if your order executes at its limit price stacks up with the *expected surplus* you would receive from the continuous market if you block an execution in the call in an attempt to execute one tick lower.

	Call Auction		**Continuous Auction**	
Q2	Surplus at $11.90 = $0.100	>	Expected surplus at $11.90	$= \$0.10 \times 0.99$ $= \$0.099$
Q3	Surplus at $11.90 = $0.100	<	Expected surplus at $11.80	$= \$0.20 \times 0.90$ $= \$0.180$
Q4	Surplus at $11.90 = $0.100	>	Expected surplus at $11.80	$= \$0.20 \times 0.10$ $= \$0.020$
Q5	Surplus at $11.90 = $0.100	=	Expected surplus at $11.80	$= \$0.20 \times 0.50$ $= \$0.100$

The response to these four questions can be generalized with reference to a *breakeven probability*, which is a probability value (such as 0.50 in Q5) that equates the surplus in the call with the expected surplus one tick lower in the continuous market. If you believe that the actual probability of execution is greater than the breakeven probability (e.g., if you think it is 0.90 as in Q3), then you should preclude an execution at that price in the call auction and attempt to buy one tick lower by placing a price limit one tick lower on your order in the call (and also in the continuous market if you do not execute in the call). With reference to Q3, you accomplish this by pricing your order at $11.80. Or, if you believe that the actual probability of execution is less than the breakeven probability (e.g., if you think it is only 0.10 as in Q4), do not block an execution in the call at the higher price.

We can drill further down into this example. Say you believe that the actual probability of execution is greater than 0.50. This leads to another question: Might you do even better by putting a limit of $11.70 on your buy order? Or, how about a limit of $11.60? And so forth. In a procedure known as *iterative dominance*, we find the optimal buy order to send to the call by assessing each price, starting one tick below your reservation price, until we get to a breakeven probability that is *higher* than the probability that you think applies. At that point, the likelihood of executing is just too small to justify placing the order there. So, go back to the previous higher tick (if selling you go back to the previous lower price), and that is your optimal limit price in continuous trading. Here is how the procedure works in our example. The breakeven probabilities for a buy order at prices ranging from $12.00 down to $11.60 are:

Price Limit for Buying		Surplus In		Breakeven Probability of Executing in Continuous
Call	Continuous	Call	Continuous	
$12.00	$11.90	$0.00	$0.10	NA
$11.90	$11.80	$0.10	$0.20	**0.50**
$11.80	$11.70	$0.20	$0.30	**0.67**
$11.70	$11.60	$0.30	$0.40	**0.75**
$11.60	$11.50	$0.40	$0.50	**0.80**

The breakeven probability in the far right column equals the surplus in the call divided by the surplus in the continuous market.

Note that the breakeven probability increases as price decreases. The reason is that, as we move to lower prices, the gain in surplus achieved by reducing your price by one tick is proportionately less. Because your incremental gain is proportionately less from taking the risk, the probability of the risk paying off must be higher. However, the actual probability of executing at lower prices in the continuous market decreases. The reason for this is that the execution probabilities are conditioned on (take account of) the fact that your order did not execute in the call. Suppose that the clearing price at the call is $11.90 and that your limit price in the continuous is $11.80—you then need a $0.10 price decrease in the continuous market for your order to execute. This could, of course, happen because of accentuated volatility in the continuous market, as we discuss in Chapter 3. What if the clearing price in the call is $11.90 and your price limit in the continuous market is $11.70? You would then need a $0.20 decrease in the continuous market, and the probability of this larger downtick occurring must be less. And so on, as you change your price to $11.60 or below.

We can now determine the optimal order to submit to the call. Identify the highest value of price in the continuous market for which you believe that the probability of executing in the continuous market is less than the breakeven probability. Perhaps, for instance, you believe that a limit order at $11.80 in the continuous market has a 0.55 probability of executing if a limit order in the call at $11.80 fails to execute, and that the comparable probability for a limit order at $11.70 in the continuous market is 0.45. The lower 0.45 probability is *less than* the breakeven value of 0.67, while the higher 0.55 probability is *greater than* the breakeven value of 0.50. Thus your optimal pricing decision is to avoid an execution in the call at $11.90 but not at $11.80, and you do so by putting a limit of $11.80 on your order (for both the call and the continuous market). In effect, the expected surplus of $0.11 (a 55 percent chance of a $0.20 surplus) in the continuous market provides a reference point for the limit price used in the call. The surplus from a $10.90 execution in the call is just $0.10, so $10.80 is the best limit price to use in the call.

Continuous Trading Followed by a Closing Call

Before proceeding with the case of continuous trading followed by a closing call, let's revisit the analytic context within which you are making your order placement decision to buy shares. Your buy order, which has an absolute price cap (a reservation price that generates zero surplus), is a *day order*; it must be filled or canceled by the end of the trading day. Purchase at a price lower than your reservation price and you get a surplus. Your goal is to maximize the expected value of this surplus, and your time frame is the current trading day. After the current session ends, news can come out, you might change your assessment of the stock for your own idiosyncratic reasons, and/or your portfolio manager might give you another order to work. What happens after the market closes is not relevant to your trading decision today. We view the current trading session myopically, and let tomorrow be another matter.

Of course, under some circumstances, you might take longer than a day to implement a trading decision. Institutional traders are commonly given several days by their portfolio managers when working large orders in relatively illiquid markets. But, at some point, there should be closure on a trading decision, and we in effect are considering this concluding point. When that point is a closing call (many exchanges end their trading days with calls), your order placement decision for the closing call is simple. Submit your buy order one tick below your reservation price (or a sell order one tick above) just as you would in the "call auctions are the only game in town" scenario.

But there is more to it than that. The more intriguing question concerns the impact that a closing call has on the order that you submit to the continuous market before the call. We deal with this partly in two sections of Chapter 3—"Should You Submit a Limit Order or a Market Order?" and "How Should You Price Your Limit Orders?" Of critical importance in the Chapter 3 discussion is the relationship between the *actual probability* of a limit order executing and the *breakeven probability* that would leave you indifferent between placing a limit order and placing a market order. Let's introduce some numbers and extend the discussion.

Your reservation price is $12.00, the lowest offer in the order book is $11.10, and you are choosing between lifting the $11.10 offer or entering a buy limit order at $10.80. You quickly determine that your breakeven

probability is 75 percent (because $0.75 \times \$1.20 = \$0.90$). You then consider the actual probability of your limit order executing. As we state in
Chapter 3: *If you believe that the actual probability of getting an execution is higher than 75 percent, submit a limit order. If you think that
the actual probability is lower than 75 percent, submit a market order.*

A closing call affects your order placement decision via its impact on
the actual probability of order execution. You submit your limit order, allow
it to sit on the book until the end of the trading session, and, at that point, if
it has not executed, it is canceled (i.e., you have entered a day order). The
closer to the end of the day that you have placed your order, the lower is the
probability that it will execute, all else the same (clearly, the actual probability of execution is less for a day order placed at 3:30 P.M. than for one
placed at 10:00 A.M.). Consequently, for an otherwise identical set of conditions, at 10:00 A.M. you are more apt to enter a limit order (which could
tighten the spread and supply liquidity), and at 3:30 P.M. you are more apt to
enter a market order (which removes liquidity and could widen the spread).

Now turn to Chapter 3's Exhibit 3.10, where the buyer's expected surplus is maximized by a limit order placed at \$10.80, and to Exhibit 3.11,
where the buyer's expected surplus is maximized by a market buy that executes at the offer of \$11.10. Here, too, the actual probability of order exe-
cution affects your optimal order placement. As the close of trading
approaches, actual probabilities fall (the probability curve shifts downward in the range below the offer) and, increasingly, decisions tilt toward
market orders, a response that leads to wider spreads.

Thomas H. McInish and Robert A. Wood were among the first academicians to observe that spreads increase significantly as trading comes to
a close.[7] We can explain this intuitively with reference to the "gravitational
pull effect." Namely, trading with certainty at a posted quote becomes increasingly attractive (all else the same) as the end of the trading day
draws near. The result of this strengthening of the gravitational pull effect
is wider spreads.

We are now in position to consider how a closing call affects your order placement decision in a continuous market leading up to the closing
call. The closing call gives you another chance to realize a surplus if your
limit order fails to execute in the continuous market. With the call as a
backstop, your expected surplus from a buy limit order strategy at the
time when you place your order in the continuous market is

$$E(S) = [Pr \times S^{Cont}] + [(1 - Pr) \times E(S^{Call})]$$

where:

- S^{Cont} is the surplus that you realize if your limit order executes in the
  continuous market.

- $E(S^{Call})$, where $S^{Call} = \max(0,\ P^R - P^{Call})$, is the surplus that you expect to realize if your limit order in the continuous market does not execute and you submit a limit order at your reservation price to the call.[8]
- Pr is the probability that your limit order executes in the continuous market.

Because the second term on the right-hand side of the equation, $[(1 - Pr) \times E(S^{Call})]$, is necessarily positive, you are more apt to place a limit order than a market order in the continuous market when continuous trading is followed by a closing call, especially as the close of trading nears and the probability of realizing an execution in the continuous market (Pr) falls.

If, with a closing call, limit orders are more apt than otherwise to be placed instead of market orders as the end of continuous trading approaches, the introduction of a closing call should result in spreads that are tighter than otherwise during this part of the trading day. Pagano and Schwartz observed a statistically significant decrease in percentage bid-ask spreads in the last hour of continuous trading on the Paris Bourse (currently Euronext Paris) following that exchange's introduction of a closing call in 1996.[9] Again, intuition is provided by the gravitational pull effect. Namely, the attractiveness of trading with certainty at a posted quote increases (all else the same) as the close of the trading day draws near, but the increase is tempered if, after the continuous market ends, you can enter your order into a closing call with a limit price equal to your reservation price.

Consider the following illustration for a trader with a reservation price of $12.00, who enters the market at 3:40 P.M. with an expected-surplus maximizing limit order to buy 1,000 shares in an order book market at $11.30.

	Probability of Execution in Continuous	Expected Surplus^{Cont} per Share	Expected Surplus^{Cont} 1,000 Shares
$11.50 (ask price)	1.00	0.500	$500
$11.40	0.85	0.510	$510
$11.30*	0.75	0.525	$525
$11.20	0.60	0.480	$480
$11.10	0.50	0.450	$450
$11.00	0.40	0.400	$400

At 3:40 P.M., in the absence of a closing call, the trader's surplus is maximized by the limit order priced at $11.30, as indicated by the "*" at that limit price.

Then, at 3:50 P.M., you enter the market with a reservation price of $12.00. But now the probabilities of execution are lower because, at this point, there are only 10 minutes left until the closing bell.

	Probability of Execution in Continuous	Expected Surplus^{Cont} per Share	Expected Surplus^{Cont} 1,000 Shares
$11.50* (ask price)	1.00	0.500	$500
$11.40	0.80	0.480	$480
$11.30	0.65	0.455	$455
$11.20	0.50	0.400	$400
$11.10	0.40	0.360	$360
$11.00	0.30	0.300	$300

At 3:50 P.M., in the absence of a closing call, your surplus is maximized by a market order, as indicated by the "*" at $11.50 (ask price).

But wait! Let's introduce a 4 P.M. call and see what happens. Now you come up with the following probability assessments for the alternative clearing prices that could be set at the closing call, along with the associated surpluses that you would receive (the columns to the right are based on submission of a buy order priced at $11.90 into the auction).

Possible Call Clearing Price	Probability of Clearing Price Being Set	Expected Surplus^{Call} per Share	Expected Surplus^{Call} 1,000 Shares	Cumulative Surplus^{Call} 1,000 Shares
$11.90		0	$ 0	$ 0
$11.80	0.05	0.01	$ 10	$ 10
$11.70	0.05	0.015	$ 15	$ 25
$11.60	0.20	0.08	$ 80	$105
$11.50	0.30	0.15	$150	$255
$11.40	0.30	0.18	$180	$435
$11.30	0.05	0.035	$ 35	$470
$11.20	0.05	0.04	$ 40	$510
$11.10		0	$ 0	$510

Note that the probabilities for the possible clearing prices (which extend from $11.80 down to $11.20) sum to 1.00. Note also that your expected surplus from a 1,000-share order with a price limit of $11.90 in the call is the cumulative value of $510 shown in the bottom right-hand cell ($510 is the probability-weighted average of the surpluses shown for each possible clearing price individually). The expected surplus of $510 for the 1,000-share order exceeds the surplus of $500 from trading by market order. Therefore, you should not submit a market order at 3:50 P.M. Should you, at that time, submit a limit order? Yes, of course. The best limit order to submit at 3:50 P.M. is $11.40 because it offers the highest expected surplus of all the possible limit prices. The best result you could hope for is that it executes because, if it does, it generates $600 surplus, which is greater than the expected surplus of $510 from the call auction.

Your strategy for placing your 1,000-share order at 3:50 P.M. is now determined: Buy 1,000 shares in the continuous market at $11.40; if unexecuted by 4:00 P.M., go into the closing call at $11.90. Your expected surplus, $E(S) = \text{Pr} [S^{\text{Cont}}] + [(1 - \text{Pr}) \times E(S^{\text{Call}})]$, is $(0.80 \times \$600) + (0.20 \times \$510) = \$582$, which is greater than the $500 surplus you would get from executing at $11.50 by market order at 3:50 P.M.

We have seen that, with a call followed by continuous trading, you enter your orders at less aggressive prices in the call. In contrast, when continuous trading is followed by a call, your incentives tilt toward liquidity-supplying limit orders rather liquidity-removing market orders, since the closing call gives you an additional chance to trade. In both cases, having one facility followed by the other enables you to place your orders less aggressively in the facility that operates first.

We can summarize:

- In a call auction-only environment, you place maximally aggressive limit orders (your limit price equals your reservation price).
- Following a call with continuous trading can result in your orders being priced less aggressively in the call—the expected surplus from a subsequent execution in the continuous market may lead you to price your order in an opening call away from your reservation price.
- Ending the continuous market with a call effectively gives you "another swing at the ball," which means that you do not have to chase liquidity as aggressively as you otherwise would in the continuous market. If the order truly is a day order, then your limit price in the closing call should be your reservation price.

A REALITY CHECK

We have set forth procedures for determining an optimal price limit to put on your call order when the call auction is followed by continuous trading, and for determining an optimal price limit to put on your continuous market order when continuous trading is followed by a call auction. No human trader can be expected to work these solutions out at a trading desk with a rapidly ticking clock pressuring the trading decision. We do not expect you or anyone else to be able to do this with scientific precision. As we have discussed in Chapter 1, if the trading decision is being made by a live trader, it must be a "blink" experience. You simply get a feel for the best way to handle your order. However, your ability to feel your way to a good pricing decision may be strengthened by practice. But practice itself is more productive when accompanied by an effective conceptual framework. It is with this in mind that we have structured a solution to the two questions we have posed: "How do I price my order in the call when it is followed by continuous trading, and how do I price my order in the continuous market when it is followed by a call?"

Computers and real-time market data that are available to traders today provide another avenue for applying our formulation. Algorithmic trading software can be developed to support order entry when continuous trading and periodic call auctions are both available, and our framework identifies the important parameters to include in the algorithms. While no human can go through the needed calculations with sufficient speed, a computer can, and algorithms based on the preceding formulations can be programmed into the computer and fine-tuned over time based on performance feedback. We discuss algorithmic trading further in Chapter 6.

OPTION VALUE OF LIMIT ORDERS IN A CALL AUCTION

We used a payoff diagram in Chapter 3 to show how the profit you receive from placing a limit order depends on your limit price and the price of the stock that you are looking to buy or to sell. The payoff diagram for the limit order resembles the payoff diagram for an option and, as we discussed, placing a limit order may be viewed as obtaining an option to buy or to sell shares if a specified condition (the price of your order) is satisfied. Let's revisit this and consider the placement of a limit order in a call auction.[10] As you will see, the payoff diagram for a call auction differs from the payoff diagram for the continuous market. This underscores the difference between call and continuous trading, demonstrating again that you should price your limit order differently in call and continuous markets.

Let the call auction operate as follows. At time t_0, the exchange opens the limit order book and, until the time of the call (time T), participants can place limit and market orders in the book without their orders being executed. At time T, the exchange freezes the limit order book and determines the clearing price of the security, which is the price at which all trades take place.

Let's suppose, as we did in Chapter 3, that you are seeking to buy one share of a security and have a reservation price of $50. As we discussed in the previous section, because limit orders execute at the common clearing price in a call auction, you should put a price of $50 on your limit buy order (unless you are large enough to believe that your order will have market impact).[11] Exhibit 4.8 shows the surplus that you can obtain from a one-share limit buy order with a price limit of $50 (your reservation price) if a liquidity event occurs.

In Exhibit 4.8, P^C is the value that a liquidity event drives the clearing price to in the call auction. The limit buy order you placed at $50 will not execute if P^C is greater than $50. For this discussion, let's ignore the possibility of an inexact cross and presume that your order will execute if P^C is $50 or below. In this case, because your order executes at the common clearing price, your surplus depends on P^C. The lower P^C is, the higher is the surplus that you will obtain.

The payoff diagram shown in Exhibit 4.8 corresponds to that of a standard put option with a strike price of $50 and an expiration date that corresponds to the time of the call auction. This is the financial asset that you receive from the placement of a limit buy order at $50 in a call auction when only a liquidity event can occur during your trading window.

Surplus

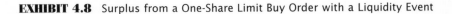

EXHIBIT 4.8 Surplus from a One-Share Limit Buy Order with a Liquidity Event

Exhibit 4.9 shows, for both the call and the continuous environment, the payoff that you will receive from your limit order executing when a liquidity event occurs. Contrasting the payoff diagrams without considering the probability distributions for P^C and P_T suggests that the payoff to a limit order in the call is superior to that in a continuous market.

Let's look at this more closely. Because it is written at $50 (your reservation price) rather than at $47 (your limit price in the continuous market), your limit order in the call auction has a positive payoff in the price range from $47 to $50; in the continuous market your limit order does not. Further, because limit orders that execute do so at the common clearing price rather than at their price limits, your limit order in the call has a payoff greater than $3 in the price range below $47; in the continuous market your limit order does not (this is Berkeley's point about price improvement).

But don't be misled. When the execution probability is also taken into account, we cannot conclude that, if a liquidity event occurs, your expected trading gain from placing a limit order in a call auction is unambiguously superior to your expected trading gain from placing it in the continuous market. The reason is that the probability of P_T reaching any given value in the continuous market does not, in general, equal the probability of P^C reaching that value in the call auction. With accentuated volatility in the continuous market, the probability of reaching $47 in the

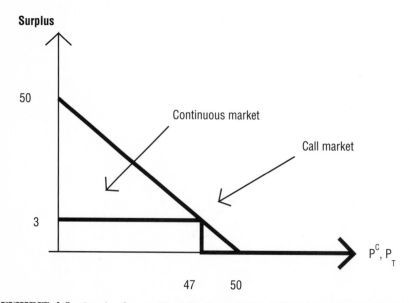

EXHIBIT 4.9 Surplus from a Liquidity Event in the Call and Continuous Markets

continuous market may be greater than the probability of P^C reaching $47 in the call.

So far, we've discussed liquidity events only. We saw in the previous chapter that the placement of a limit order in the continuous market will result in an undesirable outcome if an unfavorable news release causes your limit order to execute before you learn of the news and are able to withdraw the order. The same is the case in call auction trading, but your risk is tempered. An unfavorable news release could drive the call market clearing price below what your revised reservation price will be based on the news. A major corporate or government announcement that could take place before a call should be monitored if you are participating. But even if an adverse event occurs, your limit order will receive better treatment in a call auction than it will in continuous market trading. We can explain this with reference to Exhibit 4.10.

Exhibit 4.10 shows your payout if you place a limit buy order at $50 in a call auction and some other investors place orders because of news that you have not yet received. In Exhibit 4.10 we take P_1^R to be your revised reservation price after you have received the news. The exhibit shows the following:

- If the information event occurs without P^C being driven to your limit price of $50 or below, your order does not execute and your payout is zero. This is clearly the case if the new information is bullish.
- If the information event drives P^C below your price limit, your order executes. In this case, you profit only if the information event drives P^C below your revised reservation price. This is the case if the information is bearish but a sufficient number of other participants react more negatively to it than you do (i.e., if your reservation price does not fall as much as the reservation price of others).
- If the information event results in your revised reservation price falling below P^C, you lose. This is the case if the information is bearish, but an insufficient number of other participants react more negatively to it than you do (i.e., if your reservation price falls more than the reservation price of most others).

EXHIBIT 4.10 Surplus from a Limit Buy Order with an Informational Event

	$P^C < 50$	$P^C = 50$	$P^C > 50$
$P_1^R > P^C$	$P_1^R - P_C > 0$	$P_1^R - P_C > 0$	0
$P_1^R = P^C$	0	Not Applicable	Not Applicable
$P_1^R < P^C$	$P_1^R - P_C < 0$	$P_1^R - P_C < 0$	0

Contrasting Exhibit 4.10 and Exhibit 3.14 shows that you, as a limit order trader, do not obtain the same payoff following the advent of bearish (or bullish) news in the call and the continuous environments. First, because you place your reservation price in the call auction, your limit order will execute if P^C is in the range from \$47 to \$50, whereas your limit order at \$47 in the continuous market will execute only at \$47 and below. In this case you will profit if the information event follows (1) the advent of bullish news that does not drive P^C above your reservation price or (2) the advent of bearish news that does not drive your reservation price below the clearing price.

Further, because all executed limit orders trade at a common clearing price and not at their price limits, the advent of bearish news that changes an investor's reservation price as well as P^C does not guarantee a loss when your limit order is placed in a call auction. Only if the information event drives P^C below your revised reservation price (P_1^R) will you lose, and your loss will be less than it would be in the continuous market if the clearing price were below \$47.

What might we conclude from this? The discussion suggests that it is more attractive to place limit orders in a call auction than in a continuous market if your trading motive is to change your portfolio holdings. But if, on the other hand, you are after volatility capture, you will find the continuous market a preferable environment.

TIME TO CALL THE MARKET

Call auctions have historically been part of the landscape in Europe, and fully electronic calls are now an important, integral component of the electronic trading platforms of all major European exchanges. Until recently, with the exception of the NYSE's opening and closing calls (which are not fully electronic), they have been neither used nor well understood in the United States (unless one goes back roughly 100 years in U.S. history). Now they are a solid part of the NASDAQ market, they are included in Archipelago's market structure, they are represented by two ATSs (Instinet's and ITG Posit's crossing networks), NASDAQ is planning the introduction of several intraday crossing networks, and the Big Board is considering the call's inclusion in its new Hybrid Market. Further, depending on the definition that you use, the ATS Pipeline may also fit into the call auction space. Calls clearly are an important trading vehicle to know about and understand. Large investors with their big orders, in particular, may appreciate them as being excellent facilities for finding liquidity, particularly the intraday and closing calls that are less prone to the intricacies of bookbuilding and the challenges of price discovery.

A call auction is a very different trading vehicle than a continuous market. You should approach it differently, enter your orders differently, and expect different results. Further experimentation with TraderEx software may help to tie down this point. You might find that a hybrid combination of call and continuous is very desirable from your point of view as a user. It is also desirable for the broad market because of the sharpness that calls bring to price discovery, and the stability they can offer for intraday price formation. This is the direction that market structure has been moving in, first in Europe and currently in the U.S. In our opinion, now is the time for the market to be called.

FROM THE CONTRIBUTORS

Alfred R. Berkeley III
A Call Is Not a Call Is Not a Call

Frank M. Hatheway
The NASDAQ Crosses: A View from the Inside

James Ross
Call Market Trading—It's About Time

A Call Is Not a Call Is Not a Call

Alfred R. Berkeley III

A call auction is typically defined as a trading vehicle that pools orders together for execution (1) at a single price, (2) at a predetermined point in time, and (3) in a multilateral trade. This description fits many of the standard call auctions in exchanges around the world, and it is the definition that underlies much of the discussion in this chapter. Interestingly, each one of the three parts of this definition need not apply. It is in this very fundamental sense that a call is not a call is not a call.

A call that gathers orders for a multilateral batch could match the individual buy and sell orders at different prices; Optimark, a cleverly designed call auction vehicle, did this but did not succeed in the marketplace. The time of a call is typically preannounced, but this, too, is not a necessary requirement; calls can be held "on request." Perhaps the most distinctive aspect of a call in the eyes of many is that it pulls multiple orders together for a *multilateral trade*, rather than matching contra-side orders in *bilateral trades*, as is generally the case with continuous trading. The new ATS, Pipeline, calls the market in an individual stock "on request." Pipeline is designed to deliver multilateral trades, but it has large minimum order sizes that execute in strict price and time priority. The net effect is to deliver mostly bilateral trades. We classify Pipeline as a call auction designed to discover quantity, not price.

What then is the definition of a call? I prefer to focus not on how orders are handled, but on *what the order handling accomplishes*. So viewed, the essence of a call is that it can deliver price improvement for pre-positioned limit orders. Traditional continuous trading models do not do this. Put your limit order on the book of a continuous market and, if your order is at the top of the book in terms of price and time priority, and if a contra-side market order arrives, your order will execute *at the price at which it has been placed*.

Say your limit order is to buy 1,000 shares at $52.10. Your pre-positioned, liquidity-providing order has arrived first, but there is no way in a continuous market that a market order to sell, which has arrived second and is liquidity demanding, will execute against your order at any price lower than $52.10. None! But, curiously, the market order, which has arrived second and has taken liquidity (not supplied it) can be price-improved by a specialist or some other floor trader stepping ahead of your limit order by increasing the bid by only a penny to $52.11. If this happens, your limit order remains sitting unexecuted on the book.

The hallmark of a call auction need not be that it is a "fixed in time, multilateral trade at a single price" procedure. The essence is that it offers price improvement to pre-positioned, liquidity-supplying limit orders. As this chapter makes perfectly clear, your limit order to buy, which was entered into the call at $52.10, will execute at $51.50 if $51.50 is the clearing price at the call. All other attributes of the trade are incidental to this one very important reality—a call auction offers price improvement for pre-positioned, liquidity-supplying limit orders. Pipeline's order-matching algorithm does exactly this: It price-improves the first order that has been placed. It removes the perverse incentive to be passive and wait, and it solves the prisoner's dilemma problem (see Chapter 6).

Let's step back and consider your trading needs. The bottom line in choosing to trade in a call market or in a continuous market is clear: If you are in the market to capture volatility, you need a set of tools that will let you succeed. If you are changing your portfolio, you want to prevent others from capturing value from you, and you need a different set of tools. You need a set of tools that will hide your trading intentions from others. Let's examine the tools available.

Traders typically trade to capture volatility. They are in the market to harvest the option value inherent in displayed limit orders. These are entered by investors who need to rearrange their portfolios. Investors rearrange their portfolios for many reasons; for example, perhaps the price of oil is rising and the investor wants more exposure to oil exploration companies and less to oil-sensitive businesses like airlines.

To harvest the option value inherent in displayed limit orders, you need to be able to see displayed limit orders. This means that you need to be in an "open book" market, one that displays limit orders. You also have to trade on a market that allows you to see the book. This means that you have to be in an open book market that also serves an "open community." There are open limit order book markets that serve closed communities; the NYSE is such a market. Your limit orders are displayed, but only the specialists can see the limit order book—you cannot. No wonder the value of a "seat" (a license to trade) on the NYSE is so high. Open book markets that serve open communities include the NASDAQ and the electronic communications networks, or ECNs, like Instinet and Archipelago. Brokerage firms can connect electronically to the ECNs and to the NASDAQ, and if you use one that does, you can have nearly instantaneous access to the limit orders displayed there.

NASDAQ and the ECNs are very attractive to traders because of the information asymmetries they offer that favor traders over investors. It is harder to capture volatility on the NYSE, because you are not permitted to see the open limit order book. The NASDAQ has an opening and a closing call market. The calls are open in that you can see the orders on the book, but you lose some of the control that you might need when you can no longer cancel your order as the call nears. As this is being written, NASDAQ has announced its intentions of having three call markets during the day. Individuals will likely have access to these call markets through their brokers.

To hide your trading intentions, you need to avoid the open, continuous market limit order book facilities that are structured to advantage the trader at the expense of the investor. Hiding one's trading intentions is very important for large institutional investors because their very presence in the market tends to cause prices to change against their interests. (Hiding one's trading intentions is probably less important to individual investors, but it is worth understanding the differences in market structure, if only to understand what is happening around you.) Institutions hide their trading intentions in call markets like POSIT or Pipeline. POSIT runs marketwide calls at least every hour, seeking to maximize the volume of shares crossed (quantity discovery) and pricing *parasitically* off the major market for each stock. This means that POSIT users agree to accept executions priced off the NYSE or the NASDAQ for the stocks they have submitted. Institutional investors are able to put large blocks into the POSIT cross and not have their size or side revealed to the market if the orders are not filled.

Pipeline differs from POSIT in that it allows institutional investors to call the market in an individual stock at any time. Pipeline was designed from scratch as a new market structure in which everyone receives exactly the same information at exactly the same time, and everyone has exactly the same opportunities to act on the information. Pipeline requires large minimum orders (100,000 shares for very liquid stocks; 25,000 shares for most stocks; and 10,000 shares for rather illiquid stocks.) Pipeline differs from most call auctions in that it is a "call on request" that often results in bilateral, not multilateral trades. All orders are firm orders, so there is no backing away, and hence no information leakage. Pipeline also prices parasitically off the primary market for each stock. Most critically, Pipeline's price-improvement procedure rewards the party who has entered an order first. We also essentially give midpoint crosses rather than prices at the bid or at the ask. Pipeline, an innovation that came from the free market, is aimed at solving the wealth transfer that arises from the flaws in the design of the current continuous markets, flaws that favor traders and hurt investors. Pipeline is designed to strip the option value out of displayed limit orders by not displaying them.

From the descriptions set forth above, it is clear that call markets can and do serve different functions. Calls are being used to discover price and to open and close the NASDAQ and the NYSE markets. Calls are being used to tease out quantity in the case of Pipeline and POSIT. Pipeline's call also gives the edge to early order placers who, by pre-positioning their limit orders, supply liquidity to the market. This is the feature of call auction trading that we at Pipeline emphasize.

The NASDAQ Crosses:
A View from the Inside

Frank M. Hatheway

In 2004, NASDAQ introduced new crosses to enhance the opening and closing processes. In the terminology set forth in this chapter, these crosses are price discovery call auctions of the open limit order book variety. In creating the crosses, NASDAQ hoped to increase the choice of execution methods available to investors while preserving the central features of NASDAQ's open and competitive electronic market structure. As discussed in the main text of the chapter, some investors need to trade at benchmark prices established at the start or the end of the trading day. To meet this need, the cross design superficially resembles traditional exchange auctions, but does not rely on a single individual acting as both auctioneer and participant. Instead, NASDAQ has sought to create a fully automated, open, competitive, and transparent auction process that brings together large numbers of buyers and sellers in a single trade that resolves liquidity imbalances and improves price discovery.

Although NASDAQ had high hopes for the crosses, there were risks. NASDAQ trading had historically been done on an order-by-order basis, and the idea of combining multiple orders into a single electronic transaction was new. Would traders learn the process and adopt appropriate strategies for both retail and institutional orders? Furthermore, most NASDAQ opening and closing trades were handled upstairs, not through NASDAQ's electronic book. Would orders migrate to the book to participate in the crosses? Also, the global experience with electronic opening and closing auctions had been mixed. Some markets' auctions had not proven to be universally popular. Others had been unable to successfully balance supply and demand under all circumstances. NASDAQ's design tried to learn from these experiences, but would it work? We faced yet another risk—certain events such as derivative expirations and index rebalances are times of incredible stress for traders and trading systems. Even if the crosses proved to be successful on normal days, would they be able to handle the crush of orders at these key, critical moments?

Almost immediately after launch, the industry reacted very positively to this new way of trading NASDAQ stocks. The highpoint of the introduction of the Closing Cross occurred barely one month following the rollout, when over 330 million shares traded in over 1,600 stocks during the annual Russell Index reconstitution. The process took only 12 seconds to complete. At one point at that day's close, NASDAQ was executing 8,400 trades per second, and over 500 stocks traded more volume in that single cross than they typically did for an entire day.

Subsequent reaction to the crosses has continued to be very positive. Since the crosses launched, volume on both of them has increased by over 200 percent from a few million shares per day soon after introduction, to about 25 million shares per day by mid-2005. The peak volume day for the Closing Cross is now 425 million shares, and it is 250 million shares for the Opening Cross. The ability of the NASDAQ cross to unify multiple simultaneous buyers and sellers at a single price is unmatched by any continuous trading system.

The crosses have proved popular with a spectrum of investors ranging from small retail customers to large institutional investors. The Opening Cross has attracted predominantly retail order flow. Over half the volume executed on the open consists of regular "day" orders waiting for the trading day to start. On most days, less than 20 percent of the opening cross volume is specifically marked as "on-open." This chapter notes that large traders are wary of participating in price discovery at the open, and indeed the institutional orders have flown predominantly into the Closing Cross. Over 50 percent of the executed volume contains specific instructions to trade on the close. The typical order executed on the close is over three times the size of its counterpart on the open. Derivative expirations are unique events with the great majority of the executed volume coming from very large orders marked specifically as "on-open" or "on-close."

There have been additional benefits from the introduction of the crosses beyond the crosses' ability to execute large amounts of volume. Because of NASDAQ's competitive and transparent auction, price volatility on both the open and the close has been significantly reduced. Furthermore, the crosses attract substantial additional offsetting liquidity, typically in excess of 50 percent beyond what is necessary to meet the demands of the auctions process, as shown in Exhibit 4.11. The graph shows the liquidity at the auction price and the cumulative liquidity at 10 one-penny price ticks away from the auction price as the six-day average of daily averages for all stocks in the NASDAQ Opening Cross for the trading days September 9 through 15, 2005. To the benefit of investors, this liquidity often remains in the continuous market after the cross. Finally, the NASDAQ auction prices have been adopted as the standard for opening and closing values of NASDAQ stocks. In other words, the Closing Cross produces NASDAQ's official closing price.

The NASDAQ Opening and Closing Crosses have been very successful in providing transparent price discovery that reflects the true supply and

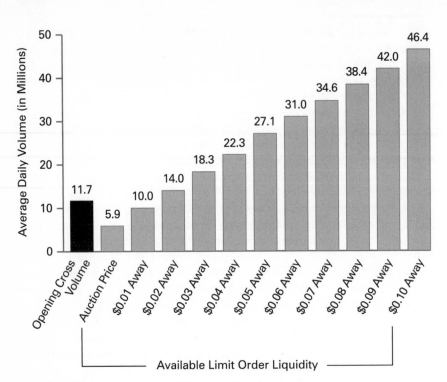

EXHIBIT 4.11   NASDAQ Opening Cross Liquidity September 9–15, 2005
Source: The NASDAQ Stock Market, Inc. Copyright 2006, reprinted with permission.

demand in the marketplace. The crosses generate opening and closing prices that are widely used throughout the industry, by major indexers, mutual funds, and investors. One clear indication of the success of adding call auction style trading to NASDAQ's existing market structure is the clamor for additional auctions to address other unique times when multiple buyers and sellers want to meet and determine a single price through a competitive, open, and transparent process.

Call Market Trading—It's About Time

James Ross

Much time and effort have been spent over the past 20 years applying technology to the financial marketplace. The evolution of electronic communications networks (ECNs) and alternative trading systems (ATSs), the focus on global straight-through processing, and the singular importance of FIX (a standardized messaging protocol for industry participants) are all potent examples of our industry's commitment to technical innovation and integration. Mix in an active regulatory agenda (decimalization and Regulation ATS), and you have a recipe for a dramatically changing and evolving marketplace. One could argue that this change has been revolutionary.

Without a doubt, market participants are faster and better organized than ever before. Technology—in the form of nanosecond order delivery speed, sophisticated order and portfolio management capabilities, and complex algorithmic strategies—has dramatically enhanced participants' relationships with the market. Buy-side traders, and sell-side as well, have many more tools at hand to analyze, create, implement, and, most importantly, control their trading strategies than ever before.

As market participants have embraced these new technologies and their numbers have exploded, the business models that supported the traditional continuous market have become less relevant. The proliferation of natural agency order flow arising from the new technologies has transformed a lumbering principal quote market into a fast-paced order-driven market. No longer do participants have to rely solely on a market maker or specialist for liquidity and price discovery. Now the newly empowered market participants, when submitting their orders, have many different venues to choose from. Primary exchanges, ECNs, ATSs, and regional exchanges are all competing for the market participants' order flow in this new financial world order.

But building this new world order on the old continuous market concept comes at a price. An order-driven market that is turbocharged with cutting-edge technology available to any and all has unleashed a torrent of financial marketplace issues. Some of these problems are linked to the highly automated nature of the order-driven market (fractured liquidity, declining trade size, and penny jumping). Other problems are due to the conflict between automation and manual processes (locked and crossed markets, and trade-through violations). Yet others are the same culprits that have always plagued market participants (inadequate block liquidity, rollercoaster price volatility in active stocks, uncertain markets in mid- and small-cap stocks, excessive transaction costs, and information leakage).

As with any new frontier, a certain reckless abandon characterizes the new financial world order. Evidenced by the issues mentioned above, it is a liquidity and price discovery free-for-all, and no matter how many ways we split a penny, slice an order, or deconstruct a second, the continuous market will never be able to keep up with the market participant's new-found efficiencies—unless, that is, the discipline of time is integrated into the market.

Call market trading embodies the perfect synthesis of time and technology. As we see with the continuous market environment, technology alone without the discipline of time fractures price discovery and liquidity. A call market, on the other hand, leverages both and unites market participants. It also supercharges liquidity and sharpens price discovery. In every way, call markets are a perfect match for the new financial world order.

Whereas participants may execute at any point in time in the continuous market, participants in a call can only submit, edit, cancel, and update during a scheduled time period (also known as bookbuilding) that leads up to the match or auction. Nothing executes until the match or auction algorithm is run at the end of the bookbuilding time period. As stated by Economides and Schwartz, "The essence of call market trading is that orders are batched together for simultaneous execution, in a single multilateral trade, at a pre-specified time, and at a single price."[12]

The factor that distinguishes call markets from continuous markets is its deliberate and disciplined usage of time. Though the constraint on time represented by the call seems limiting, it is this time discipline that can focus the liquidity and price discovery free-for-all. In a continuous market without this discipline, thousands if not tens of thousands of natural matches fail to find each other every day, and true consensus price discovery is frittered away by subsecond order executions.

That said, there are some particular areas where call markets add a distinct and unique advantage to the execution process. Let's consider this further with respect to liquidity creation, benchmark prices, price discovery, and the inclusion of a diverse set of market participants.

CALL MARKETS AND LIQUIDITY

Liquidity in a call has characteristics that make it highly unique. Whether in a cross or an auction, liquidity builds over a short period of time. Nothing is traded until the call is executed, so the bookbuilding phase of a call is extremely unique and dynamic.

In an opaque benchmark cross (identified in this chapter as type 3, a crossing network), liquidity is submitted into a central database (black box) where it waits for the match to execute. Since the building process in a cross is opaque, participants do not know who or what is in the cross. This level of opacity greatly reduces if not outright eliminates market impact and information leakage. As a result, it significantly increases the order size and thus the trade size in a cross.

While order and participant opacity is not the sole domain of a benchmark cross (continuous trading systems also successfully reduce market impact and information leakage by leveraging opacity), opacity in a cross literally takes liquidity to a higher level. As we see, opacity fuels larger order sizes, but when participating in a cross, time further links same-side orders together at the moment of execution, thereby enhancing liquidity for contra-side orders. This time-link of order flow can supercharge block executions that can rival a stock's average daily trading volume—all in the blink of an eye!

Liquidity is transparent in most auctions, as volume is aggregated at a price level. In a call auction, though, the bookbuilding phase adds a dynamic process that permits liquidity to aggregate and price discovery to evolve. As the bookbuilding phase of an auction matures, pooling liquidity can attract same-side and contra-side order flow. As the pool of liquidity grows, in a virtuous circle, larger and more competitive block liquidity is in turn attracted.

CALL MARKETS, BENCHMARK PRICES, AND PRICE DISCOVERY

Execution prices in a cross or in a price discovery call auction (the latter is identified in this chapter as type 4, an open limit order book auction) both find a consensus price, but in different ways. In a benchmark cross, a price benchmark—like midpoint of the national best bid and offer (NBBO), VWAP, or last sale—is selected prior to the cross and is applied to the executions once the cross is executed. No price negotiation is permitted. It is interesting to note that while a benchmark cross does not discover a price, hundreds of millions of shares are available for midpoint NBBO benchmark crosses every day, while the continuous market maintains spreads that usually have little volume showing on the bid or the offer. With regard to a price discovery call (type 4), a price is set which maximizes the number of shares that will trade.

One of the strongest attributes of a call auction is its time-disciplined approach to price discovery. There are two critical aspects to the call auction—the bookbuilding phase and the auction algorithm. Both give a call auction a dynamic that is absent in the continuous market. As already discussed, the bookbuilding phase enables liquidity to evolve and grow over a period of time. This is also true for the price discovery process. From the moment an auction begins, there is a critical interplay of market participants who compete for their positions in the book. Each bid and offer that has been entered is firm and cannot be deleted or made less aggressive; a price can only be increased for bids or reduced for offers.

As they compete, both bid side and offer side prices tighten until the spread is ultimately eliminated. This delivers a price at which a set of both the buyers and sellers agree (in continuous trading, this is called a locked market)—but this is only beginning, since an auction does not execute until the end of the bookbuilding phase.

Upon reaching an initial auction price, there is the unique opportunity for the bid side and the offer side to overlap (in continuous trading, this is a crossed market). Both buyers and sellers will continue to compete as liquidity builds, and they will be willing to pay more (or receive less) in order to get a block done. The more aggressive they are, the more additional liquidity will be attracted, and so on, until the end of the bookbuilding phase.

Once the scheduled time for the bookbuilding phase ends (let's say after 15 minutes), the auction book is frozen and the price at which the maximum number of shares will execute determines the single auction price. The more participants there are in the auction, the more closely will the call's clearing price be aligned with a true consensus price.

CALL MARKETS AND THE INCLUSION OF MARKET PARTICIPANTS

The key to an effective call is participation. The basic design of a call does not preclude anyone. A call's environment is conducive to any type of market participant—an institution or retail customer, an investor following an active or a passive trading strategy, a technical or fundamental investor, a hedge fund, and a market functionary or liquidity seeker. All of these are welcome.

In a type 3 opaque benchmark cross, broad participation greatly increases the chance that there will be matching tension in the cross. In a type 4 open book auction, broad participation better insures an accurate and competitive price discovery process. In either type of call, it is clearly important that broad participation means more than just many participants. Broad participation refers also to the *diversity* of investment and trading strategies that help to create the tension in a call. A call with only index fund participants trading adds and deletes from their index will be one-sided, as all clients will be selling the same stocks or buying the same stocks at the same time. So an effective call requires a diverse set of participants with diverging investment strategies and trading goals.

Passive trading strategies driven by participants such as plan sponsors, investment managers, transition managers, and even some global broker/dealer portfolio trading desks, tend to be list-based. They generally want a benchmark price, trading constraints, and the low transaction costs of a cross. Active trading strategies driven by participants such as hedge funds, sector funds, growth and value funds, market timing strategies, market makers, and specialists, tend to be stock specific. They want the transparency and dynamic price discovery process of an auction.

But by no means are the participants in a cross or auction limited to one or the other call. Passive traders frequently participate and benefit from the price discovery process by submitting orders with limits or conditions on them. Similarly, active trading strategies can leverage FIX-based technology to interact quickly and seamlessly with the block liquidity and illiquid issues available in a cross.

Without a doubt, call markets are an effective way to address many of the problems that arise from a frenetic continuous order-driven market. As the market participants have grown more efficient, so, too, must our marketplace embrace new and efficient market concepts. As this chapter clearly shows, first in Europe and now increasingly in the United States, markets have been moving to incorporate fully electronic, call market trading—and it is about *time*!

EXERCISES

1. Consider block pricing, an alternative to the walk-the-book pricing algorithm that is implemented in TraderEx. In block pricing, an arriving market order that has a size larger than the available quantity at the bid or offer will trade at one block price determined by the final limit order. If the best offer to sell is $11.20 and is good for 10 at $11.20, and there are 50 more offered at $11.30, then a market order for 11 to 60 units will trade in its entirety at $11.30.
   - Which do you feel is a fairer approach to setting trade prices in an order book system, block pricing, or walk-the-book pricing?
   - What types of traders benefit from the block pricing approach? Who is disadvantaged?
   - Would you operate differently in a block pricing market?
2. Run TraderEx in the Order-Driven/Buy-Side mode until 12 noon. Then, with the same scenario number, run the Hybrid/Buy-Side mode until 12 noon.
   - How did the 9:30 and 11:50 call auctions influence your trading and performance?
   - Would your call auction orders have changed if the call was 'The Only Game in Town'?
3. In Exhibit 4.7b, how much *larger* could your buy order be before it moves the auction price up to 11.50?
   (A: You can increase it by 108 to 128. Larger than that will move the price up.)
4. In Exhibit 4.7b, what is the largest *sell* order that a trader can enter priced at 11 without moving the price down to 11.30?
   (A: 54.)

APPENDIX TO CHAPTER 4

Further Details on Clearing Price Determination

We have stated that, in a call auction, prices and transaction volumes are set by the intersection of the cumulated bid and offer curves. If these two curves were continuous, they would, with few exceptions, lead to a clearly defined price and trading volume. In actual markets, however, cumulative bid and offer curves are not smooth but are step functions. This is because price and quantity are both discrete variables (there is a minimum price variation, and shares are normally traded in board lots). Additionally, orders tend to cluster at round integers (for instance, there are more orders with a limit of $27 than of $26.97 or $27.02).

With step functions, additional criteria are needed to set prices at the auctions. Time priority is one rule to determine exactly which orders execute if the cumulated buys and sells are not equal at the selected price. So far, so good. But step functions can lead to another problem: Two or more prices can be tied according to the primary criterion, the maximization of trading volume. What happens then?

Exhibits 4.A1 through 4.A4 illustrate the most common criteria for setting prices. The exhibits show the accumulated orders on the book, starting with market orders and then proceeding from the most aggressively priced limit orders to the least aggressively priced limit orders. As we have seen, this means that buy orders are cumulated in a descending order, and that sell orders are cumulated in an ascending order. In Exhibit 4.A1, the maximization of turnover leads to an unambiguous transaction point: 3,000 shares to buy and 3,000 shares to sell execute at $99. At $98.75 only 2,500 shares could be traded because of the available sell orders; at $99.25 the buy orders would be the limiting factor and only 2,100 shares would trade. Additional criteria are needed if two or more prices satisfy the maximization of turnover criterion.

One possible criterion (after the maximization of turnover) is the minimization of the number of unexecuted orders at the clearing price. Look at Exhibit 4.A2. Two prices, $99.00 and $98.75, lead to a trading volume of 3,000 shares. By setting a price of $99.00 a surplus of only 500 (on the sell

EXHIBIT 4.A1 Setting the Price: The Maximization of Turnover Criterion

Buy Orders, Number of Shares				Sell Orders, Number of Shares		
	Accumulated				Accumulated	
Individual	At the Price	From Highest Price	Price (Limit)	From Lowest Price	At the Price	Individual
400 + 300	700	700	Market			
....	....	....	> 100			
200	200	900	100			
300	300	1,200	99.75			
400	400	1,600	99.50	4,200	500	200 + 300
200 + 300	500	2,100	99.25	3,700	700	700
800 + 100	900	▼3,000	99.00	▲3,000	500	500
1,000	1,000	4,000	98.75	2,500	300	100 + 200
700 + 200	900	4,900	98.50	2,200	300	300
			98.25	1,900	300	100 + 200
			98.00	1,600	100	100
			< 98	....	....	....
			Market	1,000	1,500	700 + 800

side) remains; with a price of $98.75 a surplus of 1,000 shares would remain on the buy side.

If there are two or more prices that satisfy the first and second criteria, the criterion of market pressure can be applied. As can be seen in Exhibit 4.A3, two prices, $98.75 and 99.00, produce both a maximum trading volume of 3,000 shares and a minimum surplus of 1,000 shares. For both prices, the surplus is on the buy side, which drives prices up; the highest price in the set of alternative solutions, 99.00 in the example, is chosen to be the market price. If the surplus were on the sell side, the lowest in the set would be chosen.

Finally, it is possible (albeit highly unlikely) for two prices to yield the same maximum turnover, with equal surpluses, with one being on the buy side and the other being on the sell side, as is shown in Exhibit 4.A4. In this case, the price that is closest to the most recent price (typically referred to as the reference price) is selected—$99.00 rather than $98.75 in this example, because $99.00 is closer to the previous price of $99.50.

In very special situations, these four criteria may be insufficient. Additional rules are needed if too much time has past since the last reference price was set and if, in the meantime, prices in the broad market have moved to a different level.

EXHIBIT 4.A2 Setting the Price: The Smallest Surplus Criterion

Buy Orders, Number of Shares					Sell Orders, Number of Shares		
	Accumulated				Accumulated		
Separate	Per Price	From Highest Price	Price (Limit)		From Lowest Price	Per Price	Separate
400 + 300	700	700	Market				
....	....	....	> 100				
200	200	900	100				
300	300	1,200	99.75		4,700	500	200 + 300
400	400	1,600	99.50		4,200	700	700
200 + 300	500	2,100	99.25		3,500	500	500
800 + 100	900	3,000	99.00		3,000	800	100 + 700
1,000	1,000	4,000	98.75		2,200	300	300
700 + 200	900	4,900	98.50		1,900	300	100 + 200
			98.25		1,600	100	100
			98.00		....	....	....
			< 98				
			Market		1,500	1,500	700 + 800

Buy side — Surplus → 1000

Sell side — Surplus → 500

213

EXHIBIT 4.A3 Setting the Price: The Market Pressure Criterion

| | Buy Orders, Number of Shares | | | | Sell Orders, Number of Shares | | |
| | | Accumulated | | Price (Limit) | Accumulated | | |
	Separate	Per Price	From Highest Price		From Lowest Price	Per Price	Separate
	400 + 300	700	700	Market			
	....	....	....	> 100			
	200	200	900	100			
	300	300	1,200	99.75			
	400	400	1,600	99.50	4,200	500	200 + 300
	200 + 300	500	2,100	99.25	3,700	700	700
Surplus → 1000	800 + 1,100	1,900	4,000	99.00	3,000	0	0
1000	0	0	4,000	98.75	3,000	300	100 + 200
	700 + 200	900	4,900	98.50	2,700	800	800
				98.25	1,900	300	100 + 200
				98.00	1,600	100	100
				< 98	....		....
				Market	1,500	1,500	700 + 800

EXHIBIT 4.A4 Setting the Price: The Most Recent Price Criterion

Buy Orders, Number of Shares				Sell Orders, Number of Shares		
	Accumulated				Accumulated	
Separate	Per Price	From Highest Price	Price (limit)	From Lowest Price	Per Price	Separate
400 + 300	700	700	Market			
....	....	....	> 100			
200	200	900	100			
300	300	1,200	99.75			
400	400	1,600	99.50*	4,700	500	200 + 300
200 + 300	500	2,100	99.25	4,200	700	700
800 + 100	900	3,000	99.00	3,500	500	500
500	500	3,500	98.75	3,000	800	100 + 700
700 + 200	900	4,400	98.50	2,200	300	300
			98.25	1,900	300	100 + 200
			98.00	1,600	100	100
			< 98	....	....	....
			Market	1,500	1,500	700 + 800

Surplus → 500 (buy side)

Surplus → 500 (sell side)

*previous price

215

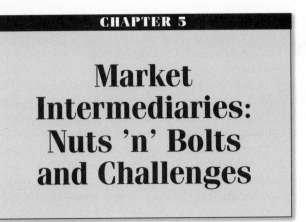

CHAPTER 5

Market Intermediaries: Nuts 'n' Bolts and Challenges

In the previous two chapters, we showed how public investors—the naturals—can meet in a pure, nonintermediated market, provide liquidity to one another, set prices, and trade. We now turn to the role of intermediaries. *Intermediation* means the participation of a third party in trading. Intermediaries fit into the value chain between the investor as the final owner of the securities, and the stock market as the price discoverer and exchange operator. Intermediaries include brokers, dealers, market makers, and specialists.

We explain how the various roles of intermediaries shape market structure decisions and have a bearing on trading decisions and outcomes. We also show how market rules and transparency affect dealers' profits. In this chapter, we view the term *intermediary* broadly, to cover the computerized intermediation functions of the market centers themselves, electronic brokers, and order routing systems. For the most part, however, when we refer to intermediaries, we have in mind the human agents involved in trading: brokers and market makers.

A *broker* handles customer orders as an agent, routing an order into the order book of an exchange or to a designated dealer intermediary. The broker may be bound by fiduciary obligations to ensure that customers receive favorable treatment in the market and obtain fair prices. In markets with *dealer* intermediaries, the dealers create value by committing capital to trade beyond the sizes that are available in the order book, or to improve on the displayed quotes in certain circumstances. Exchanges often place special obligations on intermediaries to make good, orderly markets by buying and selling from their own inventories, trading in a stabilizing manner against public orders, and taking the corresponding position risk. Currently, dealers in the equity markets are widely referred to as *market makers*. We use the two terms interchangeably.

On U.S. exchanges, a *specialist* is a designated intermediary who operates as both a broker (agent) and dealer (market maker). Each stock listed on the NYSE is assigned to one specialist firm that has an *affirmative obligation* to make a fair and orderly market for that stock. The London Stock Exchange's SETSmm system, launched in 2003, is a central order book that includes registered market makers who supplement the order book liquidity by posting continuous two-way prices. The average SETSmm security has 10 market makers providing "committed principal orders." It handles stocks that are not in the blue-chip FTSE 100 index. FTSE 100 stocks have traded in the SETS order book market since 1997.

Brokers, dealers, market makers, and specialists, along with exchanges and other trading systems, supply services to investors who are seeking to buy or to sell shares for their own investment reasons. The suppliers of trading services are referred to as the *sell-side*. Customers who require trading services (the investors) are referred to as the *buy-side* (they buy trading services). Large institutional investors (e.g., mutual and pension funds) have their own buy-side trading desks that interact with the sell-side desks.

The major U.S. equity markets include two national stock exchanges, the New York Stock Exchange (NYSE) and American Stock Exchange (AMEX); the NASDAQ Stock Market; five regional stock exchanges;[1] and several exchange-like organizations known as Alternative Trading Systems (ATSs) and Electronic Communications Networks (ECNs). The two powerhouse markets in the United States are the NYSE and the NASDAQ Stock Market. The NYSE traded 1.6 billion shares daily in 2005, and its listed domestic stocks had a market capitalization of $13.3 trillion at the end of 2005. NASDAQ traded 1.8 billion shares daily in 2005 and had a capitalization of $3.6 trillion at year-end 2005.

EMERGENCE OF THE MODERN MARKETS

The NYSE had its origins in the Buttonwood Agreement of 1792 and the adoption of a constitution and a name, New York Stock & Exchange Board, in 1817. The Buttonwood Agreement was so called in honor of a tree on Wall Street under which 24 brokers signed an agreement to impose "off-board" trading restrictions on each other and to establish minimum fixed commissions of 0.25 percent. Harking back to its previous name, the NYSE is often referred to as the "Big Board." It established its current name, the New York Stock Exchange, in 1863,[2] and will acquire its new name—the NYSE Group—in 2006.

NASDAQ started operations in 1971. A product of the *over-the-counter* (OTC) dealer market, NASDAQ is run under the regulatory umbrella of the National Association of Securities Dealers (NASD—NASDAQ stands for NASD Automated Quotations); the NASD was the parent of NASDAQ until the two organizations separated in 2002. The OTC market originated in an era when stocks were bought and sold in banks and the physical certificates were passed "over the counter." Initially, NASDAQ was not a market, but simply an aggregator and disseminator of dealer quotes, and it became known as a dealer-intermediated or *quote-driven* market. The quotes of the intermediaries establish the prices at which the naturals (investors) can trade by market order. In a pure quote-driven environment, market makers are the only source of the quotes.

NASDAQ's striking success as a system resulted in its name being applied to the market that it helped to create. Prior to the success of NASDAQ, the natural progression for a U.S. company as it grew from a small start-up to a major firm with national prominence was first to issue stock and trade in the OTC market, then to list on the AMEX, and finally to transfer its listing and become an NYSE-listed firm. This changed as NASDAQ first eclipsed the AMEX and then challenged the NYSE by retaining many of its premier listings such as Microsoft, Intel, and Cisco as they grew.

In recent years, NASDAQ has substantially reengineered its market. Robert Greifeld's contributed piece in this chapter summarizes major developments that have transformed the competitive dealer market into a modern hybrid that offers, in the words of Greifeld, "solid order-driven components [that] are now operating effectively, side by side with our NASDAQ market makers." He also underscores the important role that the competitive NASDAQ Market Makers continue to play in NASDAQ's hybrid market:

> *The NASDAQ market model is about competition. We recognize the value of intermediaries, the NASDAQ market makers, in this context. We have over 400 total participants including more than 250 market makers in the NASDAQ stock market. They play a vital role. We need them for the liquidity they provide. We need them for what they bring to price discovery. We need them for the stability that they offer the mid and small cap segments of our market and all of our listed stocks during stressful conditions.*

From the 1970s until the SEC's Order Handling Rules went into effect in 1997, the NYSE and NASDAQ gave companies a distinct choice between listing on a primarily order-driven, agency-auction market, or on a competitive dealer market. The two market structures remain different, but NASDAQ is no longer a predominantly quote-driven environment.

While the NYSE refers to its market as an agency-auction market, it has always had a dealer component through its specialists and member firms with "upstairs" market making desks. The NYSE's acquisition of Archipelago, expected to be completed by early 2006, will provide the Big Board with its first all-electronic order-driven element.

NASDAQ evolved into a hybrid quote-driven and order-driven market following the introduction in 1997 of new Order Handling Rules that were set forth by the U.S. Securities and Exchange Commission in response to artificially wide bid-ask spreads and noncompetitive dealer quote setting, brought to light by academicians Bill Christie and Paul Schultz in 1994.[3] The SEC's new rules required, for the first time, that orders from public traders be properly represented in the NASDAQ quote montage. NASDAQ's transformation into a hybrid had been reinforced by the growth of ATSs and ECNs, and we detail their operations shortly. There is now wide acceptance that these order-driven trading platforms are indeed part of the broader NASDAQ marketplace. One of these, BRUT ECN, was acquired by NASDAQ in September 2004, and a second major one, Instinet, is currently in the process of being acquired by NASDAQ.

Across the Atlantic, new trading platforms have been introduced across the board from Sweden to Spain and beyond. The London Stock Exchange, like NASDAQ, reengineered itself from a competitive dealer market into a hybrid built around an electronic order-driven platform (SETS). In Germany, Deutsche Börse's Xetra® platform, which was rolled out in 1997, is a far less intermediated venue than its predecessor, the Frankfurt Stock Exchange's trading floor (which, though much diminished, still exists). Nevertheless, market making has remained important for all of these markets, as the contributed piece in this chapter by SWX Swiss Exchange–based Frank Romanelli makes perfectly clear. Along with reviewing several types of market making functionaries, Romanelli stresses that "market making can play an important role in a nation's capital market by providing liquidity and enhancing investor confidence."

Deutsche Börse's Martin Reck directly addresses the need for special order handling for large orders in his contributed piece to this chapter. As Reck puts it, "[H]ighly transparent, electronic limit order platforms are excellent facilities for handling small, retail orders for high liquidity stocks. Dealing with large orders, even for liquid shares, is another matter entirely." With regard to large orders, Reck considers the possibility of substituting electronic "intermediation" for human intermediaries. Along with briefly reviewing the electronic platforms currently available, he describes a new order type that Deutsche Börse is currently working on for Xetra—a *volume order*—designed to enable an efficient integration of institutional-size orders with retail order flow.

In recent years, the combined forces of technology, competition, and regulation have accelerated the pace of change in market structures globally, and the pace shows no signs of slackening in the foreseeable future. Facing new rivalries, competitive pressures, and the demands of increasingly sophisticated buy-side traders, NASDAQ and the NYSE in the United States, and major market centers in Europe including Deutsche Börse, Euronext, and the London Stock Exchange, are developing what they believe to be optimal trading structures for the future. While there are few certainties to rely on, we can suggest one: Intermediation and human intermediaries will remain important for all market centers.

INTERMEDIATION ON THE NYSE

The NYSE is a hybrid market where orders for the purchase and sale of listed securities are centralized at specialists' posts on the trading floor. At the posts, the orders interact in a predominantly auction environment. The major players who operate on the NYSE's trading floor are specialists, house brokers (sometimes referred to as *commission house brokers*) and independent, direct access brokers, who once went by the colorful name *two-dollar brokers* in reference to the commission they previously charged per round lot of 100 shares. They charge far less today.

Specialists

Specialists are the most prominent intermediaries at the NYSE. As of January 2006, there are seven specialist units (down from 38 in 1997), with the two largest covering stocks that make up 49 percent of the NYSE's trading volume. In 2005, specialist principal trading accounted for about 17.6 percent of NYSE volume. As brokers, specialists match public orders that they have received with other public orders, and with the orders of other professional traders from NYSE member firms. As dealers, specialists take the other side of the trades themselves, thereby providing immediate liquidity. They also act as auctioneers, overseeing the "crowd" of floor brokers at their posts, and they "represent" orders in the limit order book. Precise NYSE rules determine who gets to trade, in what sequence, and when a specialist should and should not step in as a dealer.

NYSE-listed securities are also traded on other U.S. exchanges, in the NASDAQ market, in the upstairs broker-dealer market, and overseas under different trading rules. In spite of its rivals, price discovery generally occurs at the NYSE, and many traders prefer to have their orders routed to the Big Board. In 2005, 77 percent of the share volume for NYSE-listed issues took place on the NYSE.

Each NYSE-listed stock is assigned to one specialist firm, and all orders for a stock that are sent to the NYSE converge at the specialist post to which that stock is assigned. A specialist is bound by certain responsibilities and restrictions with regard to a listed corporation and his own trades. When trading is heavy, floor traders pack in about the post and the specialist conducts an auction. As auctioneer, the specialist is responsible for (1) ensuring that orders are handled in conformity with acceptable auction practice, and (2) determining the orders that have priority (i.e., who gets a trade).

NYSE Rule 104 is the main rule governing specialists' operations. Rule 104 says that "the function of a specialist, in addition to the effective execution of commission orders entrusted to him, is the maintenance . . . of a fair and orderly market . . . which . . . implies the maintenance of price continuity with reasonable depth, and the minimizing of the effects of temporary disparity between supply and demand." With regard to a listed company, a specialist:

- Must make at least one annual contact with an official of the corporation.
- May not be an officer or a director of the corporation.
- May not accept orders directly from officers, directors, principal stockholders of the corporation, or from the corporation itself.
- May not participate (neither the specialist nor anyone associated with the specialist—for example, a partner or clerk) in a proxy contest or in a contest for a change of management of the corporation.

With regard to his or her own trades as a market maker, a specialist:

- Cannot buy for his or her own account while holding unexecuted market orders to buy, and cannot sell for his or her own account while holding unexecuted market orders to sell, and must always give priority to equally priced limit orders. This is known as the specialist's *negative obligation* (i.e., the specialist is not allowed to trade ahead of a public order at the same price at which the public order would execute).
- May not charge a brokerage commission and be a dealer in the same trade.
- Cannot trade with an order that he or she is holding on the order book without the permission of a floor official.
- May not solicit orders in stock in which he or she specializes.
- May not accept orders from an institution, or deal directly with an institutional investor.
- Is restricted in his or her freedom to buy shares at a price higher than the last transaction price (on an uptick) or to sell shares at a price lower than the last transaction price (on a down tick). This "tick-test rule" prevents the specialist from accentuating a market imbalance.

The principal rule the specialist must observe is *affirmative obligation*, which is described in NYSE Rule 104.10(b):

> *In connection with the maintenance of a fair and orderly market, it is commonly desirable that a member acting as specialist engage to a reasonable degree under existing circumstances, in dealing for his or her own account when lack of price continuity, lack of depth, or disparity between supply and demand exists or is reasonably to be anticipated.*

Specialist operations are particularly critical at the start of each trading day. The NYSE opening bell rings at 9:30 A.M., but the market for an individual stock does not open until the specialist finds a price that balances the buy and sell orders that have entered the book for the stock. Specialists do this by matching market orders that have come in through the electronic order entry system; public limit orders and eligible market orders that come into their electronic display books; and orders from the trading crowd. This special opening is a form of call auction trading (a procedure discussed in Chapter 4).

At the opening call, a specialist establishes a price that he believes best balances the accumulated buy and sell pressures (i.e., that best reflects the market's aggregate desire to hold shares of the stock). However, the specialist may choose not to open a stock at the price that a call auction algorithm would set (namely, the price that would maximize trading volume based on public orders only). In setting the opening price, specialists will often commit their own capital by buying for or selling from their own accounts so as to balance all orders, including their own.

A specialist can request to delay an opening because of overnight news or a large imbalance between buy and sell volumes at prices close to the previous close. When the opening is delayed, the specialist sends out one or more indications of the range that the opening price will most likely be in. He is required to wait at least 10 minutes to allow orders to arrive in response to the indication, as detailed in NYSE Rule 123. When an acceptable price is found, the market for the stock is opened and trading begins.

This process can be simulated using the TraderEx software. TraderEx has a "Liquidity Provider" mode that is loosely modeled on specialist operations. Enter "Liquidity Provider" mode, and set "Initial Price" at 32.50 and "Scenario Number" at 3. We will open the stock as the specialist.

Two preopening screens are shown in Exhibits 5.1 and 5.2. Prior to opening the stock at 9:31 (Exhibit 5.1), the specialist sees orders that arrived overnight, and an indicative opening price of 32.00. After four minutes, the screen suggests an opening price of 31.80, which has an imbalance of 8 units on the buying side (see Exhibit 5.2). The specialist

TraderEx		
DAY	**TIME**	**SEED**
1	9:31:00	3

TICKER	PRICE	
	QTY	
	TIME	

MARKET	indicative	32.00
CALL	imbalance	-10

BIDS	OFFERS	
48	32.90	134
48	32.80	103
63	32.70	103
63	32.60	103
63	32.50	103
68	32.40	85
78	32.30	85
78	32.20	85
78	32.10	85
95	32.00	85
108	31.90	85
140	31.80	85
194	31.70	85
194	31.60	54
194	31.50	27
215	31.40	27
215	31.30	27
231	31.20	27
284	31.10	
314	31.00	

EXHIBIT 5.1   Exercise: Pre-Opening Screen of Liquidity Provider

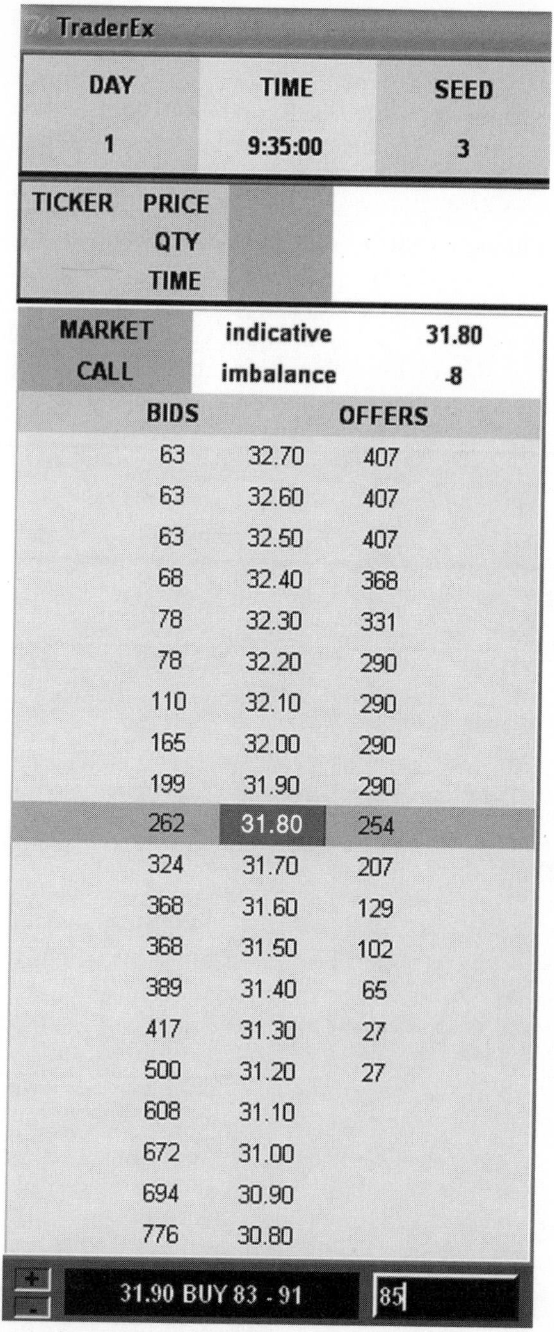

TraderEx		
DAY	**TIME**	**SEED**
1	9:35:00	3

TICKER	PRICE	
	QTY	
	TIME	

MARKET	indicative	31.80
CALL	imbalance	-8

BIDS		OFFERS
63	32.70	407
63	32.60	407
63	32.50	407
68	32.40	368
78	32.30	331
78	32.20	290
110	32.10	290
165	32.00	290
199	31.90	290
262	31.80	254
324	31.70	207
368	31.60	129
368	31.50	102
389	31.40	65
417	31.30	27
500	31.20	27
608	31.10	
672	31.00	
694	30.90	
776	30.80	

| + | 31.90 BUY 83 - 91 | 85 |
| - | | |

EXHIBIT 5.2 Pre-Opening Screen after Four Minutes

would often sell the additional 8 units to fill all of the orders at 31.80 and open the stock with 262 units trading at 31.80.

Click on the "+" button at the bottom left of the order book to increase the opening price to 31.90. To open the stock higher at 31.90, the specialist is encouraged by the system to buy at least 83 units so that the imbalance at the opening price is no more than the minimum imbalance of 8 at 31.80. The specialist is not supposed to open the stock at a price unless his participation reduces the imbalance from its minimum level, which in this illustration is 8.

As the specialist, participate in the opening trade at 31.90 by buying 85 units. The opening trade of 284 units at 31.90 leaves an imbalancen of 6—that is, 6 of the 290 units for sale at 31.90 are unfilled. The 6 units remain offered at 31.90 once continuous trading begins (see Exhibit 5.3). You are

TraderEx							
DAY	TIME	SEED	TRDS	INDEX	VOL	HI	
1	9:37	3	10	319	284	31.90	

TICKER	PRICE	31.90
	QTY	284
	TIME	9:35

QUOTE	31.80		31.90	#	TIME		SHARES	TYPE	PRICE
	32		6	1	9:35	BUY	85	LT	31.90
BIDS		OFFERS							
	32.70								
	32.60								
	32.50	18							
	32.40								
	32.30								
	32.20	25	25						
	32.10								
	32.00								
	31.90	6							
32	31.80								
54	31.70								
25	25	31.60				TOTAL	85		31.90
	31.50				[9:37] Market Order to BUY 6				
21	31.40				[9:35] 284 units traded at call price of 31.9				
28	31.30				[9:35] Call Price 31.80				
34	31.20								
53	31.10								
30	31.00								
22	30.90								
	30.80								

+>　GO　LIVE　>　>>　>>>　QUIT

EXHIBIT 5.3　Liquidity Provider Buys 85 Units to Minimize Imbalance

now long 85 units and will be hoping to sell them for more than 31.90 in order to earn a dealing profit.

To continue the exercise, beginning from the 9:36 screen with the +85 position and the settings from Exhibit 5.3, continue to play the simulation until you have worked off the 85-unit position. Take note of two things here:

1. Your quotes are initially 31.60 bid and 32.20 offered, and are good for up to 25 units. They can be adjusted like limit orders but will not be reduced in size when you trade.

2. When the specialist's quote and a limit order are at the same price, the NYSE "public order priority" rule means that the limit orders at a given price must be filled before the specialist can trade from his own position at that price.

There are several different ways specialists affect prices:

- Specialists dampen the short-run volatility of prices, but they do not peg prices. If the underlying pressure exists for a price to increase or decrease to a new level, the price goes to the new level. Specialist intervention is intended only to dampen swings that occur either because of thinness on one side of the market or as a result of the difficulties of price discovery. Fair and orderly prices are valued because they give participants more assurance that prices will not jump erratically as orders are being received and turned into trades.

- At times, the specialist is not expected to keep price changes within normal limits. When sizable price movements occur because of major stock-specific news, the market may not be able to find a new price and handle trades efficiently at the same time. Under this condition, the specialist may, with the permission of a floor official, *halt trading*. During a stock-specific trading halt, the specialist has time to assess market conditions, and traders have time to digest the news and revise their orders.

- The extreme volatility during October 1987, and especially the precipitous decline on October 19, 1987, demonstrated that the liquidity that specialists can provide to a market under stress is limited, and that trading halts for specific issues may not arrest a broad decline or a fundamental market trend. It is of utmost importance for a specialist to be able to distinguish a technical price change from a price change generated by news. If it is technical, he or she should intervene. If it is fundamental, other measurements must be taken into consideration. A specialist firm does not have an obligation to put itself out of business.

- During the 1987 crash, specialist capital proved inadequate relative to the enormous selling pressure from institutional and retail traders. The NYSE's criteria for a fair and orderly market were unsupportable when the market dropped 508 points, or 22.6 percent in a single day. Following the crash, the NYSE introduced marketwide trading halts referred to as *circuit breakers* in the hope of containing excessive volatility in the broad market. The halts are triggered when the Dow Jones Industrial Average moves up or down, 10 percent, 20 percent, or 30 percent in a specified time period.
- A specialist may also *stop a stock* (that is, guarantee an execution at a *stop price*). The request to stop a stock may be initiated at a floor broker's request for a public trader. If the specialist succeeds in finding a better price, the stop is off. Once an order is executed in the crowd at the guaranteed price, the specialist must execute the stopped order and inform the floor broker that the stop has been *elected*.

Other NYSE Intermediaries

Specialists are not the only intermediaries operating on the floor. They are joined by house brokers, direct access brokers, and technology that plays the role of an electronic intermediary.

House Brokers   Employed by the brokerage houses, these floor brokers are a link between the brokerage houses and the specialist posts. The house brokers receive orders from their firms' clients and "expose" them to the trading crowds (i.e., each order is brought to the specific post where that stock is traded). The broker will then either leave the order on the book, execute with the specialist or with another broker, or cross the trade. A cross trade occurs when the broker has both a buy and a sell order for the same stock. All floor trades must be reported to and approved by the specialist.

Direct Access Brokers   These independent brokers perform the same functions as the house brokers, but they are not employed by a brokerage house. Rather, the direct access brokers are independent firms that execute orders for their own customers (predominantly institutional customers). Minimal intermediation is involved when a buy-side customer electronically sends his order to a direct access broker, and disclosure of the institution behind the order and its trading interest can be avoided.

Technology   A number of systems have enabled the NYSE to expand its capacity and to operate faster. In 1976, the NYSE instituted its Designated Order Turnaround (DOT) system that brokers use to route orders directly to specialists' posts on the trading floor. The DOT system has been upgraded significantly, and the improved electronic order routing system became known as SuperDOT in 1984. Until 1986, DOT orders arriving at a specialist post caused a ticket to print out that was then completed when the order executed. Ticket printers were replaced by the Display Book, an electronic workstation that displays all limit orders and incoming market orders to the specialist. Currently, over 90 percent of the orders that execute at the NYSE are delivered by SuperDot.

The NYSE made its first effort to automate floor broker functions in 1993 with the Broker Booth Support System (BBSS), an order management system that is customized to the needs of floor brokers. The wireless e-Broker system was rolled out in 1997 to link off-floor computer desktops to floor brokers' wireless handheld devices. The e-Broker devices account for about 30 percent of NYSE volume, and allow brokers to receive orders, access market information, and transmit execution reports from any location on the trading floor. The choice of routing an order electronically or using a floor broker is discussed later in the chapter.

Launched in 2000, Direct+ is an automatic execution system for orders up to 1,099 shares at the best bid or offer with anonymity and no floor broker fees. The system is an ECN-like direct execution system that bypasses the floor broker and the specialist, and has an average execution time of 0.4 seconds. It handled about 10 percent of NYSE volume in the first half of 2005. As noted earlier, the Exchange is currently finalizing plans for its Hybrid Market, which is intended to provide more execution choices to NYSE users, as described by John Thain in his contributed piece in Chapter 2. The new facilities will also eliminate three current restrictions on Direct+ use: the 30-second minimum gap between consecutive orders, a 1,099-share size cap for orders, and the addition of market orders to limit orders as those eligible to trade via NYSE Direct+. Customers can opt to have their orders automatically executed via Direct+, or, if they want the opportunity for price improvement, can use floor brokers and their expertise in handling orders. In the new Hybrid Market, specialists and brokers will interact with orders electronically as well as in person. Human judgment is expected to be particularly valuable in less-liquid stocks, and during the opening and closing of trading as well as during times of uncertainty, such as when an earnings surprise or an outside event leads to market instability and price dislocation.

INTERMEDIATION AT NASDAQ

Historically, NASDAQ has been a decentralized, electronically connected market comprising geographically dispersed, competitive dealer and member firms linked together by telephones, electronic systems, and computer screens. The philosophy behind the NASDAQ dealer market has historically been different from that which characterizes the NYSE. Rules of order handling and trade execution have been simpler, and competitive forces have been relied on more than explicit regulation to promote liquid, fair, and orderly markets.

NASDAQ's roots lie in the National Association of Securities Dealers (NASD). Headquartered in Washington, D.C., the NASD has primary responsibility for regulating brokers and dealers and, in this capacity, imposes a uniform set of rules for its members.[4] NASDAQ began operations in 1971 but was not designed as an order routing or execution facility. Rather, it simply displayed market maker quotes for NASDAQ issues on terminals in brokerage offices across the country. Prior to the NASDAQ system, the OTC market was linked by telephone lines among market making and other member firms. Quotes were disseminated on daily "pink sheets" that were printed and circulated every morning.

Against this background, the real-time, electronic NASDAQ system had a tremendous impact on the efficiency of the market. It integrated the dealers' quotes, caused spreads to tighten, and improved the quality of price discovery. With this success in hand, in 1982, the NASDAQ National Market (NM) was introduced. It had higher listing standards and, for the first time, the real-time reporting of last sale prices and volumes. NASDAQ/NM market makers are required to report transaction prices and sizes to the NASD within 90 seconds of a transaction's occurrence. Issues on the NASDAQ/NM list are the largest and most actively traded stocks.

To understand the operations of the NASDAQ market, one must appreciate the services provided by dealers, the costs the market makers incur, and the dynamic pricing and inventory policies that they employ (we discuss these later in the chapter). A quote-driven market, by its very nature, is a multidealer market that is physically fragmented across the various competitive market maker firms. Any firm can make a market for any given issue with only minimal barriers to entry. Between 3 and 50 dealers typically make a market in any one stock, with the more actively traded issues such as Cisco, Intel, and Microsoft attracting as many as 100 dealers.

NASDAQ market makers do not have unique franchises in the stocks they handle. Issues are not assigned to, but are selected by, the market maker firms. When a dealer firm is registered as a market maker for an issue, it must make a two-sided market by continuously posting both bid and offer quotations for the issue. Unlike NYSE specialists, NASDAQ market makers do not have a regulatory obligation to maintain a fair and orderly market. A dealer firm is also free to stop making a market for an issue whenever it so chooses although, if it does so, it is not allowed to resume market making in that issue for 20 business days.

In recent years, NASDAQ has been reengineered to include, along with its traditional dealer market, nondealer facilities: the NASDAQ Market Center, which was launched in 2002; the BRUT ECN, which was acquired in 2004; and the Opening and Closing Crosses, which were instituted in 2004. Today, limit orders and call auctions are playing a prominent role. Nevertheless, as the contributed piece by Robert Greifeld underscores, market makers continue to play a vital role in the NASDAQ marketplace.

Limit Orders in NASDAQ

Limit orders were not first introduced into the NASDAQ market by NASDAQ but by Instinet, which started operations in 1969 as the first electronic communications network. Instinet became a limit order facility for NASDAQ stocks. It was not referred to as an ECN, however, until the latter part of the 1990s when the SEC introduced the term during its investigations, which led to the 1997 Order Handling Rules. As its name (short for "Institutional Network") suggests, Instinet was designed to be a trading system for institutional investors. The system enables customers to meet and trade electronically in an anonymous, disintermediated environment. For years, Instinet was viewed by many as an alternative to (and competitor of) the traditional NASDAQ dealer market. However, its presence has turned the broader NASDAQ marketplace into a hybrid environment. This is a benefit to its large buy-side customers (the institutional traders) and thus to the issuers that NASDAQ wishes to retain.

With its order-driven electronic platform and limit order display for customers, Instinet looks very much like an exchange. However, the company has been registered with the SEC not as an exchange but as a broker-dealer firm, and then as an ECN. Instinet had long taken the position that it is nothing more than a broker-dealer—that it operates in the upstairs market much as does any other broker-dealer firm that puts trades together for large customers. The only real difference, according to Instinet, is that it does the job electronically. This view underscores the difficulty of differentiating an exchange market from a broker-dealer firm in today's environment of network screen-based trading. The SEC's term *electronic communications network* reflects the ambiguities. Instinet went from being the only ECN in 1995, to being one of a dozen in existence at the end of the period 1997 to 2000.

After struggling to attract sufficient liquidity as an institutions-only trading system, NASDAQ dealers were welcomed into Instinet in the early 1980s. Dealers were then able to use Instinet for their own trades and, while not identified by firms' names, they were revealed as dealers in the system. In 1987, Instinet was acquired by Reuters and, in 1989, dealer anonymity was introduced, such that no Instinet user would know, either before or after a trade, who the counterparty was or whether the counterparty was an institution or a dealer. With this change, order flow to Instinet surged. Instinet, in effect, became an interdealer broker (IDB) for NASDAQ market makers. We discuss interdealer trading later in this chapter. The company has also run an after-hours crossing, referred to as Instinet's crossing network. Their flagship system, however, has always been their continuous electronic market.

Faced with the loss of market share to ECNs and ATSs, and recognizing its own lack of order-driven trading, NASDAQ began to develop its present hybrid trading platform, the NASDAQ Market Center (formerly SuperMontage), in 1999. The system helped it compete with the ECNs and shifted the NASDAQ system from an electronic quote display service to a full-fledged electronic market. The new facilities have not been easy to build. Market Center is a complex system that took the better part of five years to design and to be given regulatory approval. By the time of its launch in 2002, it had cost $107 million to develop. In addition to ECNs and ATSs, Market Center today competes with an Alternative Display Facility (ADF) that is operated by the NASD.

The NASDAQ Market Center system allows market participants to enter quotes and orders at multiple prices, and displays aggregated interest at five different prices on both sides of the market (ranging down from the bid quote and up from the ask quote). The system offers full anonymity and price and time priority, allows market makers to *internalize* orders, includes *preferenced orders*, and allows market makers and ECNs to specify a *reserve size*. That is, market participants have an option not to display their full order sizes (e.g., they can enter *hidden* or *iceberg* orders). The advent of SuperMontage has gone a long way toward completing NASDAQ's transformation from a quote-driven market to a hybrid market that includes both quote- and order-driven features.

In spite of NASDAQ's new capabilities, the electronic alternative trading systems (including two large ECNs, Instinet and Archipelago) accounted for nearly half of trading in NASDAQ stocks in 2004. In April 2005, NASDAQ announced its agreement with Instinet to acquire INET, an entity formed from Instinet's institutional-focused ECN operations, and those of Island, a rival retail-oriented ECN that had been acquired by Instinet in 2002. On December 8, 2005, the venerable INET ECN formally became part of the NASDAQ corporate structure.

The NASDAQ Crosses

Alternative trading systems (ATSs) initially brought call auction features to the broader NASDAQ marketplace. Investment Technology Group's (ITG) Posit, which started operations in the turbulent, crash month of October

1987, operates an intraday crossing network. Like Intinet's after-hours cross, Posit matches customer buy and sell orders that meet or cross each other in price, based on a crossing price that has been established in the NYSE or NASDAQ market. These crossing networks have offered an attractive alternative to institutions that are willing to trade at a market price without their orders having any effect on what that price turns out to be, and they have had some success in teasing out quantity discovery. The two major drawbacks of the crossing networks are (1) their execution rates tend to be low, and (2) if they draw too much order flow away from the main market, they can, to their own detriment, undermine the quality of the very prices on which they are basing their trades. These limitations can be overcome in a call auction environment that includes price discovery.

NASDAQ introduced a major new facility in its market structure in March 2004 when it instituted Closing Cross, and again in November 2004 when it instituted Opening Cross. As noted in Chapter 4, the two NASDAQ crosses are open limit order book call auctions. These auctions have provided NASDAQ with good systems to sharpen price discovery and lower trading costs at two particularly critical times in its trading day: at the market open and at the close.

The ECNs and ATSs

The ECNs and ATSs, developed to enable trading away from NYSE and NASDAQ intermediaries, share several characteristics. They are for-profit, order-driven operations that can include intermediaries but are not primarily based on intermediaries. They honor strict price and time priorities. They offer speed, low commissions, anonymity, transparency, and customer control over their own orders. This new environment, however, is not without its drawbacks. The multiplicity of systems has fragmented the order flow, and competition between the different markets has reduced sell-side revenue, eroded profits, and impaired the provision of market maker capital. But perhaps the tide is turning. Among other acquisitions, the recent merger activity involving the NYSE (which is acquiring Archipelago) and NASDAQ (which has acquired INET) indicates that the markets are reconsolidating.

TraderEx has a hybrid mode that combines call auctions with a continuous order book market and designated market maker intermediaries. This hybrid market structure incorporates an opening cross and intraday call auctions with an integrated price-time priority order book and dealer quote display. While it is not an exact replication of the hybrid structures at the NYSE, NASDAQ, or London Stock Exchange, the TraderEx hybrid illustrates how market makers can supplement order book liquidity.

Exhibit 5.4 shows the hybrid market screen during continuous trading.

7₺ TraderEx				
DAY		**TIME**		**SEED**
1		**10:04**		**1**

TICKER	PRICE	44.70	44.70	44.70
	QTY	3	7	11
	TIME	10:04	10:03	9:56

QUOTE	**44.60**	**44.80**
	--	15

Hit	BIDS		OFFERS	Take
CAT	44.60	45.00		DOG
DOG	44.50	45.00		PLUM
PLUM	44.50	45.00		COD
COD	44.50	45.00		TUNA
TUNA	44.50	45.10		CAT
		45.40		
		45.30	31	
		45.20		
		45.10	40	
		45.00		
		44.90	33	
		44.80	15	
		44.70		
		44.60		
		44.50		
		44.40		
		44.30		
	25	44.20		
	43	44.10		
		44.00		

EXHIBIT 5.4　TraderEx Hybrid Market Screen During Continuous Trading

When a dealer and a limit order are at the same price in the TraderEx hybrid mode, whichever was placed earliest at that price will execute first when a contra-side market order arrives. In this illustration, the order book offer at 44.80 is best, while the highest bid comes from the dealer CAT. A public market buy order would first execute against the 44.80 and 44.90 bids for 48 units. Any remaining unfilled quantity would then transact against one of the dealers' 45.00 offers. A public customer's market sell order would "hit," or sell to the market maker CAT, at 44.60.

Differences between the NYSE and NASDAQ

The NYSE and NASDAQ are both evolving into hybrid structures, but these two major market centers are likely to remain quite different from each other in several important ways.

Stocks Traded Specialists must apply for the right to be the specialist for newly listed issues on the NYSE, and the Exchange's stock allocation committee makes this decision with reference to inputs from the company and other exchange members. Issues are rarely given up by a specialist firm, and are almost never taken away. NYSE specialists operate in the secondary market only. In the NASDAQ market, broker-dealer firms are free to participate in the new issues market, although a firm that does so must temporarily give up market making for an issue in the secondary market when it acts as underwriter for the same company in the primary market.

Information Flows Specialists are prohibited from dealing directly with institutions. NASDAQ market makers, on the other hand, can receive orders directly from customers, including institutional traders. This direct contact gives OTC dealers an information advantage that NYSE specialists do not enjoy. With more contact with institutional investors, a NASDAQ market maker can better sense the motive behind an order—namely, whether it is information-motivated or instead is an *informationless* order (for example, if it is from an index fund). Some market makers maintain close contact with the firms whose securities they trade, and brokerage houses with NASDAQ trading operations commonly act in a corporate finance advisory capacity for these firms.

NYSE specialist firms have no such relationship with their listed companies. Specialists, on the other hand, have an information advantage that is not shared by the NASDAQ market makers—they see a larger fraction of the order flow because order flow is more consolidated in exchange trading.

Price Discovery Market makers sense the public's buy/sell propensities by posting quotes and observing the market's response in the order flow. Consolidation of the public order flow on the trading floor of the NYSE gives exchange specialists a more comprehensive knowledge of the buy/sell propensities in the broader market for an issue. Many traders away from the NYSE trading floor will ask for a market "look" at a stock to get a floor broker's sense of the activity and interest in it.

Regulation Competing NASDAQ market makers face fewer rules and regulatory restrictions than NYSE specialists. The dealer market relies more on the pressures of a competitive environment to discipline the dealer firms in trading with public customers. NASDAQ market makers cannot be subjected to price continuity or stabilization tests because they do not have exclusive franchises. Consequently, the rules, regulations, and surveillance of specialist operations are of necessity more elaborate on the exchanges than in the NASDAQ market.

Alternatives to Traditional Intermediaries

In most markets historically, you would enter your orders through human intermediaries. In the United States, in fact, an exchange is defined by regulators as a facility where only intermediaries meet. More recently, though, systems that offer electronic negotiation of block trades, once the exclusive domain of trading desks, have had successful launches. LiquidNet started operations in 2001, and Pipeline started in September 2004. Both facilities are alternative trading systems that enable institutional customers to meet anonymously and trade in size. Part of LiquidNet's ability to attract order flow is attributable to its customers being able to negotiate their trades with reference to quotes prevailing in the major market centers, but without any disclosure beyond the negotiating counterparties. In other words, LiquidNet's customers do not have to participate in significant price discovery (the lion's share of all LiquidNet executions are within the spread). Pipeline offers an alternative procedure for accomplishing a similar goal. With Pipeline, you can trade in size and at good prices without leaving footprints that others can detect.

In TraderEx simulations, you have direct access to the liquidity pool, but negotiation is not incorporated in the software provided with this book. Look at the example in Exhibit 5.5. In this quote-driven market, the dealer YOU* (controlled by you) and each of the four machine-generated market makers are making a two-sided market (posting both a bid and an ask quote). The bids establish the prices at which the public can sell. They are in the left-hand column, arrayed from the most aggressive

TraderEx				
DAY		**TIME**		**SEED**
1		**10:12**		**5**

TICKER	PRICE	10.80	10.80	10.90
	QTY	18	19	40
	TIME	10:12	9:59	9:55

Hit				Take
BID		**QUOTE**		**OFFER**
−	+	−	+	−	+

	BID	QUOTE		OFFER
		10.80	**11.20**	
DOG	10.80	11.00		**TUNA**
YOU*	10.80	11.10		**CAT**
COD	10.80	11.10		**DOG**
CAT	10.70	11.10		**COD**
TUNA	10.60	11.20		**YOU***

EXHIBIT 5.5　TraderEx Two-Sided Market with YOU* as a Participant

(highest) to the least aggressive (lowest). The asks establish the prices at which the public can buy. These are on the right, arrayed from the most aggressive (lowest) to the least aggressive (highest). The inside market, or BBO (best bid and offer), is the most aggressive bid (10.80) and the most aggressive offer (11.00). The quoted spread in this example is currently 20 cents.

Coping with Fragmentation

Direct market access (DMA), trading algorithms, and smart order routing are now providing an intermediary service to market participants. In addition, some new technology firms have emerged that provide order management, handling, and routing services in a fragmented environment. One of the more popular order routers is Lava, a service that is used by many of the major brokerage firms. A market order routed through Lava uses proprietary Lava technology to select a marketplace, primarily on the basis of a stock's recent trading activity. Firms such as Lava are commonly referred to as *smart order routers* or *consolidators*. In essence, they consolidate information from various markets so that the customer can get the most favorable execution across markets. For users, the fragmentation problem is diminished.

OVERVIEW OF MARKET MAKER OPERATIONS

A market maker firm trades from its own inventory as a *principal*. When public investors want to buy, a market maker firm sells *from its own portfolio*, reducing a long position or going short. When public investors want to sell, a market maker firm buys *for its own portfolio*, reducing a short position or going long. Market makers indicate their willingness to buy or to sell by their quotes. A market maker's quotes consist of two parts: a bid to buy and an offer to sell, along with the share sizes that the two quotes are good for. Public investors sell at the market maker's bid and buy at the market maker's ask.

In Exhibit 5.5, two of the market makers (DOG and YOU) have posted identical quotes on the bid side. TUNA is alone at the lowest offer of 11.00. Why do you think TUNA is offering at 11.00? It is likely that this market maker has an uncomfortably long position and is eager to sell. The TraderEx dealer quote-setting rules are based on the dealer's position and its magnitude relative to a position limit. Dealers who are long beyond a position limit lower their bids and offers and perhaps sell to one of the other market makers. They adjust their bids and offer quotes lower when their position is too long, and higher when their position is too short.

The dealer quote-changing rules were developed with input from several London-based market makers. They reviewed simulation output that included dealer positions and trades, and fine-tuned the TraderEx dealer rules by pointing out when different changes should be made as a result of the trades and the quote changes of the other dealer. The graph in Exhibit 5.6 shows how, in one simulation, dealer bid and ask quotes (two thin lines) adjusted to reflect their aggregate inventory positions. Bid and ask

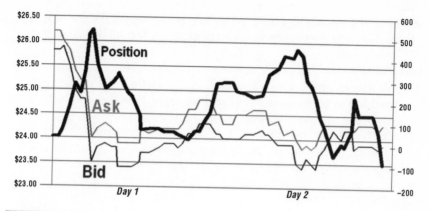

EXHIBIT 5.6 Dealer Bid and Ask Quotes Adjusted to Reflect Aggregate Inventory Positions

quotes are on the left axis, and position (right axis) is tracked over a two-day trading period. Notice that the rapid increase in dealers' long positions led to lowering of the quotes.

TraderEx's dealer strategies include the possibility of *bluffing*. A dealer that is short, for instance, but just bought stock, could lower its bid and make the lowest offer in order to draw the other dealers into lowering their quotes. If the other dealers are long, they may lower their quotes to avoid increasing their long position. In Exhibit 5.5, if TUNA succeeds in stemming quote increases in the stock, it will improve its P&L performance by covering the short at a lower price. If TUNA is a dealer with a short position, however, bluffing with lower quotes runs the risk of TUNA selling even more. Eventually, a TraderEx market maker that is short beyond a position limit will raise its quotes as many times as necessary to reduce the position risk.

In TraderEx, as in most quote-driven markets, there is no secondary rule of order execution (such as time priority), and any dealer making the best quote has an equally likely chance to receive the order. For instance, if three dealers are making the highest bid, each has a 33.3 percent chance of receiving the next incoming order to sell. This is consistent with a pure quote-driven market in which each customer selects the market maker to whom he wishes to direct an order. Directing an order to a specific dealer firm is known as *preferencing*.

Market Maker Services

A market maker firm is characterized by the nature of the transactional services that it provides to the buy side. Let us now consider these—the supply of immediacy and liquidity to individual customers, the animation of a market, and the provision of price discovery for the broad market.

Immediacy   The classic dealer role is the provision of immediacy. Buyers and sellers arrive sporadically in a continuous trading environment and need a way to meet. In Chapter 3 we show how the limit orders entered by some relatively patient participants in a continuous trading environment establish the prices at which other participants can trade immediately by market order. In the quote-driven environment, market maker quotes play this role. The market maker is continuously present, buying when a public seller arrives and selling when a public buyer arrives. The market maker is the medium through which public buyers and sellers effectively meet each other. With market maker intervention, all public participants can trade with immediacy even though they arrive at the market at different moments in time.

Liquidity   Liquidity provision is a service that is commonly attributed to market makers. In contrast to the order-driven market, a market maker firm will commonly trade for a larger size than it is quoting. A displayed quote may be an 11.20 bid for 10,000 shares, but the market maker may buy 100,000 shares or more at that price for a good customer.

As discussed in Chapter 2, attributing quote-driven liquidity to dealers is not, strictly speaking, correct. As with the order-driven market, the ultimate source of liquidity for public buyers is natural sellers, and the ultimate source of liquidity for public sellers is natural buyers. The market maker simply helps the public buyers and sellers come together and cannot be the ultimate source of liquidity. After buying shares from a public seller, the market maker hopes to sell those shares to a public buyer, and vice versa. If the quotes are set properly, and if the public buy and sell orders are reasonably balanced, the market maker's inventory will stay reasonably *flat* (close to zero). But if the public buy and sell orders do not offset each other sufficiently, an inventory imbalance will develop. When it does, the market maker is forced to reliquify by adjusting the quotes and/or by inter-dealer trading.

Animation/Catalyst   Animating a market is one of the more intriguing and least noted services provided by an intermediary. The French have used the term *animateur* to describe a market maker who has a contractual agreement with a listed company to use dealer capital to bring liquidity to the market for less liquid stocks. While that is not exactly what we have in mind here, the term *animator* is nevertheless a good one. Floor brokers who act as animators are more apt to think of themselves as *facilitators*. The facilitation may be viewed in the context of bookbuilding and quantity discovery, subjects we touched on in the previous chapter and discussed in further detail in Chapter 6.

The bookbuilding problem that characterizes a call auction opening extends into the continuous market. The major challenge is getting larger, predominantly institutional participants, because of their fear of being front-run, to reveal their orders and trade. In a recent paper, Sarkar and Schwartz report evidence, for a broad spectrum of stocks and market conditions, that orders are not attracted to an inactive market, that active trading leads to more trading, and, accordingly, that trading occurs in bursts.[5] The findings are consistent with much demand to trade being latent. *Latency* means that participants on both sides of the market are keeping their orders in their pockets to prevent the market from knowing their trading intentions. But if something sparks a bout of trading, both buy and sell orders get pulled out of the traders' pockets and a trade burst occurs.

Animation may be viewed in this context. Anyone who has observed trading in general, or the action of a floor broker in particular, has seen how the introduction of a fresh, new order into a market can stir up trading. Throw a crust of bread into a quiet country lake and you will observe a similar response—immediately, fish that you didn't see before dart in for the carbohydrates. You can look at a trading screen or at the people milling around a specialist's post on the New York Stock Exchange and observe that nothing is happening. Then, let one new participant arrive and announce an order to trade 5,000 shares of XYZ Corp., and the market for XYZ comes alive. That 5,000-share order may be just a beginning—the broker may have 45,000 more shares behind it. The important thing, at the start, is to initiate trading, so that volume picks up and prices update.

In the previous chapter, we suggested the possibility of including a market maker with an animator function in a call auction. Intermediaries who, in effect, play this role already exist in the continuous market. The point is that stocks (the mid- and small-cap stocks in particular) do not necessarily trade well with just the order flow from naturals. An intermediary is commonly needed to animate the market.

Price Discovery Price discovery is the process of finding share values that best reflect the broad market's desire to buy and sell shares. In the order-driven environment, price discovery occurs as public participants place their limit and market orders with regard to their own assessments of share value and their own beliefs about where prices might currently be heading. No single participant has individual responsibility for price discovery in a pure order-driven market.

In contrast, one set of participants does play a key role with regard to price discovery in the quote-driven environment: the market makers. They do so because the substantial portions of the aggregate order flow that they each see give them a feel for the relative balance between public buy and sell pressures. Furthermore, misjudging the order flow can be very costly for a market maker.

What is the price that the broad market is looking to discover? This question can be answered with reference to Exhibit 5.7. To simplify the discussion, let there be just one market maker, and assume that all orders are the same size so that we can plot orders rather than shares on the horizontal axis. The downward-sloping step function in Exhibit 5.7 describes the cumulated public buy orders: $D(p(t))$ is demand as a function of price at time t. The upward-sloping step function describes the cumulated public sell orders, or supply. Steps exist in the buy and sell curves because quantities arrive in discrete amounts at discrete prices. These two curves are constructed in the same way that we constructed the buy and sell curves shown in Exhibits 4.3 through 4.6 in the previous chapter with regard to the call auction. The difference is that, for the call auction, we cumulate orders that have *actually been submitted* to the market. For the market maker environment, we cumulate orders that are *expected to arrive* at each price.[6] Specifically, the expected arrival rate is the number of orders that are expected to arrive in the next brief time interval (e.g., the next half hour), depending on the market maker's bid and offer. But nobody

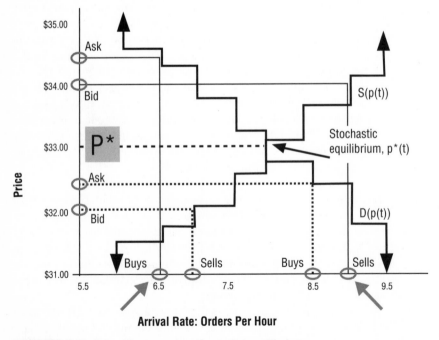

EXHIBIT 5.7 Price Discovery in a Quote-Driven Market

can be certain about future order flow. The best a market maker can do is to post the quotes, wait, and find out. For this reason, the arrow pointing to the equilibrium price in Exhibit 5.7 is labeled "stochastic equilibrium."

Assume that the buy and sell curves depicted in Exhibit 5.7 accurately describe the propensities of public participants to buy and to sell shares. The intersection of these two curves identifies the price that would equate the number of buy orders that are expected to arrive with the number of sell orders that are expected to arrive. We have labeled the price that balances the expected arrival rates P*. (See Exhibit 5.8.) This is an equilibrium value; P* here is the same as the P* in TraderEx that we introduce in Chapter 1 and show the economic determination of in Exhibit 1.2. It is a value that participants collectively are trying to discover and that everyone individually would like to know. It is the value that the market maker's quotes should ideally bracket. For instance, in Exhibits 5.7 and 5.8, P* is 33.00. If the market makers are quoting 32.95 bid, and 33.05 offer, then the expected buy and sell order arrival rates would be equal.

Market Maker Revenues

How are market makers compensated for the services they provide to the buy side? From three sources: the bid-ask spread, appropriately trading the order flow, and commissions.

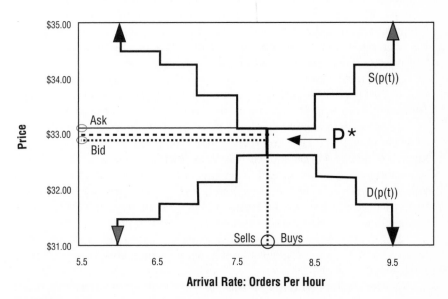

EXHIBIT 5.8 Price Discovery in a Quote-Driven Market Yields Equilibrium Value of P*

Bid-Ask Spread   A market maker firm realizes revenue from the spread between its bid and offer quotes, and the classically cited source of dealer profits is the dealer's bid-ask spread. Sometimes the spread is referred to as the "jobber's turn" (*jobber* is the older British term for market maker). If the bid and the offer are reasonably stable over time, and if the dealer repetitively buys at a lower bid and sells at a higher ask, he profits from the round trips. A *round trip* is first buying and then selling (or, for a short position, first selling and then buying). The amount of the spread is the return for one round trip. The return for just one purchase or just one sale is conventionally taken to be half of the spread. From the customer's perspective, half of the spread is commonly viewed as the price per share of immediacy. In a pure quote-driven environment, a public customer has no choice but to buy immediacy and to pay its cost. Competition among dealers should ideally drive this cost down to its minimum level.

All else equal, wider spreads lead to greater profits for market makers. Three factors in particular determine the size of the inside market spread (the gap between the best bid and offer): share price, trading volume, and the cost of market making. Share price is important because *percentage spreads* tend to be fairly constant across different price levels, all else constant. Accordingly, the *dollar size* of the spread will be higher for a higher-priced stock. For instance, a $100 stock will have a spread that, all else equal, is roughly 10 times the spread for a $10 stock.

Larger average trading volume, all else equal, results in tighter spreads: More frequent trading makes it easier for market makers to reliquify (i.e., to get out of accumulated positions, either long or short). Being able to trade down faster to a comfortable position contains a market maker's risk exposure to information change.

Higher market making costs lead to wider spreads for the same reason that higher production costs generally lead to higher sales prices in any competitive industry. We will focus shortly on the costs of market making.

Refer again to Exhibit 5.5. If the next arriving order is to buy 40 units, COD could sell at $11.10, and then raise its bid quote and buy the 40 units back at $10.90 or $11.00, and earn $0.20 or $0.10 per share. Clearly, on the one hand, with a larger spread, more revenue can be realized from a given volume (turnover). On the other hand, for a given spread, revenues are higher as the trading volume (turnover) in a stock is greater. With highly liquid stocks, a market maker profits mainly from volume, not from having a large spread.[7] Until recently, NASDAQ market maker bids and offers had to be for a minimum of 1,000 shares. Currently, they are free to size their quotes as they wish.

Market makers with long positions hope that share values will move up so that they can sell from inventory at higher prices. Market makers with short positions hope that share values will move down so that they can profit by covering their short positions (buying back shares) at lower prices. In general, market making is most profitable when prices mean revert (which, as we saw in Chapter 3, must be the case for limit order placers to trade profitably in an order-driven market). But a market maker can never know for sure. Future price changes are uncertain, and accumulating inventory (either long or short) is risky.

Exhibit 5.9 shows a book from TraderEx that characterizes a quote-driven market. There are five market makers: COD, CAT, DOG, YOU*, and TUNA. In TraderEx the quotes are good for up to 99 units, and the smallest order size is 1 unit. Select the "Quote-Driven" mode and a "Scenario Number" of 5. Simply click "+>" to advance the clock to 12:39. You will have bought three times up to that point and have a position of +90. Raise your bid to 20.90. (See Exhibit 5.9.)

After making the best bid of 20.90, advance to 12:59. You will buy two more times, and as a market maker (YOU*), you have become long 133 at an average price of 20.83. (See Exhibit 5.10.) Now it's your job to reduce the position back to 0, and seek to realize a profit by selling for more than your purchase cost.

Dealers try to avoid accumulating excessively long or short positions.

TraderEx									
DAY		**TIME**		**SEED**		**TRDS**	**INDEX**	**VOL**	
1		12:39		5		14	210	562	

TICKER	PRICE	21.20	20.80	20.80	21.20	20.80	21.20	20.90	20.90	20.80	20.80
	QTY	2	4	2	4	4	4	8	30	3	10
	TIME	12:39	12:05	11:53	11:43	11:27	11:15	11:09	11:06	11:06	10:57

Hit			Take	#	TIME		SHARES	TYPE	PRICE
				3	10:57	BUY	10	CU	20.80
BID	**QUOTE**		**OFFER**	2	10:54	BUY	40	CU	20.80
− +	− +		− +	1	9:49	BUY	40	CU	20.80
20.80	21.20								
CAT	20.80	21.20	CAT						
DOG	20.80	21.20	DOG						
YOU*	20.80	21.20	YOU*						
COD	20.80	21.20	COD						
TUNA	20.80	21.20	TUNA				TOTAL	90	20.80

EXHIBIT 5.9 Beginning of Exercise—Having Purchased 90, Time to Raise Bid

TraderEx									
DAY		**TIME**		**SEED**		**TRDS**		**INDEX**	**VOL**
1		**12:59**		**5**		**15**		**210**	**605**

TICKER	PRICE	20.90	20.90	21.20	20.80	20.80	21.20	20.80	21.20	20.90	20.90
	QTY	40	3	2	4	2	4	4	4	8	30
	TIME	12:59	12:52	12:39	12:05	11:53	11:43	11:27	11:15	11:09	11:06

					#	TIME		SHARES	TYPE	PRICE
Hit			**Take**		5	12:59	BUY	40	CU	20.90
BID		**QUOTE**		**OFFER**	4	12:52	BUY	3	CU	20.90
− +		− +		− +	3	10:57	BUY	10	CU	20.80
	20.90		21.20		2	10:54	BUY	40	CU	20.80
YOU*	20.90		21.10	DOG	1	9:49	BUY	40	CU	20.80
CAT	20.80		21.10	COD						
DOG	20.80		21.20	CAT						
COD	20.80		21.20	YOU*						
TUNA	20.80		21.20	TUNA		TOTAL	133			20.83

EXHIBIT 5.10 Next Step in Exercise—Reduce Holdings from 133 to Zero and Make a Profit

The location of their quotes is their basic inventory control mechanism. The procedure is akin to steering a boat. With a boat, the pilot adjusts the tiller and the boat responds. But the response is sloppy, depending on wind, tide, and the vessel's own momentum.

Picture a market maker who wants to reliquify after acquiring a long position of 150,000 shares. He will adjust the quotes downward. By improving on the offer (posting a lower ask), the market maker is indicating a more aggressive willingness to sell shares. By posting a lower bid, the market maker is discouraging further public selling. Alternatively, a market maker with a large short position will raise the offer to discourage public purchases and will raise the bid to encourage public sales. But after adjusting the tiller in this manner, the market maker has to wait for the public's response to bring his inventory back to a reasonable target level. Steering a boat is not always so simple, particularly at slow speeds when its response lags more.

There is another inventory control mechanism. A market maker can also trade with another market maker. This procedure is akin to steering a car. With a car on a dry road, the driver turns the wheel and the car responds immediately and exactly. It is common for one market maker who is long to sell shares (that were bought from customers) to another market maker who is short and wants to buy shares (that were sold to customers), or vice versa. The transaction is referred to as *interdealer* trading or *intramarket* volume. Before the London Stock Exchange added its SETS order book, intramarket dealing was about 40 percent of total volume, with the remainder known as "customer business."

As a market maker in TraderEx, you can trade with another market maker. Just use the "Hit" button above the bid in order to sell, or the "Take" butten above the offer if you want to buy. Also, do not be surprised if you receive an order from one of the machine-resident market makers with whom you are competing. When the market makers trade with each other in TraderEx, the size is either 10 or 30 units, at the discretion of the dealer receiving the trade request from the initiating dealer.

Trading the Order Flow   The second revenue source for a dealer is the short-term trading profits realized from successfully trading the order flow. A dealer is not a long-term investor in the stocks that he is making a market in, and is not interested, per se, in trading the stocks. Rather, having a good sense of the dynamics of the order flow and how to interact with it, the dealer is trading the *order flow*. Trading the order flow could not be profitable if share prices, except for bouncing between bid and offer quotes, followed a random walk.[8] But the dynamics of order arrival can result in prices trending in one direction and then mean reverting back toward a previous level. As we have previously discussed, mean reverting and trending behavior are attributable to liquidity events, momentum trading, and the dynamic process of price discovery.

A successful dealer has a sense of when, on net, to buy (i.e., to accumulate a long position) and when, on net, to sell (i.e., to accumulate a short position). That is, a successful dealer may anticipate when a preponderance of sell orders has depressed prices for noninformational reasons, or when a preponderance of buy orders has raised prices for noninformational reasons. The short-term price swings give market makers an opportunity to buy shares at temporarily depressed prices and to sell them at temporarily inflated prices. The market maker profits by reversing out of his position as prices mean revert. In essence, the market maker is following a contrarian strategy.

The short-term mean reversion coexists with accentuated short-period volatility, and the volatility accentuation is a profit opportunity for market makers just as it is for limit order traders. However, when trading the order flow, a market maker will incur substantial inventory swings. The venture is risky.

Commissions A market maker firm's third revenue source is commissions charged to customers. While any sell-side participant who operates in the dual capacity of broker (agent) and dealer (market maker) routinely charges brokerage commissions, dealers, historically, have not. Dealers customarily make *net trades*. That is, a customer buys at the dealer's offer or sells at the dealer's bid, and incurs no additional charge. The dealer simply earns profits from the round trips that he makes. However, following the transition to a one-cent tick in the United States that was completed in 2001, dealer spreads have narrowed and dealer revenue has shrunk to the point where some market makers are starting to charge commissions.

Market Maker Costs

Two distinctive costs characterize market maker operations: the cost of carrying an unbalanced inventory, and the cost of trading with a better-informed counterparty (the cost of ignorance).

Cost of an Unbalanced Inventory We know from portfolio theory that an investor can manage risk by proper portfolio diversification, and that a properly diversified portfolio provides the investor with a risk-appropriate expected return. A market maker, however, is not a typical investor. A market maker is buying or selling, not for his own investment purposes, but to supply shares to others or to absorb shares from others. To this end, the market maker commonly acquires a poorly diversified portfolio and, in so doing, accepts risk that could have been diversified away.

The expected return on a stock compensates for nondiversifiable risk (commonly measured by beta). What compensates the market maker for accepting diversifiable risk? The classic answer is the bid-ask spread. Whatever makes inventory control more difficult—be it preferencing, price volatility attributable to news release, relatively infrequent order flow in a small-cap stock, or the stochastic nature of the order flow—translates into more costly market making and hence wider spreads.

Cost of Ignorance The cost of ignorance is the cost of receiving an order from a better-informed trader. Assume a market maker has posted a bid at 50 and an offer at 50.10, and that, without the market maker knowing it, the equilibrium price for a stock jumps to 53. An informed trader comes in and buys at the 50.10 offer. The market maker loses from that trade because the bid and the offer will both rise, and the market maker will have sold at a lower value (50.10). After the market maker sees where prices are going, he will regret having traded with the better-informed counterparty. The principle is general: Whenever a trade is triggered by a better-informed order hitting a market maker's quote, the market maker will have ex post regret.

Stated more broadly, inaccurate price discovery is costly to a market maker. We can see this by returning to the monopoly dealer model and Exhibit 5.7. We have used P* to identify the price that best balances the expected rate of buy and sell orders, and have shown that, in equilibrium, the market maker will set the offer above P* and the bid below P*. Remember that P* is not observable in the continuous market because the buy and sell curves are based, not on actual orders, but on the number of orders that are *expected to arrive* in a relatively brief, future interval of time (e.g., the next hour). If the quotes straddle P* (as they do in Exhibit 5.7), the arrival of buys is expected to balance the arrival of sells, and the dealer's inventory should stay in reasonable balance. However, ex post, the actual arrivals of buys and sells will likely not balance exactly because actual rates generally differ from expected rates by some random amount.

More importantly, a serious inventory imbalance can develop if the market maker misjudges the location of P* or if, unbeknownst to the dealer, a news event causes P* to jump either up or down. Consider Exhibits 5.11 and 5.12. Exhibit 5.11 depicts a situation where the demand for the stock is *higher* than the market maker has anticipated, either because of mistaken judgment or the occurrence of a bullish news event that the

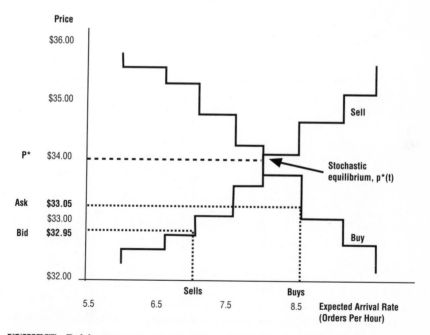

EXHIBIT 5.11 Price Discovery in a Quote-Driven Market—Market Maker Quotes Are Too Low

dealer has not yet learned about. We see that P* is 34 and that the dealer's quotes are 32.95 bid, 33.05 offered. As informed buyers jump on the 33.05 offer, the rate of sales to the public rises and the rate of purchases from the public falls. With the order flow to the market maker out of balance, the dealer quickly acquires a short inventory position. As a control mechanism, the dealer raises the quotes, hoping once again to straddle P* and to return to a flat inventory position. In the process of adjusting the quotes, however, the market maker will be buying shares at a price that is higher than the price at which he had previously sold.

Exhibit 5.12 depicts the opposite situation: The demand for the stock is lower than the market maker has anticipated, either because of mistaken judgment or the sudden occurrence of bearish news that the dealer does not yet know about. We see that P* is 32 and that the dealer's quotes are 32.95 bid, 33.05 offered. As informed sellers jump on the 32.95 bid, sales to the dealer increase and purchases from the dealer fall. Now, the market maker quickly acquires a long position. In response, the dealer will lower the quotes, trying once again to straddle P* and return to a flat inventory position. In the process of adjusting the quotes, however, the mar-

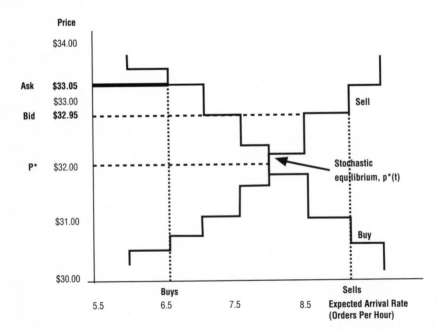

EXHIBIT 5.12 Price Discovery in a Quote-Driven Market—Market Maker Quotes Are Too High

ket maker will be selling shares at a price that is lower than the price at which he had previously bought.

Achieving accurate price discovery is not easy, and inaccurate price discovery is costly for the dealer. What compensates the market maker for the cost of ignorance? The revenue that the dealer receives from transacting with liquidity traders (who are sometimes referred to as *uninformed* traders), and it must be large enough for the costs of dealing with better-informed traders to be offset. Could dealers exist without liquidity traders? They could not. No dealer can stay in business by trading only with better-informed participants. Without liquidity traders, the market makers would close down their operations and the quote-driven market would collapse.

ORDER HANDLING AND TRANSPARENCY IN A DEALER MARKET

Now that both NASDAQ and the NYSE are hybrid structures, are intermediaries still required in trading? They certainly are. Buy-side traders are commonly faced with the challenge of working an order that ranges up to 100,000 shares, 500,000 shares, one million, or more. Wayne Wagner, chairman of the Plexus Group,[9] recently stated, "Our data show that over half of institutional decisions to trade exceed 20 percent of [a stock's] average daily trading volume."[10] These big orders may be broken into smaller pieces and fed to the market carefully over an extended period of time (up to a day or more). Alternatively, a search for a buy-side counterparty may be undertaken to bring a large buyer and a large seller together to execute a block trade (10,000 shares or more). Or a larger trade may be executed, in part or in whole, against dealer capital.

Customers trading large cap stocks in blocks, and all customers trading in mid caps and small caps, typically require sell-side assistance. With fewer shares outstanding, fewer investors and, consequently, relatively sparse order flow, the ecology of the limit order book market can break down for thinner issues. When this happens, market maker services are needed. For less liquid stocks, the market maker plays a key role in facilitating liquidity supply through quoting. With more liquid stocks, by contrast, liquidity attracts liquidity from investors who post their own orders in the market. A market maker is less needed for the frequently traded, big cap issues where the spread is narrow and there is breadth and depth in the order book. A good example is the Kursmakler (dealer) System versus the Xetra electronic trading platform in Germany. For on-exchange trading, the most liquid stocks basically trade 100 percent on Xetra, while the less liquid stocks still need the market making support of a Kursmakler.

The participation of market maker intermediaries introduces a number of market structure issues that can influence trading rules and how the market is organized. One of the most important attributes of any equity market is its *transparency*. In a transparent market, public participants can obtain accurate information about current market conditions. Transparency has two major components. *Pretrade transparency* refers to quotes and quote sizes, and *post-trade transparency* refers to transaction prices and trade sizes. Pretrade transparency is important because the quotes describe trading possibilities that currently exist (although, as noted, there can be bluffing in the setting of quotes). Post-trade transparency is important because an actual transaction means that both a buyer and a seller have agreed on a price. However, a completed transaction has occurred in the past and, as it fades into history, the market information that it has generated can rapidly become stale.

Transparency is a contentious issue in market structure. Many constituents typically cry out for more transparency. Trading requires investors to make tactical decisions: How do you time your orders? How do you size your orders? At what prices would you be willing to trade? In which market do you want to trade? Observing market maker quotes and seeing recent trades facilitates the timing, sizing, and pricing of your orders. And there is another factor: Knowing the quotes, trade sizes, and transaction prices better enables you to monitor and assess the quality of the executions that you have received.

Since 1989, the London Stock Exchange has had a system of delayed trade publication that became known as the Worked Principal Agreement regime. The regime is restricted to trades instigated by the customer that are larger than eight times the normal market size ($8 \times$ NMS) for the security concerned. NMS is the maximum number of shares in a company that market makers are obliged to deal in at the prices that they are quoting. In the Worked Principal Agreement, an institutional investor and a broker-dealer enter into a provisional agreement in which they agree on the basic terms for the trade, including limit price and size on which improvement must be sought by the broker dealer. The terms of this agreement are reported to the Exchange but are not published until after the broker dealer searches for counterparties with whom to offset the trade. The broker dealer must execute and report the trade either by the end of the trading day, or when they have found counterparties for 80 percent of the value of the trade, whichever comes first.

Transparency is commonly thought to translate into better market quality in terms of liquidity, stability, fairness, and price discovery. However, it is not clear that a more transparent quote-driven market will be more liquid. Too much transparency hurts the market makers, and this can result in their providing less capital to market making. It is also not clear that transparency adds to price stability in a dealer market. If, in a pure quote-driven market, greater transparency results in market makers committing less capital to market making, there will be less liquidity and, with less liquidity, prices will be more volatile. In a hybrid quote-driven, order-driven system, because transparency can attract limit orders, it is difficult to measure the trade-off between having more orders in the order book and having less market maker capital.

Transparency's impact on fairness is less ambiguous. A marketplace is perceived as being fairer if participants know the array of prices at which trades are being made and can better assess the quality of their own executions. Transparency is also desirable for price discovery. However, we have to be cautious with this one. If there is less liquidity in the market and prices are more volatile because market makers are committing less capital to market making, price discovery will be less accurate as well. In a less liquid, highly transparent market, investors are reluctant to put their orders on the order books where they are exposed to other market participants (exposed limit orders are more vulnerable in less liquid markets). In conclusion, we care about transparency, but greater transparency does not necessarily lead to better market quality.

To see this more clearly, put yourself in the position of a market maker. Assume that you have just acquired a sizable inventory while buying from a large mutual fund. Your customer's desire to sell has been shifted to you, and you are now in the position that the mutual fund had been in. You need to work off that position. There is a phrase in the industry that captures this: "Shares sold to a market maker are still for sale." This is because the market maker is not the final customer, despite the fact that the order is in his book (and neither is the market maker the ultimate source of liquidity, as noted earlier in this chapter and in Chapter 2).

How does this relate to transparency? The point is, having just bought from a public seller, you now want to pass the parcel on to a public buyer. Just as the mutual fund does not want others to know that it has entered the market as a seller until after the shares have been sold, neither do you want other dealers or the public to know that you are now looking to sell the shares. The success of any market maker firm depends on its ability to hide large positions, and you do not want your inventory revealed by a trade publication. While the public does not see your inventory directly, market participants can be very good at inferring it from your trades. This is why less transparency in the form of delayed trade publication may be desirable in the dealer market.[11]

In reality, markets are never totally transparent, including order-driven markets. Whether or not to reveal an order is a choice that typically faces a public investor, even when the investor has already conveyed the order to the market. Institutional investors in particular need this choice. Choice is provided to them in a number of ways by floor-based markets such as the New York Stock Exchange, and by electronic trading platforms such as that run by the Paris Stock Exchange (Euronext Paris). For instance, a floor trader on the NYSE typically reveals only parts of a large order, which he "slices and dices" and trades over an extended period of time. In Paris, large investors can enter iceberg orders, where only a part is revealed to the market and the remainder is hidden (i.e., not revealed) on the book. At Deutsche Börse (Xetra), volume orders are being considered, as discussed in Martin Reck's contributed piece.

In the NASDAQ environment, a public trader may give a large order to a market maker. The dealer may execute part or all of the order against his own inventory or seek counterparties for all or part of the order. The dealer will work any unexecuted portion of the order over time. Regardless of the specific route taken, it is not in the interest of the client and/or the market maker for the trade to be publicly revealed until the client's order has been executed in full and the dealer has reliquified. Consequently, it is not optimal for a dealer market to be highly transparent.

Anonymity is also of utmost importance for institutional customers. One way to protect against losing it is to incorporate a *central counterparty* (CCP) in the trading system. The classic clearinghouse in an equity market acts as a CCP. In so doing, a clearinghouse becomes a seller for each buyer, a buyer for each seller, and assumes responsibility for the failure of any market member to fulfill his obligations. By stepping between the two parties to a trade, the clearinghouse ensures that neither the buyer nor the seller need learn of the other's identity after the trade.

The big traders want more than anonymity, however. They want virtual invisibility. Other participants, simply by knowing that a big player is in the market looking to buy or to sell, will seek to trade ahead of the order even if the big trader's identity is not known. Others trading ahead cause the big player to incur a big market impact cost. Perhaps the best way to deal with this is to enable the big players to meet each other in a separate facility that offers minimum possible information leakage. Liquidnet and Pipeline, two new ATSs, offer such a system.

COMPETITION AND PREFERENCING

The most obvious way that market makers compete with each other is by how aggressively they set their bids and offers. If the spread is constant and the bid and offer are raised, the quotes are more aggressive on the bid side. If the bid and offer are lowered, the quotes are more aggressive on the offer side. The only way to become more aggressive on both the bid and the offer simultaneously is to narrow the spread.

Competing by aggressive quote setting is not so simple, however, because of preferencing. As we have noted, *preferencing* refers to a customer choosing to send an order to a particular market maker regardless of what that dealer might be quoting at the time. This can be done because there is no time priority rule in a quote-driven market. The public customer (this applies primarily to institutional clients) is free to pick randomly a market maker firm to whom to send an order, or to make the selection based on previously established relationships. Orders are typically preferenced to a market maker who has developed a special relationship with the customer.

What if the market maker firm that the customer chooses to trade with is not posting the most aggressive quotes? If its quote is less aggressive than the best quote on the market, the market maker is not obliged to take the order, but generally will accept it to maintain a good relationship with the customer. When a market maker does accept an order, he will typically fill it at a price equal to the most aggressive bid or offer existing at the time the order is received. For instance, if the best bid on the market is 50, a sell order preferenced to a dealer quoting a $49.90 bid will be filled at 50. This practice is referred to as *quote matching*.

Preferencing diminishes a market maker's incentive to compete via the aggressiveness of his quotes. You can sense this yourself by running TraderEx as described in the following TraderExercise. Launch TraderEx, and select the "Quote-Driven, Dealers Only" mode, and then choose the case, "Some Preferencing (Dealers not making best quotes eligible to receive orders)." (See Exhibit 5.13.) Enter a scenario number of 1, and click through to 9:54. The market order to sell 80 goes to you, even though you are not making the best bid quote. (See Exhibit 5.14.)

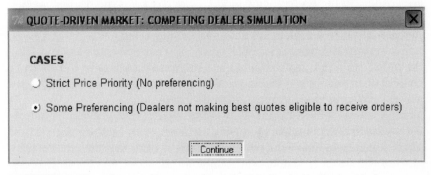

EXHIBIT 5.13 Selecting "Some Preferencing" in TraderEx Dealer Mode

TraderEx							
DAY		**TIME**		**SEED**	**TRDS**	**INDEX**	**VOL**
1		9:54		1	5	211.63	319

TICKER	PRICE	21.20	21.20	21.20	21.20	21.20	21.20
	QTY	80	4	30	60	10	55
	TIME	9:54	9:49	9:49	9:49	9:49	9:49

Hit			Take	#	TIME	SHARES	TYPE	PRICE
				1	9:54	BUY 80	CU	21.20
BID		**QUOTE**	**OFFER**					
− +		− +	− +					
	20.80	21.20						
CAT	21.20	21.20	DOG					
TUNA	21.20	21.20	YOU*					
DOG	20.80	21.20	COD					
YOU*	20.80	21.60	CAT					
COD	20.80	21.60	TUNA		TOTAL	80		21.20

[9:54] 80 SOLD to YOU* At 21.20
[9:54] Market Order to SELL 80

EXHIBIT 5.14 Preferenced Order Does Not Depend on Your Bid Quote

While a market maker firm that is quoting at the best bid or offer has a somewhat higher probability of receiving the next incoming order (especially if it is alone at the quote), the next order could still be preferenced to a market maker who is not on the inside market. Complete preferencing in a market with five market makers would mean that each has a 20 percent chance of receiving the next incoming order regardless of the quotes they are posting. In the preferencing mode, TraderEx gives the dealers making the best bid or offer quote an added 10 percent chance of receiving an arriving order. If two dealers are alone on the bid when a sell order arrives, pure price priority would give each dealer a 50 percent chance of receiving the order. TraderEx preferencing means that they each have a 25 percent chance of receiving the order, while the other three dealers each have about a 16.7 percent chance of having their offer hit.

In a market where preferencing is common practice, what does a market maker firm accomplish by raising the best bid or by lowering the best offer? It will have raised the bid or lowered the offer that the other market makers will have to match, and it may not itself receive the next order. The incentive to do this is not high unless the market maker has good reason to believe that the best posted bid and offer are out of line with the broad, underlying desire of participants to buy and sell shares.

If market makers have only a weak incentive to quote aggressively, how do they compete? By developing good customer relationships. An institutional investor will call a specific dealer house because it has received good service from that firm in the past. If a dealer either turns a customer down or executes the customer's order at an inferior price, the customer will think twice before preferencing an order to that dealer firm again.

Market makers may price-improve customer orders (we discuss this in a moment), and they can also offer an array of ancillary services that enable them to attract order flow. For instance, they may provide customers with research reports on companies, computer software, and/or data for investment analysis. They may offer direct computer links that result in faster executions than customers could achieve elsewhere, and so forth.

Because of the way in which dealers compete, their spreads tend to be wider than in an order-driven environment. In a pure order-driven market, an incoming order executes against a contra-side order that has been selected according to two strict criteria, price and time—the most aggressively priced order executes first and, if two or more orders are tied at the most aggressive price, the order that was placed first executes first. If there is a lengthy queue of orders at the best bid or offer, a newly arriving buy (or sell) order can get priority simply by being priced one tick above the best bid (or one tick below the best offer). Aggressive pricing to get ahead of the queue results in a narrowing of the spread. Because this does not occur in a pure quote-driven market, spreads tend to be wider there than in the order-driven environment.

What effect does preferencing have on market makers' profitability? More orders will be preferenced to a market maker firm that has good customer relationships. This is highly desirable for the firm. For one thing, a firm's net revenue is related to its trading volume. Additionally, a firm that sees a larger percentage of the order flow has an advantage with regard to price discovery and thus can set its quotes more knowledgeably.

Preferencing, however, is not an unmitigated good. It is excellent for a dealer firm to receive preferenced orders but, as we have seen, inventory control is then more difficult. With preferenced order flow, posting the most aggressive quote on the market does not assure that a market maker will receive the next incoming order, and posting less aggressively than the best bid or offer does not insure that the market maker will not receive the next incoming order. We have likened controlling inventory through quote changes to steering a boat, rather than a car. Preferencing certainly makes steering the boat more difficult. The greater difficulty of controlling inventory can negatively impact a firm's profitability.

Under what regime do market makers prefer to operate—one with preferencing, or one with strict time and price priorities? Preferencing is an industry practice and dealers are comfortable with it or they would not have continued the practice. Nevertheless, preferencing is a two-edged sword.

PRICE IMPROVEMENT

In addition to providing capital for trading, intermediaries facilitate order handling in two primary ways. First, they facilitate the price and quantity improvement of customer orders; and second, they facilitate the market timing of customer orders. We discuss the market timing function in Chapter 6 and its appendix.

Price improvement means that an order is executed within the spread. Namely, a buy order is executed at a price lower (and/or in larger size) than the best posted offer, or a sell order is executed at a price higher (and/or in larger size) than the best posted bid. Why might this happen?

Market makers get to know their customers. Consequently, they can differentiate between customers who are apt to be trading for liquidity reasons and customers who are likely to be in possession of new information. Liquidity-motivated customers include, for example, an indexer that is trading to rebalance its portfolio to track an index, or a mutual fund experiencing cash inflows or outflows from its investors. By contrast, a value investor with the reputation of being a good stock picker may be trading because of better information. Dealers are more apt to give price improvement to customers who they believe are trading for their own individual reasons, rather than because they are in possession of new information that will soon become common knowledge.

There are further reasons for giving price improvement. A dealer might give price improvement to a customer who has negotiated a better price. The dealer might want to give better treatment to a frequent customer, or to one with whom he is attempting to develop a better relationship. Price improvement is often provided to retail orders in the United Kingdom, where retail brokers route over 90 percent of retail orders through the retail service providers (RSPs), who not only often improve on the order book price, but also can accommodate deals for settlement on trade date (T) plus 5, plus 10, or even plus 20 days, compared with the mandatory SETS order book requirement to settle all trades for T plus 3.[12]

Price improvement has yet another important role to play. We have previously discussed the difficulty of price discovery, and the risky dealer inventory positions that can develop when the quotes do not bracket the unobservable equilibrium price, P^*. A straightforward defense against not knowing the location of P* is for a market maker to raise the offer and lower the bid (widening the spread increases the likelihood that the quotes bracket P*). Then, with a wider spread, the market maker might price-improve an incoming order that he has reason to believe is not from a more knowledgeable participant (i.e., one who might have superior knowledge of the current value of P*, or of how P* might jump once new information that he possesses becomes common knowledge).

Price improvement may be linked to price discovery in a more proactive way. A dealer might be more apt to give price improvement selectively if, at the moment that an order arrives, he observes more pressure on one side of the market than on the other. For instance, if buyers are more prevalent then sellers, sell orders are more apt than buy orders to be price-improved, and vice versa. This is particularly true for an order-driven market, such as the New York Stock Exchange, that includes specialists in its market structure.

On the NYSE, each stock is allocated to one specialist firm, and specialists play a key role with respect to price discovery for the stocks assigned to them. The process of discovering a new price level is manifest in the adjustment of the quotes and, given the quotes, in price improvement being offered predominantly to one side of the market or the other. A link between price improvement and price discovery is indicated by a relationship that has been observed by Handa, Schwartz, and Tiwari (HST 1998) between price improvement and two key variables: market balance and market direction.[13]

Market balance is measured as bid size (the number of shares posted at the bid) relative to ask size (the number of shares posted at the offer). Market direction is measured as the change of the midpoint of the best bid and offer on the market over the 15-minute interval within which a trade has been made. The HST study observed that, when the bid size is larger than the ask size (all else constant), or when the market is rising (all else constant), buyers receive less price improvement (buy prices are closer to the offer) and sellers receive more price improvement (sell prices are further above the bid). Handa et al. also found that the opposite result holds when sell orders are larger than buy orders, or when the market is falling. Under these conditions, buyers receive more price improvement and sellers receive less. These relationships indicate that price improvement is not simply a matter of good fortune and/or bargaining ability, but that it is part of the price discovery process.

Price improvement serves another useful purpose for a market center that is the primary venue for price discovery. In the United States, for instance, prices for NYSE-listed stocks are predominantly set on the NYSE even though the stocks also trade in satellite markets (e.g., the regional exchanges and various alternative trading systems). The satellite markets are said to "free ride" on NYSE price discovery. This does not please the Big Board. An interesting way for the Exchange to defend itself against free riding is to be less transparent about the prices that it sets. NYSE specialists have some ability to do this by letting spreads be wider, and then price-improving orders after they have arrived at the Exchange. The Exchange stresses that customer orders sent to another market may, as a consequence, miss an opportunity to be price-improved. Here is another way to look at it: Setting wider spreads and then giving within the spread transactions regularly helps to dilute the quality of the quotes that the satellite markets are looking to free-ride on.

Price improvement on the NYSE may be given either by a stock exchange specialist or by a floor broker who steps forward and takes the contra-side of the trade. The process of exposing an order to floor traders takes some amount of time. Interestingly, this procedure cannot be replicated by a fully electronic trading system. With an electronic platform, nanoseconds can matter and the time clock is relentless—customers must be able to hit posted limit orders and achieve immediate executions with certainty. An execution cannot be delayed, even for a split second, while a better price is being sought because, in the interim, another order might arrive and the electronic system must be able to handle it instantaneously. However, instantaneous price improvement can be given in one (and only one) way: by having hidden orders placed within the posted spread. Designated market makers do this at Deutsche Börse, the primary German stock exchange. With a hidden order between the best posted bid and offer, a market order can execute instantly at a price that has been improved vis-à-vis the posted quotes.

THE FUTURE OF INTERMEDIARIES IN HYBRID MARKETS

If intermediation is not required, you should have the option to trade in a nonintermediated environment and not pay for services that you do not need. The order-driven market discussed in Chapters 3 and 4 has desirable properties, particularly for liquid stocks, retail order flow, and markets that are not under stress. But illiquidity is a serious problem for many issues (particularly the mid and small caps), many orders are too big to be easily digested in the market (primarily those generated by institutional customers), and stress characterizes all markets on a daily basis. Accordingly, intermediaries have important roles to play. These involve, first and foremost, providing dealer capital, animating the market, participating in price discovery, and offering price improvement.

In the past, the London Stock Exchange and NASDAQ were, for the most part, pure dealer markets. On the other end of the spectrum, the Paris Bourse and other continental exchanges ran call auctions. The Tokyo and other Far East exchanges have been and currently are continuous order-driven environments that include call auctions at market openings and closings. In many exchanges historically, one also sees features of a hybrid market. A striking example is an order-driven market like the New York Stock Exchange. As we have seen, the Big Board includes specialists (who participate in trading as market makers) and other floor traders (who work orders according to their own judgment about market timing). Also included in the broader NYSE marketplace are upstairs trading rooms that include dealers who provide proprietary capital to facilitate block transactions.

In recent years, major markets around the globe have been explicitly designed as hybrids. Limit order books have been introduced in the NASDAQ market (NASDAQ Market Center) and the London market (SETS and SETSmm), and the new NYSE Hybrid itself will link the specialist to a directly accessible limit order book. Market makers are included in order-driven platforms throughout Europe, and they receive trading privileges in return for posting quotes and fulfilling certain obligations. Virtually all markets now include call auctions. These advances toward hybrids have been driven by participants who individually have different trading needs depending on the size of their orders, motives for trading, and the characteristics of the stock (or list of stocks) being traded, as well as by participants who collectively need sharper price discovery at market openings and closings. For the broad market, a hybrid structure can sharpen price discovery, provide enhanced liquidity, and help to stabilize a market under stress.

This discussion has an important bottom line. As Greifeld indicates in his contributed piece, human intermediaries will continue to have an important role to play in the hybrid structures of the future. Enabling them to operate profitably side by side with fast-market, electronic trading is not a simple matter, however. For a hybrid market to exist as such, it is necessary that the human agents retain sufficient critical mass order flow to keep them in business.

FROM THE CONTRIBUTORS

Robert Greifeld
NASDAQ Market Makers in the NASDAQ Stock Market

Martin Reck
Electronic Intermediaries for Block Trading

Frank L. Romanelli
The Importance of Market Making

NASDAQ Market Makers in the NASDAQ Stock Market

Robert Greifeld

N ASDAQ provides buyers and sellers the ability to meet electronically and directly, at a very low cost and very efficiently. Offering them the best possible service is the best thing that we can do for our other two constituencies, our issuers and the NASDAQ market makers.

In recent years, we at NASDAQ have reengineered our market. Historically, we have been a competitive dealer market. That started to change in the late 1980s with the growth of Instinet, an order-driven facility. Next a slew of new ECNs arrived following the SEC's 1997 Order Handling Rules. In 2001 and 2002 we upgraded our order display and execution systems, but they still lacked functionality and ease of access relative to our competitors.

In 2003 and 2004 we significantly enhanced our functionality with new order types and routing as well as with the acquisition of the BRUT ECN in September 2004. These actions improved the NASDAQ experience for our existing market makers as well as opening up NASDAQ to new types of participants. Another big step was taken in 2004 when we introduced the Closing Cross and Opening Cross (the crosses are discussed in Chapter 4 and in Frank Hatheway's contribution to that chapter). We have now acquired Instinet, which enables us to integrate its operations more seamlessly in our hybrid market structure. The bottom line is that solid order-driven components are now operating effectively, side by side with our NASDAQ market makers.

The NASDAQ market model is about competition. We recognize the value of intermediaries, the NASDAQ market makers, in this context. We have over 400 total participants including more than 250 market makers in the NASDAQ stock market. They play a vital role. We need them for the liquidity they provide. We need them for what they bring to price discovery. We need them for the stability that they offer the mid- and small-cap segments of our market and all of our listed stocks during stressful conditions.

When trading electronically through NASDAQ's systems, market makers and other NASDAQ participants attract investors' order flow only by having the best price. When dealing directly with investors upstairs, they attract order flow by providing both the best price and the best service. Regardless of how market makers interact with investors, they have to compete for investors' business. Competition benefits investors.

Some other markets also have intermediaries, which they call specialists, who are in a monopolist position with respect to the order flow. They are able to see and interact with customer order flow, but are not forced to compete for access to investors' orders. Our competing model doesn't allow that to transpire, and we believe our model is best for investors.

Change is not easy. Each major step that we have taken has required enormous efforts to assure that we are acting efficiently for investors, appropriately for our market makers, and in harmony with the SEC's objective of strengthening the vitality of our markets. We have been encouraged by the effectiveness of the steps we have thus far taken. We remain committed to progress and know that, for the foreseeable future, change and innovation will be a never-ending process.

Electronic Intermediaries
for Block Trading

Martin Reck

As Chapter 3 points out, highly transparent, electronic limit order platforms are excellent facilities for handling small and medium sized orders for high-liquidity stocks. Dealing with large orders, even for liquid shares, is another matter entirely. Handling large orders is a complex undertaking. At best, traders tend to avoid transparent price discovery mechanisms; at worst, they abstain completely from participating. The reason? The large traders are struggling to avoid market impact, adverse market movements, and the opportunity costs of not realizing trades in a timely manner.

What options are there for the execution of large orders? What markets can the big players turn to with their huge orders? Intermediation, either of the human or the electronic variety, is required. Accordingly, I am approaching the large order handling issue within the context of Chapter 5.

Large orders originating from the buy-side can go to market intermediaries—brokers who either seek a counterparty in the market, or who provide their own dealer capital so that a trade can be made. This interaction with the flow of block orders is *manual*—typically, the interaction between the buy side and the sell side is conducted via telephone. Manual interaction also involves sell-side brokers seeking potential counterparts (either other buy-side customers or dealers who are looking to unwind positions that they have taken while giving other buy-side players dealer-provided immediacy). Brokers charge a commission for seeking a counterparty, while block dealers commit their own capital and charge a net price that covers their costs.

Both the dealer-provided capital route and the broker-provided search procedures have their shortcomings. There is the danger of information leakage (knowledge seeps out in the market that a large order is seeking to be executed), and there is the possibility that a dealer will charge an unreasonably high price for supplying his risk capital. Electronic platforms that are alternatives to the manual interactions have recently emerged which claim to overcome these shortcomings. By and large, the electronic platforms fall into four categories:

1. Buy-side trading networks (e.g., Liquidnet).
2. Centralized order books with continuous or periodic reference price crossing (e.g., Instinet's continuous block crossing, POSIT and Instinet's intraday cross).

3. Centralized order books with a "block board" concept (e.g., Pipeline).

4. Block trading mechanisms that are integrated to the central limit order book of an exchange system (e.g., the iceberg order functionality in Deutsche Börse's Xetra.[14])

Briefly, the core market structure features of the first three categories are as follows:

1. Operating in the United States and in the major European markets, Liquidnet reads member firms' order management systems (OMS) for orders that can be matched, and it electronically notifies traders to enter into one-on-one negotiation when it finds such orders. Negotiations take place completely anonymously, as no pretrade information about contra-side identities is made available. Transaction prices for 93 percent of all trades are within the prevailing spread of the respective main market, and the prices of 53 percent of all trades are at the exact midpoint of the spread.[15] Liquidnet does not allow sell-side members to enter orders, so only a limited group of firms participate.[16]

2. Electronic crossing systems match large orders either continuously or periodically. Either way, matching prices are taken from the leading market in the respective stock, the order books are not transparent, and the orders are anonymous.

3. Pipeline takes a somewhat different approach. The Pipeline computer determines prices and matches orders using an algorithm that can give price improvement to pre-positioned limit orders. A completely closed order book sits in the center. The book shows only if an order has been entered, without revealing the side of the market (buy or sell) that the order is on. The traders' orders are all hidden, and the crossing orders are executed immediately following price-time priority rules if multiple orders match.

The mechanisms noted here all offer minimal (or no) transparency, and they all operate completely in parallel with the leading exchange market for their respective stocks. Consequently, their market structures inhibit any integration with the rest of the market. But, as stated by Schwartz and Francioni, "for the benefit of the broad market, market architecture should be structured to integrate institutional and retail order flow more effectively."[17] The question is whether, in the age of electronic stock trading, a computerized trading solution could further achieve the desired integration of markets.

Exchanges have made a logical step in this direction by introducing a specific order type, the *iceberg order*, noted elsewhere in this book (see, e.g., Chapter 3). The intention is to attract large orders to the central order books so that the liquidity on them might be enhanced. Iceberg orders are constructed as limit orders with both a hidden quantity and a visible quantity. The visible quantity is shown in the order book, the hidden part is not. Once the visible part has been executed, another portion of the hidden part of the order is displayed for further execution. So the concept of an iceberg order also restricts market transparency. But that is only for part of the individual iceberg order. The order itself is designed to concentrate liquidity and to avoid market fragmentation.

Our experience with Xetra shows the frequency with which hidden orders are being used today. About 0.7 percent of all orders submitted to Xetra are iceberg orders. The representative iceberg order in Xetra is about 12 to 14 times the normal size of an order on Xetra, and thus the number of shares submitted as iceberg orders is higher—their total representation in trading volume is about 8 percent.[18] Nevertheless, the use of iceberg orders is dwarfed by the magnitude of over-the-counter block trading that we are currently experiencing. Put the two together, and it is clear that the exchanges should figure out how to improve further on the concept of a hidden order.

Here is a promising route. An extension of the iceberg order concept was recently proposed by Budimir, Gomber, and Schweickert.[19] I can briefly describe the new order as follows. Adding two more parameters to an iceberg order—a hidden limit (defined by the order submitter) and a minimum volume (the smallest accepted order size, defined by the market operator)—results in a new order type that the authors call a *volume order*. The hidden limit is not displayed; it denotes the maximum (minimum) price that the buyer (seller) is willing to accept if there is a sufficiently large volume available on the market's contra side. That price can be more aggressive than the limit price that is one of the iceberg order parameters of the volume order.

A volume order is both a passive and an active construct. On the one hand, it behaves passively (like an iceberg order) by simply sitting in the order book with a peak part displayed, waiting to be executed. If the peak part does execute, another tranche of the order (a new peak) becomes visible on the book. On the other hand, a volume order can become active, not only when it enters the book, but also when something relevant changes on the contra side of the market.

This is how it works. A volume order has two parts, a standard iceberg part with a visible limit price and a visible peak, and a second, totally hidden part with a more aggressive but hidden limit price. When the order is entered, the system checks whether the minimum volume (the smallest allowable size of a volume order) could be executed given its hidden limit price, either against visible (i.e., regular) volume or against contra-side volume orders. Accordingly, if volume increases on the contra-side (either regular volume or volume order volume), the computer again determines if a match at the hidden limit price is possible. Volume orders can certainly match each other within the market spread if, for instance, the hidden limits of two volume orders cross within the spread. In that case, the hidden limit price of the volume order that has been sitting longer in the book will be taken as the matching price.

As Budimir, Gomber, and Schweickert discuss, volume orders are expected to provide several major benefits. They combine the concept of a limit order book with that of a crossing network or block board. They increase market liquidity by integrating the two liquidity pools, and by allowing for the full interaction of all orders, both large and small. With their active role (that is, searching for an execution with the contra side of the market), volume orders, unlike iceberg orders, can trigger additional matches and thus increase the likelihood of execution for sitting orders. Thus opportunity cost for block orders will be reduced. Furthermore, volume orders can provide additional matches for regular orders, which should make the limit order book more attractive to a spectrum of other participants, including retail customers.

To conclude, electronic intermediaries for block trading are not at all at the end of their development. In fact, they are just starting to emerge. Today's alternative trading system (ATS) solutions fragment rather than integrate the market. Exchange-based innovations that effectively integrate institutional and retail flow are feasible and desirable, as the example of the volume order shows.

The Importance of Market Making

Frank L. Romanelli

C hapter 5 discusses the various market models and their associated liquidity and price discovery characteristics. We have seen how, more and more, the U.S. markets have embraced the order-driven models that by now have long existed in Europe. In this piece I discuss the role of the market maker and how that role is becoming more and more important in the European marketplace.

SOME HISTORICAL BACKGROUND

In the past 10 to 15 years, there has been growing dissatisfaction with the market models traditionally used on both sides of the Atlantic. In the United States, quote-driven markets were the norm, but in Europe the markets were predominantly order-driven except in the United Kingdom. With the increase in automation and developments in technology, the United Kingdom adopted the U.S. NASDAQ model in 1986 for its "big bang."

The "one size fits all" syndrome is misguided. The fact is, over time, markets have tended to develop hybrid structures. But this is not enough. From a technical point of view this has worked fine but, in reality, the needs of market participants are not being met, at least not in Europe. This may have something to do with cultural differences between the market participants on both sides of the Atlantic.

In Europe, the markets were generally dominated by banks that provided a range of services for their customers, from banking to securities trading. Banks, generally acting on instructions from their clients, steered away from risk as much as possible. In the United States and the United Kingdom, the functions carried out by today's large banks were unbundled, and individuals as well as specialist firms played a large role in the markets. Firms that did nothing but make markets were quite common. It was not unknown for a dealer to carry a position overnight of a million dollars or more in one security! These firms lived or died by their ability to make a market, and taking risks was part of their everyday life.

This started to change in the United Kingdom about 20 years ago when the marketplace was opened up and banks were allowed to own brokerage and market making firms. The banks would not tolerate the high risks their dealers were taking, and a more risk-averse culture was gradually introduced into the United Kingdom. This had not been a problem in continental Europe since markets there were mostly order-driven and, when a firm did make a market, it tended do so on a fair-weather basis. That is to say, if the climate looked good, a bank would quote a price, but if it looked like clouds and rain, the bank was not willing to venture outside. Any individual bank, of course, would say that fair-weather market making "is what the other banks do."

The drivers of efficiency and cost reduction drove exchanges to unify and automate. However, the introduction of electronic exchanges did not lead to any change in the trading model per se. They simply automated the existing processes. So we currently have a situation in Europe where the traditional client limit order book is being used by so-called "market makers" who are nothing more than the fair-weather or unofficial market makers just described. This is now finally beginning to change.

TYPES OF MARKET MAKING

The order-driven market works well in Europe for blue chip securities—and so it should, since these securities are usually the liquid ones where there is a good flow of supply and demand. To place this into context, around 90 percent of the liquidity in Europe is focused on about 10 percent of the total number of European securities. For securities that are not so liquid (the small and medium caps or the companies that are newly introduced to the market), we need the kind of environment that existed when market makers competed with one another for the business and were willing to quote prices in both good and bad times.

Having briefly defined the fair-weather market maker, let's look at other types of market makers.

Primary Market Makers

Primary market makers are sometimes referred to as designated market makers or specialists, but the concept is generally to have one primary market maker responsible for a specific security or group of securities. A recent example is the International Securities Exchange (ISE). The ISE defines this intermediary as someone with significant responsibilities, including overseeing the opening, providing continuous quotations in all of their assigned securities, and handling customer orders that are not automatically executed. At the ISE, a primary market maker (PMM) has to purchase a PMM membership that entitles him to act as a PMM in a group or "bin" of stock options. One PMM is assigned to each of 10 groups of options traded on the Exchange.

An advantage of this type of structure is that market members have a point of contact who is responsible for maintaining an orderly market, and who is available to answer market questions and to resolve trading-related issues. Such a structure, aligned by industry sector, could be envisaged for a European equity exchange of the future.

Competitive Market Makers

These are market makers who are willing, and who are indeed obliged, to provide continuous two-way prices in minimum size for a certain period of time. These market makers use their own capital, research, and resources to guarantee liquidity and to compete for order flow. They will buy or sell from their own inventory and earn revenues from the difference between their bid and ask prices for a given security. There is nothing wrong with this principle, as these firms are not charities. They are in the business of making money, just like any broker or bank, by charging fees or commissions to their customers.

Some exchanges require a minimum of two or three market makers per security, and it is not unusual for some securities to have a dozen market makers or more competing for business. It is, of course, important to monitor the market maker obligations to eliminate collusion with other market makers when fixing quotes or abandoning the market when volatility is very high. Those who are there in good and bad times with competitive quotes and depth are the ones who will generally gain market share.

Issuers

The listed company in a stock market normally has no desire to make a market in its own shares, and prefers to leave this to its bank or specialist. Often the lead bank involved in the company's IPO carries out the market making role as an extension of its services. We also recognize the role that a bank may have in issuing a warrant on a company's shares and meeting a duty to buy or sell these warrants at any time at a given price. The warrant market normally has a single market maker (i.e., the issuer), but competing market makers are not ruled out. Indeed, the Skontroführer is a specialist in the German Euwax (Warrant) Exchange model who can often improve on the price quoted by the issuer. The Skontroführer can be seen as a competing market maker as well.

In summary, market makers play an important role in the markets by providing liquidity. With increased regulation and the search for best execution, spreads are increasingly tightening. The role will call for even more efficient and skillful monitoring of market data and pricing instruments to attract the buy-side.

IS MARKET MAKING COMING BACK?

In reality, market making never went away. Indeed, in Europe, the growth in the derivatives market is reinforcing the market making concept. In the equities market, we have seen that only blue chip trading on a recognized exchange is really efficient. In London there is strong resistance to the expansion of the London Stock Exchange's SETSmm trading system to include even more securities in a hybrid order book model.

Whatever the security, after a certain point, illiquidity is always with us. Up to a certain size of order, many securities are liquid. Above this order size, a large block of a popular stock usually cannot be traded immediately based on current supply and demand conditions. Some type of intervention is required, be it an interdealer broker (IDB) or some sort of alternative trading aystem (ATS), such as POSIT, which is particularly focused on block trading.

Europe needs more market making to increase the efficiency of its capital markets. Many products today are traded off-exchange in the OTC markets. What model is there that could ensure that there is a buyer for every seller in a small- or medium-size company?

WHY BOTHER?

We have argued that true market making can play an important role in a nation's capital market by providing liquidity and enhancing investor confidence. The role carries certain obligations like providing guaranteed prices or responding to quote requests from other market participants. Fair-weather market makers are usually free to operate in order-driven markets, and they do not have the obligation to always quote a two-way price (but neither do they have the advantage that everyone must trade with them). If the true market making role is also associated with carrying risk, why then would any individual or firm bother? The answer, of course, is that where there is risk there are also opportunities. The U.S. and UK markets abound with stories of market making firms paying their staffs bonuses that are at least equal to their annual salaries in good times.

European exchanges are coming under increasing threat and competition, especially with the European Union's new MiFID regulations that are due to be implemented in 2007. These regulations will remove the concentration rules adopted by some exchanges to force orders onto their centralized systems. Alternative trading systems will be officially recognized and best execution rules will be introduced. Together with a focus on the reduction of costs and the replacement of legacy systems and infrastructures, there is bound to be more consolidation ahead, similar to what is happening today in the U.S. markets with the proposed merger of the NYSE and Archipelago, and of NASDAQ with Instinet. The introduction of new market making opportunities will create a niche area for those European exchanges that are prepared to offer new services.

We have asked, "Why bother?" If market making is to be encouraged, then this question must be addressed by the European exchanges, and incentives and rewards for market makers need to be clearly defined. Numerous examples already exist, ranging from reduced transaction fees or fee holidays, to profit sharing. The budding equity trader should ask himself whether he wants to be like the rest in handling only the popular stocks, or would like to create a niche for himself in what could be a more profitable area in the future.

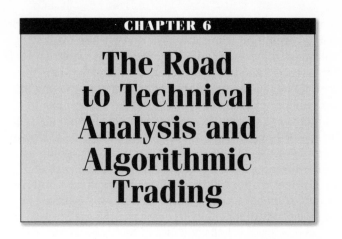

CHAPTER 6

The Road to Technical Analysis and Algorithmic Trading

W e discussed the efficient markets hypothesis (EMH) in Chapter 2, so let's begin with a recap. The EMH is one of the cornerstones of modern portfolio theory. The idea is that markets are so efficient in pricing equity shares that prices properly reflect *all* current information that is pertinent to the value of a stock, and any further trading on the basis of existing information would be profitless. By "all," we mean absolutely "all." All existing information and all anticipations of information change are properly reflected in price. This being the case, what might cause a price to change? Only *new* information, and by "new," we mean entirely "new." Unless it is truly new, it is partially anticipated, and the anticipation, as we have said, is already reflected in the stock's price. This is what is meant by information having been discounted in the market.

Can new information be predicted? No, any predictable component is already discounted in a stock's price. If the new information is entirely unknowable, can anyone say whether it will be bullish or bearish, or by how much? Of course not. Thus, who can predict what the next price change will be? Nobody. This being the case, an equity's price will change in totally unpredictable ways or, let us say, in random ways. Therefore, in a perfectly efficient, frictionless market, a stock's price will follow a random walk. Random walk can and has been extensively tested by financial economists. Early tests going back to the 1960s and before were based largely on day-to-day price movements. While these tests appeared to support the random walk hypothesis, more recent analyses of intraday (high-frequency) data are increasingly pointing to a contrary conclusion.

What would the nonpredictability of a stock's future price movements imply about the value of technical analysis and algorithmic trading? Technical analysis would be without reason and useless. Algorithmic trading could still have some applications, but its value would be much diminished. Yet technical analysis has been widely used for years by a broad array of participants, and computer-based algorithmic trading has come on board and gained enormous popularity in the past couple of years. Why might technical analysis and algorithmic trading be thought to be so valuable? This is the issue that we address in this chapter. Our focus is not on fashioning technical trading rules per se or on designing specific algorithms, but on gaining insight into their economic raison d'être.

Even if prices do not follow random walks, a real-world trading environment may still be informationally efficient. As discussed in Chapter 2, real-world markets are replete with costs like bid-ask spreads, market impact, fees, delays, trading halts and other blockages. These costs introduce correlations in the returns data, but do not necessarily imply a violation of the EMH. If the frictional costs outweigh the profitability of technical trading based on past trade price patterns, the EMH can still hold.

Yet technical analysis and algorithmic trading can have important roles to play. To understand this, we pay particular attention to the complex realities of price discovery and quantity discovery. This need not be at odds with the efficient markets hypothesis, but it certainly can raise some eyebrows. Perhaps, in light of the complexity of real-world markets and the realities faced by the participants who operate within them, we might recognize that, just possibly, our equity markets are not so efficient after all. Some of the complexities are beyond computers' capabilities. When asked "How important has algorithmic trading become?" Robert Gasser, CEO of Nyfix Transaction Services, replied:

> *It's a very useful tool, but the premise that you can turn off manual intervention and shoot a bunch of orders into an algorithm is rather naive. There's certainly a need for constant human intervention in terms of the ability to make some judgment calls based on market forces. So as powerful a force as algorithmic trading has become, I think it has reached its peak for a little while. It certainly has the capability to reduce the labor intensity, but there's always a need for human judgment.*[1]

DYNAMIC PRICE DISCOVERY

We have a story to tell. The story is one about investor behavior that underlies the dynamic process of price formation. It is one that recognizes that investors are not perfect information-processing machines. It suggests how a set of investors might interact with each other as they collectively set share values in the marketplace. In so doing, the story establishes a conceptual foundation for technical analysis and algorithmic trading.

Investor Behavior

The starting point of our story is the fact that investors are not textbook efficient, information-processing machines. No one is able to assess share values with great precision. The problem is that the information sets that get translated into security prices are too big, they are too complex, and our tools for analyzing them are too crude. Who can say, in light of a company's new earnings report, dividend policy, investment plans, regulatory situation, competitive environment, management team, the broader economic health of the country, and so on and so forth, that a company's equity is worth precisely $34.12 a share? Nobody can do this, not even a top graduate from one of the world's best business schools. John Porter's contributed piece in this chapter portrays the complexities of market information. David Segel's piece further considers how different investor types respond to news in different ways, which further complicates the translation of information into share prices.

Let's restate the question. Given all the relevant information, could any stock analyst say that a company's expected growth rate is exactly 7.000 percent? What if one analyst, in being very precise, sets the expected growth rate at precisely 7.000 percent and another, who is equally precise but somewhat more bullish, sets the expected growth rate at 7.545 percent? It is ridiculous to believe that anyone could estimate a growth rate with basis point accuracy. Not even close! But let's carry on with the story.

Take these two growth rate estimates and plug them into a simple stock evaluation model, the commonly taught dividend discount model, and see what you get. Let it be known that, one year from now, the company will pay a dividend of $1.35 a share, that its cost of capital is 10 percent, and that, with the dividend discount model, the current share value (Price) is expressed as follows:

$$\text{Price} = \frac{\text{Dividend One Year from Now}}{\text{Cost of Capital} - \text{Expected Growth Rate}}$$

Plug in the numbers. If the expected growth rate is 7.000 percent, we have

$$\text{Price} = \frac{\$1.35}{0.10 - 0.07545} = \$55$$

If the expected growth rate is 7.545 percent, we have

$$\text{Price} = \frac{\$1.35}{0.10 - 0.07545} = \$55$$

Wow! The price just jumped from $45 to $55!

The dividend discount model is, of course, a gross simplification of reality. Nevertheless, we can learn something from it. A future dividend of $1.35, a cost of capital of 10 percent, and an expected growth rate of 7.000 percent translate into a share price of $45.00. Increase the growth rate by just 54.5 basis points to 7.545 percent, and the share value jumps 22 percent to $55.00. What this model says is that anyone who misestimates a growth rate by just 0.5 percent, can evaluate the shares of this stock with only ±22 percent precision! This fuzziness in share valuation is the start of our story.

The second part of our story deals with how investors respond to a fuzzy share valuation. Ultimately, each investor decides his own share value. Each, in other words, sets his own reservation price. In the context of the example just presented, let's suppose that some investors (the gloomy bears with a 7.000 percent growth estimate) select $45.00 as their valuation, and that others (the brave bulls with the 7.545 percent growth estimate) select $55.00 as their valuation. What we have is a case of *divergent valuations* (touched on earlier in Chapter 2). In this story, the divergence of opinion is attributable to the inability to assess share values with precision. As we proceed, we keep the story simple by assuming that all investors fall into just two groups—the gloomy bears and the brave bulls.

The third and final part of our story is that investors, recognizing that their abilities to assess information are limited, communicate with each other and respond to what the others think. People talk at cocktail parties and in meetings. They listen to the often conflicting opinions of the market gurus, and they observe the behavior of prices in the marketplace. As they do, they may change their evaluations and switch from being gloomy bears to brave bulls, or vice versa. We refer to this switching as *adaptive valuations*.

Three Punch Lines

This is a three-part story. It moves from fuzzy assessments to divergent expectations to adaptive valuations, and it has three punch lines. First, the story reinforces the view of the marketplace as a network, as discussed at the end of Chapter 2. Within the network, no one participant alone establishes an equilibrium price—rather, the participants search for a price collectively. A property of a network is that, the larger it is, the more effectively it operates. This is commonly referred to as a *positive network externality*. New entrants in a network consider the benefits that they receive from being a part of it, but the benefits that their participation brings to others is, to them, an externality (of which they do not take account). We said in Chapter 2 that "as more orders converge in a marketplace, the orders provide more liquidity to each other and better price discovery results for the broad market." But customers as order placers do not individually take this into account—liquidity and price discovery are products of the network.

The second punch line of our story is that there is no unique equilibrium price for a stock. That is right, you read it correctly—a stock does not have a unique equilibrium value. Rather, the price that is ultimately discovered in the marketplace depends on exactly how information about separate valuations is communicated between the members of the group. Who has spoken first, the brave bulls or the gloomy bears? What direction has the sentiment of the group started moving in—up or down? Emotions may be contagious and self-reinforcing. Early expressions of optimism may result in higher prices prevailing; early expressions of pessimism may result in lower prices prevailing. This is a multiple equilibria environment. Multiple equilibria may not be something that you have been schooled to think about, but it is a topic of interest to economists. Thomas Schelling won the 2005 Nobel Prize in Economics for his work on how people respond in settings with multiple equilibria. We may more commonly believe that, when a market reaches equilibrium, it is a unique, single-valued solution, but a network can exhibit multiple equilibria and, in our story, an equity market network does.

The third and final punch line is in the spirit of the second. The multiple equilibria environment is *path dependent*. Assume that an important news event has occurred for a stock, and a new equilibrium value has to be found. Consistent with our story, following the news event, all participants may agree on the direction of the expected price response, but not on the magnitude. So, vis-à-vis each other, some participants will be bullish and others bearish. As the bulls and the bears trade with each other, talk with each other, and observe prices in the market, the price in the market evolves between their different valuations. Assuming no further news release, the price will eventually settle on a stable value that we can call an equilibrium. Will this value be closer to the bullish assessment or to the bearish assessment?

Path dependency means that the final, stable value that is discovered depends on the specific path that price has followed in the discovery process. In particular, the early shape of the path is critically important. If the bulls start out being more vocal, the path will start moving up, more participants (but, of course, not necessarily all) will switch to being bulls, and the final equilibrium price will be closer to the bullish valuation. The opposite will occur if the bears speak up first—the path will start moving down, more participants (but, of course, not necessarily all) will switch to being bears, and the final equilibrium price will be closer to the bearish valuation.

How the Participants Communicate

The story we have just told captures the essence of the price discovery process but is a bit vague. Let's be more precise.

We have assumed that all participants fit into one of just two groups— the brave bulls and the gloomy bears. Much can be accomplished analytically by introducing one more assumption: The information exchange between the two groups is entirely captured by a single variable, the distribution of participants between the two groups. Rather than cocktail party chatter, or market gurus, or any of the myriad different ways of looking at market data, consider just one—the proportion of participants who are bullish, represented by k, and the proportion who are bearish, represented by $(1 - k)$.

In the market, the bulls are buyers and the bears are sellers. Thus k represents the percentage of buyers, and $(1 - k)$ represents the percentage of sellers. The arrival of buy-triggered trades and sell-triggered trades can be observed in the market. Any trade that was made, for instance, at an offer price must have been triggered by the arrival of a market order to buy, and any trade that was made at a bid price must have been triggered by the arrival of a market order to sell. Thus participants speak to each other via their actions in the market that reveal each of them as being either a buyer or a seller.

As we will see, k is a very important variable. Take a look at John Porter's piece and think about how k can represent various technical factors that he refers to, such as market breadth and the number of stocks making new highs relative to the number making new lows. Then tie this in with David Segel's piece about the "mood" of the market. At this point, all of the authors are on the same page. We hope that you are, too.

We continue by first assuming that k is known by all participants. Common knowledge of k is a static framework. We then relax this assumption and let k be discovered in the market as customers arrive and trading proceeds. This is a dynamic framework. For both the static and dynamic frameworks, we assume a continuous limit order book market with no short-selling restrictions. Participants arrive at the market one at a time to trade one unit of a stock, and each either places a limit order or submits a market order that executes against a posted limit order. Bid and ask quotes are established on the market, and we take the market price to be the midpoint of the bid-ask spread.

The Static Framework

A static framework for studying the market created by the high and low valuation groups has been modeled by Handa, Schwartz, and Tiwari (HST).[2] They solve an interesting question: If some participants are willing to buy up to a price of $55, others are willing to sell down to a price of $45, and k is common knowledge, what price will clear the market? Think about it—this is an unusual setting. More typically, one thinks of buyers bidding the price up and sellers bidding the price down until a buy order crosses a sell order and a trade is made. If the orders do not meet or cross, a positive bid-ask spread is established in the market. But, in the HST setting, it looks as if we have an inverted spread, reflecting overlapping buy and sell interests at a number of prices (i.e., the market bid is higher than the market ask). With the inverted spread, could any price between $45 and $55 be a possible candidate for equilibrium? How does the market decide which value between $45 and $55 to take? As you think about this, keep in mind that we are not dealing with an economic bargaining situation. We have assumed a sizable number of atomistic participants who each step forward, one at a time, and decide either to place a limit order or to trade against a contra-side limit order by market order.

To understand this better, think about the two values, $45 and $55. These are not values that the participants transmit to the market in the form of orders. Rather, they are reservation prices, as we have previously discussed. A bull, for instance, would buy up to $55 if he has to, but may *not* be willing to pay $49 if it is likely that shares can be obtained at $48.90. Likewise, a bear would sell down to $45 if he has to, but may *not* be willing to sell at $51 if the probability is sufficiently high that shares can be unloaded at $51.10.

In this stylized framework, HST have solved for the optimal quotes for the bulls and bears to set as they post limit orders on the market. The solution yields a positive (not inverted) spread. The lower k is, the greater is the probability that the next arriving customer will be a seller. Knowing this, the now patient bulls are willing to post limit orders at lower prices, and the now aggressive bears are more eager to place market orders even though the bid quotes are lower (the bears have to be more aggressive because there are more of them). Consequently, the lower k is, the lower will be the quotes and, therefore, the quote midpoint, which we are referring to as the *price*. Or, if k is relatively high (i.e., greater than 0.50), the bulls will post higher bids (they know they must bid higher to attract bears to enter market orders), and the bears will post higher offers (they know that the bulls, not wanting to risk nonexecution, will be more apt to place market orders). Consequently, the higher k is, the higher will be the quotes and, therefore, the quote midpoint, or price.[3] In effect, k fully determines the price in this setting.

The Dynamic Framework

Paroush, Schwartz, and Wolf (PSW) have modeled the dynamic framework[4] with the assumption that k is common knowledge relaxed. Clearly, k is not known or even observable until participants sequentially arrive at the market and reveal themselves to be buyers or sellers. In this context, k discovery is equivalent to price discovery. An interesting thing happens when k is discovered while trading proceeds. In the dynamic framework, the adaptive valuations part of our story comes into play and, with it, path dependency and multiple equilibria emerge to characterize price formation.

Paroush, Schwartz, and Wolf model expectations formation (expectations of k and of the price that the market is heading toward). They also deal with individual behavior in the price discovery process, and with group dynamics. In their dynamic setting, expectations of k are revised as trading progresses on the basis of the observed arrival rates of buyers and sellers. If, early in the process, buyers predominate, the price path tends to converge on a relatively high value. Or, if sellers predominate early on, the path tends to converge on a relatively low value. The value that each price path converges on is an equilibrium value. A multiple equilibria solution results because different price paths converge on different values. Each equilibrium value is path dependent, and particularly sensitive to the initial conditions.

The PSW formulation applies directly to price formation within a relatively brief trading period (e.g., one day). However, by relaxing a few basic model assumptions—first, that a high value and a low value are fixed as in the Handa et al. analysis; and second, that k is the sole conduit for information transfer—PSW's analysis suggests that price discovery can incorporate more extended effects. How might this play out in actual trading?

Participants might pay attention to the movement of other series like the price and volume paths followed by related assets and various market indexes. They might consider recent highs and lows that a stock has set, and/or the length of time that a stock's price has remained above or below a certain benchmark value. Participants may pay attention to something like an advance/decline line. In a broader context, price discovery can play out over a more extended period of time and over a wider range of prices. Considerations about participants' behavior such as these start to build a bridge between our analysis of trader interactions and real-world price discovery, intraday volatility, technical analysis, and algorithmic trading. We will soon return to this thought.

QUANTITY DISCOVERY

One of the basic principles taught in standard microeconomics courses is that, in competitive markets, prices and quantities are set by the intersection of market demand and supply curves. The intersection of a textbook demand and supply curve does a wonderful thing—it provides a simultaneous solution for the two variables, price and quantity.

Life in the equity markets is not that simple. We considered price discovery in the previous section. In our discussion of the interaction between bullish and bearish traders, trade size was one unit. In this section, we relax the assumption that order size is fixed at one unit and redirect our focus to *quantity* discovery. Like price discovery, it is an imperfect process. Unfortunately, simultaneous solutions do not characterize our modern equity markets. The problems of quantity discovery are part of the reason. Institutional customers cannot easily integrate their large orders into the order flow. Rather, fearing market impact, they work their orders as discretely as possible, typically over extended periods of time, slicing and dicing them for delivery, one tranche at a time.

At any moment, a sizable two-sided, latent demand to trade can exist. That is, some big asset managers may be holding large buy orders in their pockets at the same time that other big asset managers are holding large sell orders, also in their pockets. When the buyers and the sellers do not find each other, mutually beneficial trades do not get made, price discovery is disrupted, and quantity discovery is incomplete.

Price and quantity discovery have, to an appreciable extent, decoupled in today's equity markets. This is not surprising. Retail customers submit small orders and are unconcerned about market impact effects. Large institutional customers could submit huge orders but do not, fearing market impact. How do the orders of the little mice and the giant elephants get integrated? Answer: The elephants either chop their orders into mouse-size pieces, or they seek to trade with each other in a separate venue at prices established in the market where the mice predominantly meet. Consequently, this is what happens. Price discovery takes place in the more central and transparent market, and quantity discovery, to an appreciable extent, takes place off-exchange. There is nothing necessarily wrong with this. It is simply how the world works.

The elephants can meet and trade directly with each other in a number of ways. Traditionally, large block trades have been made, and still are being made, in the upstairs, broker/dealer offices. Crossing networks such as ITG's Posit and Instinet's Crossing are available to the big players. Liquidnet and Pipeline have emerged as successful block trading facilities. The alternatives share one thing in common—they offer quantity discovery and either no price discovery (in the case of the crossing networks) or minimal price discovery (in the case of upstairs trading, Liquidnet, and Pipeline). Because they are decoupled, both price discovery and quantity discovery are imperfect processes. Nevertheless, if the order flow were *forced* to integrate, the result would no doubt be even more inefficient.

This takes us further down the road to understanding why technical analysis and algorithmic trading have an economic raison d'être.

Bookbuilding

The heart of the quantity discovery problem can be viewed in the context of bookbuilding. *Bookbuilding* is a term that has traditionally been used to describe what an investment banker does to build interest in a stock before bringing it to market for an initial public offering. This is not what we have in mind here. We are using the term to describe the process by which the *book*, on a daily basis, literally gets built from orders for already issued stocks traded in the secondary market. Building the book is a permanent, ongoing problem, especially with respect to institutional order flow. Chakraborty, Pagano, and Schwartz (CPS) have studied the bookbuilding dynamic in a way that is insightful for large traders.[5]

Let's start our brief description of CPS's analysis by recalling a movie you might have seen, *A Beautiful Mind*, starring Russell Crowe. Crowe played the role of John Nash, the brilliant economist/mathematician who won a Nobel Prize in Economics for having developed noncooperative game theory. His contribution to game theory, known as the Nash equilibrium, was a significant effort at demonstrating what happens when "most desirable outcomes" are sought by players in noncooperative games. Nash's basic insight was that, when people compete, they do not necessarily achieve the most desirable results that would be obtained if they instead cooperated. Chakraborty et al. recognized this behavior in the context of the equity markets, and they formally modeled it. Their objective was to obtain, using a game theory structure, an understanding of the dynamics of bookbuilding.

John Nash applied the Nash equilibrium to a game known as the "Prisoners' Dilemma" that we can describe with reference to Exhibit 6.1. Assume that two prisoners, prisoner A and prisoner B, have both been accused of a serious crime, and that they are being interrogated in separate cells. Neither knows what the other has revealed or may reveal. They are found guilty (or not) and are punished (or not), depending on what each of them says when interrogated. The alternatives, for each, are either to keep quiet, or to squeal and incriminate the other. If they both keep quiet, instead of facing a very serious charge like the death penalty, they get off with only a minor charge. As they would both be relatively satisfied with that outcome, that outcome for both of them is the best outcome in this game.

Now for the dilemma. Both prisoners have an incentive to deviate from the "do not confess" option. Each will fare better by squealing and incriminating the other if the other keeps quiet. In this situation, the squealer (say prisoner A) gets no punishment and can walk free, while the other prisoner (B) receives the most serious punishment. So A has an incentive to incriminate B. For the same reason, B has an incentive to squeal on A so that B can go free. The bottom line is that both are incented to incriminate the other, even though both would be better off if they both

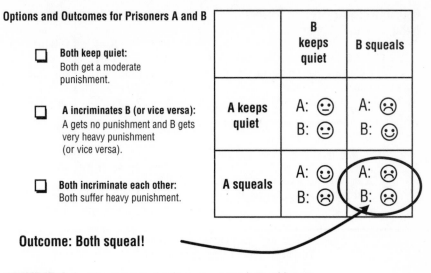

Options and Outcomes for Prisoners A and B

☐ **Both keep quiet:**
Both get a moderate
punishment.

☐ **A incriminates B (or vice versa):**
A gets no punishment and B gets
very heavy punishment
(or vice versa).

☐ **Both incriminate each other:**
Both suffer heavy punishment.

Outcome: Both squeal!

EXHIBIT 6.1   The Prisoners' Dilemma—A Nash Equilibrium

kept quiet. Consequently, both prisoners squeal. The two of them wind up
with heavy sentences and are in a worse situation than if they had cooperated instead of having competed with each other.

The Nash equilibrium can be applied to the world of trading, as shown
in Exhibit 6.2. Chakraborty et al. consider the situation where there are
two large traders with large orders to execute. Assume that trader A is
looking to buy a block of stock at the same time that trader B is looking to
sell a block of stock. Let each know that the other is out there (of course,
rarely do they know this), without either of them knowing when the other
will show up. Assume the market opens with a visible, open-book call auction. The question for both traders is, "Should I enter my order in the
opening call auction, or go to the market after the morning call?"

Chakraborty et al. show that trader A and trader B will both hold their
orders back from the opening call. The reason is the same as it is for the
prisoners' dilemma. Here, it is the traders' dilemma. Comparable to the
prisoners' dilemma, the optimal outcome for both would be for both to go
to the opening call. In this case, the two would meet and provide liquidity
to each other. In so doing, they would both happily achieve an execution
with little or no market impact.

But, as is the case with the prisoners' dilemma, both traders have an
incentive to deviate from the mutually beneficial strategy. Trader A will
say, "It makes sense for me to hold my buy order back and to wait for
trader B to sell and push the price down. By being patient, I will be able to

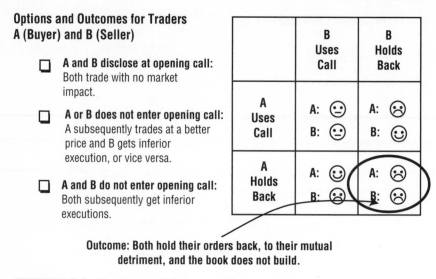

Options and Outcomes for Traders A (Buyer) and B (Seller)

☐ **A and B disclose at opening call:** Both trade with no market impact.

☐ **A or B does not enter opening call:** A subsequently trades at a better price and B gets inferior execution, or vice versa.

☐ **A and B do not enter opening call:** Both subsequently get inferior executions.

Outcome: Both hold their orders back, to their mutual detriment, and the book does not build.

EXHIBIT 6.2   The Traders' Dilemma—A Variation on Prisoners' Dilemma

buy at a lower price." The same logic holds for trader B: Wait for A to come in, buy, push the price up, and enable B to sell at a higher price. For each of them, holding back (which is equivalent to not telling the truth) while the other places an order in the call would lead to an excellent result. On the other hand, not holding back when the other does and going into the call alone would lead to a very bad result. It's a leader-follower game in which both want to follow.

Consequently, as with the prisoners' dilemma, they both do what is undesirable for the two of them collectively—they both hold back from the opening call. The result? Both traders go to a market that is less liquid and wind up paying for their decisions in terms of higher market impact costs. Nevertheless, A's behavior is not irrational, and neither is B's. Each is following a self-interested, self-optimizing trading strategy given his expectations of what the other will do. These conclusions are not based on any assumption of investor irrationality. They are based on the very rational idea that every trader is out for his own self-interest. Nevertheless, at the end of the day, each participant winds up with an undesirable outcome. That is the nature of a Nash equilibrium.

The outcome of the two traders' strategies underscores the problem of bookbuilding. What can be done about this? From the point of view of market design, how can a market's structure be changed to avoid the undesirable Nash equilibrium? Chakraborty, Pagano, and Schwartz focus on one solution in particular. They suggest that an intermediary—an entity like a direct access broker, the classic exchange specialist, or an upstairs market maker—should take an active role in bookbuilding. They see the intermediary as a facilitator who can animate a market. The animation process may involve anonymously providing capital, not to supply liquidity per se but to get the big buyers and sellers to step forward and supply liquidity to each other. By posting an order to sell, the animator may encourage buyer A to step forward (A would not have to worry as much about market impact because the anonymous animator's contra-side order is there). Seeing the activity and buyer A's order, seller B might then come forward and compete with the animator for A's order. As this happens, the animator can step aside and let A and B trade with each other.

The institutional customers should be able to trade with each other if, in fact, they are on opposite sides of the market. How common is it for natural buyers and sellers to both be present and looking to trade at the same time in the neighborhood of the same price?

Two-Sided Markets

When both buyers and sellers are looking to trade at the same time in the neighborhood of the same price, a market is said to be *two-sided*. The extent to which markets are two-sided is an empirical issue, as is the magnitude of any unexpressed, latent demand to trade. The latency of demand is not observable, however. It can only be inferred from market data. Sarkar and Schwartz have done this in their study of the two-sidedness of markets and the clustering of trades.[6] Their study is based on the complete quotation and transaction records for a matched sample of 41 NYSE stocks and 41 NASDAQ stocks for the period January 2 to May 28, 2003.

The study classified each trade according to the side of the market (buyer or seller) that triggered it. The classification rules are simple. Any trade that is closer to the asking price is classified "buy," any trade closer to the bid is classified "sell," and any trade at the spread midpoint is classified "buy" if the last recorded price change was positive, and "sell" if the last recorded price change was negative.[7] The authors then recorded the count of buy trades and sell trades in each half-hour interval, for each NYSE and NASDAQ stock, throughout the sample period. Trades were also classified as being relatively large or small, and the half-hour windows the trades occurred in were classified according to time of day (opening, midday, or closing), and according to whether there was relatively little information change or much information change at or around the time of the window.

What Sarkar and Schwartz found is that, for all of the various conditions considered—marketplace, trade size, time of day, and information environment—the markets are systematically two-sided. The two-sidedness is evidenced by the observation that, for each of these conditions, the arrival of more buy orders in a half-hour window is positively associated with the arrival of more sell orders for that half-hour window. In other words, the arrival of buy-triggered trades is positively correlated with the arrival of sell-triggered trades. The positive correlation between the number of seller-initiated and buyer-initiated trades in a half-hour period is highly pervasive and significant for stocks assessed individually, for NYSE stocks assessed collectively, and for NASDAQ stocks assessed collectively. In effect, the presence of buyers demanding liquidity leads sellers to demand liquidity as well, and vice versa.

Trade Clustering

Sarkar and Schwartz also found that trades tend to cluster in certain half-hour windows, and that two-sidedness characterizes the clusters. They established this by contrasting the distribution of the observed number of trades in half-hour windows with what would be expected if trade arrival was a random process. Visualize it this way. For a stock, classify the number of trades observed in each specific half-hour window in the sample period as being either high (H), medium (M), or low (L), based on the observed distribution of trades for that stock over all half-hours. Then count the number of half-hour windows over the entire sample period that are classified as H, M, or L.

The study found that the number of H and L half-hour windows is large, and that the number of M half-hour windows is small, compared to what the expected numbers would be if trade arrival were random. This is evidence of clustering—namely, systematic trade clustering causes more of the windows to be classified H, the sparsity of trades in other windows results in more of them being classified as L, and fewer are classified M. It appears that there is a feast or famine element to trading. When the market is quiet, it remains quiet for a while. But when trading picks up some speed, it gains momentum, there is a burst, and because of these bursts, a substantial number of H windows show up in the data. Importantly, the H windows (the trade bursts) remain predominantly two-sided.

What do the two-sided bursts suggest? Sarkar and Schwartz link them to the portability of trades—portability in time, that is. There need not be anything magic about trading precisely at, say, 10:35 in the morning, or immediately on receipt of an order. Asset managers generally do not have an immutable demand for immediacy. Four separate surveys of institutional investors' trading practices and preferences, covering U.S., European,

French, and Australian participants, portrayed a remarkably consistent picture. As summarized by Schwartz:

> *Many buy-side traders indicate that they are typically given more than a day to implement a large order. They frequently delay trades to lower their trading costs, commonly break up large orders for execution over time, and regularly take more than a day for their large broken up orders to be executed completely.*[8]

What matters to asset managers is the price of the trade, and they are commonly willing to work their orders patiently so as to get a better price. Many participants, particularly the large ones, time the placement of their orders. They wait for conditions to be propitious before stepping forth to make a trade. Until they are spurred to take the orders out of their pockets, their demand to trade remains latent, and the liquidity that they could bring to the market is latent. While demand remains latent (unexpressed), quantity discovery is incomplete, just as CPS's theoretical bookbuilding model suggests would be the case.

What triggers a trade burst? We know that order flow attracts order flow. We observe that trading triggers more trading. Then, eventually, the pace of activity subsides. Beyond these observations, there is much that we do not know. The exact genesis of a trade burst may be as obvious as one floor trader in front of a specialist's post announcing a desire to trade or as elusive as the genesis of a hurricane. Different observers of the market may have different views about this. It certainly makes the marketplace a very interesting environment, and it underscores why market data on volumes as well as prices are so important and valuable to traders. It also underlies some of what David Segel may be thinking about when he assesses the mood of the market.

We are now in a better position to understand why technical analysis and algorithmic trading have something to offer the many participants who see their value and use them.

TECHNICAL ANALYSIS

There is a widespread belief in the industry that useful trading information can be gleaned from charting price movements from the recent past (including trade-to-trade data from the current trading day) using techniques referred to as *technical analysis*. Technical analysis involves basing predictions of future price changes on observed patterns in recent market data (prices, trading volume, block trading activity, short interest, put-call ratios, implied volatility, and so forth).

Conventional academic opinion is that these predictions are ineffective. This certainly would be the case if markets were frictionless and share prices followed random walks. But, as we stress in this book, trading is not costless, and prices do not follow random walks. This reality is far more widely recognized by academicians today than it was a decade or so ago. Nevertheless, profitable trading based on predictions culled from historical data would still not be possible if markets are informationally efficient (remember the efficient markets hypothesis), and conventional academic thinking has continued to remain on the side of the EMH.

Welcome to Technical Analysis Territory

The dynamic price formation discussed earlier in the chapter suggests a violation of random walk, but does not necessarily lead to a rejection of the EMH. As we saw with two investor types (the brave bulls and the gloomy bears), a stock's price has a trading range—a high value (e.g., $55.00) that can be considered a *resistance level*, and a low value (e.g., $45.00) that can be considered a *support level*. According to Michael Kahn:

> *Resistance is simply a price level at which sellers become just as aggressive as buyers, and the forces of supply and demand are somewhat in balance. . . . The converse is true for support as buyers step up to become as aggressive as sellers and prices stop falling.*[9]

We are now entering technical analysis territory.

Recall that there is one important market indicator in our discussion—the proportion, k, of participants who are buyers. At each event (i.e., the arrival of each new participant), the bid and ask quotes are based on k, and price is taken to be the midpoint of the bid-ask spread. If k is greater than 0.5, buyers are aggressive (as Kahn puts it), and price in this example will be above $50.00, the mid-point of the stock's trading range. If k is less than 0.5, sellers are aggressive and price will be less than $50.00. Let's consider the case where buyers are aggressive (k is greater than 0.5).

Suppose that by some event (e.g., the 10th) in the trading session, the best estimate for k is 0.6, and all participants know it. This means that the actual probability that a buyer will arrive at the 10th event is 60 percent, and the quotes will reflect this by moving up. If a buyer does arrive, k at the next event (e.g., the 11th) will be reestimated to be greater than 0.6 and, accordingly, the quotes and price will be yet higher. So, too, will the probability that a buyer will arrive at the 11th event. The whole thing will be repeated again at the 12th event, and beyond. Each time a buyer arrives, k gets higher and price rises. This translates into price trending upward in the foreseeable future (of course, all bets are off if information change occurs, but that is a risk we all run, including the market technicians). Wouldn't this imply a profitable trading opportunity? Why not buy now and flip the shares soon after at a higher price? Ignoring the risk of information change, as of the 10th event, you would win 60 percent of the time. That is a very good bet, wouldn't you say?[10]

At second glance, the bet may not look so good, if trading costs are brought into the picture. If a limit order is used to acquire the shares, 60 percent of the time the order will not execute (for a buy limit to exercise, a seller must arrive). If the limit order does execute and you then have to flip the shares, a limit order strategy would be a particularly risky way to go about unwinding your position. With this one, let's forget about the limit order strategy. A momentum player is more apt to acquire shares by market order and then to flip them by market order. Accordingly, the shares will have to be purchased at the (higher) ask and subsequently sold at the (lower) bid. For the round trip to be profitable, the bid at the time they are sold would have to be higher than the ask that was posted when the shares were purchased.

Is it possible to trade profitably this way? Of course, but perhaps not on average. Remember, all participants know what is happening. All know that what one clever trader could win, someone else would lose (in this context, trading is a zero-sum game). But it would be easy for each and every participant to defend against being a loser by simply bidding lower and offering higher. In other words, the spread would widen sufficiently to nullify any possibility of anyone profiting, on expectation, from any trending with a short-term strategy. This shows how trading costs can leap in and rescue the efficient markets hypothesis.

Of course, in real-world markets, some participants, armed with high-speed computers, extensive live data feeds, connectivity to trading systems, and the right kind of algorithms, could still squeeze profits out of the order flow. An ability to do so would be a particularly insightful rejection of the EMH. But any evidence that would lead to the venerable hypothesis's rejection is generally kept under wraps for pecuniary purposes. We certainly would not expect to see it laid out in a research paper published in an academic journal.

Fond Memories of the EMH

The EMH is elegant, compelling, extraordinarily difficult to refute, and humbling. It stands as a warning to all aspiring, young masters of the universe, armed with what they might think are magic formulas by which they will earn millions. The EMH says that nobody with only publicly available market information and what might appear to be a crystal ball will be able to (1) know the future path that prices will follow, and (2) trade profitably on that knowledge. For one thing, prices should, and to a large extent do, reflect existing information. For another, trading is not costless. For yet another, any exploitable predictability in price changes can be viewed as an intertemporal arbitrage opportunity—shares can be bought at one moment at a relatively low price and sold at another moment at a higher price. As is true with arbitrage trading, the very act of trading eliminates an exploitable pattern. Consequently, any and all arbitragable opportunities are exploited and eliminated, the predictable powers of the technical analysts (the Darth Vaders of the trading world) are annihilated, and the EMH (Luke Skywalker) is rescued.

At least, so goes conventional academic thinking. One prominent academician, Burton Malkiel, has argued this quite forcefully. In 1973, he wrote,

> *Technical analysis is anathema to the academic world. We love to pick on it. Our bullying tactics are prompted by two considerations: (1) the method is patently false; and (2) it's easy to pick on.*[11]

Is technical analysis patently false? Not all academicians agree. Lawrence Summers argues that an inability to reject the EMH is not a sufficient basis for accepting it. Summers cites evidence provided by Modigliani and Cohn, by Shiller, and by Arrow, among others, that "certain asset prices are not rationally related to economic realities."[12] In light of Summers' own demonstration that large valuation errors need not be reflected in significant correlation patterns, he writes,

> *The standard theoretical argument for market efficiency is that unless securities are priced efficiently, there will be opportunities to earn excess returns. Speculators will take advantage of these opportunities by arbitraging away any inefficiencies in the pricing of securities. This argument does not explain how speculators become aware of profit opportunities. The same problems of identification described here as confronting financial economists also plague "would be" speculators. If the large persistent valuation errors considered here leave no statistically discernible trace in the historical patterns of returns, it is hard to see how speculators could become aware of them.*[13]

But, as we have noted, with the advent of high-frequency data, evidence that dependency patterns do exist in stock returns has strengthened. In short, the EMH is not looking as stellar as it once did. Summers had some rather strong feelings about this. Shortly after the dramatic market plunge on October 19, 1987, he was quoted in the *Wall Street Journal* as saying that the efficient markets hypothesis is "the most remarkable error in the history of economic theory."[14]

Thirty years earlier, the famous financier Bernard Baruch expressed his view of the link between information and stock prices:

> *The prices of stocks—and commodities and bonds as well—are affected by literally anything and everything that happens in our world, from new inventions and the changing value of the dollar to vagaries of the weather and the threat of war or the prospect of peace. But these happenings do not make themselves felt in Wall Street in an impersonal way, like so many jigglings on a seismograph. What registers in the stock market's fluctuations are not the events themselves but the human reactions to these events, how millions of individual men and women feel these happenings may affect the future.*[15]

We are playing a different ball game if what matters are human reactions to events rather than the events per se. Now, the link between information and security prices is considerably more intricate (especially if information encompasses the world), and behavioral considerations are far more important.

We have just presented three views of the market: Burton Malkiel (1973), Lawrence Summers (1986 and 1987), and Bernard Baruch (1957). Which conceptualization is closest to your own?

Let's now circle back and consider the road that we have been following. We wish to understand why, in principle, technical analysis and algorithmic trading can deliver value added. We have been focusing on price discovery and quantity discovery as dynamic, imperfect processes. This is not what is generally taught in MBA programs. In standard business school classes on stock selection and portfolio formation, the reasoning conveyed is that a stock's value is uniquely linked to current information. If you know the current information, then you know what the current price should be. Further, all investors with the same information will translate that information into the same share price. If this were the case, share prices could be found in the upstairs offices of the security analysts without reference to the marketplace where trades are made. We teach that current price is known, that it is future prices that are uncertain, and that investing involves risk only because we do not know what the future will bring.

This is not reality. As we have stressed, information sets are vast, and our analytic tools imperfect. When assessing the information sets, we do not come up with precise valuations and, more importantly, different analysts do not come up with the same valuations. Consequently, the marketplace is characterized by divergent expectations, which are, in turn, accompanied by adaptive valuations—we learn more about value by seeing what other traders do. As a consequence, stocks do not have unique equilibrium values. They have path-dependent, multiple equilibria values.

Welcome to Behavioral Finance

The path we are following opens a door to behavioral finance and, as it does, raises myriad questions. How do participants behave in this divergent and adaptive environment? How do they communicate with each other? What signals do they respond to? What patterns in the transaction records give participants confidence that a price, right now, for the current, brief, trading moment, is reasonable? No trader wants to make a purchase or complete a sale and then moments later look stupid because it was a bad trade. Does a head-and-shoulders pattern reveal that a current price level really is not supportable? If price pierces a support or resistance level, does this mean that the market will actually be going lower or higher? It is certainly valid to answer questions such as these with the use of statistical analyses of current and past market data.

This is what technical analysis is all about. Technical analysis need not be viewed as a way of predicting values that will be realized sometime in the future. Technical analysts commonly describe their work as studying data generated by the actions of people in the market so that they, the analysts, might better determine the right time to buy or sell a stock. The analysts may be viewed as looking not to predict the distant future, but to determine the color of the market at the current time so as to know just when and how to submit their orders.

In other words, in our nonrandom walk setting, technical analysis can be a valuable tool to have for assessing price movements that are likely to occur right now, in the current session, as the broad market searches for appropriate consensus values. For instance, a common practice of technical analysts is to locate a support level (a lower bound) and a resistance level (a higher bound) for a stock, based on the issue's recent trading range. If either of these bounds is neared but not penetrated, a technical analyst might expect the stock's share price to reverse course and stay within its current trading range. However, if either of these bounds is pierced, a signal is sent to the market that the stock's value has indeed shifted to a new level. David Segel, in his contributed piece, puts it this way:

> In a rational market, it should make no difference at what level a stock trades. For example, imagine a stock that is making new highs, touches $100 per share, and then retreats. In a random walk world, price action is haphazard and offers no interpretive data, but most traders would argue that if such stock fails to break through $100 a second and then a third time then its retreat from that resistance point is likely to be substantial. They know equally well that if the stock trades through and closes above $100 then this level will likely turn from having been the previous resistance level to being a new support level!

Support and resistance bounds, of course, are not readily apparent, but are assessed based on the skill and experience of the trader. The trader might attempt to profit by using a reversal (contrarian's) strategy if price appears to be fluctuating between the two bounds, or a momentum strategy if a support or resistance level is pierced. Exhibit 6.3 shows support and resistance levels at work in a one-day TraderEx simulation run. The market and P* prices are about $22.25 at the outset, slightly above the previous day's support level of $22. About 15 minutes into the day, P* drops to $21.30, triggering informed selling and momentum sell orders. Market prices overshoot P* and reach a low of $20.55, at which point price rises up to a resistance level from the day's open of $22.20. Informed trading then pulls price back down from the resistance point toward the current P* level of $21.30.

The point is, it is not just the future that is unknown. The current period is also uncertain. Prices do not change simply because information has changed. They change because they are involved in a search process. It is a search for a stable value, for a value that an economist might call equilibrium, for a value that has been validated by the market. The search can involve a good deal of volatility (the divergent views on value and the constant updated estimates of k provide a basis for understanding this intraday volatility). When you invest, you might be thinking of holding a position for a year or more. Yet, when you trade, you are thinking of the next 30 minutes (or seconds). Price movements within the next 30 minutes (or seconds) may have little to do with underlying information change. They may simply reflect the dynamic behavior of the order flow. You will operate well in this environment, not based on how well you have assessed a stock's fundamentals, but according to your knowledge of its order flow. At this point, you are not trading the stock—you are trading the order

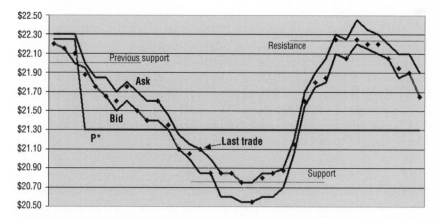

EXHIBIT 6.3 Support and Resistance Levels in a TraderEx Simulation

flow. When it comes to trading the order flow, you do not research the fundamentals. It is the dynamic properties of the stock's intraday price movements that you need to know about. This is when technical analysis is most useful.

As you apply it, in whatever way you find has the most value for you given the type of trader you are, we wish you the best of luck for the next 30 minutes (or seconds).

ALGORITHMIC TRADING

Algorithm (-ith'm) n. [altered (after arithmetic) < ALGORISM] math. *Any special method of solving a certain kind of problem; specif., the repetitive calculations used in finding the greatest common divisor of two numbers (called in full* Euclid's algorithm).
—*Webster's New World Dictionary*

Algorithmic trading—the automated, computer-based execution of equity orders via direct market-access channels, usually with the goal of meeting a particular benchmark
—*Domowitz and Yegerman*[16]

Algorithmic trading. It covers automated trading in which large orders are broken up and sent into the marketplace according to predetermined quantitative rules. These rules could be based on a number of historical volume patterns, the current day's price and volume activity, as well as other trading systems.
—*Nina Mehta*[17]

It is remarkable how strikingly different two children of the same parents can be. So it is with technical analysis and algorithmic trading. Both have their origins in the costs, nondisclosures, blockages, and other frictions of the marketplace. Both are based on the use of market data. But, from this point on, the two emerge as very different creatures. However, we are getting ahead of our story.

For as long as we can remember, our academic colleagues have talked about algorithms while talking about problem solving. For many years now, the term has also been applied to trading. The contributed piece by Paul Davis, "Algo History at TIAA-CREF," gives a good sense of how deep the roots of algorithmic trading go at one of the largest and most important of all institutional fund management firms. If a broad definition of the term is applied, all professional traders are operating on the basis of algorithms. So it is not new in that sense. In the last couple of years, however, computerized algorithmic trading has become a hot ticket.

Automated algorithmic trading services are now being offered by many broker/dealers and are being widely used by buy-side traders. *Traders Magazine* reported that a recent study showed that 60 percent of buy-side firms are now using algorithmic trading tools for order execution.[18] Where there is so much smoke, there must be fire. Algorithmic trading has to be offering something of considerable importance. Wherein lies its value?

Back to the mantra of the EMH: If markets were frictionless and share prices followed random walks, technical analysis would be fruitless. So, too, would be algorithmic trading. In fact in a frictionless, capital asset pricing model (CAPM) world, there would be no trading as we know it—with continuous, costless pushes of a magic button, the share holdings in all portfolios would continuously maintain their desired weights. Harry Potter could not ask for more magic than that. But, as we have said any number of times now, trading is not costless and random walks are not a reality. Consequently, price discovery is not highly accurate, nor is quantity discovery reasonably complete. This reality makes trading of major importance and sets it apart from investing as a distinct operation. Institutional participants in particular are acutely aware of this.

Algorithmic Trading vs. Technical Analysis

Like technical analysis, the value of algorithmic trading lies in the intricacies and imperfections of price and quantity discovery. However, while the two may share a common raison d'être, they differ from each other in very important ways. Algorithmic trading is a set of rules—in fact, it is sometimes referred to as *rules-based trading*. A trading rule states that *if* this, that, and perhaps some other conditions are satisfied, *then* I want to submit this order, cancel that order, and so on. In fact, TraderEx's machine-resident market makers are algorithmic traders who follow simple rules based on their current inventory positions relative to their position limits, the direction of their last trade, and the quote changes of the other dealers. The rules specify when they will match the inside bid or offer quote, make a new best bid or offer, come off of the inside bid or offer quote, or initiate a trade with another dealer. TraderEx's market maker algorithm was developed with inputs from several experienced market makers in the London equity market.

Technical analysis, on the other hand, signals price changes that are likely to occur. If a stock's price has moved in such and such a way, then we expect that it likely will have a particular pattern next, and so on. Rules, however, can be layered on an analysis of recent price and volume records, and technical analysis and algorithmic trading can be used in combination.

Algorithmic trading is computer-based, while technical analysis and charting predates the computer. Technical analysis is typically used to search for profitable trading opportunities; the major use to which computer-based algorithmic trading is currently being put is to control trading costs. Domowitz and Yegerman, taking algorithmic trades to be all orders "executed through computerized model-based trading strategies and implemented through algorithmic server technology," report that "the vast majority of these executions follow a volume weighted average price (VWAP) strategy."[19]

There are further differences to note. The economic raison d'être of technical analysis lies primarily in the intricacies of *price* discovery; algorithmic trading has much to do with the intricacies of *quantity* discovery. Technical analysis can be applied to very short-term, intraday price movements, as well as to longer term, multiday price patterns; algorithmic trading is strictly a short-term trading application. Technical analysis can be undertaken by all traders, small and large alike; algorithmic trading is for the big players—the ones who incur the big execution costs.

Algorithmic Trading and Quantity Discovery

Our earlier discussion in this chapter of quantity discovery started with the bookbuilding problem as it applies to large traders. Large buyers and large sellers need each other for the liquidity that they can mutually provide one another, but they surely do not step forward and shout, "Hey, I have 150,000 shares to sell, does anybody want them?" Or, "I'll buy 275,000 shares, who wants to sell them to me?" This might be fine for 100 shares or even 1,000, but for 150,000, or 275,000, or half a million, or more? Small orders do not have market impact—the big ones do.

As we have stressed in this book, the profitability of a portfolio manager's stock selection can be seriously undermined if the investment decisions are poorly implemented in the marketplace. Consequently, large players come to market with much care. The buyers and sellers might sense each other's presence, but they wait for each other to move first, and not exactly with a "please, after you" sense of politeness. This is the bookbuilding problem previously discussed. A buyer pushing price up is good for the seller; a seller pushing price down is good for the buyer. Neither wants to be caught on the short end of the stick. This leads to Chakraborty, Pagano, and Schwartz's prisoners'/traders' dilemma problem that we have looked at. The big guys hold their orders back and, as they do, the liquidity that they could provide each other remains latent. Sarkar and Schwartz's empirical study suggests that much of the time an appreciable amount of liquidity may be latent.

Alternatives exist. Crossing networks such as ITG's Posit and Instinet's Crossing, and block trading systems such as Pipeline and Liquidnet, are enabling large customers to come together with anonymity and to trade in size. But these systems need prices to base their trades on. As we have noted, the prices come from the main market centers. The centralized, transparent markets, however, do not cater to the large trades. From New York to London, Frankfurt, Paris and beyond, many of the orders these venues receive from big customers have either been entered as hidden (iceberg) orders or have been sliced and diced and fed into the market, tranche by tranche, over an extended period. Put this all together, and the stage is set for algorithmic trading. Another good example involves the optimal placement of a limit order in a call auction that is followed by continuous trading or in a continuous market that is followed by a call, as we discussed in Chapter 4.

The Sarkar and Schwartz observation that trades tend to occur in bursts further sets the stage.[20] Quantity is not being discovered as long as orders remain in traders' pockets. What is it that triggers the transformation of this latent liquidity into active orders and produces a trade burst? What occurrences in the marketplace pull the orders out of the traders' pockets? Traders have decision rules concerning when to be patient and when to move forward aggressively. If the conditions are met, trades occur. A good algorithm specifies those conditions for an individual trader, depending on the size of the order that he wishes to execute, the liquidity and volatility characteristics of the stock to be traded, the time pressure from the fund manager for the trade to be made, and the willingness of the fund manager and the trader to take risk.

Where the Rubber Meets the Road

Let's bring this down to earth, to where the rubber meets the road. Picture yourself at the buy-side desk of a large mutual fund. Your portfolio manager (PM) has just instructed you to sell 300,000 shares of Xyz.com, a stock that trades on the NYSE. You are given one day maximum to get the job done. Average daily volume (ADV) for Xyz.com is 700,000, and the stock's intraday price volatility is high. Your PM will be displeased if the average price you receive for your sells is less than Xyz.com's volume weighted average price (VWAP) for the day. Price for this stock commonly changes swiftly, and trading opportunities can present themselves quickly and disappear in a flash. If word leaks out about what you are trying to do, you can get slaughtered in the market. How do you cope with this? What kind of trading strategy do you formulate? What set of trading tools do you need to implement your strategy?

Electronic trading can have major advantages here. Most importantly, it can give you anonymity, control over your order, and speed. A good strategy may be to go first to the crossing networks and/or block trading facilities and see what you can get done. Then, with what remains, slice and dice and time the placement of each tranche of your big order according to an algorithm. Give part of your order to a direct access broker on the NYSE floor (without, of course, disclosing that you have more to do). Go to INET and/or to Archipelago when they are offering liquidity. Track market data, be patient, and step forward when an opportunity presents itself or the market looks like it is about to move away from you. As you proceed, trade as much as you can while keeping the average price that you are getting for your sells above the day's VWAP. Moving those 300,000 shares in a day and beating a VWAP benchmark in a fast-moving market when the ADV for Xyz.com is only 700,000 shares is not easy. Computer-based rules and electronic order handling can be an enormous help to you. As Domowitz and Yegerman document, VWAP trading is a major use to which algorithmic trading is being put.

Here is another situation. You have just been given a list of 100 stocks, some of which have to be bought, and others sold, to keep your fund's portfolio in line with a market index that the fund is tracking. Strategic decisions that you have to make in this setting include which names to trade aggressively, which to be patient with, and which stocks could be replaced by other stocks with similar characteristics if, at any given time, they are easier to trade. This is called basket trading with substitutions. Again, algorithmic trading tools are a huge help with all of the alternatives and contingencies that are involved.

Trading Tools and More

There is more in the buy-side trader's arsenal. Being computerized, algorithmic trading can be united with electronic order management and execution management systems that are being widely used by the buy-side traders. This allows for the convergence of portfolio management analytics and execution tools (see Domowitz and Yegerman, and Domowitz and Krowas for further discussion).[21] Relevant information flows to be tied together include the trading characteristics of individual stocks, performance benchmarks, historic measures of trading costs, and historic measures of broker performance. The costs and risks of alternative trading strategies can be projected, and the information structured and made available on the user's trade blotter. You can even come up with a pretrade prediction of what your trading costs will be. If a fund manager is indifferent between two trades to alter the portfolio, go with the one that has the lower expected trading cost.

Computer-based algorithms may enable a buy-side trading desk to operate efficiently and cost effectively in a fast-moving market, but what happens when many buy-side desks undertake algo trading? Do fast markets become faster? No doubt. Data traffic into the exchanges and ECNs has grown far faster than overall trading volumes, as more orders are submitted and then canceled and replaced at different prices. In so doing, does the procedure destabilize the market? It depends. Some algo rules might be destabilizing, but others might stabilize prices. How effective is this for everybody collectively? Think about it. If everyone gets better weapons to fight with, can the average player be better off?

Do the algo traders leave footprints in the transaction records that market technicians and other algo traders can pick up? They sure can if they do not take proper care to cover their footprints. Algorithms now exist for reverse-engineering the algorithms of others so that their trading intentions might be discovered and front-run. The antidote to this is the use of sophisticated strategies. Hiresh Mittal of ITG was quoted in *Traders Magazine* as saying:

> *An algorithm must randomize how it sends orders into the market, how it prices orders, and the way it cancels and replaces those orders. Otherwise, someone could see that order coming and prepare to make money on it.*[22]

Human Algo Traders

A computer-based algorithm may be considered an electronic intermediary, doing the work that a broker would have done. Reciprocally, a floor trader may be viewed as a human algorithm. We conclude this section by discussing the floor trader's role in working not held (NH) orders on the floor of the NYSE to implement a switching strategy—first wait for the market to come to you so that you can be a liquidity provider but, if it looks like the market is about to move away, step forward, spark a trade, and grab liquidity before it gets away from you. Handa, Schwartz, and Tiwari (2004) found that this smart order algorithm translates into lower execution costs. We provide further description of order handling by floor traders in the Appendix to this chapter.

The floor traders could base their market timing on a variety of variables and market conditions, and different floor traders might give different weights to different inputs. Handa, Schwartz, and Tiwari write:

> *There are a number of . . . ways in which a floor trader may add value: (1) the trader might obtain knowledge of the presence of a contra party, mitigating price impact; (2) the trader could "round up" multiple counterparties, again cushioning the impact by trading in what may be viewed as a spontaneous call auction; (3) the trader could anticipate periods when liquidity is high and trade more often and in large sizes during such periods; (4) the trader could avoid trading in periods when trading is low; and (5) the trader may possess superior ability to read momentum in the market and to time trades accordingly.*[23]

This points the direction for some computer-driven algorithms. Handa, Schwartz, and Tiwari looked at two key variables: (1) the imbalance between buyer-triggered and seller-triggered trading volume in 15-minute intervals (a variant of the variable k), and (2) the price trend established by the 15 most recent trades. They found that the probability of trades being triggered by floor brokers handling NH orders was related to these two variables and that, when the trades were so triggered, trading costs, on average, were lower. This meshes with the promise of algorithmic trading.

Viewed broadly, algorithms have historically been used by traders, although not many of them in the past may have even known the term. What is new is the prevalence of computer-based algorithmic trading. As exciting and promising as it might be, computer-driven trading does leave human judgment out of the equation, even as it reinforces the speed with which events can occur. Some might feel that today's markets are getting too fast, that they are being overly driven by computers and computer technology.

An analogous situation concerning baggage handling at the Denver International Airport was reported recently in the *New York Times*.[24] Ten years ago, according to the *Times* article, Denver introduced a computerized baggage-handling system that "immediately became famous for its ability to mangle or misplace a good portion of everything that wandered into its path." The article went on to say that, "Sometime over the next few weeks, in an anticlimactic moment marked and mourned by just about nobody, the only airline that ever used any part of the system will pull the plug."

Like baggage, orders have to be routed, handled, and delivered somewhere. But unlike Denver's baggage-handling system, computer-based algorithmic order handling is working, and it will not meet a similar fate. Nevertheless, it is important to note the role of the human element. Regardless of the computer's power to process information and deliver performance for the buy-side trader, it would be a big mistake to believe that, for a long time to come, it will be safe to take the human element out of trading.

FROM THE CONTRIBUTORS

Paul L. Davis
Algo History at TIAA-CREF

John H. Porter
The Complexity of Market Information

David Segel
The Mood of a Market

Algo History at TIAA-CREF

Paul L. Davis

Equity portfolio management at TIAA-CREF Investment Management LLC covers the gamut of investment styles. There are international and domestic portfolio managers; growth and value managers; large and small cap managers; fundamental, quantitative, passive, and index managers. Not only must the trading desk be sensitive to today's PM needs, but it must anticipate and prepare for tomorrow's needs. We began our development of the CREF automated trading platform in the late 1980s in response to a portfolio management approach designed by Eric Fisher, the senior quantitative analyst at the time. Algorithmic trading is one tool on that platform.

Eric and his team developed an automated valuation–based strategy that was designed to stay very close to, and ahead of, its benchmark portfolio. Such strategies are tried frequently now, but at the time there were few investment management firms running serious money using such an approach. Eric had a very unusual insight related to trading. He simulated our strategy over and over again, randomly selecting only a part of the daily trade list. He found that, if the strategy really had an alpha (could beat the benchmark) and if our trade list executions were essentially random, we could achieve superior performance without executing all of our orders. Trading costs could be kept low by trying to buy at the bid and sell at the offer (be a liquidity provider instead of a liquidity demander) and by regularly participating in the crossing networks that had just been developed. We reported Eric's research and the structure of our trading system in 1991 at a Berkeley Program in Finance Seminar.

The inherent dangers of our approach were (1) that the alpha we found in our tests might not be sustainable going forward, and (2) there could be a selection bias against us as we traded because, unlike the simulations, the orders from our trade lists that would actually get executed might not be a random selection. Fortunately, we avoided both pitfalls. We beat our benchmark, the S&P 500 initially and the Russell 3000 later on, in 9 out of 10 years until the onset of the dot-com bubble in the late 1990s. Our valuation methodology failed to add value during the bubble. Even if we had executed our trade lists in their entirety and at no cost, we would not have beaten our benchmark. But long before we moved away from that investment strategy, we concluded that the electronic trading tools we had developed had broad applicability. These tools became available for all portfolios and became the core of the trading environment used by all of our enhanced index, passive, and index portfolio managers.

The trading platform that we developed in the late 1980s and early

1990s was an amalgam of a trading system and an order management system. There was very little third party order management system (OMS) software or trading software available at the time. Our traders could control all trading activity from a single platform. While our present algorithms are fully automated, our early algorithms required a more hands-on approach. Most of the orders directed to this trading platform arrived as baskets of orders. The algorithms ordered the stocks by importance and the traders were at the controls. For example, the trader could select those industries with the most severe, unwanted exposures and trade only those industries using SuperDOT and, after their development, the ECNs. There were automatic pilot features as well. Traders could turn on algorithms that would maintain a supplying liquidity stance in the sense that the algorithm would cancel and replace orders so that buy orders would stay positioned at the bid, and sell orders at the offer. Other early algorithms would reposition orders in response to moves in futures and industry returns and in response to trading imbalances.

Beginning in the late 1980s, we captured all real-time data for every stock we traded. Tick-by-tick prices, trade sizes, bids and offers, and bid and offer sizes were stored in data sets that were merged with records of our trades for analysis and feedback into the trading process. Based on this data, we made an interesting observation that we reported at a Paine Webber conference in the early 1990s—the effectiveness of our trading using a five-minute time horizon determined the overall effectiveness of our trading. That was not the case for any one trade. For example, if we bought IBM at 10:30 at a price that was lower than the price of IBM at 10:35, the trade may or may not look good versus the end-of-day price. However, when we aggregated all of our trades over different time periods, we found that average outperformance over a five-minute window implied average outperformance for the day. (Needless to say, the cross-sectional standard deviations of longer time horizon returns were higher than those of five-minute returns.) This was all the more remarkable given our effort to be a liquidity supplier and not to push prices. Either our alphas were being realized immediately or our trading strategies were effective—or both.

Most algorithms in the marketplace today are targeted to a benchmark price. The most common benchmark price used is VWAP, the volume weighted average price. Some are implementation shortfall strategies in which the benchmark price may be the price when the order first arrives in the trading system, or the opening price. Our work with real-time tick data suggested a different path. We postulated that traders (at least our traders and our algorithms) are investors with very short time horizons. The critical decisions to be made—when to pull the trigger; at what price; or how many shares can be put into the market—should be made with the hope of beating the market in that stock over the next few minutes. We speculated that success in that endeavor would lead to good results when trading costs are computed across large samples using any of the standard benchmarks. This appears to be the case.

The CREF Stock Account was set up in 1952 as the equity pension vehicle for college and university faculty and staff. It is presently valued at over $100 billion. For most of its history, it has consisted of various subportfolios, with each subportfolio either focusing on a different part of the global market or using a different portfolio management approach. The CREF Trading System (CTS) was originally designed for one of these components. As our product line grew, CTS was restructured to trade all portfolios in the CREF family of accounts. A change in strategy was needed, however. Either we hire more traders to control and oversee trading across many portfolios, or we continue down the automation path. The latter approach was chosen. We thought that we had the experience needed to design a flexible algorithm that would meet the foreseeable needs of all of our basket trading. We were right.

The algorithm had to be part of a complete trading environment. The environment had to accommodate the algorithm, crosses among portfolios, and trading on crossing networks as well as other trading modalities. All of this is integrated on the CTS platform. The CREF Trading System runs on several computers at two sites over 1,000 miles apart. Any computer can handle the entire trading load, but the workload is divided across installations in order to quickly recover from almost any type of outage, however severe. Every execution is recorded at both sites in real time and recovery, if ever needed, would be immediate.

The algorithm we use continues to evolve. The next big developmental push is based on a simple observation. Even though algorithmic trading might appear quite complex, compared to what a trader (the human algorithm) does, it is straightforward. A trader evaluates an order and can try to get it done in any number of ways. These include trading it electronically, perhaps giving it to a broker on the floor of the NYSE, asking a broker for capital, or putting it on an ATS. The type of order will determine the approach. Given the nature of liquidity—sometimes it is there and sometimes it is not—a trader will have a difficult time anticipating what will happen and what the trade will cost. On the other hand, an algorithm will use the same strategy for all orders. An algorithm, if it could speak, could tell the portfolio manager what will happen with much more confidence. A conversation might go something like this:

> **Mr. Algorithm:** Hey, Ms. P.M., that order is right in my wheelhouse. I can do it in about three hours, slicing and dicing, and it ought to cost you about 15 basis points compared to the arrival price.

Ms. P.M.: Okay, Mr. Algorithm, go to it.

Mr. Algorithm: You may not have noticed, but it took you so long to get back to me that there is only one hour left in the trading day. Are you sure you don't want to wait until tomorrow morning? I will have to be three times as aggressive to get it done and you can anticipate at least three times the trading costs. If you insist on doing it now, I recommend you give the order to a trader and have the trader look for pockets of liquidity.

Ms. P.M.: Sorry about the delay. Let's wait until tomorrow morning.

The danger a user of an algorithm faces is not knowing the limits of the algorithm. Our goal is to communicate those limits pretrade and in real time to the traders and the portfolio managers. By assigning orders to algorithms and traders more systematically, we can better meet our trading objectives, including lowering trading costs.

The Complexity of Market Information

John H. Porter

Equity prices are influenced by myriad factors, some of which derive from attributes specific to the individual company in question. A broader set of variables relates to macroeconomic aggregates such as employment and inflation, which influence prices at a market level, resulting in a systematic impact on individual securities or sectors. The macro determinants of equity pricing can be divided into three areas: the fundamental, the technical, and the psychological. My purpose here is to review these three areas that critically affect macro decision making in the equity arena and to give some practical examples of each.

FUNDAMENTALS

Macro or top-down analysis may be considered to be more challenging than the specific or bottom-up approach. In effect, all market participants have access to the extensively analyzed macroeconomic variables and have less of an advantage against those who, operating in a more narrowly defined space, obtain security-specific information. Moreover, macro analysis not only requires the correct forecast of the relevant variables—it also must gauge the extent to which the expected outcome is not already reflected in current market prices.

Perhaps the most critical macroeconomic variables relate to both fiscal and monetary policy. The former can have a direct influence on stock prices via government spending. For example, defense and security-related companies benefited greatly from the increased military spending in the aftermath of the terrorist attack on September 11, 2001. Fiscal policy can also have an indirect effect via its influence on interest rates; however, that is more the domain of monetary policy. When the central bank is tightening the availability of credit, the interest rate applied to discount future earnings streams rises, causing stock prices to decline.

Unfortunately, applying the result of the most assiduous macroanalysis to investment decision making can be equivocal at best. For example, equity investments have always been considered to be a robust long-term hedge against inflation to the extent that the nominal value of the goods produced by corporate assets rises along with the general price level. However, if the central bank should act to offset the impact of higher inflation by raising interest rates, stock prices could fall for the aforementioned reasons.

Other types of fundamental variables include the slope of the yield curve (when short-term interest rates exceed long-term rates, an inverted yield curve suggests that the economy will experience a recession); the role of government in the overall economy (the greater the share of government spending in GDP, the lower the overall level of productivity in the economy); the change in corporate bond yields (falling corporate bond yields are considered to be positive for stock prices); and the number of corporate bankruptcies (increasing business failures are clearly a negative factor for general stock valuations).

Finally, the relevant fundamentals can vary with respect to secular changes in the economy or cyclical extremes. At present, the U.S. current account has registered the highest deficit with respect to GDP in the postwar period. If the dollar were to fall precipitously to correct this imbalance, the stock market would in all likelihood suffer. Even a partial liquidation of the significant foreign holdings of U.S. government and agency debt would result in an abrupt rise in interest rates. The significant leverage of households, much of which is linked to the housing sector, could be considerably imperiled with an obvious impact on equities.

TECHNICALS

Technical analysis can be summarized as the identification of patterns in past price and volume movements that can be used to project future prices. Despite the widespread use of technical analysis by market participants, standard academic thinking is that it does not have any predictive power. This debate is captured in the academic literature regarding the efficiency of markets. (For a detailed discussion of the three types of market efficiency, see Burton Malkiel's *A Random Walk Down Wall Street*). The semi-strong version of the efficient markets hypothesis posits that excess risk-adjusted returns cannot be achieved using publicly available information.

Nevertheless, there are those who maintain that certain technical indicators can serve as useful inputs into the investment decision-making process. (A strong proponent of these types of indicators is the renowned Ned Davis of Ned Davis Research, Inc.) These indicators are thought to reflect the intrinsic health or strength of the overall market. Trend and momentum are statistical concepts designed to measure price direction and rates of change, respectively, thereby enabling the action of the market itself to dictate the investment outlook. To the extent that markets trend, the identification of this attribute can lead to profitable investment strategies. From a macro perspective, it is important to equally weight industry group price indexes and to use appropriate filters (e.g. moving averages) to discern trends more finely. Momentum indicators merge both price and trading volume to determine the strength and general health of the market. Comparing the rate of change of stock indexes using various time periods is useful to detect possible inflection or turning points.

Market breadth, or the relative number of securities in a given index that advance or decline on a specific day, is another technical indicator which measures the internal strength of the market. This metric can also be extended to the number of stocks that achieve a yearly high in price compared to those making new yearly lows. Since market tops take time to form, a price peak is more probable when moving averages are reaching higher levels without confirmation from an increasing number of stocks making yearly highs. Conversely, markets tend to make cyclical bottoms rather abruptly. To this effect, a market bottom, characterized by a vast majority of new yearly stock lows, indicates that a selling climax has occurred with a price reversal in the offing. Finally, a relatively balanced split between stocks making new yearly highs and those making new yearly lows is indicative of a general lack of breadth and is therefore considered negative. When the majority of stocks are making new highs for the year (or new lows), the existing bullish (bearish) trend receives confirmation. This type of indicator helps the investor distinguish a bear market rally from a bull market, as well as the price extremes oftentimes associated with the end of a bull market.

There are many other types of technical indicators used to determine market strength. A diffusion index reflects the number of stocks whose price is advancing over a given time period compared to those whose price is declining. An advance/decline line can be constructed, subject to some smoothing function, to measure the magnitude of the overall trend. A variant of this approach compares the number of stocks making new highs during a specified time interval to those making new lows. This technique is particularly useful to project stock index highs, as these are often preceded by an increasing number of weekly highs on individual stocks.

Myriad statistical variables have been constructed to determine the inherent fundamental health of the market. Moving averages, previously identified as useful in the discovery of market trends, can also be applied to gauge the breadth of an index. A significant percentage of stocks trading above their moving averages, for example, signals a confirmed uptrend.

Oscillators have been developed to identify periodic sideways and trendless market environments. In addition, this statistic can signal short-term market extremes within a trend, commonly referred to as overbought or oversold conditions. Stochastics, for example, are a type of oscillator that delivers this signal by measuring the velocity of the security's price. Finally, a trend that is nearing completion can often be discerned by divergence and a loss of momentum reflected in the oscillator. A classic example of divergence is the appearance of an equal number of new highs and new lows.

PSYCHOLOGICAL

Psychological factors are very important in technical analysis to the extent that they underlie the behavior of market participants and often contain harbingers of future market moves. This area of macro analysis is based on the premise that the majority of investors make collective mistakes, being bullish at the top of the market and bearish at the bottom. Market sentiment, perhaps the most widely recognized indicator of this particular category, is a gauge of speculative activity of market participants derived through polling investors on their specific views and positions. A quantitative approach to measure how investors are positioned is known as the *Commitment of Traders Report* prepared by the U.S. Commodity Futures Trading Commission (CFTC). If the large speculators are all positioned in the same directional fashion, it is highly likely that the market will move in the opposite direction. In other words, if speculative market participants have already bought, there will be no one left to push the price higher. As such, the path of least resistance is down.

Another indicator of sentiment which reflects the propensity for risk taking in the market is the measure of future volatility (VIX). This index is particularly useful for identifying extreme market lows which occur when investors engage in the panic liquidation of security holdings. Market bottoms are often associated with resurgent fear in the investor's psyche, leading subsequently to an upward spike in the VIX.

A final type of sentiment analysis focuses on savvy investors who are privy to better information than the naive speculator. One statistic that is tracked quite closely is insider sales. If managers of a company are liquidating significant amounts of stock, there is presumably little justification to buy.

Sentiment can also be derived by various statistics that purport to gauge supply and demand. Increases in share supply linked to initial public offerings or secondary stock offerings are often associated with downward pressure on prices. Similarly, the aggregate amount of cash holdings relative to household assets constitutes a proxy of potential demand. For example, stock prices tend to benefit from an elevated cash/asset ratio on the balance sheet.

The techniques delineated here have proven to be useful tools in the macro approach to equity investment. However, they are only one part of the process. Micro variables such as the valuation of individual stocks, as well as macroeconomic aggregates such as inflation and income, should also play a prominent role in investment decision making. Markets aren't totally efficient, but they are still tough to beat. As such, all relevant variables should be carefully considered in order to improve the likelihood of successful investing.

The Mood of a Market

David Segel

When explaining market movements and sentiment, traders often claim that the market "has a personality." This may sound simplistic and even dismissive, particularly when viewed against a sizable body of academic literature that supports the efficient markets hypothesis (EMH). If the market is made up of numerous rational individuals all acting independently, how can it have a personality?

The trader's view represents a different perspective. Traders like to see the market from the top down and they are aware that, in the short term, markets aren't perfectly efficient. In fact, markets are often emotional, subject to the responsive whims and quirks of the agents who collectively create their makeup. Not only do markets behave with distinct sociological behavior patterns, but different markets have different personalities. This makes sense, as any given product will have a different constituency of active users.

TRADER TYPES DIFFER

Think of the collective body of users who traded Microsoft, Oracle, or AMD during the dot-com boom of the late 1990s. Who were the participants in these markets? Some were investors who had managed their portfolios well. Some were looking to lock in their wins, and others were willing to take risks with their profits. Some were institutions that, with clients' interests in mind, needed to be vested in the bull market opportunity. These players were thinking about winning, and their behavior reflected this. Users in these categories reacted to short-term news and price movements with particular responses. In the late 1990s, they may have been collectively acting out of confidence, as the broader market rally of the previous years had encouraged them with successes, with a cushion, and, perhaps most importantly, with profits that could be used to take risks.

Compare this dynamic to that of a money market as it responds to a surprise news event such as a terrorist attack or a natural disaster. The market participants are different. It is likely that they represent large investors or asset managers who are approaching the market from an alternate portfolio perspective. They may be driven by a need for protection, they may need fast responses, and they may be described by various flavors of greed or of fear. Their sociological profile is inherently different. Consequently, their market behavior is also different.

Having been active in the market for almost 20 years (during which time, almost without exception, I have had real-time market exposures), I am intimately aware of the need to be in touch with the short-term structural makeup of the market that I am trading. I must have a feel for the psychology of the other participants who are also active in it. It is important to look beyond the mask of the apparently efficient market, and to recognize that markets are made up of orders. The people who create these orders represent a complex panoply. However, as a trader, I am less interested in using this information for analyzing and explaining why the market has done what it has done. I am much more interested in figuring out what the market will do next. The hows and whys are less important than the "what next." My requirement is to understand the market players' interpretations and the actions that will follow.

This chapter talks about price and quantity discovery. It refers to a variable called k, the ratio of the number of active buyers (bulls) who are in the market relative to the number of active sellers (bears). What does this variable k really represent? In my opinion, it represents the aggregate *mood* of the market. Will the participants collectively support a higher price level, or are they going to pull out and let the price drop? Do they feel comfortable trading at the prices that they see, or are they holding back their orders so that their true desires to buy or to sell are not revealed to others? Ultimately, from a trader's point of view, the name of the game is price and quantity discovery.

So how do you begin to understand the personality of the market? In his book, *Blink* (also mentioned in Chapter 1), Malcolm Gladwell suggests that the human brain has a clearly discernable ability to process and interpret vast amounts of disparate pieces of information, all in fractions of a second, in the "blink of an eye."[25] He is right. We see this in the market all the time. Participants, represented by orders, are constantly expressing their views, their interpretations, their preferences and their biases. With so much to take in, where should we start to understand it all?

UNDERSTAND THE PARTICIPANTS

Market participants have a diverse range of objectives. They display different trading characteristics, and they vary in their influence and impact. Take a look at the equity markets at any point, and the order book will contain interest from a range of users—fund managers, index arbitrageurs, long-short hedge fund traders, day traders, derivatives traders, ordinary retail customers, and many more. Each type of participant will have a different trading characteristic. Each will approach the market differently in terms of

- Frequency of trades.
- Time horizon (how long they hold their positions).
- Size of trades.
- Speed of response to news or price actions.

If we look at the mid-2002 example of the European life insurance companies being forced to sell part of their equity portfolios to satisfy regulatory solvency requirements, we see that they had a significant market impact, and we learn that reading the flow of their orders was essential for anyone who at the time was trading these markets. The low trading frequency, long time horizon, huge size, and relatively slow response time of an insurance company stands in marked contrast to the activity of a proprietary trader. The trader is far quicker in responding to news, probably trades with a high frequency, and no doubt has a much shorter holding period. Therefore, to effectively read the market, you need to know the full range of users, their characteristics, and when they are likely to be active.

To stay on the pace you must look at the same information as the other participants. An increased efficiency of information dissemination and a better understanding of it have increased the correlation between different products and asset classes, creating both opportunities and risks. If you are trading in the equity markets it is not just company earnings and corporate activity of which you need to be aware; interest rates, commodity prices, consumer confidence figures, and even the weather, all play an increasing role in moving the market. Think of it as a jigsaw puzzle, in which each fresh piece of information or knowledge that you fit to the board helps you see the whole picture more clearly.

HOW TECHNICAL LEVELS AFFECT THE MARKET

Once again, here is a challenge to the EMH. In a rational market, it should make no difference at what level a stock trades. For example, imagine a stock that is making new highs, touches $100 per share, and then retreats. In a random walk world, price action is haphazard and offers no interpretive data, but most traders would argue that if that stock fails to break through $100 a second and then a third time then its retreat from that resistance point is likely to be substantial. They know equally well that if the stock trades through and closes above $100 then this level will likely turn from having been the previous resistance level to being a new support level!

There are two possible explanations. First, *anchoring and adjusting* is a powerful human psychological thought process—known, observed levels become important reference points. Second, everyone has the same tools and even if only a fraction of the participants believe the logic, if the whole market is looking at the same levels, the levels effectively become self-fulfilling prophecies. Consequently, regardless of your academic standpoint, it is important to understand the basic angles and principles of technical analysis.

CROWD THEORY

Crowd theory is another challenge to the EMH's suggestion that market participants are independent and rational. The cautionary tales of the classic market bubble stories make fascinating reading and provide invaluable lessons. From the Dutch Tulip bubble in 1624, to the South Sea bubble of the 1720s, to the late 1990s tech rally, in each case mild hysteria stepped in to disrupt rational behavior. Anyone not familiar with the first two should read one of the numerous texts on the subject because, as Mark Twain stated, "History never repeats itself, but it certainly rhymes."

Sometimes the market will just want to go up, and there is no supporting fundamental reason. Quarter-end window dressing is a good example. Pick any example and inherent to it is the sociology of the market. Although users have powerful interpretive capacities, they are human, with human responses, with fear and greed and ego that ultimately impact, or in some cases even dominate, their decision making.

SUMMARY

I want to encourage you to take the time to get to know your market. If Malcolm Gladwell is right, we can get to know the participants and their motivations, and from that we can interpret why a market's mood is what it is. We might even appreciate what this information means in terms of short-term price movements.

I also encourage you to monitor the broader trends. Probably the largest trend in evidence at the moment is the increasing correlation between products, markets, and asset classes. This is a function of both technological change and the emergence of hedge fund style trading. Technological advancement means that more information is available faster, and that more powerful analytical tools are available to process it. Hedge funds have led the way in cross–asset class trading, using strategies known as global macro, convertible bond, and capital structure arbitrage. All of this means that the market structure has changed.

Like it or loathe it, globalization has made the world a smaller place. The financial markets have progressed in a similar fashion, and their personalities have shifted as well. Just when you've learned to understand the participants and the key external factors, just when you have gained insight into the market's personalities, the market moves on, providing you with another fresh challenge.

APPENDIX TO CHAPTER 6

Order Handling and Market Timing on a Trading Floor

In this chapter, we have examined the basis for technical analysis and algorithmic trading. In markets with real trading frictions and latent, unexpressed demands to trade, both can be essential tools. A fine-tuned trading algorithm can be seen as functioning like a skilled floor trader. In this Appendix, we consider in further detail the market timing operations of a human intermediary—a floor trader at the NYSE.[26]

Consider an NYSE floor trader who has just been instructed to buy 100,000 shares of ABC Corporation for a mutual fund. A price limit would typically be stipulated, but the order is not a typical limit order and it is not placed on a limit order book. Rather, it is an NH order.

NH stands for "not held" to time or to price. Holding a broker to a time means that a market order must be executed as quickly as possible after it has been received. Holding a broker to a price means that he must execute the order at a price that is at least as good as the one that was available when the order was first received. For instance, if a floor broker receives an order to buy 500 shares at market and can lift an offer at 25, that broker is held to executing the market order at 25 or better. This requirement does not apply to an NH order. With an NH order, the floor trader works the order patiently, attempting to obtain a better execution for the customer. Consequently, the floor trader and the customer both accept the risk of eventually receiving an inferior execution or no execution at all. NH orders are sometimes referred to as *discretionary orders*. With a discretionary order, the broker is not held to a time or a price.

A floor trader with, for example, a 100,000-share NH buy order will typically proceed as follows. The broker will keep the order hidden in his pocket, will work it over an extended period of time, and will turn it into trades one piece at a time according to the broker's judgment and sense of market timing. The special handling enables the floor broker to execute each tranche of the order in response to market events as they occur. By hiding the unexecuted portion of the NH order and working it carefully, the floor trader is striving to contain any market impact cost attributable

to others knowing about the order and front-running it. He is also attempting to balance market impact (the cost of being too aggressive) with the
opportunity cost of missing the market (the cost of being too patient). The
balancing act calls for knowledge of current market conditions, and it requires finesse.

With limit order book trading, a limit order is first placed on the book
where it sits for some period of time and is then turned into a trade if and
when a contra-side market order arrives. Note the following about the
procedure:

- The limit order book environment offers each participant a choice between two strategies: (1) place a limit order, be a liquidity supplier,
  and wait; or (2) place a market order and demand immediate liquidity.
- An order on the book reflects conditions that existed when it was
  placed, and a stale limit order results in a transaction price that does
  not properly reflect current market conditions.

Neither of the above applies to an NH order. Working an NH order
with finesse is a mixed strategy. Floor traders attempt to be liquidity suppliers, hoping that the market will come to them. However, if current conditions indicate that the market is likely to move away, a floor trader will
step forward with all or part of the order and trigger a trade. In other
words, the floor trader will switch between being a liquidity supplier and
being a liquidity demander. Successful switching behavior requires a good
knowledge of current market conditions.

Given today's technology, large buy-side traders can obtain extensive
knowledge of current conditions at their trading desks, and many are able
to control their own orders without the services of an intermediary.
Whether the physical presence of intermediaries on a trading floor conveys a further informational advantage remains a subject of debate in the
United States, although most of the European markets have by now
closed their floors. Nevertheless, some evidence suggests that working
NH orders on a trading floor does help contain trading costs.

As orders on the book and in the crowd of traders on the floor change,
a floor trader monitors the color of the market and decides whether to
step ahead of the limit order book by offering a better price, or to trade
with another contra-side floor trader, or to wait patiently for a more ad-
vantageous opportunity. In making this decision, the floor trader assesses
the market in a number of ways, including the order imbalance for the
stock, the current price behavior of related stocks and market indexes,
the mood of traders on the floor, and the amount of time remaining in the
trading day.

Let's return to the floor trader who is working the NH order to buy 100,000 shares of ABC Corp. Assume a situation where the day is young, the market fairly flat or drifting down, and sell orders on the ABC book outweigh the buys. Under these conditions, the floor trader will wait patiently for the price of ABC to fall. Perhaps it does. Perhaps part of the 100,000-share order gets executed. But then let the broad market turn bullish. As it does, new limit orders to buy ABC are placed on the book, and a surge of market buy orders thins out the sell side of the book. As the buy-sell imbalance reverses, traders in front of the ABC post get excited, and by now the 4:00 P.M. close is approaching. Under these conditions, our floor trader who is working what initially was a 100,000-share buy order steps forth aggressively and initiates a trade (or a sequence of trades).

By operating in this fashion, a successful floor broker can better control trading costs for the customer. A smoother integration of a large order into the market also conveys benefits to the broader market in the form of less erratic price discovery and an attending reduction of intraday price volatility. Nevertheless, the services of a floor broker are not costless and, around the world, exchange floors are being replaced by fully electronic trading platforms. We anticipate that market timing will increasingly be facilitated by electronic intermediation.

CHAPTER 7

Performance Measurement

W hether you are an active individual trader, are working at the trading desk of an asset management firm, are a sell-side broker or dealer, or are at home playing the TraderEx simulation, you will no doubt want to have some way of knowing how well you are doing.

Measuring a trader's performance is not as straightforward as one might initially think. How do you separate the short-term returns you might get from trading, from the longer-run returns that you might realize from investing? How do you distinguish the returns you achieved by being skillful, from the profits that you captured (or lost) through chance? How do you know whether the returns you have realized are appropriate given the risks that you have incurred in the process of gaining them? Have you properly controlled your execution costs? When you trade, are you getting the best execution? Are there reasonable benchmarks against which to assess your performance?

These are among the issues that we address in this chapter.

THREE SIMPLE PERFORMANCE MEASURES

Let's look at three simple measures of trading performance: (1) a straightforward profit computation, (2) trading surplus, and (3) comparison with a performance benchmark. Each has its uses for certain traders at certain times, but each also has its shortcomings.

Profits

The most straightforward trading performance measure is your profit. Profits can take two forms—realized and unrealized. Trading profits are *realized* when a stock inventory position is closed out—that is, returned to zero—and the cash account shows a clear addition or subtraction. Here is an illustration: Start with zero shares and zero cash, buy 20,000 shares at $60.00. Next, sell 8,000 at $60.10, and then sell 12,000 at $60.05. The initial trade cost $1.2 million, and the two sales generated $1,201,400 in proceeds, leaving the trader with a flat position in the shares, and a cash position and *realized profit* of +$1,400. (See Exhibit 7.1.)

When you have an open, nonzero share position, you can assess the mark-to-market value of your open position, and your *unrealized profit*. Long trading positions are generally marked-to-market at the bid price, and short positions are generally marked-to-market at the offer. At 10 A.M. in the current example, the trading position is +12,000, and assume for illustration purposes that the bid is $60.01. As a result, you would have a realized profit of $800 ($0.10 gain per share times 8,000 shares sold) and an unrealized profit of $120 ($0.01 times 12,000 still held), for a total mark-to-market profit and loss (P&L) of +$920.

As the illustration shows, your P&L is the dollars that you have received from selling shares minus the dollars that you have paid out to acquire them, adjusted for any current inventory position that you might have. The inventory adjustment is made by marking your current position to market and adding its value to your profits if it is a long position, or subtracting its replacement value if you have a short position that you will have to cover. In TraderEx, shares are marked-to-market by multiplying a long position by the highest bid quotation, or by multiplying a short position by the lowest offer. The mark-to-market measure can be misleading, however, if your open position is larger than the market's bid or offer sizes—you could not unwind your long position entirely at the bid or your short position at the offer, but would have to accept less aggressive and less profitable prices on the book.

EXHIBIT 7.1 Example of Realized Profit

Time	B/S	Shares	Price	Cash Position	Share Position
9:00 A.M.				$0	0
9:41:25 A.M.	Buy	20,000	$60.00	−$1,200,000	20,000
9:55:49 A.M.	Sell	−8,000	$60.10	−$719,200	12,000
10:03:01 A.M.	Sell	−12,000	$60.05	$1,400	0
				$1,400	**0**

When a trader is seeking to fill a large buy or sell order, a major problem with the profits measure is that it reflects two things: trading profits (or losses) and investment profits (or losses). Perhaps you have traded well, but your portfolio manager (PM) has given you a buy order in a stock that turns out to be a dog; perhaps you should get high marks and your portfolio manager should get a different job (or vice versa, if the stock selection was on target but you have traded poorly).

That said, anyone with a very short-term horizon and a trading strategy based predominantly on intraday market movements, who has returned to a flat position, might find a simple profit calculation meaningful. This group includes market makers, position traders, short-term market technicians, and day traders. These participants are commonly thought of as trading the order flow, rather than trading as investors in the stock. These people typically do not care much about the stock itself or its fundamentals. They ask just one question "Can I trade the order flow profitably?" A straightforward profit computation will provide a good answer to that question.

A simple profits calculation could also give useful feedback in the context of TraderEx. The TraderEx simulation is a trading game, not an investment game. Your software package gives you no information about the fundamentals. If you feel that you can trade the order flow profitably and would like to give it a try, go for it. Your risk is that the underlying, unobservable equilibrium price, P^*, introduced in Chapter 1, might drop when you have a long position, or might rise when you have a short position. But if you try your hand at being a day trader, that is the game you are playing.

See if mean reversion and a cagey use of limit orders will enable you to be a profitable TraderEx trader. Remember, however, that on any one play of the game, you might win or lose, not because of your ability, but because of your luck (or lack thereof). Much depends on the unpredictable path followed by P^*. Only by assessing your profits, on average, over enough plays of the game, will you be able to tell how well you are doing. If your profits, on average, increase as you become more familiar with the simulation, you will know that your abilities as a trader are improving.

Trading Surplus

In Chapter 3 we introduced the term *reservation price*. A reservation price reflects what a portfolio manager believes the stock is worth. It is the PM's responsibility to set it as a target price. This is the maximum price at which the PM would be willing to buy, or the minimum price at which he would be willing to sell. With a reservation price in hand, your performance as a trader can be measured by the difference between your PM's reservation price and the price at which you have traded. This difference is your *trading surplus*. Say you were instructed to buy 5,000 shares with a cap (reservation price) of $45.00, and that you succeeded in acquiring the shares at $42.90. You have profited to the tune of $3.10 a share, or $3,100 in total. Fantastic! Let's go down to the pub and celebrate!

Not so fast. It may be an interesting idea to assess the performance of the trader according to the trading surplus, and the performance of the portfolio manager with reference to the reservation price, but the world does not work that way. For one thing, a PM may not reveal his true reservation price to the trading desk. More importantly, the PM may not be impressed by a $3.10 a share surplus. What if you buy shares at $42.90, moments later the stock is trading at $42.50, and over the rest of the day the average transaction price drifts down to $42.10?

The TraderEx simulation can present you with large orders to buy or to sell. The program will not tell you that your PM is attaching a reservation price to the shares. An assessment of your own performance as a trader should focus on the price you have traded at relative to the prices you could have traded at if you had handled your orders differently. When it comes to assessing performance, a portfolio manager may not give a hoot about how well a trader has done relative to a reservation price. The big question is how the trader did relative to the array of buying and selling prices established on the market. Keep in mind, however, that your own actions can affect the sequence of prices and trades against which you are assessing yourself.

Performance Benchmarks

Here is another way of measuring your trading performance—choose a benchmark and see if you can beat it.[1] The benchmark might be a stock's VWAP, closing price, or whatever else you believe relevant. Beating the benchmark is called *capturing alpha*. Marcus Hooper focuses on this in the piece that he has contributed to this chapter, "The Quest for Trading's Holy Grail—Alpha!"

Why is alpha a holy grail? In part, because a good benchmark is very hard to find. What prices in the marketplace does it make sense to be assessed against if you are working a large order for an institutional investor? Given the multiplicity of values that are traced out in the continuous market, which should be used as a benchmark? A daily opening price is one possibility, and a daily closing price is another. The opening price is irrelevant, however, if a news event or a P* jump (in the terminology of TraderEx) has caused prices to change after the opening and before you have traded. Similarly, the daily closing price is not a good benchmark if a news event or P* jump has occurred before the close but after you have traded. Further, opening and closing prices are noisy measures—the opening is volatile because of the complexity of price discovery, and the close is volatile because participants are seeking to close out positions and fill orders that they have been working with relative patience during the trading day.

A third benchmark averages the opening and closing prices along with the high and low prices for the day. This benchmark suffers from the shortcomings just described for the opening and closing prices taken alone. Throwing in the daily high and low does not help much. While this benchmark is typically referred to as "open, close, high, low (OCHL), we prefer to sequence the letters as LHOC, which can be pronounced "L-hock," so that it rhymes with "ad hoc."

The benchmark that is most widely used by traders and PMs in the United States and Europe is the *volume weighted average price* or VWAP, which is pronounced "Vee-Wap." The use of VWAP assumes that the relevant benchmark is the price at which an average (representative) share has traded during a relevant interval of time (e.g., a trading day). According to this benchmark, any participant who bought below this average has traded well, as has anyone who has sold above it. A variant of VWAP is TWAP (time weighted average price).

Compared to the first two benchmarks, VWAP may appear to be the best of the lot. After all, when you are buying shares, why not contrast your purchase price with the average price paid per share by all other participants. Or, when you are selling, why not contrast the price received with the price at which the average (representative) share has been sold during the same short span of time.

Serious questions can be raised, however, about the VWAP benchmark. It suffers from the same basic problems as the first two benchmarks (changes in P* can make it irrelevant, and intraday prices typically are highly volatile). Further, a full day's price history is not applicable if, for instance, a buy-side trader receives the order from the portfolio manager in the later part of the afternoon. Would it be better for the benchmark to reflect only the prices from the time the buy-side trader has received the order until the end of the day? The problem then would be that the trader's own executions increasingly define the average, as the window over which the average is computed tightens around the trader's order. The same problem exists when prices over the full day are used but the market for the stock is thin and the trader's order is large. That is, the executions that occur for a 500,000-share order for a stock that, on average, trades 300,000 shares a day are bound to have a sizable impact on the benchmark against which it is being assessed. Much too much impact: Your trades will determine VWAP, which dilutes its value as an objective benchmark.

Another major problem with the VWAP performance benchmark is that it creates an incentive for traders to time their orders with respect to the benchmark, a practice that can lead to higher trading costs. For instance, if prices are rising toward the end of a day, continued purchases could drive your average buying price, for the day, above the performance measure. So why not wait for the next day before buying more shares? The next day prices may be even higher, but in that case so, too, will be the benchmark. Consequently, you can receive high scores on both days from the assessment even though trading costs are effectively higher. The same is true if you are looking to sell and prices are falling as the day progresses. If the price decline continues into the next trading day, you may beat the benchmark on both days by postponing sales to the second day, even though you sell at lower prices on the second day than you otherwise could have.

There is more. Roughly speaking, you cannot account for a substantial part of a day's market volume (e.g., a fifth) and not fall awry of VWAP. Traders seeking to be at or better than VWAP are forced to hold back portions of their large orders, filling them over several days, and often over a week or more, as a means of staying within or near the VWAP benchmark. When a large number of institutional traders in the market behave in this fashion, share prices naturally fail to reflect true levels of demand, and the relevance of VWAP as a benchmark is undermined. VWAP merely reflects those small portions of various orders that are actually brought to the market each day in the expectation that they are too small to affect the market price significantly.

A VWAP trader can chase a stock several percentage points up or down over a period of days, appearing skillful against VWAP while often damaging the fund's performance. Chan and Lakonishok's (1995) finding that market impact costs are significantly higher when measured for trade *packages* rather than for individual trades underscores the flaws inherent in VWAP as a trading performance benchmark.[2] American Century Mutual Funds reported that its broker who ranked best under a VWAP methodology ranked *worst* under a methodology that accounted for share price movements the day after the trades were made.

Having stated all of these VWAP criticisms, we now suggest that this performance benchmark may still give some useful feedback in the context of TraderEx. VWAP is a noisy performance benchmark because P* is not constant throughout the day. But one of VWAP's biggest problems in actual markets, that it can be gamed, need not be a shortcoming for you in the TraderEx environment. If you complete the orders you receive by the end of each day, gaming is not an issue. If you run the simulation for two days or more, you can game VWAP in TraderEx, but who cares? In fact, try doing so—it would be a good exercise. But avoid gaming VWAP if you want an unbiased measure of your own trading performance. The simulation is only a learning tool, and it includes a VWAP statistic so that you can use it to assess your performance if you wish to do so.

TRANSACTION COST ANALYSIS

If you have gotten the impression that there is no truly good performance benchmark, you are correct. Is there an alternative, another route to follow? There is. It is known as *transaction cost analysis*, or TCA. This route involves directly measuring the cost of each transaction. Recent developments in computer technology, analytic skills, and data availability have greatly facilitated transaction cost analysis. The availability of transaction data and econometric skills have enabled us to understand more clearly just how sizable an impact these costs can have on portfolio returns. Domowitz, Glen, and Madhavan have found that, for an equally weighted global portfolio of stocks, execution costs account for 23 percent of returns when portfolios are turned over twice a year.[3]

As discussed in Chapter 1, there are two broad categories of costs—explicit and implicit. The explicit costs are dollar amounts that could be printed on your transaction slips; they include commissions, fees, and taxes. The implicit costs are not visible and are not printed on your transaction slips; they include the bid-ask spread, market impact, and opportunity costs. As documented by ITG, "[T]he major components of execution costs are implicit costs (most importantly the price impact of the trade) that account for 75 to 90 percent of total costs."[4] TCA focuses primarily on implicit costs, which is the more difficult of the two to calculate. So do we—there are no explicit costs in the TraderEx software, only spread, market impact, and opportunity costs.

The Implicit Costs of Trading

In this section, we take a closer look at the components of the implicit costs of trading and how they might be measured. The comprehensive cost is referred to as *implementation shortfall*; its components are the spread, market impact, and opportunity costs.

Implementation Shortfall   Implementation shortfall is the overall difference between the price of a stock at the time the trading instruction is generated by the PM, and the actual price obtained when the order is executed. It captures the gap between the hypothetical position that you would have in a friction-free market with costless trading, and the actual position that you wind up with because trading is not costless. Implementation shortfall results from the bid-ask spread, market impact, and opportunity costs.

The Bid-Ask Spread   The bid-ask spread imposes a cost for traders using market orders. It can be measured in three ways: quoted spread, effective spread, and realized spread.

The *quoted spread* is what is visible in a market's advertised bid and offer quotes. For round-trip transactions (first establish and then unwind a position), traders pay a spread cost by buying at the higher offer price and selling at the lower bid. If the quotes are $52.22 bid and $52.26 offer, the spread is $0.04.

The *effective spread* captures a trade's immediate market impact cost or any price improvement received. It is the difference between the midpoint of the bid and ask, and what investors actually pay or receive for a stock, times two.[5] Immediate market impact occurs when a large buy order executes above the offer, or a large sell order executes below the bid (you can see this if you enter a market order in TraderEx that is larger than the bid or offer side). Price improvement works as follows. In many markets, hidden orders, negotiated trades, and undisclosed interest can lead to trades taking place inside the quotes. For instance, if the quotes are $52.22 bid and $52.26 offer, an arriving sell order may be price-improved by a buyer and trade at $52.23. For a seller-initiated trade, the effective spread is twice the difference between the quote midpoint and the trade price. For this example, the quoted spread is $0.04, while the effective spread is

$$2 \times (\$52.24 - \$52.23) = \$0.02$$

For buy orders, the effective spread is twice the trade price minus the quote midpoint.

If all buy orders paid the ask and all sell orders received the bid, then the effective spread would be the same as the quoted spread. When an order receives price improvement, the effective spread is less than the quoted spread. However, if the immediate effect of a large order is an execution outside of the current quotes, the effective spread is wider than the quoted spread. Academic studies increasingly focus on effective spreads rather than quoted spreads, because the effective spread accurately reflects prices actually paid or received by customers.

The *realized spread* accounts for permanent price changes or *price innovations* (as they are sometimes called) that can occur as trading progresses. Eliminating any price innovation isolates the temporary price effect, which is the true market impact cost of a trade. The effective spread does not capture this if the temporary effect is not instantaneous (front-running, for instance, can cause a noninstantaneous, temporary effect). The realized spread is similar to the effective spread, except that it uses the quoted midpoint some minutes (commonly five) *after* the order is executed.

Let's consider the realized spread with regard to a large buy order that executes at a higher price because of its size. There are two possible ways to capture the temporary price impact of this large trade: (1) match the trade price with a preceding price to see how much price has been pushed up, and (2) match the trade price with a following price to see how much price falls after the temporary impact of the large buy order has faded. The second approach is preferred because only the following price can properly filter out any price innovation and capture the market impact cost from the mean reversion in price that occurs as the impact of the large trade fades.

It is desirable to be buying in a rising market and, with the *following price* being used to measure the realized spread, the realized spread can be reduced or even be negative for a well-timed execution. There is a further problem with the procedure, however. Our demonstration in Chapter 6 that price formation can be a multiequilibrium, path-dependent process implies that the large buy order can have a more lasting price impact. To the extent that this happens, the following price will be higher than otherwise because of the order itself and, consequently, the market impact of the large order is underestimated. For the preceding example, if five minutes after the seller-initiated trade at \$52.23 the quotes are \$52.21 bid and \$52.26 offer, then the realized spread is

$$2 \times (\$52.235 - \$52.230) = \$0.01$$

Market Impact   As just discussed, market impact is measured by the realized spread. Market impact costs are incurred because a stock's price is influenced by the PM's orders and trades. Market impact is measured by how much the executed price differs from a chosen benchmark, such as the quote midpoint or the last trade price. Market impact is a price concession—the discount or premium for large orders—that needs to be made to get the trade done. It may also reflect information seepage or poor trading skill. Traders try to control market impact by breaking up orders and trading them over a period of time in order to conceal information about the full size of the order. Of course, the risk is that the market price will move against the trader during that time, and that opportunity or timing costs will then be incurred. Such delays or cancellations may reduce the return more than market impact would have.

Opportunity Cost   Opportunity cost is the cost of forgoing an option to take an action. In trading, opportunity cost is the cost of waiting and deciding not to trade when the PM really wants to buy or sell. If a trading desk receives an order to buy ABC Corporation's stock when the price is \$50 a share, but fails to act during a period when the price rises to \$51, the opportunity cost is \$1 a share. Opportunity or timing costs are measured as the price change that occurs while all or part of an order is being held awaiting additional liquidity, or is being metered out in smaller pieces into the market's current ebb and flow. Opportunity cost can be an interday cost, if a large order is broken up. Some have argued that trading cost analyses are biased, that they underestimate true costs because doable trades are overrepresented, and the costs of missed trades or cancelled orders are not factored in.

In the illustration presented in Exhibit 7.2, a portfolio manager decides to sell a large stock position at a time when the midpoint of the quotes is $51.95. The order is given to a broker who eventually finds a counterparty buyer willing to pay $51.80. A large block sell order executes at $51.80, which imposes $0.15 in implementation shortfall on the portfolio. Transaction cost analysis would use the midpoint or last trade price at the time of the buy or sell decision as a benchmark for calculating implementation shortfall. After the decision to sell was made, the buy-side trader took five minutes to consider whether to use an ATS, an algorithm, or different brokers. The buy-side trader instead gives the order to a sell-side firm that takes five minutes to find a bidder for the entire block at $51.80, three cents below the bid. Five minutes after the trade, the sell order's temporary price impact is evident, as the midpoint has moved up two cents to 51.90 from 51.88. However, the market's closing price suggests that any delay to completing the trade would have increased timing costs and the implementation shortfall.

To summarize, the implementation shortfall of $0.15 (the difference between $51.95 and $51.80 is 29 basis points) consists of $0.08 ($51.88 minus $51.80) in market impact costs (of which $0.05 is from the bid-ask spread) and $0.07 ($51.95 minus $51.88) in timing costs.

You can generate further examples yourself using TraderEx. Assume that you are given an order to sell 500 units just after the open. First use the "Order-Driven, Proprietary Trader" mode, and then the "Quote-Driven, Dealers-Only" mode, to build a short position of 500 by 12 noon. Use the same scenario numbers. What implementation shortfalls do you then incur?

Using Transaction Cost Analysis

Wayne Wagner and Melissa Spurlock, in the piece they have contributed to this chapter, give the big picture about the use of transaction cost

EXHIBIT 7.2 Illustration of a TCA for a Large Sell Order

Price				
Ask $52.98	A 51.95	A 51.93	A 51.94	A 51.87
Midpoint **51.95**	M 51.91	M 51.88	M 51.90	M 51.82
Bid 51.92	B 51.87	B 51.83	B 51.86	B 51.77
		*Trade **51.80**		Last 51.78
Decision to sell	Give order	Trade	Post-trade	Close
3:30 P.M.	3:35 P.M.	3:40 P.M.	3:45 P.M.	4 P.M.

analysis (TCA). They explain how a careful TCA assessment can be used to improve the interaction between a portfolio manager and his traders, to sharpen the operations of the buy-side trading desk, and to monitor the effectiveness of external brokers and other agents who are also relied on to process trades for the institutional investor.

The most obvious application of TCA is to assess the cost of a trade after it has been made. Post-trade analysis is useful for assessing the performance of a trader and for sharpening a desk's trading strategies. Keep in mind, however, that individual trades can be impacted by a myriad of market events and that, when it comes to assessing performance, attention should be paid as well to averages computed over a sufficient number of trades. At the same time, TCA can also be used to flag individual trades which appear to be outliers that require investigation.

Another use of TCA is to guide the formation of trading strategies. For instance, benchmarks can be established to assess the relative costs of trading aggresively and of trading patiently. Additionally, TCA can be used to assess the effect of order size on market impact costs for stocks with varying size and volatility characteristics. It can be used to evaluate the performance of traders and brokers. In the past few years, TCA has, with increasing success, been used for pretrade analytics that forecast or predict market impact costs in a way that better coordinates the management of trading costs and risk control. As we learn more about the relationship between order placement and transaction costs, TCA gains critical importance as a tool that a buy-side trader must have. An integral part of this analysis is risk management, the topic to which we next turn.

RISK MANAGEMENT

Trading entails risk. If you trade aggressively and your inventory position mounts (either long or short), your returns may at times be large but, in the process of realizing them, the risks that you have taken might be unacceptable. If you trade too impatiently you may incur unnecessarily large market impact costs. If you trade too cautiously, you might miss an opportunity to buy or to sell shares. Effective trading necessarily entails risk management, and any assessment of your performance should take account of the risks that you have incurred.

What Risk Involves

Risk has a number of different facets. Comprehensively viewed, it includes operational and transfer risk, counterparty risk, and market risk.

Operational and Transfer Risk   While not directly related to trading decisions, both technical and human failure may cause transfers of either money and/or title to fail. These risks can be controlled by the inclusion of a central counterparty (CCP) or clearinghouse. The classic clearinghouse in an equity market acts as a CCP.[6] In so doing, a clearinghouse becomes a seller for each buyer, and a buyer for each seller. The CCP assumes responsibility for the failure of any market member to fulfill his obligations to deliver (either shares or cash).

In principle, the liability of a clearinghouse is shared by each and every participant. All participants are obligated to fulfill all trades that they have executed. To mitigate the risk of a member failing, the clearinghouse holds margin (mostly covered by collateral) against open positions from its members. A clearinghouse does not guarantee delivery on settlement day but, given its strict regimes, it generally manages to achieve very high settlement rates for the due dates.[7]

Counterparty Risk   Counterparty risk is the risk that the trading counterparty will not fulfill his obligation either to deliver securities or to pay cash. This could occur as a result of cash or solvency problems. This risk is particularly serious in cross-border trading. For smaller members, the failure of a large counterparty may force them out of business. Like operational and transfer risk, counterparty risk is best controlled by the inclusion of a CCP in clearance and settlement.

Market Risk   Market risk can contribute to counterparty risk because changing share prices affect the amount required to replenish an open position (i.e., the margin requirement). Market risk, in the very end, is perceived and understood as volatility, and volatility is an important parameter for margin calculations. The margin calculation should ensure that the clearinghouse has enough collateral to cover the replacement cost of the position over the nonsettled period. The margin requirement is calculated on the basis of the net open positions.

Because market risk has the broadest relevance to trading, we next discuss it in more detail.

Market Risk

For long-term investors, trading is the process by which a desired portfolio is achieved. Astute trading can enhance longer-run portfolio performance, while poor trading can seriously erode your portfolio returns. All traders face market risk because of the uncertainties concerning the prices at which trades can be made. As we have seen, if you move too aggressively to acquire or dispose of shares, you incur market impact costs; if you move too cautiously, and the price change that you anticipated occurs before you have acquired or disposed of the shares, you incur opportunity costs.

Sell-side market makers trade to accommodate customer demands for immediate liquidity but, in the process, acquire inventory positions that have to be worked off. New recruits at broker/dealer trading desks are very constrained in terms of the orders they are allowed to handle and the inventory positions they are permitted to acquire (see David Segel's piece in Chapter 1).

Day traders and other market technicians may trade to exploit what they perceive to be patterns in prices and quotes but in the process they, too, may acquire unacceptably large inventory positions. Try playing TraderEx aggressively as a proprietary trader, and track your profits and inventory positions (both long and short). You might note that, in simulation runs where you have acquired a large inventory position (either long or short), your profits have been either extremely good or quite miserable, and not much in between. This reflects one of the big risks that you incur as a trader.

Risk Aversion

One of the key tenets of modern portfolio theory is that we are all risk-averse. That does not mean that we will not accept risk (which, of course, we do), but that we must be compensated for accepting it. For equity trading, risk is defined with regard to the volatility of share prices, which can be measured by the variance (or standard deviation) of returns. Other measures can also be used, such as a stock's high-low price range over, for instance, a daily interval. The compensation for taking risk is the return that an investor expects to receive when holding shares of a stock.

The variance of returns is a good risk measure when returns are normally distributed around their mean.[8] The mean of the distribution is the stock's expected return. With a normal distribution, any draw that is a given distance above the mean has the same probability of occurring as a draw that is the same distance below the mean. In dollar terms, any possible win (a draw above the mean) has the same probability of occurring as any comparable loss (a draw that is an equal distance below the mean). It is similar to flipping a fair coin: The probability of a head equals the probability of a tail. Recognizing this, you might ask, why would we all be risk-averse if, in the risky situations that we face in the equity markets, expected gains equal expected losses? Shouldn't we all expect to come out even, if the expected return is zero? If this is the case, shouldn't any positive expected return be enough to satisfy us? The answer is clearly no, and we all know it. The expected return must be sufficiently positive to compensate for our aversion to taking a risk. We explain this further in the Appendix to this chapter.

Variance

We measure risk in terms of the variance (or standard deviation) of returns. Variance (or standard deviation), however, is sensitive to the period over which we measure the returns that we are taking the variance of. To measure variance, we must first specify the length of time over which returns are measured. As a long-term investor, you would be interested in the variance of longer-run (e.g., annual) returns. As a day trader or market maker, you would care about the variance of shorter-run (e.g., daily) returns. You might also be interested in knowing that the intraday pattern of variance is U-shaped.[9] That is, volatility has been documented to be greatest at the beginning and the end of the trading day, and lowest in the midday periods. The bottom line is that variance is a standard measure of volatility, but it varies depending on the measurement period in question.

Volatility is the key motive for hedging in both cash and derivative markets. You can have a stock and option portfolio that is *delta neutral* (which means that the stocks are combined with options in just the right proportions to be hedged against price movements) while you may be looking to gain from the time or volatility value of the position. Delta neutrality does not, however, come without cost—hedging always lowers returns, and you pay for it in terms of your expected portfolio performance.

As explained in the Appendix at the end of this book, "Prices and Returns," obtaining an appropriate variance measure for different measurement intervals would be straightforward if a stock's returns were not correlated over time (i.e., if a stock's price followed a random walk). You could measure variance for any interval, say a one-day interval, and apply it to any other interval by multiplying the daily measure by the number of days in your longer interval. For instance, under a random walk, the variance of five-day returns (expressed as a rate per five days) is five times the variance of daily returns (expressed as a rate per day).[10] Prices do not follow random walks, however; short-run returns are autocorrelated. A time series is said to be autocorrelated if its value at one point in time is correlated with its value at another (not necessarily adjacent) point in time. This autocorrelation, because it tends to be negative, is manifest in the variance of short-period returns being larger relative to the variance of longer-period returns than would be the case if prices did follow a random walk. That is why it is important to use a very short-term measure of variance for risk management from a trader's perspective.

Risk of Carrying an Unbalanced Portfolio

It is well established in modern portfolio theory that diversification reduces risk, and that the returns an investor can expect to receive for accepting risk compensate only for that risk which cannot be eliminated by proper portfolio diversification. A portfolio that is not properly diversified is *unbalanced*. An unbalanced portfolio is not among the set of efficient portfolios. A trader's portfolio may become unbalanced because transaction costs (including the cost of portfolio monitoring and submitting orders) have inhibited trading. Or a trade may have been sought but not realized because the contra-side order that was hoped for did not arrive at the market.

Market makers have received special attention in the academic literature because of the nondiversifiable risk that they routinely accept as a standard part of doing business. As discussed in Chapter 5, a customer seeking immediate liquidity can buy at the market maker's offer, or sell to the market maker at his bid. In the process of servicing this customer (and others), the market maker can acquire an unbalanced inventory and accept diversifiable risk. The market maker gets to that inventory position by having posted bid and offer quotes and then having waited passively for customer orders to arrive. A long position will result if public sell orders predominate, and a short position will result if public buy orders predominate. What compensates for this willingness to accept diversifiable risk?

Before answering, let's reiterate. Positive expected returns compensate all investors for holding a long position in a stock. However, the risk premium, as we have said, is only for accepting nondiversifiable risk. The market maker who has acquired shares in order to service the public's demand for immediacy will have accepted risk that he could have diversified away from without lowering the expected return. The market maker who has acquired a short position in the process of selling shares has accepted risk that must be compensated for in alternative ways. If the expected return to a position does not provide adequate compensation, what does?

The bid-ask spread of the market maker's quotes provides some compensation for the risk of trading with public customers who are seeking immediacy. This risk is greater, the sparser and more uncertain the order flow is for a stock (inventory rebalancing is typically more difficult with thinner stocks). The risk of an unbalanced position is also greater when the stock is more price volatile. In the face of price volatility, market makers typically wish to trade down to a sleeping position before the close of each trading session.

In short, risk management for a market maker involves, first and foremost, adjusting his quotes (and hence bid-ask spread) so as to have proper inventory control, as discussed in Chapter 5. Market makers, like limit order traders, also benefit from prices more generally following a mean-reverting path that encompasses larger swings than the simple bounce between the bid and the offer.

Risk of Trading with a Better-Informed Trader

The market maker also runs the risk of trading with a better-informed customer. In this respect, a market maker is not alone—limit order traders accept this same risk, as discussed in Chapter 3. Anybody who has posted a quote or a limit order has in effect extended an option to the public, and that option can be exercised by any customer, including one who, being better informed, knows that the option is mispriced. This can be visualized with respect to P*, the equilibrium price in TraderEx. If P* jumps above the offer, an informed trader will shoot in a buy order. If P* drops below the bid, an informed trader will shoot in a sell order. A market maker, limit order trader, or you will always lose when trading against the informed order flow in TraderEx.

What compensates traders and market makers for accepting this risk? Once again, the bid-ask spread is a major part of the answer. This can be understood by classifying customers as either liquidity traders or information traders, as done in Chapter 5. Liquidity traders are presumed to be informationless; their orders are motivated only by their own idiosyncratic needs for cash. Thus, the arrival of a liquidity-motivated order to buy does not imply that a stock's price is too low, and neither does the arrival of a liquidity-motivated order to sell imply that it is too high. Consequently, market makers and limit order traders both benefit from trading against the liquidity-driven order flow. The market maker sells at the higher offer, buys at the lower bid, and earns the spread. A limit order trader likewise sells at a higher price (his offer), buys at a lower price (his bid), and saves paying the spread. The returns thereby received compensate for the losses incurred when the counterparty to the trade is not a liquidity trader but a better-informed customer.

In this context, risk management for a market maker or limit order trader involves setting quotes so that the expected benefits from trading with liquidity customers will exceed the expected costs of trading with better-informed players. Recognizing this, consider the market maker and the bid-ask spread. Widening the spread is a defensive move against the informed traders (the wider the spread, the further P* has to jump to get outside of the spread). However, there is no bound on the size of the P* jumps, and the spread can never be widened enough to provide total protection against trading with a better-informed participant. But widening the spread also increases transaction costs for the liquidity traders, which reduces the number of liquidity-driven orders that the market maker can expect to receive. Accordingly, here is the situation: A spread that is too narrow yields insufficient revenue from liquidity traders and leaves the market maker unnecessarily exposed to the informed customers, and a spread that is too wide yields diminishing protection against informed players and reduced revenue from liquidity traders. Somewhere in between is the ideal spread to set. Establishing and maintaining it is an important aspect of risk management for the market maker.

BEST EXECUTION

Further attention has been drawn to performance measurement and TCA by a regulatory obligation called the *best execution* obligation.[11] Best execution has been a significant objective in the United States since the enactment of the U.S. Congressional Securities Acts Amendments in 1975. In mandating the development of a National Market System (NMS), the 1975 Amendments set forth the goal that investors' orders be provided the opportunity to be executed, consistent with efficiency and best execution, without the participation of a dealer.

A best execution obligation has more recently gained attention in the European arena. In London, the publication of the Myners Report in 2001 led to a protracted debate about (1) whether traditional fund management contracts give managers adequate incentives to minimize transaction costs, and (2), if not, what to do about it.[12] In 2004, the European Parliament adopted the Markets in Financial Instruments Directive (MiFID), which is slated to take effect in mid-2007. A best execution obligation is one of the key provisions in the Directive.

Simply stated, a best execution obligation refers to the responsibility of a broker/dealer intermediary or asset manager to execute customer orders at the best possible price with minimum broker/dealer intervention. But what does best execution really mean? The U.S. Congressional Act did not say, and a widely accepted empirical definition has not since been developed. Some of the very same difficulties in defining good performance are reflected in the ambiguities that surround the notion of best execution.

The Association for Investment Management and Research (AIMR) issued a major task force report on best execution in 2001. In the introduction, the report states:

> *Therefore, it is not feasible to define a single measurement basis for best execution on a trade-by-trade basis. Instead, the Guidelines focus on establishing processes, disclosures, and documentation, which together form a systematic, repeatable, and demonstrable approach to show that best execution compliance is consistent and effective.*[13]

The Investment Company Institute (ICI), in its comment on the AIMR Report, puts this more strongly:

> *We recommend that the (AIMR) Guidelines clarify that best execution is not a quantifiable concept and that statistical measurements can be only one part of the overall assessment that firms may make in examining best execution.*[14]

The problem is multifaceted. First, market impact costs and opportunity costs are not subject to being measured with precision on a trade-by-trade basis.[15] Second, as we have discussed, good benchmarks for assessing trading performance are difficult to define. Additionally, different kinds of orders require differential handling, depending on the needs of a trader, the size of an order, and the liquidity of the market for the shares being traded. In other words, the execution that is "best" depends on the particulars of the specific case at hand. Further, how does one measure best execution for orders that are broken into smaller pieces for execution over an extended period of time? And how does one specify a common set of best execution procedures to apply to a broad, diverse population of participants?

When the concept of best execution was set forth in 1975 in the United States, institutional participation was far less than it is today, and the best execution requirement was fashioned primarily with regard to retail order flow. Currently, however, attention has turned to institutional investors, a group for whom the requirement is appreciably more difficult to fulfill.

Implementation Problems

For three reasons in particular, the extension of a best execution requirement to the institutions is extraordinarily difficult to implement. First, more than price matters. Execution quality for a large participant depends on an array of trade characteristics. In addition to price, institutional investors also care about speed of execution, certainty of execution, and anonymity. Immediacy matters to the institutional customer largely because the mere knowledge that an order is being brought to market can move market prices. When traders receive an indication that a large order to buy (sell) is coming to the market, they may try to buy (sell) ahead of it. The practice is referred to as front-running. Anonymity (and, even more, invisibility) is desirable for controlling market impact costs. The importance of each of these characteristics depends on the needs of the individual trader, the attributes of the specific stock being traded, and the motive for trading (e.g., information or liquidity reasons). Clearly, one size does not fit all, which makes an objective definition of best execution very difficult to come by.[16]

The second problem is that *best execution* is not subject to simple definition. Institutional customers typically break up their orders for execution over a series of trades over an extended period of time. Wayne Wagner has reported that 80 percent of institutional orders are larger than half of a stock's average daily trading volume.[17] It is clear that the big funds are forced to reduce their trading interest to a size that markets can accommodate. That is, because of the difficulty of integrating large orders into a predominantly retail order flow, they "slice and dice" their orders. The large funds also time the placement of their orders. Consequently, best execution cannot be simply defined with regard to a snapshot picture of prices that are available at a given moment in time. Rather, it must include the optimal timing of orders over a series of trades. If a snapshot assessment is difficult, an assessment of a sequence of trades is close to impossible. What is needed is a benchmark, such as the volume weighted average price (VWAP), against which to assess a realized sequence of executions. Unfortunately, as we have discussed, VWAP is a poor post-trade benchmark, and a good alternative is not readily available.

Third, market structure is imperfect. A best execution obligation cannot be reasonably imposed in any market where the structure is not working well for institutional investors. Today's markets are geared to accommodate retail-sized trades averaging less than 1000 shares per execution, and the big traders are trying to fit their large pegs into these tiny holes. Moreover, the pegs are growing larger while the holes are becoming smaller. NYSE average trade size, which peaked at 2,303 shares in 1988, had declined to 343 shares in June 2005. Concurrently, block-trading volume (trades of 10,000 shares or more) on the Big Board dropped from 51.1 percent of reported volume in 1988 to 27.9 percent in June 2005.[18]

The responsibility for excessive trading costs also lies with the buy-side participants themselves. This is because their focus on minimizing trading costs is often undermined by soft dollar arrangements. In the words of Harold Bradley, "Clearly, soft dollar agreements play an important role in the execution decision and are often in direct conflict with an investment firm's fiduciary duty to the client."[19] The problem is that, through soft dollar arrangements, asset managers receive costly research, computer systems, and other support services from the sell-side firms, using client assets (rather than firm expense budgets) as payment.[20] Hopefully, with the increased attention currently being given to best execution procedures and to the measurement and containment of transaction costs, the industry will be weaned from its soft dollar practices.

Best Execution and Transaction Cost Analysis

An ability to quantify transaction costs and to use smart order routing systems does not necessarily allow one to quantify and to obtain best execution.

Transaction costs are typically measured ex post (i.e., after a trade), and smart order routing systems can only attempt to control transaction costs. Best execution depends on knowing ex ante (i.e., before a trade) what execution costs will be and, if taken literally, means that the very best of all possible trades has been made.

Best execution is a broader concept than transaction cost analysis. A best execution obligation carries with it a fiduciary responsibility. The AIMR report states:

> *When one looks closely at the chain of responsibility as trades go from the idea to completion stage, it can be seen that responsibility for securing best execution is shared by many. These responsibilities can be thought of as being hierarchical: investment management traders operate within parameters established by managers, brokers follow instructions specified by investment management traders, and exchanges execute their procedures according to the submissions of brokers.*[21]

Measurement Problems

Let's take a closer look at the difficulties encountered when trying to apply the concept of best execution. We start by taking a simplistic view. Assume a market characterized by a sizable number of small, priced orders and, for a moment, focus myopically on a single point in time when a little incoming order arrives and triggers a trade. In this environment, best execution means that the little incoming order executes at the best counterpart price available (i.e., that a sell order transacts at the highest posted bid, and that a buy order transacts at the lowest posted offer). If all orders are consolidated on a single book, best execution is assured by the price priority rule of order execution (namely, that the most aggressively priced orders trade first). If the marketplace is geographically fragmented, best execution requires that, through intermarket linkages and/or integrated quotation displays, a newly arriving customer can find, access, and execute against the most aggressive counterpart quote in the broader market.

In the situation just described, a snapshot picture is taken to determine whether a participant has received best execution. The snapshot is the configuration of prices across markets at the specific moment when a trade is made. Emphasized in this picture is the size of the bid-ask spread and the depth of the book at the bid and offer quotes.

Let's move away from the static setting. Allow a participant to also decide just when to step forward with an order and trade. This is the dynamic environment within which professional buy-side and sell-side traders operate. Namely, they time their trades in accordance with current market conditions (as discussed in the Appendix to Chapter 6).

In the dynamic environment, bid-ask spreads and market impact effects continue to play a role. But very importantly, there is a third factor: price discovery, as we discussed in Chapter 6. To an appreciable extent, accentuated intraday price volatility reflects the dynamic process by which a market searches for the price that best reflects the broad desire of participants to hold shares of a stock. Price discovery, because it is a complex, dynamic process, makes best execution far more difficult to measure. The question is no longer one of simply obtaining the best possible price for an incoming order at the time of its arrival. The trader must also pick the best possible time to step forward with the order and trigger a trade.

But what is the best time? Against what value should an execution be assessed? In a dynamic environment, a performance benchmark is required. With a benchmark, best execution does not mean getting the best price. Rather, it means matching or bettering the benchmark. But, once again, we note that a good benchmark is not readily available.

Best Execution as a Procedure

Given the problem of finding a good benchmark against which to judge trades, attention has turned away from assessing best execution with reference to the transaction costs incurred for a trade, to assessing the investment/trading procedures that have been followed. Ananth Madhavan of Barclays Global Investors has stated:

> *The bottom line is, the AIMR guidelines do not prescribe how firms should measure best execution. Rather, they focus on the procedures by which firms check that client portfolios are in fact being properly handled. It is not a trade-by-trade process. Rather, what AIMR is looking for is that managers, traders, and brokers put into place a set of processes that will ensure that considerations involving trading are carefully looked at during day-to-day operations.*[22]

Natan Tiefenbrun of Instinet views best execution holistically. As he put it:

> *[Best execution] should be a holistic term. This is what we should be very focused on—how to get a money manager to look at the entire process, from end to end. How do we minimize all of the frictions that exist between the portfolio manager and the trading desk, and between the trading desk and a broker? How do we mitigate the conflicts of interest that exist?*[23]

Viewing best execution as a procedure is a meaningful development, and some progress might be anticipated. However, problems still remain. In particular, the definition of best execution procedures cannot be formulated without reference to the participants to whom they are applied. What is best is different for a buy-side participant than for a sell-side participant, for an active fund versus an index fund, for a broker/dealer intermediary versus a market center, and so forth. Wayne Wagner put it this way:

> *But it gets complicated. These decision processes are all very different. Consequently, what represents best execution for a hedge fund that wants immediate execution, may not apply to [someone who is] . . . running index funds and therefore is interested in achieving lowest possible costs.*[24]

It is also different for a momentum manager who simply has to get the shares that his portfolio manager has decided on into the portfolio, no matter what the cost.

Moreover, procedures should not be specified in such detail that agents are micromanaged. If agents are not given some leeway to make their own decisions, what is their value-added?

New Tools and Choices for the Buy-Side Trader

The landscape is changing rapidly for buy-side traders. Market structures are evolving, and technological capabilities for connectivity and order management are exploding. In both the United States and Europe, transaction cost analysis is becoming considerably more prevalent and sophisticated. What implications does all this have for the buy-side trader?

Let's be clear: Minimization of trading costs has never been the only objective of institutional participants. As noted earlier, the widespread practice of bundling trade execution services with soft dollar products (such as research) that are paid for with commission dollars, in the opinion of many, has resulted in excessive execution costs, and has imposed a competitive barrier for any new, alternative trading facility that may offer lower trading commissions and the possibility of better executions. Enforcement of best execution practices may help to rectify these problems. As Ted Aronson has remarked:

> *For the first time in 27 years, there will be a significant, and I mean significant, decrease in the use of soft dollars, in the related sins of directed trading, and all that sort of stuff. That will be the most important result of the AIMR task force guidelines.*[25]

Because of the size and complexity of the job that buy-side traders are trying to accomplish, larger traders will incur higher transaction costs, and the challenge of handling institutional-size orders will continue to be formidable. The very care that institutions take in approaching the market with their large orders makes it hard for them to meet and to provide liquidity to one another. Breaking into the flow of the continuous market and getting anything close to best execution will remain difficult.

So-called "Star Wars" technology in market centers and trading rooms is not a panacea. Electronic order book markets that are the main trading platforms throughout the European equity markets and U.S. ECNs are very efficient at handling retail order flow for blue chip issues. Gathering the liquidity that institutions require remains a challenge, however, particularly for the mid- and small-cap issues (look again at Martin Reck's piece in Chapter 5). With some undesirable consequences, electronic linkages also accelerate the speed with which events can take place (to wit, James Ross's piece in Chapter 4). This means that one trader's order can tap into a liquidity pool with lightening speed, but still lose out to a competing order that arrived a few nanoseconds ahead of it. Electronic connectivity enables buy-side trading desks to access liquidity pools with minimal broker/dealer intermediation; nevertheless, intermediaries are still needed and liquidity pools are still fragmented.[26]

Computer technology, along with bringing speed and connectivity to trading, has also paved the way for algorithmic trading, a topic discussed in Chapter 6. With algorithmic functionality, you can essentially establish a strategy rather than an order. Your strategy can state that, if a set of conditions is satisfied (e.g., a change in the price of the stock, the price of a closely related stock, the number of shares of the stock that have traded in a preceding brief interval of time, and/or the value of a market index), then you will purchase 5,000 shares. The inclusion of more relevant conditions on the order should provide the participant with better execution. *Better* does not mean *best*, however, and if liquidity is fragmented, best execution remains an elusive concept that is very difficult to make operational.

The proper timing of orders by a buy-side trader can lead to less costly, more profitable, trading. Conventional thinking among both practitioners and academicians is that some traders, being patient, are willing to be liquidity providers and place limit orders, while others who, being eager to trade quickly, place market orders that are liquidity demanding. However, as discussed in Chapter 6, professional traders commonly use a switching strategy. For example, a trader, upon receiving an order from the portfolio manager, might initially be patient, hoping that the market will come to him. However, if market conditions indicate that price is likely to move away, the buy-side trader will switch from being a liquidity supplier to being a liquidity demander. He will step forward with an order and trigger a trade. This is what market timing and algorithmic trading are all about.

Handa, Schwartz, and Tiwari[27] used a 15-minute market imbalance measure (a ratio of buy-side or sell-side trading activity to total trading activity in a 15-minute interval) to reflect current market conditions. They found, using data provided by the American Stock Exchange, that orders handled on a not held (NH) basis by floor brokers are timed in relation to current market conditions, and that this timing results in lower market impact costs. (For further discussion, see the appendix to Chapter 6.) Similar benefits may be realized with inputs from the buy-side trading desk that is now empowered with new tools and choices.

Best Execution in a Hypercontinuous Market

As discussed previously, institutional traders commonly break their orders up for submission to the market over an extended period of time. This creates overhang in the market and sets the stage for momentum trading. The net result is a diminution of order size and an acceleration of order arrivals and cancellations. The order flow, especially under stressful conditions, may fracture; the quotes can become less meaningful; and the market can become hypercontinuous and difficult for buy-side traders to follow. By *hypercontinuous*, we mean that trades are occurring with such high frequency, and that transaction-to-transaction price volatility is so accentuated, that price discovery breaks down. These disruptions to price discovery make the work of the buy-side trader considerably more challenging.

Some institutional investors tend to avoid trading at, and close to, market openings. One can readily understand why—the big players want to *know* the prices, not *set* them, and they have less confidence in the quality of price discovery at and near the opening. Volatility in the first half-hour of the day is strikingly high in the NYSE, NASDAQ, London, Frankfurt, and Paris markets. This is the time when markets are most apt to become hypercontinuous. Volume is strikingly low for the opening half-hour in London, a market that is heavily institutionally dominated. An institution may, however, be pressured to trade at or near market openings when seeking to obtain a VWAP price for the day.

A picture of what can happen at the open is presented in Exhibit 7.3, which displays transaction information for a major NASDAQ stock, Cisco, on October 18, 2005, a representative and normal day. The time window charted here extends from the 9:30 A.M. open until the millionth share had traded just five and a half minutes later at 9:35:34 A.M. The previous day, October 17, Cisco's closing price had been $17.17 (as indicated by the diamond on the left axis). On October 18, the NASDAQ Opening Cross took place at 9:30:01 with 208,253 shares trading at $17.10. In the next five and a

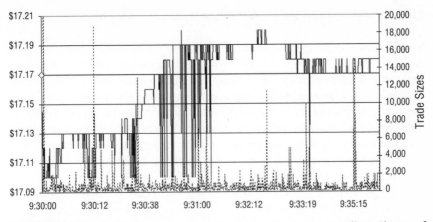

EXHIBIT 7.3 Trade Prices and Sizes in Shares for the First Million Shares of Cisco Traded on October 18, 2005.
Source: Reuters.

half minutes, 1,170 trades took place—a rate of 3.5 per second! The right axis shows the individual trade sizes that sum to one million. The average trade size in this five-minute period was 683 shares, and the median trade size was 400 shares, with 10 blocks of 10,000 shares or more executing. By the end of the day, 40.8 million Cisco shares traded with a low of $16.97, a high of $17.20 (a range of 1.35 percent), and a closing price of $16.98.

Throughout the five-and-a-half-minute opening period, the spread was generally $0.01. The difference between the 9:30 A.M. price and the 9:35 A.M. price was $0.08, and the low to high price range was $17.10 to $17.20, or 0.6 percent—just in this five-and-a-half-minute window. We interpret this as an example of fractured price discovery that can occur when a market becomes hypercontinuous. Understandably, many buy-side traders prefer not to navigate in these waters. When the currents become treacherous, best execution ceases to be a viable goal.

Another example of what could happen at the open is also provided by Cisco in the days before decimal pricing and NASDAQ's Opening Cross.[28] On January 22, 2001, from its 9:30 A.M. opening to 10:00 A.M., 7.995 million shares of Cisco traded in 9,761 separate trades (5.42 trades per second) that averaged 819 shares each. Throughout the half-hour period, the spread was generally $\frac{1}{16}$ or $\frac{1}{8}$ of a point, and the difference between the 9:30 A.M. price and the 10:00 A.M. price was $\frac{1}{4}$ point. However, prices over the 30-minute interval ranged from a high of $40\frac{63}{64}$, to a low of 40, nearly a $1 (or 2 percent) swing! This is a clear case of fractured price discovery in a hyper-continuous market. While this is just one example, it certainly suggests why NASDAQ was motivated to improve the market's opening price behavior by introducing its Opening Cross (as discussed in Chapter 4).

MEASURING THE PERFORMANCE OF A MARKET CENTER

We have seen that price discovery can go awry, especially when a market becomes hypercontinuous. The buy-side traders themselves are understandably very averse to discovering price. This aversion is reflected in the widespread use of VWAP trading, a practice that, ironically, can increase their trading costs, as we have noted. VWAP and LHOC are fallacious benchmarks. Buy-side traders and their portfolio managers should understand that trading practices designed to beat an erroneous benchmark can be costly. They should also understand, and increasingly do, that better market structure is needed.

You go to the market and trade. As a retail customer, you are apt to look primarily at the commissions you are charged, but the quality of the executions that you receive is also very important. For institutional customers, both commissions and transaction prices are critically important, and they are being assessed carefully. Whether you are big or little, the price at which you trade may or may not be reasonable in light of current market conditions, and your performance as a trader may not look good. You may have paid too much for a purchase or received too little for a sale. It is important to stress that this can happen, and that it might not be your fault. The quality of executions that you achieve very much depends, not just on your order placement decisions, but also on the efficiency of the marketplace to which you have sent your orders. If a market becomes hypercontinuous under stressful conditions, best execution becomes a vacuous concept. In its discussion of best execution obligations, AIMR (2001)[29] also notes that markets and exchanges should "continually . . . seek to develop faster, more efficient, and more reliable systems and structures to ensure that their marketplace maintains fair, transparent, and equitable trading practices." Consequently, the responsibility for providing best execution also lies with the market centers themselves.

Marcus Hooper, in his contributed piece to this chapter, suggests that prices established in the market depend on market structure, not just on an intraday basis, but over more extended periods of time as well. The thinking is compatible with our discussion in Chapter 6 of the price discovery process. Hooper's point in saying this is that market structure can affect a trader's performance (i.e., his ability to beat a trading benchmark or, in the lingo of the profession, to capture alpha). We can refocus the thought: Because market structure can affect price formation in the marketplace, market centers should themselves be subjected to a performance measurement. And they are in any number of ways—by each other, by government regulatory agencies, and by consulting firms.

Improving market quality should be the overriding objective of a market center. The important question is how to implement it. It is inappropriate to focus myopically on a factor such as the bid-ask spread simply because spreads are easily measured. An assessment of intraday price volatility, a variable that may capture a broader array of transaction costs, is advisable. Of particular importance is the magnitude of price volatility during the first and last minutes of the trading day. On an ongoing basis, price discovery is particularly difficult during these periods, and an assessment of market quality is most meaningful at these times when the market is under stress.

A market center has the obligation to reduce trading costs for the broad spectrum of investors who are its customers. As Martin Reck says in his piece in Chapter 5, to meet this obligation, order flow from the disparate groups of investors who inevitably characterize a market must be appropriately integrated. Only if this is accomplished will good price and quantity discovery be achieved.

The quality of price discovery and of quantity discovery should be assessed with regard to two variables: (1) the level of intraday price volatility and (2) institutional order size. The fact that institutions show only small parts of their orders to the market should be closely monitored and assessed by the market centers. The coexistence of high intraday volatility and small institutional order size would indicate that market quality is low, and that best execution is inordinately difficult to achieve.

Electronic limit order book markets are good trading platforms for the retail order flow for liquid, large-cap stocks. Unfortunately, the economic structure of a continuous, order-driven market breaks down when the order flow it receives is low. Even for big-cap stocks, plain vanilla electronic markets do not offer sufficient liquidity for large orders. While allowing for hidden (iceberg) orders helps, further market structure is needed for handling institutional order flow. Additional structure is now provided in the U.S. and European markets by (1) the inclusion of crossing (either on an exchange, as does Deutsche Börse, or on an ATS such as POSIT or Instinet); (2) the use of price discovery call auctions (predominantly by NASDAQ and the European exchanges); and (3) new, electronic block trading systems (such as Liquidnet and Pipeline).

A reasonable containment of transaction costs and best execution is easier to achieve in a consolidated market than in a fragmented market. Consolidation has two dimensions. Along with the spatial integration of orders, good market structure also requires an appropriate *temporal integration* of orders. Temporal fragmentation can be every bit as damaging to market quality as its spatial counterpart (as James Ross stresses in his contribution to Chapter 4). The inclusion of predetermined meeting points in time, be they crosses or price discovery calls, enables participants in general, and institutional traders in particular, to meet in an orderly fashion and to provide liquidity to one another with minimal price dislocation.

Our previous discussion of Exhibit 7.3 and the information it contains about the first half-hour of trading in Cisco on October 18, 2005, highlights a reality of the continuous market. Orders execute against each other at fluctuating prices in trades that are generally bilateral. When the trades are small and are separated from each other by subseconds, the price fluctuations are not efficient adjustments to new information. Rather, they are a manifestation of price discovery noise, which, at times, can be chaotic. During the opening 30 minutes of trading for Cisco back on January 22, 2001, price discovery appears to have been in disarray. Far better would it have been then for the traders in Cisco to have had the opportunity to meet at a single point in time, so that their orders could be executed at a single price in one large, multilateral trade. NASDAQ now offers that possibility with its newly instituted Opening Cross (discussed in Chapter 4).

As noted, multiple call auctions are now included in the European equity markets, NASDAQ now opens and closes its trading with an electronic call auction facility, and the calls are attracting meaningful order flow. Nevertheless, many institutional participants continue to avoid trading in the opening minutes. Presumably, they prefer to wait until prices are more clearly established before stepping forward with their orders. We suggest that continuing attention be given to the architecture of existing call auctions to assure that they have appropriate functionality for institutional investors.

As we have discussed, institutional investors in both the United States and Europe need a good benchmark against which to assess the quality of their trades. The standard benchmarks (VWAP and LHOC) do not do the job. Your trade should not be assessed against an average of a day's worth of poorly discovered prices. Rather, well-discovered prices that participants can have confidence in are needed. Pooling multiple orders in a properly structured call auction is the best way to produce prices that are worthy of being used as benchmark values.

With the introduction of closing calls in the European and NASDAQ markets, confidence is beginning to build in the closing price.[30] If this continues, more orders will be attracted to the closing auctions. In a virtuous circle, this will, in turn, reinforce the quality of price discovery at the close. At some point, the closing price may earn its status as a widely accepted benchmark. If volume also builds for the opening and possibly intraday auctions, these calls as well will produce values that could be used as benchmarks. The benchmarks produced in the call auctions could then be treated as safe-harbor values for a best execution obligation.

What about intermediaries? Currently, much attention is being given to the introduction of new electronic technology for order routing and information dissemination. This technology keeps making it easier to find the other side of a trade. Direct market access (DMA) is increasingly being sought and obtained by institutional customers. Block trading systems such as Pipeline and Liquidnet are rapidly growing in popularity. Hence, the role for intermediaries is diminished. Nevertheless, intermediaries will continue to be needed to resolve imbalances, to facilitate handling large orders for big-cap stocks, to animate trading, to make the mid-cap and small-cap markets viable, and to play a special role for all stocks when markets are under stress.

Four basic trading modalities are required for an efficient market model: (1) the limit order book continuous market, (2) call auctions, (3) a market maker quote-driven component, and (4) a block trading facility. Combining these four modalities into an efficient hybrid is far from simple. To some extent, the objective may be attained with ATSs providing separate modalities as niche players. Strong central exchanges can also provide the requisite interfaces and run the modalities. Whichever way, additional market quality improvements are needed and, for some time to come, achieving an acceptably efficient hybrid marketplace will remain a challenge.

BEST EXECUTION AND PERFORMANCE RECONSIDERED

Candide, portfolio manager for Voltaire's Best Possible World Fund, has just received several trade reports.[31] Five thousand shares were bought at $35.10 at a time when the market was offering 4,000 at 35 and another 1,000 were available at $35.10. "Excellent," she exclaimed. "Compliance won't flag the trade, and just think of all the free research I have received from that broker, and also those prime New York Knicks basketball tickets that he sent me." Next, 10,000 shares of another stock were sold at $28 at a time when the market was showing a bid for 8,000 shares at $28.05. "Wonderful—no red flags," she bubbled. "I sold all those shares immediately." Then 100,000 shares of another stock were bought in 20 tranches over the course of five trading hours at an average price of $42.65 (the volume weighted average price for the period was $41.75). "I'm thrilled," Candide shouted. "Just wait until you see what the VWAP will be tomorrow!"

How would you rate the performance of Candide's trader? Did he satisfy a "best execution" criterion? What is "good" and what is "best" is in the eyes of the beholder. If you are like Candide, the answers are that the performance was "good" and that the "best" criterion was met. But any criterion that can make a bad execution look good (or a good execution look bad) must be questionable. The bottom line is that best execution is a multifaceted concept that is difficult to define and even more challenging to measure. In large part this is because the quality of executions received by participants depends, not only on their individual needs and trading decisions, but also on the characteristics of a specific trade or package, on the stock being traded, on the objective of the participant requesting the execution, and on conditions existing in the market as the order is being executed.

With regard to transaction cost analysis, we have come a long way in sharpening and refining our tools for assessing transaction records and quantifying the costs of trading. There is substantially more trade data to analyze today, and as the total costs of trading have become more visible, buy-side customers have increasingly realized the extent to which poor trading can seriously erode portfolio performance. As a consequence, the buy-side professionals have improved the handling of their own orders, and they are increasingly putting pressure on the sell side to increase the efficiency of our trading systems.

As market structures continue to evolve, liquidity pools will deepen, the costs of trading will decrease, and the returns that you will realize from your portfolio as an investor will rise. What about trading as a profession? As Alfred Berkeley suggests in the Foreword, efforts should be made to "rebalance the structure of the market to 'neutral,' where neither the investor nor the trader is advantaged." Nevertheless, markets will forever remain imperfect. Trading will forever remain an important activity that is distinct from investing. Markets, facilities, and trading tools are forever changing, and new ways of trading will continue to emerge. Knowing how best to handle your orders and to capture your alpha involves a learning process that will never end. We hope that, as a student of the equity markets, you come out on the winning end.

FROM THE CONTRIBUTORS

Marcus Hooper
The Quest for Trading's Holy Grail—Alpha!

Wayne H. Wagner and Melissa Spurlock
How Intelligent Traders Enhance Their Skills with a
TCA Report

The Quest for
Trading's Holy Grail—Alpha!

Marcus Hooper

What could the Holy Grail possibly have to do with alpha? A couple of things. Both are obscured by mystery and uncertainty. They both offer numerous possible paths to enlightenment. Both offer few clues to the right direction. With respect to alpha, let's follow one path and see where we end up.

Whether you trade for a hedge fund, are an asset manager, or are a principal trader (market maker), you are usually seeking to outperform. We call it going after alpha. Capturing alpha involves beating your benchmark. Where does the alpha come from? You can generate alpha from a better understanding of the path followed by P^*. I am not thinking of the P^* in the TraderEx simulation software which follows a random walk, but of the discussion in Chapter 6 that shows that price discovery is a path-dependent process that results in a multiple-, not single, equilibrium situation.

By its very nature, the path-dependent, multiequilibrium framework opens the possibility for longer-run alpha capture. If you are a successful long-term investor or a short-term trader, go for it. However, you may identify pricing divergences that correct over time, as a statistical arbitrage fund does. Or you could exploit structural trading inefficiencies (in other words, act like a principal trader and earn your alpha from things like the market spread). So we have several categories of alpha: short-term, longer-term, and price divergence alphas. Then there is what I call structural alpha, where some traders gain or lose alpha due to market inefficiencies. A principal trader creates alpha from exploiting temporal fragmentation, which happens when traders agree on price but not on a point in time to meet.

A problem with having these various forms of alpha is that, depending on your trading role, an alpha capture strategy can work for you or against you. If you trade structural alpha, you stand to lose to a P^* alpha investor whose view is more correct than yours. You try to earn your alpha from, say, the market spread, but as P^* moves in the direction some better-informed investor has correctly anticipated, you lose. As the other investor's P^* alpha creates gains for him, your structural alpha creates losses for you because your stock position is opposite to the other investor's. That's bad news for you but good news for the other investor.

The key point here is that certain types of alpha are closely related to trading methods and market structure. The example just given shows a transfer of alpha occurring due to the existence of a principal trader. Another example would be the case of a statistical arbitrage or hedge fund that would find it harder to create alpha if the market prohibited or limited short-selling.

Let's stay with the relationship between alpha and market structure. It makes sense that change in market structure impacts the way structural alpha is created, lost, and transferred. The example of the principal trader is one obvious way for us to see this in action. Similarly, when we think of short term P* alpha, it probably makes sense that market structure changes would have an impact. If you're trading short-term movements, then the market structure must surely affect the way those short-term movements happen. Let's say that we base our market on a periodic call auction process where trades, as discussed in Chapter 4, can only occur at certain moments in the day (as opposed to continuous real-time trading). The lower frequency of pricing points (auctions) with the call market structure, and the simultaneous increase in volume at each call, means that short-term price volatility decreases. That's because there is less opportunity in the short term for divergent execution prices to occur because more trades meet at the same point in time and a better consensus on the equilibrium price is achieved. Thus the opportunity for short-term P* alpha creation is reduced because there are less opportunities to exploit pricing inefficiencies.

What about longer-term P* alpha? Can changes in market structure affect the long-term price movements? In practice, that's the same as saying that the underlying trading mechanism can alter the fundamental long-term valuation of a company—how does that sound? I think most of us would probably say that it doesn't make any sense. How could the way we trade alter the long-term valuation of a company, when that valuation is based on long-term cash flows, forecasts, and revenues?

Believe it or not, it can and does make sense, and I'll do my best to prove it. Think of a quote-driven market. The quote-driven process has an implicit embedded price stabilization process. Principal traders make quotes that are usually in relatively large quantities. The principals are in the market day after day, and their quote sizes reflect their available level of risk—not necessarily any actual underlying market supply or demand. The principals don't move their quotes when they receive orders in very small quantities—why bother? That is the embedded price stabilization: Principals only move their prices when they encounter a large order or have accumulated so many small orders that they have a large net imbalance in their book position.

Now think about an electronic order-driven market. The order book reflects revealed supply and demand, and often comprises only very small order sizes—traders don't want to show the full extent of their orders. When traders try to bring large orders into an order book, they often have to execute numerous trades in small tranches to complete a large order. In any system with simultaneous bids and offers, a movement in one of those prices affects the midprice for the share. Thus, in an order-driven market it is entirely natural for the midprice to be highly volatile when compared to a quote-driven process.

The order-driven process creates an interesting supply/demand dynamic. In a quote-driven market, a small number of principals each see large proportions of the supply and demand, and so are well placed to form an opinion of P*. But in an order book there may be hundreds of individuals, each with his own thoughts about P*, all trying to execute efficiently against large numbers of very small orders. This causes a dilution of knowledge of the supply and demand, and means that any individual trader is very poorly positioned to know the real P*.

I have a hypothesis about this: The general lack of knowledge of P* in an order-driven process exacerbates price volatility. I further hypothesize that, while this is mostly evidenced in short-term volatility, it can also create a negative feedback process that leads to significant and sustained price runs and reversals over relatively lengthy periods. This in turn means that shares can trade at wide divergences from what one might think would be their long-term P*, or fundamental valuation.

Can I prove this? If nothing else, I'll try to show that there is some strong anecdotal evidence in support of my hypothesis. To this end, I have sought to identify two unusual events that would need to occur in conjunction:

1. A total shift from one market mechanism to another (say from quote- to order-driven).
2. A share performance that shows a clear and consistent long-term price trend—by long-term, I mean several years.

These are both highly unusual events. The best recent example that we have had on my side of the Atlantic of a fundamental shift in market structure is the London Stock Exchange's move from a quote-driven system to its new SETS order-driven system. The structural change was applied to the top 100 shares in the UK market. Due to corporate activity (M&As and all that) over the period chosen, the sample size reduced further.

From this smallish sample size, I need a company with a really long-term, consistent share price trend to be able to evidence relative change in the long-term volatility; I chose to work with a six-year period. A lot of changes can happen to a company's fortunes over six years, and with a sample group of fewer than 100 companies, I did not have great expectations of finding any clear, obvious examples. That is, until I looked at the chart shown in Exhibit 7.4 for GlaxoSmithKline. This stock seems to have a clear six-year price trend which is, overall, very close to a straight line.

The top half of the exhibit is the price chart, and the bottom half is the average 14-day returns momentum, which is my indicator of longer-term price movement, or volatility. The vertical line located at the month of Oc-

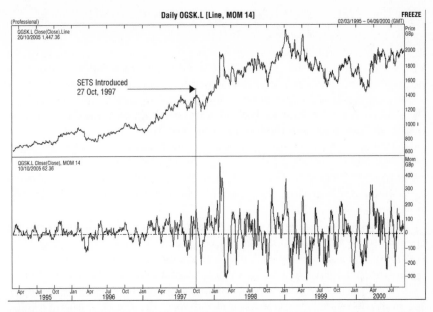

EXHIBIT 7.4   Volatility of GlaxoSmithKline Increased Dramatically After October 1997.

Source: Reuters.

tober 1997 marks what I see as the onset of greater volatility. Would you agree with me that there is a clear difference between what is to the left and what is to the right of that line? Would you hazard a guess as to when the SETS order-driven market was introduced? Let me enlighten you: It was introduced on 27 October, 1997.

Of course this is just one example, and not a full statistical analysis. But clearly something happened to radically change the longer-term price momentum. Equally clearly, something seems to have started sometime around October 1997. As a trader with 20 years of experience, I have perceived that even small changes in market microstructure can create large downstream effects. Hopefully, I have at least partly persuaded you that this might be so.

So where does this path take us in our search for alpha enlightenment? First, trading costs impact alpha (of course, we all know this). Second, we need to make the further connection that market structure often defines the trading costs in the first place. Third, don't dismiss the possibility that market structure may significantly impact not just medium- to long-term price runs and reversals, but long-term alpha as well. Fourth, isn't market structure fun! Now let's see if we can find the Holy Grail.

How Intelligent Traders Enhance Their Skills with a TCA Report

Wayne H. Wagner and Melissa Spurlock

You've gone for your annual medical checkup, and the doctor has in hand the results of the testing. What you would like to know, bottom line, is "Is there anything wrong with me? And if so, what is the problem, and what can I do to correct it?" The natural human tendency is to want to hear, "You're in fine shape." But the purpose of the medical test is not feel-good affirmation, but an unbiased probe to uncover problems and devise corrective actions.

A transaction cost analysis (TCA) annual or quarterly report performs the same role as the medical checkup. The report will show an array of information, including an overall evaluation followed by a set of detailed diagnostics that highlight trading performance in specific areas. While it is valuable to drill down into the details of individual trades later, it can be far more beneficial to evaluate and enhance the entire implementation process.

The goal is to identify and analyze what works while finding the areas that need improvement and to make the necessary enhancements. The trade desk is, in fact, a cost center. Portfolio managers are charged with making money for the firm by producing solid returns. A trader's job is not to generate alpha through trading, but rather to add value by minimizing the cost of implementing the portfolio manager's ideas.

The key to finding areas of potential improvement is to look for outlying numbers—the places where the results are not as good as the benchmark. Overall results might interest a board of directors or a chief investment officer, but the search for areas of performance improvement—the potential "sicknesses" in the trading—will be found in the outlying segments of a diagnostic report. The search for improvement potential falls into three areas:

1. Are the orders from portfolio managers delivered in a manner that promotes or impedes good trading results?
2. Are the processes used to execute these orders up to the task? Do they sufficiently distinguish and apply the best techniques for handling orders of varying characteristics—domestic versus foreign orders, orders for large-cap versus small-cap stocks, urgent versus nonurgent orders, liquidity-demanding versus liquidity-supplying orders, and so forth?

3. Are the agents that are relied on to process trades—the brokers, algorithms, trade venues, and exchanges—up to the task to which I apply them, or are there better alternatives available depending on my goals?

ORDERS FROM PORTFOLIO MANAGERS

Many professional traders lament disconnect that can occur with a portfolio manager who has little contemporary trading experience. Close cooperation, effective communication, and mutual understanding between a portfolio manager and his trader are essential to good execution—and superior performance. Some types of dissonant behavior between portfolio managers and traders can be discovered by asking the following four sets of questions:

1. Is the manager clear in his instructions? Can the trader identify urgent orders based on the instructions given? For example, a manager dealing with a cash flow problem should specify a time frame for completion in order to source liquidity in the most timely and efficient manner. He may need to pay a bit more than if he had a broader time frame in which to execute.

2. Are the order releases poorly timed—for example, late in the afternoon or after significant adverse price moves in the stock?
    *   By looking at a "time slice," a trader can demonstrate to the portfolio manager that orders given after the market has opened or late in the day can significantly lag those given earlier.
    *   Particularly when a manager is trading on semi-public information, he may wait for a reversal before giving the order to the trader. The trader, however is in a better position to determine the probability of a jump or reversal.

3. Does the manager try to override the trader with limit orders and add-on orders?
    *   The trader is the link in the implementation process most closely connected to the market. While the manager still may need to determine through limits whether he has enough alpha to justify paying for a trade, it is important that this information be shared with the trader. Many studies have shown that a trader who is given discretion adds more value over time and also becomes more confident and adept.
    *   A common complaint is that portfolio managers will give a market order for the record, but then stand with the trader and micromanage the process, not allowing the trader to source liquidity on his own.

- Add-on orders can increase costs as well. A manager who holds back part of the order may miss opportunities to discover trade blocks, generally a more efficient way of executing large orders.
- Another problem with add-on orders can be leaving a consistent footprint in the market. If you continue to trade the same stock day after day, counterparties will start to watch for you and prices often begin to reflect anticipation of your demand.

4. Does the manager size the order to reflect market liquidity? In a similar vein, have assets under management grown to the point where implementing the portfolio manager's strategy has been compromised?
   - This is fast becoming a key driver in the ability to contain costs and even complete trades. In recent years, timing costs seem to be rising relative to impact costs, suggesting that finding liquidity is an increasing problem.
   - As markets have become more efficient, managers are turning to less traditional investments such as small capitalization stocks, real estate investment trusts (REITs), and emerging market equities. The volume in these stocks can be spotty and the stated volumes can be misleading as they trade in blocks and sometimes by appointment. Managers need to understand the true capacity of their funds by doing a regular liquidity review.

Excessive costs that derive from these behaviors cannot be resolved by the trader in isolation. The manager must understand how his behavior affects the trader's ability to secure timely and low-cost trade completions. The trader is often at a distinct disadvantage in these discussions, especially if the portfolio manager has a reputation for having brilliant investment skills. Seeing the effects in black and white via a TCA report will facilitate meaningful discussions about these matters. A trader can talk, yell, and bang his head against the wall, but nothing speaks louder than real numbers!

TRADING PROCESSES

It is helpful to begin this discussion by acknowledging that all serious professionals will apply their best skills as experience has taught them to. But best execution is not synonymous with "the best I know how to do." Professional growth is a continuous learning experience. Growing that experience requires inputs from outside the received knowledge, such as:

- Discovering that a previously accepted process is no longer producing the same quality of results. This applies particularly to new markets or to old markets as they become more efficient.

- Discovering through innovation and experimentation a new process that works better. The use of new and evolving technology is key. A PM and trader must stay ahead of or at least with the curve, not behind it. The key is to automate the easy stuff and free up time for the challenges.
- Education, both formal and informal—reading, studying, discussing, participating in forums and affinity groups. Traders are often compared to their peers. Good traders know what the peers are up to. Don't be afraid to share ideas; share yours and you will get theirs. Then put good ideas to use in your own process.
- Studying a TCA report and finding anomalous results. Look for outliers, both positive and negative. Learn to analyze strengths and weaknesses and act to improve on both. Don't get bogged down by looking at just one or two trades. It takes many observations to find the trends that will help guide an effective strategy.

It should be noted that reading TCA reports with an open mind is a difficult undertaking. It is very easy to fall into the trap of the eye registering only what the mind already thinks it knows. For this reason, TCA reports are probably better discussed in a group, or with an experienced consultant, rather than in isolation.

Once a problem has been identified, the real work starts: What can be done to improve the results? Curiously, the problems often seem to solve themselves once they have been clearly identified. For example, the discovery of hidden costs in the form of delay and missed opportunities provides a whole new perspective for a trader who had been thinking solely of commissions and market impact costs. Once the trader really gets it with respect to hidden costs, trader behavior will mutate to encompass the newly formed objective of minimizing total cost.

The exciting part about breaking down costs into these components is that the largest parts of the slippage, these normally hidden costs, are the ones that are largely within the trader's ability to control and improve. Commissions can be driven down by a few pennies, and market impact can be largely out of a trader's hands. But a trader can work to control delays and missed opportunities for real cost improvement.

At other times, new ideas need to be introduced. Where does algorithmic trading work best? What do other traders do when they need to draw liquidity in a hurry? Electronic venues continue to gain in flexibility and popularity, but are only as good as their application proves them to be. The traders who achieve good results using these new venues are the ones who are careful to monitor the results in real time and who can learn from their successes and failures.

MONITORING THE AGENTS

Traditionally, most traders identify their key skills in terms of their ability to control the agents (brokers) selected to perform the executions. Whom do I trust with this order, and how much information do I release to them? These are the primary firing-line decisions that traders make. Traders, all conditioned by past experience, become exceedingly paranoid and thereby adept at real-time monitoring of agents. Is the stock behaving as I would expect? Am I getting my fair share of the volume crossing the tape? And especially, do I see any signals that my agent is working primarily for some other customer or for his own pocketbook?

It is useful to complement this watchdog activity with two levels of summarization based on TCA analyses. The first level is overnight: An objective analysis of the previous day's trading can create short-horizon feedback looks where brokers delivering unsatisfactory performance can be apprised of the fact in time to make corrective measures. This daily analysis can further allow for good communication back to the portfolio manager. Ideally it can also be used to help a trader determine his trading game plan for the following day.

It is also useful to take a longer-term perspective, say quarterly or annually, which is based on much larger trading samples. Doing so will focus attention on several more overriding issues:

- For the brokers whom we use regularly, are we directing to them the kinds of trades that play to their strengths? Not all brokers are going to be equally good at NYSE versus NASDAQ, Europe versus Far East, large cap versus small cap, routine trades versus high-liquidity demand, and so forth. Who needs another generic broker? The first question when meeting a prospective broker should be "What differentiates you?" Find out if they have a specialty that fits with some of your more obscure order flow.
- Are our peers getting better execution from the same brokers whom we use and, if so, why? Evaluate your coverage. Sometimes a desk will see far better numbers from the same brokerage with different sales traders. Be aggressive in demanding a change in coverage if the relationship is not working. Your broker should understand you, your style, and your goals. In addition, develop relationships with your brokers. Try to concentrate flow without compromising the ability to use specialty or niche brokers when necessary. Don't squeeze every last quarter-penny from the commission. A relationship needs to be profitable for both sides in order to work.

- Who should be in our stable of brokers? Most TCA reports will provide cross-client universes that show how brokers perform for many customers. These reports can be used to identify brokers who should be added to the stable because of their proven ability to handle certain types of trades.

Stepping back from the frenzy of the daily activity helps traders gain perspective. Examining problems in manager/trader relationships, execution of trading strategies, and the monitoring of agents helps investment management firms truly understand how the moving parts relate to one another. Transaction cost analysis reports and outside interpretations can greatly facilitate that review. Past experience with well-functioning trade desks clearly shows that TCA makes good managers, traders, and brokers even better.

APPENDIX TO CHAPTER 7
Explaining Risk Aversion

Risk management is important because we are risk-averse. Instinctively, we know this, but what precisely does it mean? In this Appendix, we offer a brief discussion of risk aversion that follows the standard academic line of reasoning.

The key insight is that investors do not assess dollar returns per se, but the utility of dollar returns. *Utility* is an economist's term for the subjective personal pleasure that an individual gets from a good, service, income, or wealth. For instance, how do you feel in utility terms when you earn $100,000 a year? How would you feel if instead you earned $200,000? All else equal, you would feel better, but probably not twice as good.

Assume that for you (and for all other investors), the incremental utility of having one more dollar declines as the number of dollars that you have (i.e., your wealth) rises. For instance, with incremental utility diminishing, if your income doubles from $100,000 to $200,000, your happiness goes up but by less than 100 percent. This decreasing incremental utility translates into your being adverse to taking a risk, and to your therefore requiring compensation for accepting the risk. To see this, consider a fair bet that has a distribution of alternative payouts that is centered on zero (i.e., the expected payout is zero). Will you take the bet?

With your incremental utility of dollars diminishing, the utility gain attributable to any positive dollar payout must be less than the utility loss from the comparable, mirror image negative dollar payout (e.g., if your payout from the bet is +$100, your gain in happiness is less than the amount of happiness you would lose if your payout is –$100). Consequently, if your expected *dollar* payout is zero, your expected *utility* payout must be negative, and you will not accept the bet. Now assume that the dollar payout is symmetrically distributed around a positive mean. Will you take the bet? Yes, if the expected dollar payout is *sufficiently* positive. Further, the greater the variance of the payout distribution, and/or the greater your risk aversion (the faster your incremental utility falls as the payout increases), the greater the positive expected dollar payout must be for you to accept the risk and take the bet.

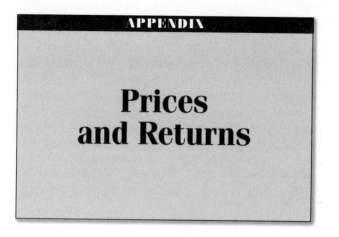

Prices
and Returns

T he measurement of returns (price changes) and returns volatility enters the discussion in several of the chapters, most notably Chapter 1 (the size of information-driven price changes in the TraderEx simulation), Chapter 2 (the accentuation of intraday volatility), and Chapter 7 (risk and returns variance). In this Appendix, we present technical details regarding the measurement of returns. We also explain the effect of measurement interval length on the mean and variance of returns, on the market model beta parameter, on the variance of residual returns, and on the market model R^2.

THE MEASUREMENT OF RETURNS

Each transaction price in a continuous market reflects the interaction of at least two orders—a buy order and a sell order. Each return that is established reflects two separate transaction prices—the price at the beginning of the period over which the return is measured, and the price at the end of the period. All told, prices and returns are complex results of informational change, liquidity change, technical trading, and the mechanics of the market. A price exists at a specific moment in time. A return reflects a change in price over a given period of time. We start our discussion of the measurement of returns by considering the time dimensions involved in their measurement.

The Time Dimension

The time dimension enters the measurement of returns in a number of ways: $(T + 1)$ points in time establish T time intervals; t identifies the tth interval, with the value of t increasing from 1 to T. The return for an interval is given an index that corresponds to the index for the interval. Thus r_t is the return over the interval $(t - 1)$ to (t). If the length of the interval is changed, then the index on the return corresponds to the point in time that demarcates the end of the longer period. That is, R_T denotes the return from 0 to T if the full span is referred to, and r_T denotes the return from $(T - 1)$ to (T) if the Tth (last) short interval is referred to. Using this notation, the relevant time dimensions are as follows:

- *Points in time:* $T + 1$ points in time extend from the first (0) to the last (T).
- *Time intervals:* T time intervals are indexed $t = 1$, $t = 2$, . . . , $t = T$, with the index on each interval corresponding to the count on the price observation at the end of that interval.
- *Time span:* The overall time span is of length T, and it comprises T short intervals.
- *Interval length:* The length of each interval is point in time t minus point in time $(t - 1)$ (e.g., one day or one week).
- *Unit period:* Both the overall time span and the shorter time intervals are measured as multiples of a *unit period of time*. For instance, if the unit period is one day, then both the time interval $(t - 1)$ to t and the overall time span, T, are measured in days.
- *Common period:* A return measured for one interval of time (such as a week) can be expressed as a rate per some other interval (for instance, per year). Converting all time rates into a common period sometimes facilitates analysis and evaluation.
- *Compounding frequency:* Interest can be compounded once per time interval, more frequently, or, in the limit, continuously.
- *Calendar time:* For theoretical analysis, time can be treated as an abstract concept. For empirical analysis, actual price observations are located in calendar time. With seasonal variability, secular trends, and/or nonstationary returns distributions, the exact location of the span $t = 0$, $t = 1$, . . . , $t = T$ in calendar time will affect the observed price behavior. Location in calendar time may be altered in the large by, for example, using 2005 prices instead of 2003 prices, or in the small by using daily opening prices instead of daily closing prices.

PRICES

The term *price* can refer either to a transaction price or to a bid-ask quotation. *Transaction prices* are prices that have been established for trades already made. *Quotation prices* are ex ante expressions of the willingness of buyers and sellers to trade. We generally restrict the use of the term *price* to transaction prices and refer to bid-ask prices as *quotes*. The behavior of prices and quotes is studied by analyzing their change from one point in time to another.

Price changes are *returns*. Price changes computed by using points of time that are separated by an interval of specified length (such as one day) are identified as pertaining to that period (for instance, *daily returns*). Price changes computed for a sequence of prices recorded at the points of time that trades occur are *transaction-to-transaction returns*. For the most part, we deal with returns measured for specified time intervals.

In empirical work, prices are adjusted for stock and cash dividends paid during an interval so that the return measured for the interval is the total return—capital gains plus dividends. Therefore, if the closing price of a stock at time $(t - 1)$ is 50, the recorded closing price at t is 49, a dividend of $.25 a share is paid, and t is the ex-dividend date, the adjusted price at t is 49.25, and the price change from $(t - 1)$ to t is

$$49.25 - 50 = -0.75$$

Similar adjustments are made for stock splits. For instance, immediately following a 2 for 1 split, the price of a share is adjusted by multiple 2.

RETURNS

Price changes (returns) can be measured as price relatives, as dollar amounts, or as percentages. Arithmetic percentages can be converted into logarithmic values or into growth rates.

Assume a time span from 0 to T divided into equal intervals indexed $t = 1, t = 2, \ldots t = T$.

The *price relatives* are

$$\frac{P_T}{P_0} = \left(\frac{P_1}{P_0}\right)\left(\frac{P_2}{P_1}\right)\cdots\left(\frac{P_T}{P_{T-1}}\right) \tag{A.1}$$

For the time interval (0, 1) we can write

$$P_1 = P_0 + \Delta P_1 \tag{A.2a}$$

$$P_1 = P_0(1 + r_1) \tag{A.2b}$$

$$P_1 = P_0 e^{g_1} \tag{A.2c}$$

where ΔP is the *dollar return*,

$$\Delta P_1 = P_1 - P_0 \tag{A.3}$$

r_1 is the *percentage return*,

$$r_1 = \frac{\Delta P_1}{P_0} = \frac{P_0 + \Delta P_1}{P_0} - 1 = \frac{P_1}{P_0} - 1 \tag{A.4}$$

r_1^* is the *logarithmic return*,

$$r_1^* = \ln(1 + r_1) \tag{A.5}$$

and g_1 is the *growth rate*,

$$g_1 = \ln\left(\frac{P_1}{P_0}\right) \tag{A.6}$$

where ln indicates the natural logarithm (to the base e, $e = 2.7182\ldots$).

Generalizing for a succession of periods, $t = 1, \ldots, T$:

$$P_T = P_0 + \Delta P_1 + \ldots + \Delta P_T = P_0 + \sum_{t=1}^{T} \Delta P_t \tag{A.7a}$$

$$P_T = P_0(1 + r_1)\ldots(1 + r_T) = P_0 \prod_{t=1}^{T}(1 + r_t) \tag{A.7b}$$

$$P_T = P_0 e^{g_1}\ldots e^{g_T} = P_0 \prod_{t=1}^{T} e^{g_t} \tag{A.7c}$$

For the overall time span we can also write

$$P_T = P_0 + \Delta P_T \tag{A.8a}$$

$$P_T = P_0 (1 + R_T) \tag{A.8b}$$

$$P_T = P_0 e^{g_T} \tag{A.8c}$$

where R_T is the percentage return over the whole time span. Equations (A.7) and (A.8) give

$$\Delta P_T = \sum_{t=1}^{T} \Delta P_t \tag{A.9a}$$

$$1 + R_T = \prod_{t=1}^{T} (1 + r_t) \tag{A.9b}$$

$$e^{g_T} = \prod_{t=1}^{T} e^{g_t} \tag{A.9c}$$

Taking logarithms of equation (A.9c) gives

$$g_T = \sum_{t=1}^{T} g_t \tag{A.9d}$$

It follows from equations (A.9a) through (A.9d) that

- The average price change over the time span of length T is the arithmetic average of the price changes over the T short intervals that comprise it.
- $(1 + R_T)^{1/T}$ is the geometric mean of the $(1 + r_t)$. (The geometric mean of n observations is the nth root of the product of the n observations.)
- g_T is T times the arithmetic mean of the g_t.

Let $R_T^* = \ln(1 + R_T)$ and $r_t^* = \ln(1 + r_t)$. Then, from equations (A.7b) and (A.8b), we have

$$\ln\left(\frac{P_T}{P_0}\right) = R_T^* = \sum_{t=1}^{T} r_t^* \tag{A.10}$$

From equations (A.8b) and (A.8c) we have

$$(1 + R_T) = e^{g_T} \tag{A.11}$$

Taking logarithms of equation (A.11) gives

$$R_T^* = g_T \tag{A.12}$$

The growth rate g_T is, therefore, a logarithmic return.

As seen in equation (A.7b), the $(1 + r_t)$ are multiplicative returns; it follows from equation (A.9b) that $(1 + R_T)^{1/T}$ is a geometric mean return. Multiplicative returns, geometric means, and especially the variance of multiplicative returns are cumbersome to deal with; additive returns, arithmetic means, and the variance of additive returns are not. For this reason, microstructure analysis frequently uses logarithmic returns (r^*) instead of arithmetic returns (r); the r_t^* are additive, and we can treat their arithmetic mean and variance.

THE INTERVALING EFFECT

The *intervaling effect* is the way in which measures of returns behavior change as the measurement interval is varied. The relevant return measures include the following:

- Mean return (stock and index)
- The variance of returns (stock and index)
- Market model beta
- The variance of residual returns
- Market model R^2

Following the previous discussion, taking logarithms of

$$\frac{P_T}{P_0} = \left(\frac{P_1}{P_0} \right) \cdots \left(\frac{P_T}{P_{T-1}} \right)$$

gives

$$R_T^* = \sum_{t=1}^{T} r_t^* \tag{A.13}$$

Let the short time span $(t-1)$ to t be the unit period. The intervaling effect is the effect on each of the five measures of increasing the interval T over which the long-period return, R_T^* in equation (A.13) is measured.

Mean Return (Stock and Index)

Taking means of equation (A.13) and assuming the returns distribution is stationary, gives

$$E[R_T^*] = \sum_{t=1}^{T} E[r_t^*] = TE[r^*] \tag{A.14}$$

where E is the expectations operator.

It is clear from equation (A.14) that the mean logarithmic return increases linearly with T. For instance, the average weekly logarithmic return expressed as a rate per week is five times the average daily logarithmic return expressed as a rate per day.

The Variance of Returns (Stock and Index)

Taking the variance of equation (A.13) gives

$$\text{Var}(R_T^*) = \sum_{t=1}^{T} \sum_{u=1}^{T} \sigma_t \sigma_u \rho_{t,u} \tag{A.15}$$

where σ_t (σ_u) is the standard deviation of returns in the tth (uth) short period

$\rho_{t,u}$ is the correlation between the tth short period return and the uth short period return, $t, u = 1, \ldots, T$

The correlation between returns affects the relationship between the variance of the long-period return and the variances of the short-period returns. Because of this, the intervaling effect on variance depends on the correlation pattern in security returns. This correlation is *serial correlation*: the correlation between the returns in the time series $r_1, \ldots, r_T$.

To simplify the discussion, assume the following:

1. The returns distribution is stationary ($\sigma_t = \sigma_u$ for all short periods $t, u = 1, \ldots, T$).
2. $\rho_{t,u}$ is the same for all $|t - u|$. That is if $t = 8$, $u = 5$, and thus the returns are three short periods apart, the correlation between these two re-

turns is identical to the correlation between any other pair of returns that are three short periods apart (the ninth return and the twelfth return, the seventh and the fourth, and so on).

From assumption (1) we can write

$$\sigma_t \sigma_u = \text{Var}(r^*) \quad \text{for all } t, u = 1, \ldots, T \tag{A.16}$$

From assumption (2) we can write

$$\rho_{t,u} = \rho_{1,1+s} \text{ for } s = |t - u|, s = 1, \ldots, T - 1 \tag{A.17}$$

To illustrate, consider the following. Let the correlation between the return for $t = 4$ and the return for $u = 6$ be $\rho_{4,6}$. Because $|4 - 6| = 2$, the correlation is, by assumption (2), the same as the correlation between return 1 and return 3. Using the notation in equation (A.17), the correlation between return 1 and return 3 is $\rho_{1,1+2}$ (that is, $s = 2$ in this case). Equation (A.17) shows that $\rho_{4,6} = \rho_{1,3}$, an equality that follows from assumption (2).

How many $\rho_{t,u}$ are there in the series $t, u = 1, \ldots, T$ that are equal to $\rho_{1,1+s}$, for any $s = 1, \ldots, T - 1$? Consider the case where $T = 8$ and $s = 3$. The pairs of returns that are three periods apart in the set of eight returns are (1, 4), (2, 5), (3, 6), (4, 7), and (5, 8). There are $(8 - 3) = (T - s)$ pairings. Generalizing for all T and s, and substituting equations (A.16) and (A.17) into equation (A.15) gives

$$\text{Var}(R_T^*) = T\text{Var}(r^*) + 2\,\text{Var}(r^*)\sum_{s=1}^{T-1}(T-s)\rho_{1,1+s} \tag{A.18}$$

Equation (A.18) shows that the variance of logarithmic returns increases linearly with T if there is no intertemporal correlation in the returns (that is, if $\rho_{t,u} = 0$ for all $t \neq u$). It also follows that, for any value of $\text{Var}(r^*)$, the long-period variance $\text{Var}(R_T^*)$ will be larger if the intertemporal correlations are predominantly positive and will be smaller if the intertemporal correlations are predominantly negative.

Market Model Beta

The market model beta for a stock can be written as

$$\beta_i = \frac{\text{Cov}(R_i^*, R_m^*)}{\text{Var}(R_m^*)} \tag{A.19}$$

From the intervaling relations defined previously for the variance term, and given that

$$\text{Cov}(R_i^*, R_m^*) = \sigma_i \sigma_m \rho_{i,m}$$

it is clear that a stock's beta will be independent of the differencing interval if there is no intertemporal correlation in security returns [that is, if $\text{Var}(R_{iT}^*)$ and $\text{Var}(R_{mT}^*)$ increase linearly with T, and if the cross-correlation $\rho_{i,m}$ is the same for all T]. By contrast, intertemporal correlation in returns will introduce an intervalling effect on the beta coefficient. With serial cross-correlation, the use of short-period returns causes beta estimates to be lower for relatively thin issues and higher for the largest issues.[1]

The Variance of Residual Returns

The *variance of residual returns* behaves in the same way as the variance of returns—it increases linearly with T in the absence of serial correlation, at a faster rate in the presence of positive serial correlation, and at a slower rate if the serial correlations are predominantly negative. Residual variance is further affected if beta itself is dependent on T, with the effect depending upon the impact that the intervalling effect on beta has on the average absolute size of the residual term.

The Market Model R^2

The squared coefficient of correlation for a regression equation shows the percentage of the variation in the dependent variable that is explained by change in the independent variable. For the market model regression,

$$R^2 = \frac{\beta_i^2 \text{Var}(R_m^*)}{\text{Var}(R_i^*)} \tag{A.20}$$

There will be no intervaling effect on R^2 if there are no intertemporal correlation patterns in security returns. This is because, in the absence of such correlation, beta is independent of T, and $\text{Var}(R_m^*)$ and $\text{Var}(R_i^*)$ both change linearly with T. However, intertemporal correlations cause an intervaling effect on R^2; the effect depends on the intervaling effect on beta and on the intervaling effect on the variance of R_m^* in relation to the intervaling effect on the variance of R_i^*. R^2 generally falls considerably as the differencing interval is shortened from, for example, monthly measurements to daily measurements or shorter.

About the Authors and Contributors

Alfred R. Berkeley III is CEO of Pipeline Trading Systems, LLC, an alternative trading system for equity block trades. Previously, he was president and then vice chairman of the NASDAQ Stock Market, Inc., from May 1996 to July 2003. Prior to NASDAQ, he was managing director and senior banker in the Corporate Finance Department of Alex. Brown & Sons, Inc., financing computer software and electronic commerce companies. Berkeley joined Alex. Brown & Sons in 1972 as a research analyst and became a general partner in 1983. From 1985 to 1987, he served as head of information services for the firm. In that capacity, he was responsible for all corporate information services, including both the firm's back and front office technology. Berkeley then moved to Alex. Brown's Merger and Acquisition department where, from 1987 to 1989, he developed the firm's technology practice. He is a trustee of Johns Hopkins University, Kintera, Inc., and Webex, Inc. He is a member of the National Infrastructure Assurance Council and serves on several other nonprofit and for-profit boards.

Paul L. Davis is a managing director at TIAA-CREF Investment Management LLC. TIAA-CREF is a national financial services leader and the premier retirement system for higher education and research employees. Further information can be found at http://www.tiaa-cref.org. Davis joined TIAA-CREF in 1983 after working at Prudential Securities in New York. Before his career on Wall Street, he taught mathematics at Lehigh University, Manhattanville College, and West Virginia University. He has an undergraduate degree from West Virginia University and a doctorate in mathematics from Carnegie Mellon University.

Reto Francioni has been the CEO of the executive board of Deutsche Börse AG since November 2005. Before that, he was president and chairman of the board of SWX-Group. Prior to assuming that position, he was co-CEO of Consors Discount Broker AG, Nuremberg. In 1993, Reto Francioni was named to the executive board of Deutsche Börse AG, where he was responsible for its entire cash market. In 1999,

373

he became deputy chief executive officer. Earlier in his career, he held management positions in the securities exchange and banking industry, and was a director of the corporate finance division at Hoffmann LaRoche AG, Basel. Reto Francioni has a law degree and PhD in law from Zurich University and is a professor of economics and finance at Zicklin School of Business, Baruch College, City University of New York (CUNY). He is the co-author with Robert Schwartz of the book *Equity Markets in Action* (New York: John Wiley & Sons, 2004).

Robert Greifeld is president and chief executive officer of NASDAQ Stock Market, Inc. (NASDAQ: NDAQ), the largest U.S. electronic stock market. Since joining NASDAQ in May 2003, Greifeld has taken steps to sharpen the company's strategic direction, focusing it on becoming the premier U.S. equities market. The market's mission is to provide the most efficient, transparent trading platform for investors by leveraging NASDAQ's advanced trading technology; to capture the majority of U.S. IPOs; and to attract listings from competitive exchanges. Tapping his 20-year industry experience and leadership with electronic trading systems, Greifeld has led a significant enhancement of NASDAQ's trading offerings. In March 2004, he oversaw the launch of NASDAQ's Market Center—a newly integrated system capable of accommodating the trading of NASDAQ, NYSE, AMEX-listed securities and exchange-traded funds on a single electronic platform. In January 2004, Greifeld spearheaded NASDAQ's innovative "dual listing" program, which for the first time allowed NYSE-listed companies to list on NASDAQ. This innovative initiative made worldwide news and significantly ratcheted up the debate regarding efficient electronic markets versus manual, floor-based exchanges. Greifeld has been a vocal advocate for modernizing market structure and increasing public company CEO attention on the performance and quality of stock markets for the benefit of company shareholders and all investors. In May 2004, Greifeld led NASDAQ's decision to acquire BRUT ECN from SunGard Data Systems (NYSE: SDS). The BRUT acquisition provides NASDAQ trading systems with additional capabilities, including advanced order routing. Most recently, in April 2005, NASDAQ announced a definitive agreement to purchase the INET ECN.

Greifeld is an active speaker on financial market structure and regulatory issues. He has been vocal in Washington regarding enhancements to Sarbanes-Oxley for small companies and the use of stock options as a tool for business and economic growth. Greifeld has addressed organizations including the Investment Company Institute, the National Press Club, and the World Economic Forum.

Prior to joining NASDAQ, Greifeld was an executive vice president with SunGard Data Systems Inc., a $6.2 billion market cap company, where he was responsible for all of SunGard's sell-side businesses and its buy-side transaction routing businesses. While serving as president and chief operating officer of Automated Securities Clearance, Inc. (ASC) from 1991 to 1999, Mr. Greifeld led the team that created the Brokerage Real-Time Application Support System (BRASS) and made it the industry standard trade order management system for NASDAQ stocks.

Greifeld holds a master's degree in business from New York University, Stern School of Business, and a BA in English from Iona College. His graduate school thesis was on the operation of the NASDAQ Stock Market. Greifeld is an avid runner and has completed four marathons. He was recently named chairman of the USA Track & Field Foundation. Greifeld lives in Westfield, New Jersey, where he resides with his wife and three children.

Frank M. Hatheway is chief economist of the NASDAQ Stock Market, Inc., and is responsible for a variety of projects and initiatives to support the NASDAQ market and improve its market structure. Prior to joining NASDAQ, Dr. Hatheway was a finance professor at Penn State University and a researcher in market microstructure. He has authored academic articles in the *Journal of Finance*, *Journal of Financial Intermediation*, and other leading finance journals. Dr. Hatheway has served as an Economic Fellow and senior research scholar with the U.S. Securities and Exchange Commission. Dr. Hatheway received his PhD in economics from Princeton University.

Richard D. Holowczak is presently an associate professor of computer information systems and is director of the Bert W. and Sandra Wasserman Trading Floor, Subotnick Financial Services Center, in the Zicklin School of Business, Baruch College, City University of New York. He holds a BS in Computer Science from the College of New Jersey, an MS in Computer Science from the New Jersey Institute of Technology, and MBA and PhD degrees from Rutgers University. His research focuses on digital libraries, electronic commerce and networked information systems. He has published articles in *IEEE Computer Journal*, *IEEE Transactions on Knowledge and Data Engineering*, *Communications of the ACM*, *Online Information Review*, and *ACM Computing Surveys*. His research has been supported by the professional staff congress at CUNY, NASA, and the National Science Foundation. He is a member of the IEEE Computer Society and the Association for Computing Machinery (ACM).

Marcus Hooper, for 17 years, traded and managed trading desks for large asset management firms, including the Investment Management divisions of HBOS, Dresdner, and AXA. Marcus now develops and implements trading technology for the Global Electronic Trading Solutions team at Bear Stearns International Limited. Marcus has been actively involved in industry committees and advisory groups looking at financial markets regulation, market structure, transaction cost analysis and the application of electronic trading technology. He has provided input and direction to several projects carried out by organizations including the Investment Managers' Association, the British Bankers' Association, the London Investment Banking Association, the Financial Services Authority (FSA), the European Commission, the London Stock Exchange, and FIX Protocol Limited. He has published papers on financial market behavior, including studies on best execution, electronic and alternative trading systems, and transaction cost analysis. Marcus is very proud to have lectured to executive MBA programs in the United States, and has been a nominated speaker for AIMR's educational program.

Peter Jenkins was named senior vice president, Institutional Client Group, of the New York Stock Exchange. Mr. Jenkins reports to NYSE President and Co-COO Catherine Kinney. Mr. Jenkins is responsible for overseeing the NYSE's relationship with the buy-side community and key individual buy-side stakeholders, including mutual funds, public and corporate pension funds, nonprofit organizations, and hedge funds. Prior to joining the NYSE, Mr. Jenkins was managing director and head of North America Active Equity Trading for Deutsche Bank Asset Management. Before that, Mr. Jenkins served as head of Global Equity Trading for 16 years. Prior to that, Mr. Jenkins spent three years as a senior trader at Cigna Investment Management. He began his career as a trader at Scudder Stevens and Clark Investments in 1980. Mr. Jenkins graduated from the University of Connecticut in 1980.

Michael S. Pagano has been an associate professor of finance at Villanova University since 1999. Professor Pagano has conducted several empirical analyses related to various issues in market microstructure, financial institution management, risk management, cost of capital estimation, and interest rate determination. He has published in numerous finance journals such as the *Journal of Financial Economics, Journal of Banking and Finance, Journal of Portfolio Management,* and *Financial Analysts Journal.* In addition to serving on the editorial boards of two academic journals, Professor Pagano has been a Fulbright scholar at the University of Costa Rica and has received awards for both teaching and academic scholarship.

Prior to earning his doctorate and joining the Villanova University faculty, Professor Pagano spent over 10 years in the financial services industry. He holds the Chartered Financial Analyst designation and has experience both in commercial lending activities at Citibank and in investment valuation analysis at a financial consulting firm, International Capital Markets Corp., as well as Reuters PLC. In addition to his duties at Villanova University, Professor Pagano has been a consultant to several companies including Citibank, Paine Webber, Fidelity Investments, GTE

Investments, Philadelphia Suburban Corp., Aqua America, and Bank Julius Baer.

John H. Porter, CFA, joined Barclays Capital in June 1998. He is a managing director responsible for the global strategic bank portfolio as well as a member of the Management Committee. Prior to joining Barclays Capital, Mr. Porter was principal and chief economist at Summit Capital Advisors. As principal at Moore Capital Management from 1993 to 1996, Mr. Porter was in charge of the European office, where he contributed to the formulation of macro-orientated investment strategies and directly managed a portion of the firm's capital. Prior to joining Moore, Mr. Porter was chief investment officer at the World Bank, where he was responsible for the management of a US$30 billion international bond portfolio. He was previously the senior macroeconomist on North Africa, responsible for structural adjustment lending. He received his BA from Harvard University in 1976, PhD in cognitive psychology from the Sorbonne in 1980, and MA in international economics from Columbia University in 1983.

Gerald Putnam is the founder and chief executive officer of Archipelago Holdings, Inc., the parent company of the Archipelago Exchange (ArcaEx), the nation's first totally open, fully electronic stock exchange. Jerry has attracted major investors to Archipelago from both the institutional and retail financial services sectors. He has developed a deep understanding of the securities industry through his involvement in institutional and derivative sales at several major brokerage firms in New York and Chicago. He was at Walsh Greenwood from 1983 to 1987, moving to Chicago in 1985 to open their institutional sales desk. From there, he gained further experience at Jefferies & Company, Paine Webber, Prudential, and Geldermann Securities, Inc. Moving into the electronic trading arena in 1994, Jerry founded Terra Nova, an online broker-dealer, and was its president until January 1999.

Jerry received a bachelor of science degree in economics with a major in accounting from the University of Pennsylvania, Wharton School, in 1981. In January 2000, he was inducted into the Entrepreneurship Hall of Fame sponsored by the University of Illinois at Chicago. In October 2000, he was named one of *Time* magazine's Outstanding Innovators.

Martin Reck started his career as assistant to the executive board of Deutsche Börse AG in 1993, and became head of the Xetra market model develpment team in 1997. From 1997 until 1998 he was in-house consultant in IT/operations at Deutsche Bank AG. In 1998 he returned to Deutsche Börse AG as head of market design and functionality for Xetra. In 1999 he took the project lead of Deutsche Börse's e-commerce initiative and became CEO of Xlaunch AG in 2000. Since January 2003, he has been managing director of Deutsche Börse and head of Group Functionality.

Martin Reck graduated in computer science in Dortmund, Germany and holds a PhD in information systems from the University of St. Gallen, in Switzerland.

Rainer Riess is managing director of stock market business development at Deutsche Börse and the Frankfurt Stock Exchange. He is responsible for customer relations, services, and marketing for traders, investors, and issuers of all cash market activities of Deutsche Börse AG, comprised of the electronic trading system Xetra and the Frankfurt Stock Exchange. Currently, almost 300 member institutions from 18 countries use the Xetra system. Altogether, the cash market of Deutsche Börse is comprised of more than 50,000 stocks, bonds, exchange-traded and actively managed funds, certificates, and warrants. His past experience within Deutsche Börse Group has included managing the Primary Markets department for all listing business, creating the Neuer Markt, and shaping the development of the German and European equity market and its regulatory structure. He worked on several product innovations such as the exchange-traded funds business (XTF segment) and new index concepts, as well as the internationalization and product and service strategy of Deutsche Börse AG. As a member of the CBOT/EUREX a/c/e Alliance management committee, he worked on the implementation of the Eurex system in the United States.

Rainer Riess holds a master of arts degree in economics from the Johann Wolfgang Goethe University in Frankfurt, and an MBA from the University of Miami. He is a former Fulbright scholar.

Frank L. Romanelli is responsible for market and business development at the SWX Swiss Stock Exchange. Prior to his appointment in February 2002, he worked on numerous strategic IT projects for UBS. He has over 30 years experience working on IT projects around the globe, and his balanced experience in IT and investment banking culminated in his being appointed partner of the Logica Consultancy Group, responsible for the development of their investment banking consultancy practice across Europe. In the latter half of his career he has specialized in trading and stock exchange systems and has worked for many stock exchanges in Europe, the United States, and the Far East. Throughout his career he has held numerous management and strategic consultancy positions. In the late 1960s and early 1970s he played a key role in the development of business and database management systems and lectured on standards and methodologies for system design. He has published numerous articles on technological and business subjects, including the challenges facing stock exchanges and a strategic appraisal of trading and systems technologies in Western Europe. He is married with two children and lives in the United Kingdom.

James Ross is CEO of MatchPoint Trading, a financial technology company that specializes in call market trading and technologies. MatchPoint is committed to providing innovative benchmark matching and single price auction trading services to exchanges, broker dealers, and institutions. Mr. Ross began his career in call market trading in the late 1980s when he joined Instinet's nascent equity crossing business as a sales assistant. Over the next 14 years, Mr. Ross was intimately involved in the promotion, development, operations, and finally the management of the global crossing business at Instinet. In addition to overseeing the U.S. equity crossing business, Mr. Ross also championed many international crosses, the first local Japanese crossing venture (called JapanCross), as well as the first foreign exchange (FX) cross. As a specialist in call market trading, he has spoken on numerous industry panels about the benefits of crossing and call market trading. He lives with his wife and two children in Westport, Connecticut.

Robert A. Schwartz is the Marvin M. Speiser Professor of Finance and University Distinguished Professor in the Zicklin School of Business, Baruch College, CUNY. Before joining the Baruch faculty in 1997, he was professor of finance and economics and Yamaichi Faculty Fellow at New York University's Leonard N. Stern School of Business, where he had been a member of the faculty since 1965. Professor Schwartz received his PhD in economics from Columbia University. His research is in the area of financial economics, with a primary focus on the structure of securities markets. He has published over 50 refereed journal articles and 14 books, including *Equity Markets in Action: The Fundamentals of Liquidity, Market Structure, and Trading* (New York: John Wiley & Sons, 2004), co-authored with Reto Francioni, and *Reshaping the Equity Markets: A Guide for the 1990s* (New York: Harper Business, 1991; reissued by Business One Irwin, 1993). He has served as a consultant to various market centers including the New York Stock Exchange, the American Stock Exchange, NASDAQ, the London Stock Exchange, Instinet, the Arizona Stock Exchange, Deutsche Börse, and the Bolsa Mexicana. From April 1983 to April 1988, he was an associate editor of the *Journal of Finance*, and he is currently an associate editor of the *Review of Quantitative Finance and Accounting*, the *Review of Pacific Basin Financial Markets and Policies*, and the *Journal of Entrepreneurial Finance and Business Ventures*. He is also a member of the advisory boards of *International Finance* and the *Journal of Trading*. In December 1995, Professor Schwartz was named the first chairman of NASDAQ's Economic Advisory Board, where he served until spring 1999. He is developer, with Bruce Weber, of the trading and market structure simulation, TraderEx (http://etraderex.com/).

Uwe Schweickert joined Deutsche Börse in 1999 after receiving a diploma in economics at the Freie Universtät, Berlin. He headed the research team for cash markets, and currently participates in Trading and Clearing Market Design, developing the market structure for cash and derivatives markets. His expertise centers on future competitive and regulatory developments in securities market structure, with a special focus on electronic equity markets. His current responsibilities include market design, competitive intelligence, and European regulation issues.

David Segel is the founder and CEO of the Mako Group, one of the leading market makers globally in volatility trading. His trading career began as a pit trader of sugar options in Manhattan's CSCE in 1987. Since then he has actively traded as a member of many of the world's exchanges, including the CBOE, LIFFE, and Eurex. Mako is a lead liquidity provider in many exchange-listed contracts with particular focus on financial options on Eurex and LIFFE. David attended Yale University and graduated in 1986 with a BA in physics and philosophy. David is a U.S. national, and since 1992 he has lived in London, England, with his wife Tina and their three children, Stephanie, Kate, and Henry.

Melissa Spurlock is Senior Consultant at ITG, Inc., and former Vice President of Plexus Group. She joined the Plexus consulting team in 2004, after serving as head trader for Grantham, Mayo, Van Otterloo (GMO). Melissa specializes in the evaluation of trading strategies and implementation, including composition and use of program trading, and the use of capital in determining trade execution venue.

Melissa has experience in the creation and review of best execution documentation and compliance reviews with regulatory agencies. She founded and built the trading desk at GMO, was a director of Global Quantitative Trading, and a registered representative at Prudential Securities, Series 3. She has created proprietary order management and trading (OMT) applications, including position reporting and online best execution measures. Melissa attended Boston University, where she earned a bachelor of arts degree.

John A. Thain has been chief executive officer of the New York Stock Exchange since January 15, 2004. Mr. Thain had been president and chief operating officer of Goldman Sachs Group, Inc., since July 2003 and was previously president and co-COO from May 1999 through June 2003; he had been a director since 1998. He was president and co-COO of the Goldman Sachs Group, LP, in 1999. From 1994 to 1999, he served as chief financial officer and head of operations, technology, and finance. From 1995 to 1997, he was also co-COO for European operations.

He is a member of the MIT Corporation; the Dean's Advisory Council at MIT/Sloan School of Management, INSEAD; the U.S. National Advisory Board; the James Madison Council of the Library of Congress; and the Federal Reserve Bank of New York's International Capital Markets Advisory Committee. He is also a member of the French-American Foundation and the Board of the Trilateral Commission, as well as a governor of the New York-Presbyterian Foundation, Inc., a trustee of New York-Presbyterian Hospital, and a general trustee of Howard University. Mr. Thain received an MBA from Harvard University in 1979 and a BS degree from Massachusetts Institute of Technology in 1977.

Jean-François Théodore is chairman of the managing board and chief executive officer of Euronext NV, the leading European exchange created in September 2000 from the merger between the Amsterdam Exchange, the Brussels Exchange, and ParisBourseSBFSA. Euronext has since been enlarged to include the Porto and Lisbon Exchanges and has acquired the LIFFE, the UK derivatives market, of which Mr Théodore is member of the board.

Born in December 1946, Jean-François Théodore holds a law degree from the University of Paris and is a graduate of the Institut d'Etudes Politiques de Paris and the Ecole Nationale d'Administration (ENA).

Wayne H. Wagner is a Consultant at ITG, Inc., and Former Chairman of Plexus Group, a Los Angeles–based firm that provides implementation, evaluation, and advisory services to U.S. and global money managers, brokerage firms, and pension plan sponsors. Mr. Wagner and Plexus Group were chosen as the 1999 Consultant of the Year by *PlanSponsor* magazine. Investment News named him one of the "Power Elite 25" for 2001. Plexus Group is an independent subsidiary of JPMorgan Investor Services Company, a division of JPMorgan Chase. Mr. Wagner is author and editor of *The Complete Guide to Securities Transactions: Improving Performance and Reducing Costs* (New York: John Wiley & Sons, 1989). His most recent publishing effort is a popular investment book written with friend Al Winnikoff, entitled *Millionaire: The Best Explanation of How an Index Fund Can Turn Your Lunch Money into a Fortune* (Renaissance Books, 2001). He has written and spoken frequently on many trading and investment subjects. He has received two Graham and Dodd Awards from the *Financial Analysts Journal* for excellence in financial writing. Mr. Wagner served as a regent of the Financial Analysts Seminar and served on the AIMR Blue Ribbon Task Force on Soft Dollars and the AIMR Best Execution Task Force. Mr. Wagner was a founding partner of Wilshire Associates and served as chief investment officer of Wilshire Asset Management. Earlier, Mr. Wagner participated in the design and operation of the first index funds at Wells Fargo Bank. In an earlier century Mr. Wagner earned an MS in statistics from Stanford University and a BBA in management science/finance from the University of Wisconsin.

Bruce W. Weber is associate professor of information management at the London Business School, where he teaches courses in information management, financial information systems, and trading and financial market structure in MBA, masters, and executive programs. He has an AB degree in applied mathematics from Harvard University, and a PhD in decision sciences from the Wharton School of the University of Pennsylvania. His research examines IT-driven competition in financial services and securities markets and has been published in a number of journals. He is developer, with Robert Schwartz, of the trading and market structure simulation, TraderEx (http://www.etraderex.com/). Prior to joining the London Business School in 2003, he was on the faculties of the Stern School of Business, New York University, and Baruch College of the City University of New York, where he was founding director of the Wasserman Trading Floor, Subotnick Center, a 60-workstation financial market education center with analytic software and real-time price feeds.

René Weber is senior vice president and heads the Bank Vontobel's European Food and Beverage/Luxury Goods Equity Research Team. He has been working as an analyst for close to 20 years at Bank Vontobel AG (Zurich/Switzerland). He attended the University for Applied Science of Business and Administration, St. Gallen.

Claudio Werder is a senior vice president and heads Bank Vontobel's European Life Sciences Research Team. He has been working as a pharmaceuticals and medtech analyst for more than 20 years at Bank Vontobel AG (Zurich/Switzerland). He attended the University of Zurich.

Notes

CHAPTER 1   Getting a Grip on Trading

1. Robert A. Schwartz and Bruce W. Weber developed the simulation model for TraderEx. Oliver Rockwell wrote the software for the TraderEx version that is packaged with this book. TraderEx is owned by TraderEx LLC, which includes Schwartz, Weber, and William Abrams. We have developed more complex versions of the simulation, as well as a networked product that enables multiple players to interact with each other and with the machine-generated orders. Information about these enhancements can be found on our web site, www.etraderex.com.
2. Of the 72 questionnaires completed, 54 percent of respondents were based in the United States, 19 percent in Canada, 11 percent in Australia, 8 percent in the United Kingdom, and 7 percent in continental Europe. Robert A. Schwartz and Benn Steil, "Controlling Institutional Trading Costs: We Have Met the Enemy, and It Is Us," *Journal of Portfolio Management* 28, no. 3 (Spring 2002): 39–49.
3. Malcolm Gladwell, *Blink: The Power of Thinking Without Thinking* (Boston: Little Brown and Company, 2005).
4. The trichotomy of trading motives—information, liquidity, and technical—is fundamentally consistent with Fischer Black's formulation set forth in his December 1985 presidential address to the American Finance Association (Fischer Black, "Noise," *Journal of Finance* 41, no. 3 [July 1986]: 529–543). Black focuses on participants' trading on noise as if it were information, and emphasizes that without noise traders, informed participants would not be able to trade. The reason is that noise trading provides the camouflage informed traders need to avoid obvious detection, which would result in the information they possess being incorporated into price before they can trade profitably on it. Our technical traders can be thought of as Fischer Black noise traders, and we too incorporate them, along with liquidity traders, in order that informed participants have the ability to trade profitably on their information.
5. We are developing more complex versions of the simulation with news and other securities, as well as a Web-based networked market that will enable multiple players to interact with each other live. Information about these enhancements can be found on our web site, www.etraderex.com.

6. See Richard D. Holowczak, "Incorporating Real-Time Financial Data into Business Curricula," *Journal of Education for Business* 81, no. 1 (September/October 2005).
7. We have a substantial, if not leading, presence in many products listed on the large derivatives exchanges, including Eurex, Euronext.liffe, CME, and CBOT.

CHAPTER 2   All About Liquidity

1. Peter L. Bernstein, *Against the Gods: The Remarkable Story of Risk* (New York: John Wiley and Sons, 1996).
2. For further discussion, see Robert Schwartz and Reto Francioni, *Equity Markets in Action: The Fundamentals of Liquidity, Market Structure & Trading* (New York: John Wiley and Sons, 2004), Appendix B.
3. *The crowd* refers to floor traders on an exchange who have come together to trade, on either an agency or a proprietary basis. A floor trader typically does not reveal an order to the market until, in response to current market conditions, he steps forward with a piece or all of the order and participates in a trade. In an electronic environment, the concept of a crowd can be applied more generally to participants who use computer technology to work their orders.
4. Peter Landers, "Drug-Data Chasm Punishes Small Investors," *Wall Street Journal*, October 6, 2003, c1; and "Heard on the Street: Small Investors Face Handicap in Drug Sector," *Wall Street Journal Europe*, October 6, 2003.
5. The data were "culled from thousands of pharmacies nationwide to give subscribers day-by-day tallies of the number and sales value of prescriptions filled."
6. See Shmuel Nitzan and Jacob Paroush, *Collective Decision Making: An Economic Outlook* (Cambridge, England: Cambridge University Press, 1985).
7. James Surowiecki, *The Wisdom of the Crowds* (New York: Anchor Books, 2005).
8. Ibid., page xiv.
9. The category "missed trades" is not relevant when a trade does in fact occur. Thus, for our purposes, the 29 bps should perhaps be eliminated from the total. However, the category is relevant at the end of a holding period when the portfolio manager seeks to unwind the position but fails to do so. In any event, one could recalculate the total as wished, but we have chosen to stay with the total as reported by Plexus.
10. On January 3, 2006, Plexus Group was acquired by Investment Technology Group, Inc., with whom Wayne Wagner is now a consultant.
11. Testimony of Wayne H. Wagner, House Committee on Financial Services, March 12, 2003.
12. Deniz Ozenbas, Robert A. Schwartz, and Robert A. Wood, "Volatility in U.S. and European Equity Markets: An Assessment of Market Quality," *International Finance* 5, no. 3 (2002): 437–461.
13. Our discussion is based on a model presented by Puneet Handa, Robert A. Schwartz, and Ashish Tiwari in "Quote Setting and Price Formation in an Order Driven Market," *Journal of Financial Markets* 6 (2003): 461–489.

14. In addition to the official trading day, executions are realized in "after-hours trading" and "pre-open" trading.
15. The *efficient market hypothesis* (EMH) can be stated as follows: Excess returns cannot be realized from information that is contained in (1) past prices (this is referred to as *weak form efficiency*), (2) public information including past prices (this is referred to as *semi-strong form efficiency*), and (3) all information including public plus inside information (this is referred to as *strong form efficiency*).
16. Thomas Copeland, "A Model of Asset Trading Under the Assumption of Sequential Information Arrival," *Journal of Finance*, September 1976.
17. M. Barry Goldman and Avrham Beja, "Market Prices vs. Equilibrium Prices: Returns Variance, Serial Correlation, and the Role of the Specialist," *Journal of Finance*, June 1979.
18. For further discussion, see Kalman Cohen, Gabriel Hawawini, Steven Maier, Robert Schwartz, and David Whitcomb, "Friction in the Trading Process and the Estimation of Systematic Risk," *Journal of Financial Economics*, 1983: 264–278; and Kalman Cohen, Gabriel Hawawini, Steven Maier, Robert Schwartz, and David Whitcomb, "Estimating and Adjusting for the Intervaling-Effect Bias in Beta," *Management Science*, January 1983: 135–148.
19. Clemons and Weber (1996) examined this proposition with experimental economics, and found that without significant incentives, subject-traders remained in a liquid market even when an alternative market was available and had lower commissions. Eric Clemons and Bruce Weber, "Alternative Securities Trading Systems: Tests and Regulatory Implications of the Adoption of Technology," *Information Systems Research* 7, no. 2 (June 1996): 163–188.

CHAPTER 3   How to Use Limit and Market Orders

1. Xetra® is a registered trademark of Deutsche Börse.
2. See Robert A. Schwartz and Bruce W. Weber, "Next-Generation Securities Market Systems: An Experimental Investigation of Quote-Driven and Order-Driven Trading," *Journal of Management Information Systems* 14, no. 2 (1997): 57–79.
3. For further discussion of the placement of limit orders in a continuous order-driven market, see Puneet Handa and Robert Schwartz, "Limit Order Trading," *Journal of Finance*, 1996, 1835–1861.
4. If you have taken an economics course that covered the theory of consumer choice (individual indifference curves, demand curves, and all of that), you might recall the use of the term *utility function*. A consumer determines the allocation of income between (let's keep this simple) two goods, x and y, according to the price of each and the utility obtained from each. The utility obtained from each is described as the consumer's utility function. The consumer also has a utility function for total income (or wealth). It can be shown that the consumer will be risk-averse if his utility increases in ever-decreasing amounts with equal increases in dollar income (or wealth). In this situation, the objective of the individual, when faced

with some risky alternatives, is not to maximize *expected dollar* income (or wealth) but the *expected utility* of income (or wealth). For the case that we are dealing with, the trader, by maximizing the expected dollar gain from trading, will maximize the expected utility of his wealth. The reason is that, while the gain is measured in dollars, it is determined by the trader's reservation price, and the trader's reservation price reflects his risk aversion. For a proof and further discussion, see Thomas Ho, Robert Schwartz, and David Whitcomb, "The Trading Decision and Market Clearing Under Transaction Price Uncertainty," *Journal of Finance*, March 1985, 21–42.

5. For the analytical formulation pertaining to the existence of the bid-ask spread, see Kalman Cohen, Steven Maier, Robert Schwartz, and David Whitcomb, "Transaction Costs, Order Placement Strategy, and Existence of the Bid-Ask Spread," *Journal of Political Economy*, April 1981, 287–305.

6. Ibid.

7. See Cohen et al., "Transaction Costs," for a mathematical proof.

8. These alternatives are discussed in some detail in Robert A. Schwartz and Reto Francioni, *Equity Markets in Action: The Fundamentals of Liquidity, Market Structure and Trading* (Hoboken, NJ: John Wiley & Sons, 2004), Chapters 5 and 8.

9. We assume that the option is European (namely, that it can be exercised only at the expiration date), not American (namely, that it can be exercised at any time up to and including the expiration date).

10. T. E. Copeland and D. Galai, "Information Effects on the Bid-Ask Spreads," *Journal of Finance* 38 (1983): 1457–1469.

11. N. Beiner and R. Schwartz, Chapter 6, "The Option Properties of Limit Orders in Call and Continuous Environments," in R. Schwartz, ed., *The Electronic Call Auction: Market Mechanism and Trading, Building a Better Stock Market* (New York: Kluwer Academic Publishers, 2001).

12. The payoff diagram in Exhibit 3.13 corresponds to that of a binary put option that pays a fixed amount of $3 if the stock price is equal to or below its strike price of $47, and that pays nothing if the stock price is above its strike price. This is the financial asset that the investor receives from placing a limit buy order at $47 in a continuous market when only a liquidity event can occur during his trading window.

13. "Triple-witching" day is the third Friday of the month that ends each quarter. It marks the simultaneous expiration, at the intraday auction, of DAX stock options, DAX index options, and futures.

CHAPTER 4   Choosing between Continuous Trading and a Periodic Call Auction

1. For further discussion of the properties of call auction trading, see Kalman J. Cohen and Robert A. Schwartz, "An Electronic Call Market: Its Design and Desirability," in *The Challenge of Information Technology for the Securities Markets: Liquidity, Volatility, and Global Trading*, Henry Lucas and Robert Schwartz, eds. (Homewood, IL: Dow Jones–Irwin, 1989), 15–58; Nicholas

Economides and Robert A. Schwartz, "Electronic Call Market Trading," *Journal of Portfolio Management*, Spring 1995, 10–18; and Robert A. Schwartz and Reto Francioni, "Call Auction Trading," in *Encyclopedia of Finance*, Cheng Few Lee and Alice C. Lee, eds. (New York: Springer Science+Business Media, 2006).

2. Archishman Chakraborty, Michael S. Pagano, and Robert A. Schwartz, "Bookbuilding," working paper, 2006.

3. There is an exception to this. If the continuous market uses *block pricing* as distinct from *walk-the-book pricing*, a limit order will be price-improved if it is included in a block trade that would otherwise trade through the limit order. This can occur if an incoming order is larger than the number of shares posted at the best bid or offer. Block pricing means that all of the shares in the trade were executed at the same price (the lowest bid or the highest ask to which the block drove the price). Walk-the-book pricing means that each share from the limit order book that is included in the trade executes at the price at which it was posted. Thus there is no price improvement for booked limit orders with walk-the-book pricing.

4. This section has been adapted with permission from M. Pagano and R. Schwartz, "NASDAQ's Closing Cross: Has Its New Call Auction Given Nasdaq Better Closing Prices? Early Findings," *Journal of Portfolio Management* 31, no. 4 (Summer 2005): 100–111.

5. William Vickrey, "Counterspeculation, Auctions, and Competitive Sealed Tenders," *Journal of Finance* 16 (1961): 8–37.

6. The U.S. Treasury runs auctions for new issues of government bills, notes, and bonds. Recognizing that not all investors are expert securities traders, the auction allows for noncompetitive bids that agree to accept the discount rate or yield set at the auction by the competitive bids. Noncompetitive bids are limited in size, and the close time is usually earlier than the competitive close time.

7. Thomas H. McInish and Robert A. Wood, "An Analysis of Intraday Patterns in Bid/Ask Spreads for NYSE Stocks," *Journal of Finance* 47, no. 2 (June 1992): 753–764.

8. We write $E(S^{Call})$ because the specific clearing price that will be set at the call is uncertain. Notice that $S^{Call} = \max(0, P^R - P^{Call})$ because your order to buy in the call executes only if $P^{Call} \leq P^R$.

9. Michael S. Pagano and Robert A. Schwartz, "A Closing Call's Impact on Market Quality at Euronext Paris," *Journal of Financial Economics* 68 (2003): 439–484.

10. This section has been adapted with kind permission of Springer Science and Business Media from N. Beiner and R. Schwartz, Chapter 6, "The Option Properties of Limit Orders in Call and Continuous Environments," in R. Schwartz, ed., *The Electronic Call Auction: Market Mechanism and Trading, Building a Better Stock Market* (New York: Kluwer Academic Publishers, 2001).

11. To simplify the discussion, we are ignoring the possibility of rolling an order that does not execute in the call auction into the continuous market.

12. Nicholas Economides and Robert A. Schwartz, "Electronic Call Market Trading," *Journal of Portfolio Management* 21, no. 3 (Spring 1995): 10–18.

CHAPTER 5   Market Intermediaries:
Nuts 'n' Bolts and Challenges

1. These are the Boston Stock Exchange, Chicago Stock Exchange, the Pacific Stock Exchange (acquired by Archipelago in 2005), Philadelphia Stock Exchange, and the National Stock Exchange (formally the Cincinnati Stock Exchange).
2. For further history, see James E. Buck, ed., *The New York Stock Exchange, the First 200 Years* (Essex, CT: Greenwich Publishing Group, Inc., 1992).
3. William G. Christie and Paul H. Schultz, "Why Do NASDAQ Market Makers Avoid Odd-Eighth Quotes?" *Journal of Finance* 49, no. 5 (1994): 1813–1840.
4. NASD established the *Rules of Fair Practice*. These apply to the financial integrity of member firms, sales practices (including a maximum 5 percent markup policy, which prevents NASD members from profiting unreasonably at the expense of their customers), market making, and underwriting activities.
5. See Asani Sarkar and Robert A. Schwartz, "Two-Sided Markets and Inter-Temporal Trade Clustering: Insights into Trading Motives," working paper, 2006, and Chapter 6 for further discussion.
6. The formulation is in Mark Garman, "Market Microstructure," *Journal of Financial Economics*, June 1976.
7. The European blue chips are a good example. Handling these issues, which are traded in electronically order-driven open order books, is a pure volume, small-margin business.
8. If a stock's returns are not correlated over time, the stock's price is said to be following a *random walk*. We discuss this further in Chapters 2 and 6.
9. On January 3, 2006, Plexus Group was acquired by Investment Technology Group, Inc., with whom Wayne Wagner is now a consultant.
10. Remark made at the Securities and Exchange Commission's Market Structure Hearings, New York City, October 29, 2002. Plexus gathers and analyzes trading-related data from more than 115 money management firms that, collectively, represent approximately 20 to 25 percent of exchange volume worldwide.
11. It is important to distinguish between two terms: *trade publication* and *trade reporting*. Trade publication is the public dissemination of a trade price. Trade reporting more narrowly means reporting a trade to a regulatory authority: the NYSE, the NASD, and/or the SEC in the United States. Reporting does not expose the inventory positions of the dealer that traded to other dealers. It is the publication of large trades (putting them on the ticker tape) that market makers wish to delay. By rule, both large and small trades on NASDAQ must be reported within 90 seconds of execution. These trade reports are then instantaneously disseminated to the public.
12. The best-execution brokers also offer price improvement, which is a percentage improvement on the best price in the market in return for guaranteed volumes of business. Under the EU's Markets in Financial Instruments Directive (MiFID, which goes into effect in 2007), they will *not* be able to do this, as they would have to advertise this price on the market, which would then automatically become the best price. Under MiFID, RSPs will

be classified under Article 27 as "Systematic Internalisers," who will be required to publish "firm quotes" for liquid stocks quoted on regulated markets. *No* price improvement will be allowed on trades below standard market size (ranging from €7,500 up to €100,000). Systematic internalisers must continuously publish quotes during trading hours, make quotes readily available, and maintain a record of all quotes. This is to ensure that there is fair competition between the RSPs, other systematic internalisers, and the regulated markets. In the United Kingdom this is (for the top 350 equities) the SETS/SETSmm order book.

13. Puneet Handa, Robert Schwartz, and Ashish Tiwari, "Price Improvement and Price Discovery on a Primary Market: Evidence from the American Stock Exchange," *Journal of Portfolio Management*, Fall 1998.
14. See www.deutsche-boerse.de, *Xetra Release 7.1 Market Model Equities*, 13.
15. See www.liquidnet.com/news/news.jsp.
16. See www.liquidnet.com/company/about.jsp.
17. Robert A. Schwartz and Reto Francioni, *Equity Markets in Action: The Fundamentals of Liquidity, Market Structure and Trading* (Hoboken, NJ: John Wiley & Sons, 2004), 149.
18. See Rainer Riess and Uwe Schweickert's contribution to Chapter 3 of this book.
19. See Miroslav Budimir, Peter Gomber, and Uwe Schweickert, *Volume Discovery: Leveraging Liquidity in the Depth of an Order-Driven Market*, discussion paper, June 2005, Chair of e-finance, University of Frankfurt.

CHAPTER 6 The Road to Technical Analysis and Algorithmic Trading

1. Editorial Staff of *Securities Industry News*, "For Best Execution, Future Is Spelled TCR," August 8, 2005.
2. Puneet Handa, Robert A. Schwartz, and Ashish Tiwari, "Quote Setting and Price Formation in an Order-Driven Market," *Journal of Financial Markets* 6 (2003): 461–489.
3. Handa, Schwartz, and Tiwari also show that the spread narrows as k goes to either of its extremes of 1 (buyers only) or 0 (sellers only). At the extremes, expectations are no longer divergent and the spread collapses. The spread is at a maximum when k is 0.5, the midpoint of its range.
4. Jacob Paroush, Robert A. Schwartz, and Avner Wolf, "Trading, Price Setting and Volatility in Equity Markets Under Divergent Expectations and Adaptive Valuations," working paper, 2006.
5. Archishman Chakraborty, Michael Pagano, and Robert A. Schwartz, "Bookbuilding," working paper, 2005. Material in this section is adapted with kind permission of Springer Science and Business Media from a presentation of the paper by Pagano at a conference at the Zicklin School of Business in May 2004. See Chapter 1, "Getting the Trades Made," in J. A. Byrne, A. Colaninno, and R. Schwartz, eds., *Electronic vs. Floor Based Trading* (New York: Springer Science and Business Media, 2005) for the edited transcript.

6. Asani Sarkar and Robert A. Schwartz, "Two-Sided Markets and Inter-Temporal Trade Clustering: Insights into Trading Motives," working paper, 2006.

7. The procedure is known as the Lee-Ready algorithm. See Charles Lee and Mark Ready, "Inferring Trade Direction from Intraday Data," *Journal of Finance* 46 (1991): 733–746.

8. For the quote and surveys by Economides and Schwartz (the U.S. market), Schwartz and Steil (the European market), Demarchi and S. Thomas (the French market), and Douglas and C. Thomas (the Australian market), see Robert A. Schwartz, ed., *The Electronic Call Auction: Market Mechanism and Trading* (New York: Kluwer Academic Publishers, 2001).

9. Michael Kahn, "Getting Technical," *Barron's*, October 5, 2005.

10. In the strict form of the Paroush, Schwartz, and Wolf model, the process by which k and price evolve has a fair game property.

11. Burton Malkiel, *A Random Walk Down Wall Street* (New York: W.W. Norton & Company, 1973), 116.

12. Lawrence H. Summers, "Does the Stock Market Rationally Reflect Fundamental Values?" *Journal of Finance* 41, no. 3 (July 1986): 591–601; Kenneth J. Arrow, "Risk Perception in Psychology and Economics," *Economic Inquiry* 20 (January 1982): 1–9; Franco Modigliani and Richard Cohn, "Inflation, Rational Valuation and the Market," *Financial Analysts Journal* 35 (March/April 1979): 24–44; and Robert Schiller, "Do Stock Prices Move Too Much to Be Justified by Subsequent Changes in Dividends?" *American Economic Review* 71 (June 1981): 421–436.

13. Summers, "Does the Stock Market Rationally Reflect," 598.

14. *Wall Street Journal*, October 23, 1987.

15. Bernard M. Baruch, *My Own Story* (New York: Henry Holt, 1957), 84.

16. Ian Domowitz and Henry Yegerman, "The Cost of Algorithmic Trading: A First Look at Comparative Performance," © ITG Inc., March 2005.

17. Nina Mehta, "Algorithms Out of Control?" *Traders Magazine*, March 2005, 24–30 and 34.

18. Ibid.

19. Domowitz and Yegerman, "The Cost of Algorithmic Trading."

20. Sarkar and Schwartz, "Two-Sided Markets."

21. Ian Domowitz and Henry Yegerman, "Measuring and Interpreting the Performance of Broker Algorithms," © ITG Inc., 2005; Ian Domowitz and John Krowas, "Where Risk Control Meets Cost Control in Analytics Development," *Journal of Investing*, Fall 2004, 1–6.

22. Mehta, "Algorithms Out of Control?"

23. Puneet Handa, Robert Schwartz, and Ashish Tiwari, "The Economic Value of a Trading Floor: Evidence from the American Stock Exchange," *Journal of Business* 77, no. 2, pt. 1 (April 2004): 331–355.

24. Kirk Johnson, "Denver Airport Saw the Future. It Didn't Work," *New York Times*, August 27, 2005, A1 and A11.

25. Malcolm Gladwell, *Blink: The Power of Thinking Without Thinking* (Boston: Little, Brown, 2005).

26. This Appendix draws, with permission, on Puneet Handa, Robert Schwartz, and Ashish Tiwari, "The Economic Value of a Trading Floor: Evidence from the American Stock Exchange," *Journal of Business* 77, no. 2, pt. 1 (April 2004): 331–355, © 2004 by the University of Chicago. All rights reserved.

CHAPTER 7   Performance Measurement

1. Material in this section has been modified with permission from Robert A. Schwartz and Benn Steil, "Controlling Institutional Trading Costs: We Have Met the Enemy, and It Is Us," *Journal of Portfolio Management* 28, no. 3 (Spring 2002): 39–49.
2. L. K. C. Chan and J. Lakonishok, "The Behavior of Stock Prices Around Institutional Trades," *Journal of Finance* 50 (1995): 1147–1174.
3. Ian Domowitz, Jack Glen, and Ananth Madhavan, "Liquidity, Volatility, and Equity Trading Costs Across Countries and Over Time," working paper, Pennsylvania State University, January 2000.
4. www.itginc.com/research.
5. The difference between the trade price and the quote midpoint is multiplied by 2 because the effective spread is defined with respect to the quote midpoint. For instance, if you buy at the ask quote, your effective spread is 2[Ask − Midpoint] = 2[A − (A − B)/2] = A − B.
6. All of the major global equity, options, and futures markets have central counterparty clearinghouses.
7. For further discussion, see Robert Schwartz and Reto Francioni, *Equity Markets in Action: The Fundamentals of Liquidity, Market Structure and Trading* (Hoboken, NJ: John Wiley & Sons, 2004), Chapter 10, "Clearing and Settlement."
8. More precisely, returns are more nearly lognormally distributed and risk is better measured by the variance or standard deviation of log returns. For ease of exposition, we simply refer to the variance of "returns." See the Appendix at the end of this book for a further discussion of the measurement of returns, means, and variances.
9. For further discussion and references, see Deniz Ozenbas, Robert A. Schwartz, and Robert Wood, "Volatility in U.S. and European Equity Markets: An Assessment of Market Quality," *International Finance* 5, no. 3 (Winter 2002): 437–461.
10. If prices follow a random walk, this exact linear relationship holds for the variance of *logarithmic* returns.
11. Material in this section has been modified with permission from R. Schwartz and R. Wood, "Best Execution: A Candid Analysis," *Journal of Portfolio Management* 29, no. 4 (Summer 2003): 37–48. We also discuss best execution in Schwartz and Francioni, *Equity Markets in Action*, Chapter 11.
12. See P. Myners, "Review of Institutional Investment: Final Report," HM Treasury, London, March 6, 2001. For further discussion, see R. Brealey and A. Neuberger, "Treatment of Investment Management Fees and Commission

Payments: An Examination of the Recommendations Contained in the Myners Report," *Fund Managers Association*, October 2001; and Neuberger's
discussion in Robert A. Schwartz, John A. Byrne, and Antoinette Colaninno,
eds., *Call Auction Trading: New Answers to Old Questions* (New York:
Kluwer Academic Publishers, 2003).

13. See Association for Investment Management and Research (AIMR), "Trade
Management Guidelines" (Charlottesville, VA, November 12, 2001), 2.
14. Letter to the AIMR. See A. Lancellotta, Letter to the Association for Investment Management and Research, Re: Proposed AIMR Trade Management
Guidelines, Investment Company Institute, Washington, DC, February 12,
2002.
15. More meaningful measures can be obtained by averaging measurements over
a substantial number of trades.
16. George Sofianos, in "Trading and Market Structure Research," Goldman
Sachs, May 2001, presents a framework for evaluating and comparing the execution quality for large institutional orders. His analysis considers commissions, execution shortfall for filled orders, fill rates, opportunity costs for
nonfilled orders, and information content.
17. See Wagner in Schwartz, Byrne, and Colaninno, *Call Auction Trading*.
18. See www.nysedata.com/factbook.
19. See H. Bradley, "Views of an 'Informed Trader,'" reprinted by AIMR (2002)
from the AIMR proceedings, *Organizational Challenges for Investment
Firms* (Charlottesville, VA: AIMR, May 2002). Bradley also made this statement in his testimony before the Congressional Subcommittee on Capital
Markets, Insurance, and Government Sponsored Enterprises, March 12, 2003.
20. For further discussion, see Schwartz and Francioni, *Equity Markets in Action*, Chapters 5 ("Institutional Order Flow") and 11 ("Regulation").
21. Association for Investment Management and Research, "Trade Management
Guidelines."
22. Comments made at the Baruch College Conference, "A Trading Desk's View
of Market Quality," April 30, 2002. At the same conference, Minder Cheng,
also of Barclays Global Investors, presented details of a specific assessment
procedure that is used by his firm. The discussions are in Schwartz, Byrne,
and Colaninno, *Call Auction Trading*.
23. Remarks made at the Baruch College Conference, "A Trading Desk's View of
Market Quality," April 30, 2002. The discussion is in Schwartz, Byrne, and
Colaninno, *Call Auction Trading*.
24. Wayne Wagner's remarks were made at the April 30, 2002, Baruch College
Conference. The discussion is in Schwartz, Byrne, and Colaninno, *Call Auction Trading*.
25. Remark made at the April 30, 2002, Baruch College Conference. The discussion is in Schwartz, Byrne, and Colaninno, *Call Auction Trading*.
26. In Wayne Wagner's words, "Love them or hate them, institutional traders
still need market makers. It is a relationship built upon mutual need:
searching for liquidity, bringing companies to market, providing research,
referrals, and soft-dollar services." In Schwartz, Byrne, and Colaninno, *Call
Auction Trading*.

27. Puneet Handa, Robert Schwartz, and Ashish Tiwari, "The Economic Value of a Trading Floor: Evidence from the American Stock Exchange," *Journal of Business* 77, no. 2, pt. 1 (2004): 331–355.
28. This example was supplied by Global Instinet Crossing.
29. AIMR, "Trade Management Guidelines."
30. Pagano and Schwartz, in "A Closing Call's Impact on Market Quality at Euronext Paris," *Journal of Financial Economics* 68 (2003): 439–484, found that the introduction of a closing call in the Paris market did improve the efficiency of price formation at the close.
31. Material in this section has been modified with permission from R. Schwartz and R. Wood, "Best Execution: A Candid Analysis," *Journal of Portfolio Management* 29, no. 4 (Summer 2003): 37–48.

APPENDIX   Prices and Returns

1. For a rigorous derivation of the intervaling effect bias in beta, see K. Cohen, G. Hawawini, S. Maier, R. Schwartz, and D. Whitcomb, "Friction in the Trading Process and the Estimation of Systematic Risk," *Journal of Financial Economics* (1983): 264–278; and K. Cohen, G. Hawawini, S. Maier, R. Schwartz, and D. Whitcomb, "Estimating and Adjusting for the Intervaling-Effect Bias in Beta," *Management Science* (January 1983): 135–148.

About the CD-ROM

TraderEx Computer Simulation

The CD features an interactive computer simulation designed to provide readers with hands-on experience in making tactical trading decisions, and implementing them in different market environments. The simulation exercises are an invaluable tool for deepening understanding of how the structure of trading influences actual trading behavior. Users enter orders or set quotes into a computer-driven market that generates order flow, responding directly to participants' orders. Participants see their results in real time, and analyze them with the performance measures provided during and after play. Continuous order driven and quote driven markets are simulated, along with call auctions and hybrid combinations.

CD-ROM TABLE OF CONTENTS

1) Welcome
2) Different Market Structures and Seven Ways to Play
    a. Order-Driven: Buy-Side Trader
    b. Order-Driven: Proprietary Trader
    c. Order-Driven: Liquidity Provider
    d. Quote-Driven: Dealers only
    e. Quote-Driven: Dealers and Order Book
    f. Hybrid: Buy-Side Role
    g. Hybrid: Dealer Role

3) Parameter Selection for Simulation Runs

4) Market Opens and Runs for the Selected Number of Days

5) Performance Measurement at End of Run

MINIMUM SYSTEM REQUIREMENTS

- IBM PC or compatible computer with 386 or higher processor
- 128 MB RAM
- 5 MB hard disk space
- CD-ROM drive
- SVGA monitor with 256 Color
- Windows 95 or higher

USING THE CD WITH WINDOWS

To run the setup program, do the following:

1. Insert the CD into your computer's CD-ROM drive.
2. A window will appear with the following options: Install, Explore, and Exit.

   Install: Gives you the option to install the supplied software on the CD-ROM.

   Explore: Enables you to view the options in a directory structure. A menu should bring you directly to a list of contents—you can start the simulation or view a ReadMe file.

   Exit: Closes the autorun window.

   If you do not have autorun enabled, or if the autorun window does not appear, follow these steps to access the CD:

1. Click Start, select Run.
2. In the dialog box that appears, type d:\setup.exe, where d is the letter of your CD-ROM drive. This brings up the autorun window described in the preceding set of steps.
3. Choose the Install, Explore, or Exit option from the menu. (See step 2 in the preceding list for a description of these options.)

INSTALLING THE SOFTWARE

Click on the install button and follow the instructions on the screen to install the software. After the installation is complete you can launch the program or open the TraderEx directory to view the output files from the Windows Start menu by selecting TraderEx.

USING THE SOFTWARE

More detailed instructions can be found in Chapter 1 of *The Equity Trader Course + CD*.

USER ASSISTANCE

If you have trouble with the CD-ROM, please contact Wiley Product Technical Support at (800) 762-2974. Outside the United States, call (317) 572-3994. You can also contact Wiley Product Technical Support at http://support .wiley.com/. John Wiley & Sons will provide technical support only for installation and other general quality control items.

Programs are not warranted to be error-free. To place additional orders or to request information about Wiley products, please call (877) 762-2974.

CUSTOMER NOTE

Index